nother quality book from

**Specialist Knowledge
Services**

aint Aldhelm   research
0 Paul Street, Frome   publications
omerset, BA11 1DX   literary & book
l: Frome (0373) 51777   consultancy

TOWARD THE LIGHT

TOWARD
THE
LIGHT

A MESSAGE TO MANKIND
FROM
THE TRANSCENDENTAL WORLD

PUBLISHED BY
MICHAEL AGERSKOV
TOWARD THE LIGHT PUBLISHING HOUSE, ApS.
COPENHAGEN, DENMARK
1979

The original was published
in Copenhagen, Denmark, in 1920
under the title
"Vandrer mod Lyset"

TOWARD THE LIGHT PUBLISHING HOUSE, ApS.
"Vandrer mod Lyset"'s Forlag, ApS.
22 Købmagergade, 1150 Copenhagen K,
Denmark

ISBN 87-87871-50-5

Library of Congress Catalog Card Number:
79-9599

Published under the auspices
of
The International Foundation for "Toward the Light",
Copenhagen, Denmark.

PRINTED IN DENMARK by DYVA BOGTRYK-OFFSET GLOSTRUP

Contents

I n order to avoid any misunderstanding, and to meet possible allegations that I should be the originator of this work, I, who served as intermediary between our world and the transcendental, do hereby declare:

1. That the Message which through my agency has been conveyed to humanity stems neither from my *supraconscious* nor from my *subconscious*.

2. That I am fully aware that I have served merely as the necessary instrument for the intelligences who have manifested themselves.

3. That I have wilfully neither deleted anything from, nor have I added anything to, the messages that I was given, but have in every way tried to render them as lucidly as lay within my power to do.

Johanne Agerskov
(née Malling-Hansen)

In the Preface by my husband on one of the following pages, it is stated: "Those who read these writings should neither judge nor condemn until they have closely considered every thought in this book. Then they should let their *conscience* be the judge." In spite of this clear warning, many people, with little or no knowledge of the present work, have shrugged their shoulders whenever it was mentioned in conversation and said: **"It is of course nothing but spiritualism!"** I hereby repudiate such condemnatory statements. My husband and I have from the very beginning of our work been engaged in **psychic research,** which is much, much more than spiritualism. Never have we called upon the spirits of the dead in order to communicate with them as spiritualists do, **for such acts are against the laws of God!** On the contrary, **I was called upon** from the transcendental world – from the spiritual leaders of mankind – with a request that I should communicate with and in various ways assist them in their work for the benefit of humanity. (See "Some Psychic Experiences", pages 9 and 11).

For many years we worked under the guidance and influence of these high spiritual intelligences, pursuing courses which the so-called spiritualists do not, and cannot, pursue. The results of our psychic research are presented in the principal work "Toward the Light", in the two Supplements "Questions and Answers I & II", in "The Doctrine of Atonement and the Shorter Road" and in "Greetings to Denmark".

If, despite my husband's and my own serious warnings, people continue to speak of "Toward the Light" and its supplementary works as spiritualism, they will merely reveal **their own spiritual level** to their more clear-sighted and understanding fellow human beings.

May, 1939
Johanne Agerskov
(née Malling-Hansen)

PREFACE

The work that is hereby entrusted to humanity has come into being by means of intuition and inspiration through a female intermediary, my wife Johanne Elisabeth, née Malling-Hansen.

The book is divided into the following main parts: *Ardor's Account,* a historical presentation from the earliest times to our day, two ethical-religious speeches, *The Speech of Christ* and *The Speech of God's Servant* with related *Parables,* and a *Commentary* to Ardor's Account, chapter by chapter – except for chapters 18, 20 and 21. To this has been added a *Summary* of ethical, religious and philosophical content. The *footnotes,* unless otherwise indicated, are by the intermediary's spiritual guide, who is also the author of the Commentary and the Summary.

The Biblical names occurring in this work have been conveyed by the authors as they are known to the Danish people.[1]

Further information about the circumstances surrounding the provenance and compilation of this work can be found in the more detailed Postscript, page 337, which is by the same author as the Commentary.

The main purpose of this work is to enlighten human beings on their origin, God's relationship to them, and the struggle between Good and Evil, Light and Darkness; and also to impart the true teachings of Christ, freed from the inventions and distortions of the centuries. In this respect it continues and concludes the work of the reformers of the Church.

As for the remainder of the content, reference is made directly to the text itself.

The transcendental world has requested that the following *warning* be given to all who come into possession of this book:

Those who read these writings should neither judge nor condemn until they have closely considered every thought in this book. Then they should let their *conscience* be the judge. Once their conscience has spoken, then they can speak and write according to its dictates.

---

[1] The names used in this translation are, of course, those known to the English-speaking peoples. – Translators' note.

But everyone should bear in mind that those who speak against their conscience sin against the divine within themselves, they commit that which the Bible terms "the blasphemy against the Holy Ghost", and of which Christ says (see Ardor's Account, page 55): "But that which you have sinned against the holy within you, that shall you not be forgiven until you have suffered for it and repented of the evil you have done. Yea, I say unto you: beware the Day of Judgment; for then shall your words bear witness against you, then shall your words judge you."

Finally I wish to state that my sole task as publisher[1] of this book has been to present the work as accurately as it was received by the intermediary. (See the preceding statement).

New Year's Eve, 1919
The Publisher

The second edition has not been changed.

March, 1925
The Publisher

Since the authors of "Toward the Light" and its supplementary writings belong to a spiritual world, a world infinitely higher than ours, a human being was needed to represent them on Earth. They therefore addressed themselves to my husband and asked him to undertake this work, and he readily accepted. Although my husband passed away several years ago, in this third (Danish) edition, and in all subsequent editions, the name of the publisher will be his, whether I or anybody else will be performing the actual task of publishing the book.

May, 1939
Johanne Agerskov
(née Malling-Hansen)

---

[1] Michael Agerskov uses the Danish word *"udgiver"*, which means either "publishing house" or "the person on whose initiative a work is published." In the case of "Toward the Light" and the related works, it is the latter meaning that applies. – Translators' note.

Translator's Preface

Although "Toward the Light" was published in Denmark in the spring of 1920, the present work, published under the auspices of The International Foundation for Toward the Light, is the first foreign language version to become generally available.

The basic principle underlying this translation has been one of accuracy and strict adherence to the Danish original. However, since the main sections of the work originate from different transcendental authors, each has presented its own translation problems.

Ardor chose to give his Account a solemn, poetic and slighty archaic form, in which the graphically descriptive formulation is sustained by the metre and alliteration. In our efforts to emulate this style in the English language, we have avoided the use of modern words and constructions and given special attention to the euphony of the text.

The Speech of Christ presented somewhat different problems. In the answer to Question No. 12 in the Second Supplement, it is stated that Christ specifically aimed at producing a New Testament style of language, in the hope that this would make it possible for people to recognize him. This seemed to constitute a direct invitation to the translators to adopt the vocabulary and grammar of the Gospels, but this did not in fact turn out to be feasible. One major difficulty was that Christ touches upon many subjects in his Speech for which no biblical terminology exists. Another consideration was the fact that the grammar of the New Testament in the "King James" Bible is much further removed from modern English than the language of the Danish New Testament is removed from modern Danish. The compromise chosen in order to resolve this dilemma has been to adopt a modified biblical style with the more obtrusive archaisms removed.

The Parables, which were also given by Christ, resemble those given in the Gospels both in form and style, so that in this case the more archaic language seemed fully appropriate.

The Commentary to Ardor's Account and the Concluding Summary both cover a wide variety of subjects, that in many cases imposed a complex sentence structure on the Danish original. This led to many that has in many cases imposed a complex sentence structure on the Danish original. This led to many attempts during the translation process to simplify the text by breaking the long sentences down into a number of shorter statements. However, almost invariably such attempts involved committing the translation to one particular interpretation out of several that in principle existed in the Danish. Although in most cases the correct interpretation may have seemed obvious, this was not always the case, and the principle of accuracy therefore in practice dictated the sentence structure of that part of the translation.

The foregoing remarks apply equally to the supplementary works "Questions and Answers I & II". Here again, the effort has been to avoid any interpretation of the original text. In the few isolated cases where this for some reason was unavoidable, we have provided an explanation in the form of a footnote. English readers may thus rest assured that no interpretations have knowingly been made, that they are now placed on equal terms with Danish readers, and that the text will amply reward those who undertake the close study that it demands.

The Translators
August, 1979

FORGIVE YOUR ENEMIES!

I greet you in the name of our God and Father!

———

I Ardor, have been sent to you by the Almighty to answer your questions, and I have promised to form my thoughts so that the words by which the thoughts are rendered can be understood by human beings.

But I ask you to remember that the word is but the means whereby divine thought is revealed unto human beings; for many believe that the word is in God, and of God, but this is not so. Words, in the form you know them, are of earthly origin. But the simpler the word, the more clearly will it convey the thought, which comes from God and is in God – *Thought* – the source of all that is.

1.

Has God Existed through all Eternity, and is God a Personal Being?

Through all eternity Darkness was everywhere.
In the Darkness was the Light; in the Light were *Thought* and *Will*.
But Thought and Will *were not in the Darkness.*
In the Light was the seed of all that is good, but in Darkness was the seed of all that is evil.

Unknown eternities passed.
Slowly, Thought and Will were drawn toward each other.
Slowly, the Light spread, it became brighter and purer.
It was dawn.

Unknown eternities passed.
Thought and Will drew more closely toward each other.

1* C

The Light spread more and more, it shone with radiant beauty.
It was morning.

Again, unknown eternities passed.
Thought and Will drew closer still toward each other.
The Light welled forth everywhere, it blazed clear, fair and glorious.
It was day.

Again, unknown eternities passed.
Thought and Will became united.
Then there arose from the Light, by the power of Thought-Will, a blazing figure, a spiritual Being – *God.*
But in the same moment God caused twelve radiant figures, spiritual beings, to emerge from the Light. And these became the Helpers of God, God's Servants.
And this was the beginning of time.
But no human being is, and no human being ever will be, able to gauge the eternities that have passed from the beginning of time until this day, your time.

When God arose from the Light, Darkness was vanquished, but not destroyed. By the power of Thought-Will, He brought Darkness under the concealing waves of the sea of Light.

To separate and to purify the evil and the vile, God causes Darkness to flow through His flaming Being in eternally swirling waves. Slowly, Darkness diminishes, but when that day will come when all evil and everything vile has been absorbed by the Light and purified by God's flaming Self is known unto Him alone, who is all-knowing.

When God arose from the Light, He was perfect – all-knowing, all-loving, almighty. And He endowed His Helpers with much knowledge, much love and much power.

By Thought and from the Light, He formed and created a vast Kingdom, perfect in its glory.

By Thought and from the Light, He formed and created abodes for Himself and for His Helpers.

Then God became *the Creator.*

But I can describe nothing of this Kingdom and of these abodes, *nothing* that can be comprehended by human beings. For compared with the glorious Kingdom of God even the most beautiful place on Earth is misty and cold.

2.

How did the Angels Enter the Kingdom of God, and what is their Relationship to God?

Possibilities for infinite forms of life rested in God, for God bore all creation within Him.

By Thought and from His own flaming Being, He formed and created thousands upon thousands of glorious, graceful figures – spiritual beings – *the Angels.*

And He endowed them with wisdom, with love and with power; and He gave them all abodes in His vast Kingdom.

Then God became the Father.

When God and His twelve Helpers emerged and arose from the Light they were two within themselves, for they bore within their nature all that is male and all that is female.

But the beings God created from His own Self were created to be one within themselves, to be man and woman, destined to fulfil and complement each other in wisdom and in love, destined to be separate for ever – to be two – and yet be one.

God bestowed His deep, His infinite love upon these, His own children, for they were *of* Him, *with* Him and *within* Him. And *He* was truly in them all.

And they lived a life of splendour and joy in God's Kingdom.

And God endowed them with the power and the will to study and to learn. And His Helpers instructed them in the laws and the secrets of the Light; taught them to form and to create by Thought and from the Light.

But the Helpers of God had not the power to solve the mystery of life, which only He knew – He who was, and is, the Lord of Thought and Life.

3.

How and for what Purpose did God Create the Globes of the Universe?

Many aeons passed.

The Father rejoiced in the progress of His children in wisdom and in love.

Behold, there arose in God the thought of creating new beings.

And He decided to create them beautiful and good, with possibilities open to them of attaining, under the guidance of His elder children, the same fulness of wisdom and love.

And He decided to prepare dwelling places for His still uncreated children, dwellings in which they could live a life of beauty and joy, striving toward the fulness of the Light, and toward His Kingdom of Glory.

Then God laid the plan and gave the laws for the making and being of the Universe.

By Thought and from the Light, God formed and created four mighty suns, and in their fiery bosoms He laid down numerous forms of life.

Borne in space by God's Thought, holding fast to one another by equal attraction, by equal repulsion, these glowing suns swing two and two, opposite each other, in eternal orbit about God's Kingdom.

But from these mother suns, all the globes of the Universe were hurled out and formed.

Borne and arranged in space by God's Thought, they all swing in fixed paths, according to given laws.

4.

Were Human Beings Created by God? From where and for what Reason have Sin and Death Come to Afflict the Human Race?

Many aeons passed.

Then God saw that dense fogs veiled certain of the globes that He had formed. And He saw, in His wisdom, that after some eternities had passed these would serve as dwelling places for the beings He thought to create.

Behold, then He chose one globe, your world – the Earth.[1]

By Thought and from the Light, God formed a radiantly splendid spiritual world about the fogs and vapours of the Globe, that the Light from this realm of beauty might pervade and shine upon the Earth and mould it in the likeness of the spiritual ideal that He had formed.

Slowly, the Light spread over the Earth to ready it for life, to

---

[1]) Ardor refers here to the Globe by the name that mankind later gave to it.

make it fruitful, and to draw from its bosom the dormant possibilities for the many forms of life.

Some eternities passed.

Then God saw that the fogs about the Globe were lighter and less dense. And He knew, in His wisdom, that after a time the Earth would near its completion.

Then God spoke unto His children.

And He said: "I, your Father, wish to give you a part in My creation, for I shall create new beings, create them from My own Self and from the strong radiations of the Globe. I shall create them beautiful and good, with possibilities open to them of receiving, under your guidance, everything through the Light. And they shall live a life in beauty and joy on one of the globes that I have formed, on the one which I have chosen for that purpose. In the fulness of time shall I choose from among you some, and unto these shall I give a dwelling in the world I have created about the Earth; for from there shall they lead My youngest children, lead them along the paths of the Light, until they reach My Kingdom of Glory. But the chosen leaders may, when they so desire, return unto their abodes in this My Kingdom, that they may rest; for no work is done well, if it is not accompanied by rest."

And God bade His Helpers to show them the Earth and the world which encompassed it, and whereafter it had been formed.

And they all went forth unto this world.

But God's Helpers instructed His children in much of what was to come. And they understood that their Father would give them a difficult task to fulfil.

Some time passed.

God's children spoke among themselves of whom their Father would choose. And many of the Eldest believed that the choice should fall upon them.

And they often went unto this new-formed world about the Earth and remained there at length, and they were much pleased to abide there, for it was truly beautiful.

Some time passed.

Then some of the Eldest said: "Why does our Father not create? Behold, the Earth is now ready for habitation. Why, then, does our Father tarry?"

But at that same moment God caused His voice to be heard in warning.

And God said: "My children, return unto your abodes in My

Kingdom; for I have not chosen you; only they are fit who have *patience.*"

And they all heard the voice of their Father. But they returned not; for they still believed that the choice should fall upon them.

Again, some time passed.

Then one of the Eldest said: "Still our Father tarries and we grow impatient. Let us seek to solve the mystery of life and create the new beings ourselves; for then will they be *our* children, and our power over them will be greater yet."

And they all became of one mind.

By thought and from the Light, the Eldest sought to form and to create spiritual beings. But they were not able to solve the mystery of life.

Then they grew still more impatient. And some said: "We know that life dwells also in Darkness. Let us avail ourselves thereof."

Once more God caused His voice to be heard.

And God said: "My children, return unto your abodes in this My Kingdom; for I have not chosen you; only they are fit who have *patience.* But you, who waver between good and evil, between Darkness and the Light, you are not worthy to lead others. My children, I say unto you: never will you fathom the mystery of life that is in the Light, though you seek through all eternity; for you arose not by *the strength of your own will,* you were formed and created by Me, your Father, formed and created from My own Self. But you, who are of Me, though you have the power to create from Darkness, the power to solve its mystery of life, yet I say unto you: *do not concern your-selves therewith! For the life of Darkness is not everlasting! For in Darkness is the seed for all that is evil – for sin and for death!* But should you nevertheless avail yourselves of evil and call yourselves its masters, beware, lest you become its *servants!*"

And they all heard God's voice.

But they heeded it not; for they were greatly impatient.

Then the Elder of the Eldest stood forth.

And he said: "Our Father says that the life of Darkness is not everlasting; *but we know not this to be so!*

"Let us seek to create from Darkness, and is the life thereof *not* everlasting, then shall we return unto our abodes and remain there to await our Father's call."

Once more God's voice sounded unto them.

And God said: "My son! Why do you concern yourself with evil? Beware, lest you become its *servant!* For I alone am the Lord Al-mighty.

"Know you, My son, that the beings that you can draw forth from Darkness by the strength of your thought will never bless you, but only curse you and that whereof they were created. For you shall know that each life, however wretched and lowly it may be, will always strive toward the Light, toward that which became victorious through *Me*. My son, do you avail yourself of evil, then will Darkness bind you and all who follow you – bind you – *until your children have learnt to pity you rather than curse you*.

"My son, My children! I have spoken unto you, that you may choose that which is right."

And they all heard God's voice. But none took heed; for they were all of one accord.

Then God, their Father, fell silent; for God *compels* no one to do that which is right. But He looked with sorrow upon their conduct.

Much time passed.

By the strength of Thought-Will, the Eldest sought to draw forth Darkness from the concealing sea of the Light.

Slowly the Light receded and Darkness broke forth.

In heavy waves it whelmed over them, flowed through them, bound them to itself, defiled and bewildered their thoughts.

In heavy waves Darkness surged through their glorious world, ravaged it and laid it waste, while dense fogs laid their dwellings in ruin and took away the pure, radiant colours, while evil vapours spread everywhere.

In heavy waves Darkness whelmed over the Globe, made it fruitful and brought forth some of the many dormant forms of life.

But the Eldest saw with horror the destruction of all that was beautiful.

And they said: "How came this to pass? For this was not our will, for this was not in our thoughts.

"Truly, the power of Darkness is awesome!"

Much time passed.

God's Youngest children grieved deeply over the evil that had come to pass.

And they agreed to go forth unto the ravaged Kingdom to call back their brothers and sisters.

And they all departed to that place.

The Eldest heard their calling voices, and they all listened. But the calls sounded distant and faint, and the Eldest dared not answer; for they could not see the radiant figures of their brothers and sisters;

for the fogs and vapours of Darkness covered all.

Then the Youngest grieved still more.

And they returned once more unto God's Kingdom of Glory; but they were not able to forget the evil they had seen.

And they went unto their Father.

And they said: "Father, forgive our brothers and sisters! Father, bid them to return!"

But God answered them and said: "I *bid* no one to do that which is right; it is not I, but their evil deeds that bind them to Darkness. But for the sake of your *prayer* will I sound My voice unto them at the passing of each aeon of time, that they should remember that which they have forsaken, and repent of what they have done. For are they able to repent, then will the Light in their hearts loose them from the binding power of Darkness and draw them back unto their rightful Home; and I, their Father, shall forgive them; for I love you *all*."

Then the Youngest fell silent, for they saw that their Father's grief was without bound.

Much time passed.

The Eldest sought to create anew their ravaged Kingdom, but they were not able to do this. Dense fogs and vapours overturned and laid waste all that they sought to build up. And they were homeless amid their imperfect dwellings.

All was barren and dark.

And there was no gladness.

Much time passed.

Then the Elder said: "We are not able to make this straight, for we lack the power to do so. Let us descend unto the Earth, for I see that *there* is Darkness also."

And they all descended to that place.

But then became their horror greater still; for Darkness was there still darker, the fogs still more dense, and the vapours exceeding hot.

But life was everywhere.

For Darkness had drawn forth many forms of monstrous, hideous and awesome creature; for Darkness had brought forth manifold foul and pallid growths. Devoid of order, these sprouted and grew among each other – small, large and mighty.

But these ugly growths and these hideous creatures were to the Eldest the first forms of plant and the first forms of beast upon the Earth; for they had not seen how Darkness had corrupted all that was already created under the radiance of the Light; for they had not seen how Darkness had made fruitful and called forth some of the manifold dormant forms of life.

But filled with wonder, the Eldest beheld the evil and the hideous.

Mighty beasts waded in the swamps and tramped upon the Earth. Some moved ponderously through the air, others meandered through the waters, many let out roars and terrifying cries.

All was disorder and confusion.

The Eldest saw the beasts multiply and bring forth new creatures.

And they saw them attack one another, hurl one another to the ground, tear and trample one another asunder.

But those that fell unto the ground rose not again.

And the Eldest saw that the torn bodies of the beasts slowly dissolved and soaked into the ground, while evil vapours spread everywhere. And they saw dark shadows rise from the torn bodies, saw them slowly absorbed by the Darkness that compassed them about.

Then the Elder said: "Truly, the life of Darkness does not endure; for we see the earthly bodies dissolve and soak into the ground, and we see the spiritual bodies be swallowed up by the Darkness that is about them. Thus, all returns to that from which it was taken. Truly, this is *death!* The power of Darkness is awesome!"

And they wandered further across the Earth.

But everywhere was the same life, the same confusion.

Then the Elder said: "These creatures we can never lead, for we have not the power. But let us now carry out our thought: to form and to create earthly beings after our own likeness; let us endow them with the power and the will to multiply and bring forth new beings. For we have seen that not the *single being,* but the *kind* lives on. And when we have formed and created our children, then shall we lead them, that they may become rulers over the Earth, and we shall give them such power that they can make themselves lords over these beasts."

And the Eldest became all of one mind, for they thought that this was good.

But then God's voice sounded unto them; for an aeon had passed from the time when God had promised his youngest children that He would help their fallen brothers and sisters.

And God said: "My children, I, your Father, speak unto you, that you may remember that which you have forsaken, and repent of what you have done; for are you able to repent, then will the Light in your hearts deliver you from the binding power of Darkness and draw you back unto your righful Home; and I, your Father, shall forgive you."

The Eldest heard God's voice; but it sounded distant and faint.
And they all were filled with fear.
And they dared not answer.
Then God fell silent; for He *compels* no one to do that which is right. But He looked with sorrow upon their conduct.

Much time passed.
By thought and from the radiations of Darkness and of the Earth, the Eldest tried to form and to create earthly beings in their own likeness. But their thoughts were confused, and they made many vain attempts.

Again much time passed, while they sought to fashion the images of their thoughts in the earthly clay.
And after much toil and after much trouble, the Eldest succeeded in forming creatures that were able to breathe and to live in the dense fogs and vapours of the Earth.
These beings were the first of the human race. But they were not beautiful in any way, neither were they good, nor were their creators able to endow them with power, but only with the lust for power.
Truly, human beings were not formed and created by God, but were formed and created by God's eldest, fallen children.

5.

Have Human Beings no Right then to Call themselves Children of God?

When the human beings had been formed and created, the Eldest chose lands and places that were raised somewhat above the swamps and the waters.
And they led the new beings there, that they might make themselves lords over the Earth and over the beasts.
But when the human beings awoke to life and saw the mighty beasts, they fled in great fear and terror. Some sought shelter in the densely entwined growths; some dug caves, dug them with their hands in the steep slopes; others fled into the bleak mountains; and none dared come forth until hunger drove them out in search of food. Then they fell upon the smaller beasts, killed them and sucked their blood.
Thus they sustained life.

By thought the Eldest sought to influence and to guide their creatures. But the streams of thought from the Eldest were evil and sinful, and they led human beings to perform many wicked, many dreadful deeds.

The human beings were not able to see their creators, but when they perceived the streams of evil that emanated from the thoughts of the Eldest, they fearfully raised their hands toward the sun of the Earth, which shone with a reddish glow through the fogs.

And the Elder said: "Behold, our children seek help from the Light of the Earth, our children turn away from us, away from Darkness."

The human beings looked upon one another with evil in their eyes, they fought, they killed one another, and the living sucked the blood of the dead.

But the Eldest saw the spiritual bodies of the dead rise slowly from the ground and walk among the living.

And they saw these dead wander about, without thought, without will, without aim. They saw them as pale shadows, living and yet without life.

And some of the Eldest said: "The spiritual bodies of human beings are *not* absorbed in the Darkness that is about them, but the earthly bodies dissolve and return to that from which they were taken.

"Why then does Darkness not absorb the spiritual bodies?"

But the Elder answered them and said: "When we formed and created these beings from the radiations of Darkness and of the Earth, we forgot to withhold our own selves, and some of that from which we ourselves were formed and created flowed with the waves of Darkness into the spiritual bodies of our creatures. And no matter how faint it may be, we know that the Light, which is of our Father, can never be quenched; and these shadows will continue to be for all eternity."

Then some of the Eldest answered: "This is fearsome; for this *was not our will*. Let us seek to withhold our own selves, that no more shadows shall live and yet be without life."

Much time passed.

The human beings were like unto the beasts, they lived like them, mated like them, and their offspring became abundant.

And the streaming waves of Darkness drew a spiritual force of life from the Eldest, and imparted it to all new-born human children.

And the Eldest sought to break the power of Darkness, sought to withhold their own selves, but they were not able to do this, for Darkness bound them.

Then said some of the Eldest: "Truly, we are *the servants of Darkness;* for we are not able to free ourselves from those we have created, we are not able to withhold our own selves, Darkness pervades us, Darkness binds us. And the human shadows will continue to be through all eternity."

The Elder answered them and said: "Let us persevere, until at last we become the masters of Darkness!"

But they who had spoken would not hear him, for they were not with him. And they said unto one another: "Let us remain in our ravaged Kingdom, let us remain in our imperfect dwellings, and nevermore venture unto the Earth; for we have no power to make straight this confusion."

Much time passed.

The human beings continued to multiply. And they went forth across the Earth; but their shadows followed them. And these became ever greater in number.

Some of the shadows found their way unto the ravaged Kingdom, drawn by the thoughts of the Eldest.

But then were the Eldest filled with dismay.

Many fell silent. And for them there was no joy, for they grieved profoundly.

The shadows entered the imperfect dwellings, wandered about in the ravaged Kingdom without thought, without will, without aim – living and yet without life.

And the Eldest saw this.

But they had not the power to help them.

Then the voice of God sounded unto them once more; for another aeon had passed.

And the Eldest all listened.

But the voice of God was distant and faint.

And God said: "My children, I, your Father, speak unto you, that you may remember that which you have forsaken, and repent of what you have done!"

Then some of the Eldest answered.

And they cried out: "Father, Father, be merciful toward these wretched shadows, our creatures! Father, grant them the everlasting life of the Light, that they shall not live for ever and yet be without life! Father, be merciful! Forgive us our evil deeds!"

When they had thus cried out, the voice of God was heard once more; but then it sounded beautiful and clear.

And God answered them, and He said: "For the sake of your

prayer shall I take your children into My care. For the sake of your *prayer* shall I make *your* creatures *Mine,* and I shall bestow upon them a portion of My own Self, give them of eternal life.

"My children, suffer the remorse in your hearts to draw you unto your rightful Home. I, your Father, forgive you; for I love you all!"

But they who did not answer when God spoke saw their brothers and sisters depart from the ravaged Kingdom, borne by the radiant waves of the Light.

And Darkness closed behind them; and it grew darker yet about those who remained there.

But God provided His repentant children with abodes in distant parts of His vast Kingdom.

And He said: "Remain here in peace and rest until the Light has pervaded you and purified you; remain here until I call upon you, that you may help your creatures, help them to journey forward toward the Light, toward My Kingdom!"

And God went unto His youngest children.

And He said: "My children, some of your elder brothers and sisters are returned; bid them be welcome; for they have suffered much.

"My children, I, your Father, have promised these, your brothers and sisters, to take their creatures into My care and to make them My children. Behold, I shall bestow a spark of My own radiant Being upon every human shadow, that they can thereby strive forward, *through numerous lives on Earth,* from the deepest Darkness unto My Kingdom of Glory. My children, I, your Father, know that aeons must pass before the last human being is delivered from the bondage of Darkness and from life upon the Earth. But likewise do I know that you, My children, can shorten this time greatly, if you will suffer your radiant spirits to be bound unto earthly bodies, if you will live as human beings live, and suffer as human beings suffer, that you may bring the Light of the Spirit unto the Earth, that your future brothers and sisters can more easily find the way unto My Kingdom of Glory.

"My children, you shall *not be compelled* to go unto the Earth; but would you do this of your own free will, then I, your Father, shall *thank you.*"

The Youngest all fell silent; for they dared not answer; for they remembered the evil that they had seen.

But when they had all remained silent for a time, the eldest of the Youngest stood forth.

And he said: "Father, I am ready; I shall bring the Light unto the children of the Earth, I shall be like them, I shall live among them and seek to help them, they who shall be my brothers and sisters. Father, send me unto the Earth!"

But then they all cried out: "Father, we are ready. We will help our future brothers and sisters, that in time they may enter Thy Kingdom."

Then God looked fondly upon them all.

And He said: "My children, you have chosen that which is right. I, your Father, thank you. But I say unto you: should human beings have struggled forward without your help, should they have fought alone against Darkness and striven through sufferings and sorrows, through sin and through death, until they had reached their rightful Home, then would *their* glory have become greater than *yours, then would human beings become the first, and you would become the last;* for then would they themselves have had to strive forward to all that I, your Father, have given you. But are you able to keep your promise, to help your earthly brothers and sisters, then will you *all* be equal when in time you gather in My House, and I, your Father, will love you *all.*"

And God turned toward the eldest of the Youngest.

And He said: "My son, you were the first who was prepared to bring the Light unto the Earth. Through you this work of the Light has begun, through you shall it also be fulfilled. To you I grant the power to lead human beings forward through numerous earthly lives, until you deliver them from the Earth, that they may journey further along brighter and happier paths. And your brothers and sisters shall all obey you. But I, your Father, shall stand by your side, that you shall not grow weary. And in the fulness of time shall you bring unto human beings the greatest of all, which is *Love;* for you shall teach them to love one another, teach them to do good unto all who suffer. And I, your Father, shall guide you in your journeying upon the Earth."

And God spoke further unto His children.

And He said: "Your Father's blessing shall follow you all; your sorrows shall be My sorrows, your sufferings shall be My sufferings; and your sins shall I forgive and blot out if you repent and if you pray; for all of you will sin, for the power of Darkness is awesome! My children, I say unto you: *never strive against that which is good, against that which is true; never strive against love, against compassion, and never turn away from the Light that is within you! For then will Darkness bind you, for then will you forget Me, your Father, and then will you delay your work, delay your progress toward the high goal!"*

And they all promised to obey, they all promised to follow their elder brother.[1]

6.

Are the many Earthly Lives of Human Beings Predetermined by God?

When the Youngest had promised to let themselves be bound unto earthly bodies, had promised to live as human beings, God gave them a certain time, that they might prepare themselves for their difficult task.

In this time of preparation, God laid the plan and gave the laws for the life and being of mankind in the time to come.

Then God became the Keeper.

But God saw that dwellings were wanting for the future human spirits. And He resolved to fashion dwelling places for them.

By Thought and from the Light, God formed and created six spheres. And the first of these He laid about the ravaged Kingdom and the Earth, and the next He laid about the first.

And God created the spheres in such manner that they brightened, through numerous shadings, from shimmering dawn to clear and glorious light. And He created many dwellings in all of the spheres, that none of His future children should be without a home.

And God ordained that while embodied upon the Earth the human spirit *should itself prepare for the next earthly life* by the striving of the free will toward the Light and the good, and by the striving of the free will against Darkness and against evil.

And He ordained that the spirit, when upon death delivered from the earthly body, should be drawn unto that place, unto that dwelling it had itself prepared through its deeds; prepared with that purity, with that wisdom and love that the spirit had attained through the struggle and suffering of life upon the Earth.

And God ordained that the spirit, after each completed life upon Earth, might for a time abide in its dwelling, there to reflect upon the life just ended, to repent, to rest, to learn and to prepare for the coming journey.

Thus, through numerous lives on Earth, prepared by its own struggles and victories, should the human spirit rise slowly from the

---

[1]) The eldest of the Youngest is known to mankind by his earthly name: Jesus of Nazareth – the name he bore in his fifth, and last, incarnation.

early dawn of its first dwelling, to the clear and glorious Light of the
final dwelling in the final sphere. And there, the eldest of the
Youngest, by you called *Christ*, should receive the human spirit, and
in the name of the Father deliver it from the Earth, that it might
journey further along brighter and more beautiful paths.

When God had fashioned and ordained all these things, He bade
His Helpers to gather the shadows. And God's Helpers gathered
together all the shadows from the Earth and from the Kingdom
ravaged by Darkness.

And behold, there was a mighty host, legions of legions!

And God bestowed upon each shadow a spark of His own radiant
Being. And He took them all into His keeping, to a place He had
prepared for them far from the Earth, that in peace they might abide
there, until the divine radiance was become one with their bodies of
shadow. And thus endowed with life could they once more be bound
unto human bodies, to begin their journey toward the high goal.

7.

In what Manner were the Spiritual Bodies of God's Children Bound to Human Bodies? And in what way did the Youngest Bring the Light unto Mankind?

When God had taken the shadows into His keeping, He went unto
His youngest children.

And He said: "Behold, all is made ready, and the hour is come
when you must make good your promise. I, your Father, have made
new dwellings for you in the last of the spheres that I have laid about
the Earth and the ravaged Kingdom. In these dwellings shall you
abide while you work for mankind, in these dwellings shall you rest
when you return from each completed life upon the Earth.

"My children, I, your Father, have so ordained that not all of you
shall walk upon the Earth at once. Some shall be embodied now,
some shall help your elder brother to guide the journeying of mankind, and others shall hold vigil and protect those brothers and
sisters who are among human beings, that they should not go astray.
My children, I have so ordained that you shall not grow weary; and
when the first of you return, then shall *they* rest while others walk
upon the Earth. Thus for a time will you all be among those who
lead, for a time among those who rest, for a time among those who
guard and protect, and for a time shall you live among the suffering
human beings."

Then God chose some of the Youngest.

And He said: "My children, be you the first to go forth unto the Earth!"

And God blessed them, and He said: "When you are become as human beings and perceive the evil that issues from your fallen brothers and sisters, *then pray you for them, but curse them not,* for pray you for them, then will your tender thoughts reach unto them, and more readily will remorse awaken in their hearts."

When God had spoken thus, the Youngest all went unto the new dwelling places.

But they whom God had chosen to be embodied as human beings were brought by God's Helpers and by their brothers and sisters unto the Earth, and there bound by the life-giving cord of the Light to human children yet *unborn.* And God took their thoughts, took their remembrance; and of the Light of the spirit they kept but that which they had promised to bring unto mankind.

But when the fulness of time was come, and the children should be born, the Youngest that were bound to the unborn children's bodies drew nearer and nearer unto them. And at the moment when they were born unto life, the spiritual bodies of the Youngest – guided by the Will of God – were laid as a mantle about the new-born, and they took the form of their earthly bodies, while the life-giving cord brought the stream of Light from the spiritual unto the earthly body. And only death could sever the bond and deliver the spirit anew.

Thus became God's children united with human bodies, and thus will all spiritual bodies, according to the laws of the Light, be bound unto those of the Earth.

But when the first of the Youngest were become as human beings, *earthly time* began; for until that hour all had been disorder and confusion.

While century followed century and millennium followed millennium, the Youngest led mankind forward toward the Light.

Human beings learnt much from their leaders, learnt to shape their simple thoughts in speech and characters; for the first human beings had no speech. As beasts they uttered manifold cries to give warning, draw attention or show joy, fear, anger or revulsion.

Slowly human beings received more and more knowledge.

And they learnt to kindle fire with flint and wood, learnt to fashion implements with which to work and to defend themselves, learnt to protect themselves against the beasts and to take heed of the places whence flaming fire, rocks and scalding vapours gushed out from the depths of the Earth.

Thousands of centuries passed.

But unto each new generation the Youngest brought more and greater knowledge.

Slowly the waves of the Light streamed across the Earth. In many places new and better kinds of beast arose. But some of the monstrous and hideous beasts died out, for God made their offspring frail, and these were not able to multiply.

More pleasing and more useful plants sprang forth everywhere. Human beings learnt to till the soil and put some of the beasts to useful service, and they learnt to harvest the stems and leaves of plants and trees and their fruits. They learnt to hew the mountain rock and build their dwellings thereof. And they learnt to shape likenesses of themselves and of the beasts in wood, in stone and in coloured clay, to adorn their dwellings therewith.

Thousands upon thousands of centuries passed.

With each passing century the human body became more graceful, the spirit more full of Light, and human thought became more pure and lucid.

And the Youngest sought to bring mankind knowledge of a higher Power, a spiritual Being who ruled over and ordained all things. But the simple thoughts of human beings were not able to conceive of that which was not visible to their eyes, and they bowed down in worship of the sun of the Earth that shone upon them, prostrated themselves before the glowing sun, which gave them light and dispersed the fogs of the Earth.

Thus human beings continued, century after century, millennium after millennium, to worship the power that to them was the highest – the radiant and blazing fire of the sun.

Generation after generation, human beings journeyed forward toward the Light.

Through passing centuries they journeyed forth, seeking toward the goal, guided by God's youngest children in their human embodiment.

Thus were the purifying streams of the Light drawn across the Earth; thus was brought the Light of the Spirit unto human beings.

8.

How did the Eldest Look upon the Work of the Youngest for the Benefit of Humanity?

But the Eldest who were in the ravaged Kingdom followed with wonder the conduct of their younger brothers and sisters. And Darkness, which flowed through them without cease, confused their thoughts still more and aroused anger in their minds; and they agreed to strive against their younger brothers and sisters, agreed to draw mankind back into Darkness; for the Eldest *would not* that their creatures should belong to the Light.

And then began the struggle between the Eldest and the Youngest.

The Youngest taught mankind to live in purity, in love and in peace with one another.

But the Eldest taught them to envy and to persecute one another, to live in sin and wickedness; taught them to gather themselves into mighty armies, to march against one another, to kill, plunder and rob; taught them to seize by force nations, cities and riches to which they had no right.

And the Youngest taught mankind to make good, wise and just laws.

But the Eldest taught them to make evil, unjust, and unwise laws.

The Youngest taught that one man and one woman should live their lives together; taught human beings to love and care for their offspring.

But the Eldest taught men to take many women, taught women to take many men; for in this way they were neither able to love nor care for each of their offspring. Indeed, many did not even know their own children, nor were they concerned with their lives.

And as centuries were added to centuries, millennia to millennia, Darkness compelled the Eldest to strive without cease against their younger brothers and sisters; for with each century the power of Darkness over the Eldest increased, their thoughts became still more confused and they were able to think only evil and to desire evil; for they were truly the *servants of Darkness.*

And the Eldest continued to cast stones in the path of the Youngest.

Many fell and many grew weary; but God, their Father, raised up the fallen, sustained the weak, forgave and blotted out that in which they had erred and sinned.

God, their Father, sustained them and strengthened their courage.

And they all journeyed onward, striving against Darkness, striving for the Light and striving for the good.

But when an aeon had passed from the time when some of the Eldest answered God's calling voice in repentance, God sounded His voice anew to call upon those who were still in the ravaged Kingdom.

Only few answered Him; for only few repented of that which they had sinned. But God forgave the repentant, for He loved them all. And the streaming waves of the Light carried them away from the ravaged Kingdom. And it grew still darker about those who remained.

And once more, century after century passed, millennium after millennium.

And the Youngest sought to impart unto humanity greater knowledge of that which was not visible to the earthly eye; sought to teach that the highest power was God; taught that God was a merciful and loving Father, who loved them all and would draw them all unto His Kingdom.

But the Eldest whispered unto mankind that the highest power was a god of wrath and vengeance, taught that those who would not bow down before his stern divinity, would be cast into the pit, there to languish for ever.

And they taught them to worship many gods, to carve images in wood and stone and to bow down before these lifeless objects. Taught them to appease divine wrath by pouring out the blood of humans and of beasts upon the altars, which had been built unto these images that were without life and without power.

While centuries passed, while millennia followed millennia, the thoughts of mankind became confounded, and they confused all that they learnt; for they were not able to separate the evil from the good, to separate Darkness from the Light; for the Eldest continued to beset the Youngest in their work.

And they drew Darkness closely across the Earth, and Darkness awakened the inner forces of the Globe to a fearsome, flaming eruption. And the greatest of those realms that the embodied Youngest had created upon the Earth was laid waste and sank into the sea. Few only were able to flee from the death and destruction; for the waters flooded away most of the mighty land.

And the Youngest grieved over that which was lost.

But God, their Father, sustained the weak and strengthened their courage.

And they journeyed onward, striving for the Light, striving for the good.

Again, century followed century, millennium followed millennium; once more, the Youngest brought more and greater knowledge unto mankind, taught them anew to build mighty empires and great nations, to raise beautiful cities and glorious dwellings; taught them to mine the ores and many-coloured, sparkling stones of the mountains, to adorn with these their dwellings and adorn their bodies.

And the Youngest sought anew to impart unto human beings greater knowledge of that which was hidden from the earthly eye. And some few learnt to receive messages from the world that they did not see.

But invisible to human beings, the Eldest beset the Youngest in their work.

And they drew Darkness closer about the Earth; and they taught human beings some of the hidden powers of Darkness, taught them once again to worship the many gods, taught them to commit wicked deeds by worshipping and by calling upon the powers of Darkness.

Thus human beings journeyed gradually forward, in dawning and receding ages, toward the Light, guided by the Youngest from knowledge to greater knowledge, while the Eldest sought to draw them back, draw them under the power of Darkness.

9.

Did the Eldest Continue to be Invisible to Human Beings? Were none of them Incarnated on Earth?

Many thousands of centuries had passed since the time God had last let His voice be heard by the Eldest. Then said one of those who had remained in the ravaged Kingdom: "Behold! We continue to live in Darkness and misery. Still we have not been able to bring Light and beauty unto our dwelling places, we have no power to bring back into the Darkness those we created. Let us seek to become human beings, and live among them as do our younger brothers and sisters; for we have seen that remembrance of life with our Father is blotted out from their memory while they walk upon the Earth. Let us bind ourselves to earthly bodies; for then will the remembrance of our wretchedness, of our lack of power and our sufferings also be blotted out from our memories and while we are as human beings we shall rejoice once more in possessing power, wealth and glory."

They all listened to these words and spoke much thereof; for they all wished to forget their sufferings.

But then God spoke unto them *in warning*.

And God said: "My children, commit not this act; for it will bring much strife, much misery and a great many sufferings upon mankind, your creation, and you it will profit nothing. My children, seek to repent of the evil that already you have done, then I your Father shall forgive you, that you may return unto your rightful Home. But are you still not able to repent, and would you, against My word, bind yourselves unto earthly bodies, then should you know that *all* of you must walk under the laws I have given for the progress of mankind. Then must you strive from Darkness unto the Light, then must you walk the paths that human beings walk; but this will become sorely trying for *you*, for Darkness will gather closely about you, and you will become greater than human beings, *greater in sin, in vice and in wickedness*. For the fear and terror of Darkness will never depart from you, and your sufferings will become very great.

"My children, I, your Father, have spoken unto you, that you may choose that which is right. Take much thought ere you commit this act, *My children, take much thought!*"

And they all heard God's voice, but they listened in silence, for they were not able to repent.

Then the Elder of the Eldest stood forth.

And he said: "We wish our creatures no harm, we seek only to forget our sufferings. Surely we shall not feel greater fear and terror among human beings than we feel in this our ruined home; surely we shall not find greater suffering among them than we find here.

"Behold, how the sun of the Earth shines and glows! It brings warmth and beauty unto all who live upon the Earth. Is this not better than the cold and Darkness which reign here? Behold the splendid dwellings of the people, their proud temples, the magnificent mansions of their princes! Is this not better than our crumbled ruins? Behold their splendid raiment, their golden adornments with the many-coloured glittering jewels! Behold the riches they possess, and the riches yet resting in the bosom of the Earth and of the mountains! Is this not better than our nakedness and the filthy rags with which we seek to cover ourselves? Behold the nations and splendid cities of the Earth, the tall luxuriant vegetation, the many-coloured flowers, clear streams and mighty seas! Is this not better than our barren rocks, our murky and fog-shrouded waters? Is this not better than the evil vapours that well forth everywhere in our realm?

"Truly, we wish our creatures no harm. We wish only to share in their riches and splendour, we seek only *to forget our sufferings.*"

Then they all cried: "We wish our creatures no harm, we seek only to forget our sufferings."

God, their Father, answered them not; for He *compels* no one to do that which is right. But He looked with sorrow upon their ways.

And the Eldest sought to bind themselves unto earthly bodies – but they were not able to do so; only the Elder possessed the power to do this, for his power was great. And when his brothers and sisters implored him to stand by them, he promised to help them *all.*

Slowly the Elder journeyed from place to place across the Earth, and he bound his brothers and sisters unto human bodies yet unborn, bound them with the life-giving cord of Darkness. And he sought to take their memory, but he was not able to blot out all of it. Lust for power remained in their hearts, and the memory of the fear and terror of Darkness stayed with them all.

But when the Elder had helped his brothers and sisters, he would bind himself to an unborn human body. But behold! This he was not able to do; for he possessed not the power to blot out his own memory.

And the hour came when the Elder stood alone.

Alone and unseen by human beings, he wandered across the Earth. Alone with his fear and terror, he roamed the ravaged Kingdom. In heavy waves Darkness surged through his body, oppressing his mind and confusing his thoughts still more.

Then *hatred* awoke in his heart.

He raised his hands toward the heavens and cursed his God and Father, the source of all creation.

Then he stretched his hands toward the Earth, cursing his creatures, cursing his younger brothers and sisters, cursing those brothers and sisters who forsook him and left him to be alone.

But at that same hour God's voice sounded to him *in warning.*

And God said: "My son, cease your curses, for they profit you nothing. My son, I, your Father, say unto you: the hour will come when in humility, with grief and remorse, you will humble yourself before human beings and seek to obtain their forgiveness. My son, make it not harder for your creatures to forgive you, by adding your curses to the evil you have already prepared them: sin, suffering, misery and the bitterness of death. My son, cease your curses, for they profit you nothing, and I, your Father, grieve over you."

The Elder heard God's voice, but he answered not; *for Darkness and hatred bound his mind and his thoughts.*

Troubled times overtook mankind; for the Eldest grew up among them, and they became greater than human beings, greater in sin, greater in hatred, and they sowed the evil seed of Darkness everywhere.

Some of the Eldest were born to rule, and they wielded the scourge of power over all the peoples beneath them. And they laid the yoke of bondage upon men and upon women, that they should serve them and be slaves unto their evil lusts and desires. And they surrounded themselves with much magnificence and much splendour. They took many women, abused and slew numerous men and women. They warred continually with neighbouring kings and princes, conquered much land, many cities and great riches, conquering all by force and cunning. And they sent thousands upon thousands of warriors to their death; for their lusts were insatiable. *For they were evil and cruel, haughty and proud.*

But in their hearts they were cowardly and vile, for the fear and terror of Darkness was upon them.

Many of the Eldest were born to serve in the temples, born to be priests and priestesses of the gods. And they wielded the scourge of power over the peoples, over the kings and over the princes; for they spoke with much authority, threatening with stern retribution from their god, or gods. And all bowed down before them, bowed down in fear and submission.

The priests were counsellors to the kings and to the princes; but they gave evil and wicked counsel.

And they sought to conceal the sinful acts that were committed in the hidden chambers of the temples, for some of the priestesses of the gods were harlots.

The priests gathered together great riches, plundering by force and stealth, and they heaped up the gold in the treasure chambers of the temples.

But still they continued to seek more riches, to seek greater power; for their greed was insatiable. *For they were evil and cruel, haughty and proud.*

But in their hearts they were cowardly and vile, for the fear and terror of Darkness was upon them.

Troubled times overtook mankind.

Again, the inner forces of the Earth broke forth in flaming eruption. Again, a mighty realm sank into the sea. Thousands upon thousands of human beings perished, while mountain rocks crushed the magnificent temples, crushed the splendid dwellings, while the floods swept away all without trace. Only few were able to flee. But those who fled spread far and wide, travelled in smaller bands across nearby islands unto lands that to them were new and unknown.

But the Youngest grieved deeply for that which had been lost, grieved deeply over the evil seed of the Eldest; for they saw it spring forth everywhere, and they saw it bear manifold fruit.

But God, their Father, comforted them and strengthened them, and they journeyed onward, striving for the Light, striving for the good.

The centuries passed, millennium was added to millennium, human beings spread more and more across the Earth, moving farther and farther away from their first dwellings and homelands. And they built new realms, new nations; and each nation lived according to its own laws, governed under the rule of one man or of several men.

But those who had moved far away from their first homelands knew nothing of their forefathers, and they were no longer able to speak the tongues their fathers spoke.

Troubled were the times on Earth; for the Eldest still let themselves be embodied among human beings, and much evil, much wickedness spread everywhere.

And whenever the Eldest at death were freed from their earthly bodies, Darkness drew them back unto the ravaged Kingdom. But they implored their elder brother to bind them once more to new bodies; for they yearned to walk in the light of the Earth, in power and in glory.

And the Elder, who was the obedient Servant of Darkness, bound them anew to human bodies yet unborn. But often he bound them against his will, for his hatred was turned upon those who had failed him. *And Darkness compelled him, for the power of Darkness is great.*

But each time that the Eldest returned unto the ravaged Kingdom, after a completed life upon the Earth, remembrance of the times before their first embodiment became more faint and distant. For the Elder was not able to restore to them all that he had blotted out from their memory.

Remembrance grew still more distant, grew still fainter; but the fear and terror of Darkness never left them.

And while the centuries passed, some of the Eldest grew weary of life among human beings, and they remained in the ravaged Kingdom; for they feared to let themselves be embodied; for they feared to reap the evil seed which they themselves had sown.

And by the power of Thought-Will they sought to build likenesses of earthly dwellings and cities; and in these dwellings and in these cities they re-lived their lives on Earth.

But with their evil thoughts they continued to draw Darkness closer about the human beings, *their own creation.*

Troubled were the times on Earth.

Again, the inner forces of the Earth broke forth in mighty eruption.

Again, one of mankind's mighty realms was swept away. Blazing fire and glowing rocks ravaged and destroyed all, while the Earth opened in gaping chasms, while proud mansions and splendid cities crumbled and were swept away. Thousands upon thousands of human beings perished. Only few were able to flee from the glowing, all-engulfing torrents of fire.

And the Youngest grieved for that which had been lost.

But they sought persistently to draw the Light unto the Earth; for God, their Father, gave them still greater strength, gave them still greater power, and they strove mightily against the Eldest who were embodied upon the Earth.

Century was added to century, millennium unto millennium.

Once more the Youngest taught human beings to build realms, to found new nations, to raise new cities.

And they brought more and ever more knowledge unto human beings; taught them to gaze into the vastness of space, taught them to follow the paths and orbits of the glittering stars. But human beings were able only dimly to discern part of the greatness that encompassed the world in which they lived.

Troubled were the times on Earth; for the visible Eldest gained greater and greater power over mankind; for they tore down what the Youngest built up; for they continued to sow their evil seed everywhere and they won ever greater victories over the Youngest.

Ever more heavily Darkness descended upon the Earth. Mankind grew ever more wicked, sank ever deeper.

And the time came when many of the human spirits, when at death released from their earthly bodies, were not able to ascend unto the dwellings that God had given them in the spheres about the Earth. For their vices and evil desires bound them to the places where they had formerly lived while their mortal bodies were alive.

And then the spirits of the dead began to walk among the living, walk in their homes, in their temples, and in the palaces of the kings and princes. Wherever people went, the spirits of the dead walked beside them, whispering to them evil and sinful thoughts. Yea, they even sought to tempt human beings to commit the dreadful deeds of Darkness.

And there arose much chaos and confusion.

But some people were able to see the dead, and they spoke thereof unto others, and they were much afraid; for this strengthened many in their belief in an evil Deity, who fought with the highest God for dominion over humanity, for dominion upon the Earth.

And much fear was born in the hearts of human beings.

Troubled were the times on Earth. And the Youngest grieved over the advance of evil, and only few dared descend unto the Earth to fight against the powers of Darkness.

But these few brought great knowledge and much learning.

And they taught human beings to ponder the being and existence of nature, sought to open their eyes unto good and to evil, to the pure and to the impure. With clear words and compelling speech they sought to strengthen them in their belief in a just, all-embracing God, sought to bring them knowledge of the eternal struggle between Darkness and the Light.

And they taught mankind to search out some of nature's hidden laws, and to derive benefit from the knowledge gained. They taught them to render their thoughts, their yearnings, joys and sorrows in melodious verse; taught them to express the deep probings of their thoughts in wise and profound teachings.

And they taught mankind to build glorious temples, splendid dwellings, mighty vaults with marvellously curved arches, supported by slender columns, richly adorned with representations in many forms of animal, and most artistically entwined leaves, flowers and fruits.

And they taught them to form and to carve images of the human body and the imagined likenesses of gods and goddesses with care and artistry in the white stone of marble. And with these splendid works the human beings adorned their temples and their dwellings.

But the Youngest were not able to break the power of Darkness.

And when more than a hundred centuries had passed since the first embodiment of the Eldest, the Youngest were much disheartened, and only few ventured unto the Earth to strive against Darkness.

Then came the hour when many of the Youngest were gathered in the outermost sphere about the Earth. And they spoke much of the troubled times that were, and of the troubled times to come. And they counselled among themselves as to which course they should follow in order to vanquish Darkness.

But they continued to be much disheartened, and one of them said: "We are no longer able to lead mankind; for we have no power to do so. Behold, disorder and confusion abound!

"Many human spirits trespass against the laws our Father gave them. Behold, thousands upon thousands of their dwellings in the spheres stand empty, while the spirits, bound by their vice and lust, walk upon the Earth among the living. But we are not able to call back our earthly brothers and sisters, nor are we able to deliver them from the power of Darkness.

"And behold, some of our elder brothers and sisters in the ravaged Kingdom have sought, by the power of Thought-Will, to imitate earthly regions, cities, and dwellings, and in these shadow-realms they re-live again and again their last earthly lives. Unto these shadow-realms, by thought and by will, they draw numerous human spirits, bound in sin, to be slaves unto their evil lusts and desires. And we know that our brothers and sisters remain in the ravaged Kingdom so as to evade the laws to which they freely submitted at the time of their first incarnation.

"We know that they act in this way so as not to reap the evil seed which they themselves have sown, so as not to be overtaken by their own evil deeds. All this we know; but we have no power to bring our brothers and sisters under the laws they have forsaken. We shall never be able to do this!

"Nor shall we be able to guide mankind. Indeed, when, at our Father's bidding, we appeared before them in our full glory, without earthly form, to strengthen their faith in our Father's Divinity, we were able to awaken them to reflection for but a short time. Soon, they sank once more into sin and into vice.

"Truly, *we have fought – but we have not overcome. Humanity is lost.*"

Then spoke the eldest of the Youngest.

And he said: "Break we not the promise that we gave our Father, then is humanity not lost. And we shall never break it; for do we this, then are we not worthy of His trust.

"And you must remember: *you have all promised to follow me, your elder brother;* behold, I say unto you: let us beseech our Father to help us; for He alone has counsel, He alone is able to set right all these things. Let us pray unto our Father for help; for He has promised to sustain us, for He has promised to lead us. Truly, I ask of you, stood He not often by our side, raised He not the fallen, strengthened He not the weak and comforted the disheartened? Showed He not often the way, when we saw it vanish in Darkness? Verily, let us pray unto Him to give us still greater strength and still greater power, that we may overcome; for you should remember: not only have we promised to lead mankind unto our Father's Kingdom, we have also promised to win back our elder brothers and sisters. And furthermore, while we live as humans among the human beings, we can give our brothers and sisters much help in the arduous journey of their earthly lives. We can meet them with love, we can help them to bear their burdens, seek to remove stones from their path; we can sustain them and take them with us. And I ask all of you, what joy have we, so long as our elder brother is against us, so long as we feel his hatred and his curses? Verily, let us all pray unto our Father for help; *for He alone has counsel."*

But when he had spoken, they all fell silent, for they searched their hearts.

And again, they spoke much among themselves, until they were all of one accord. Then they said: "Brother, we shall follow you; for we know that your words are true!"

And they all went forth unto God's Kingdom.

But the eldest of the Youngest stood forth.

And he said: "Father, we come to Thee with our sorrows; for Darkness has conquered us. We come to Thee to ask of Thee to grant us greater power and greater strength, that we may reach our goal."

Then God, their Father, looked upon them all with love.

And He said: "My children, be patient, for only those who are *patient* will overcome."

And God walked among them, and He spoke unto each one, and He said unto them all: "I, your Father, thank you that none of you broke the promise you gave Me; for the temptation was very great. My children, I say unto you: put not exceeding trust in the power and strength which is yours, but be mindful that I, your Father, will give you all the power and all the strength that you need, so long as you strive for the Light, for the good, and for the true!"

And God spoke further.

And He said: "I, your Father, *compel* no human beings to follow the laws which I have given for their progress. Of their own free will must they walk under these laws. But so as to lighten your burden, at the last hour of every passing century shall I let My voice be heard by all human spirits bound in sin. And I shall speak unto them, that repentance may awaken in their hearts, that the Light may draw them back unto their empty dwellings."

And God comforted the weak, and He strengthened them all.

And He spoke further.

And He said: "My children, when you are embodied once more among human beings, then *pray* for those who are bound by evil; for the loving thoughts of your *prayer* will awaken repentance in their hearts, and then will the streams of the Light carry the repentant back unto their dwellings, which stand empty. My children, I, your Father, ask of you: seek all of you, while you walk among mankind, to remember your eldest brother and *to pray for him;* for then will you be victorious!"

And God turned to the eldest of the Youngest, and He said: "Behold, my son, I shall send a multitude of your brothers and sisters unto the Earth that they may guide humanity. And I shall send many unto the Jewish people; for thence I hear the most cries for help and sustenance; for there the people sigh under the yoke of sin. My son, prepare yourself; for in a short while shall you follow your brothers and sisters. The times are evil, and mankind is in dire need."

But the son answered Him and said: "Father, I am ready. Thy Will be done!"

Then God blessed them all.

And He sent a multitude unto the Earth; and many He sent unto the Jewish people.

But when all the Youngest were departed, God let His mighty voice be heard over the entire Earth by all the human spirits that were bound by sin, bound by Darkness. And they all ceased in what they were about; for God called upon each one; for He named each one.

Many were those who heeded God's calling voice; but a great many more remained in Darkness. For they were still not able to repent, and only those who answered God, their Father, were borne by the streaming waves of the Light back unto the empty dwellings.

And they remained for some time in the spheres in order to be purified, to rest and to learn – until they should once more journey onward in new lives upon the Earth.

But before a century had ended, God summoned the eldest of the Youngest.

And He said: "My son, are your ready? For the time is nigh, when according to your promise to Me, your Father, you shall walk upon the Earth among mankind.

"Teach human beings to love one another, as brothers and sisters, teach them to love the Light and to shun the evil and sinful deeds of

Darkness. Strengthen them in that which is good, strengthen them in that which is true. Teach them to have faith in Me, their God, the Father of their spirit."

But the son answered Him and said: "Father, I am ready."

Then God spoke further.

And He said: "My son, it may happen that your journeyings will be burdensome and hard, for many are the ways that you may walk among human beings. The times are evil, for Darkness reigns over all the Earth, and it will be hard for you to find the proper path. My son, are you ready?"

But the son answered: "Father, say unto me, shall I choose the right way?"

God looked fondly upon him, and He said: "I, your Father, will not *choose* the way for you. I will but show you the way that can lead unto the goal, and none can know beforehand whether you will fulfil your task.

"My son, hear me, for I shall seek to guide you: pray you for your eldest brother while you are as a human being, then will the loving thoughts of your prayer awaken repentance in his heart, then will he return unto his rightful Home in My Kingdom. And is your brother saved, then will Darkness have no servant to oppose you, then will the way of your journey be easier and more full of the Light, for then will mankind see in you the being that you are. Many will love you, and only few will hate you."

And God spoke further.

And He said: "My son, should you *not* remember your brother and forget to *pray* for him, then will he strive against you, then will the road of your journey be stony and dusty. The thorns will sting you, only few will love you, many will hate you, mock you and persecute you. Yea, *human beings* will bring you death – death upon the cross. Such will be their gratitude for the gifts that you bring them.

"My son, your Father asks of you: are you still ready?"

Then the son bowed down his head, and for a time he stood silent; for he searched his heart.

But his love for suffering humanity impelled him. He looked steadfastly upon his Father and answered: "Father, I am still ready. But Father, forgive me, should I not find the right path while I live upon the Earth; for Thou knowest Darkness; Thou knowest that its power is awesome."

Then God embraced His son, and He said: "I, your Father, shall lead you, that your journey should not be exceeding hard; but I say unto you: always heed My voice when I speak unto you; for then will you never go astray."

3 C

And God spoke further.

And He said: "Behold, My son, I shall ask one of your brothers to go with you upon your journey, that he may carry some of your burden and remove some of the stones from your path."

And God chose one of the Youngest. And he promised to go with his brother.

Then God spoke unto them both.

And He said: "Sustain each other, bear each other's burden, do not fail!"

And God blessed them, and He took away their memory; but He let them keep a faint remembrance of the times that were before the creation of mankind. God did this so that the eldest of the Youngest should never doubt who he was, nor ever doubt the truth of the words that he should speak unto human beings. God did this so as to help them work together, that the younger brother should not fail the elder.

And He sent them both unto the Jewish people.

But one was called *Jesus of Nazareth and the other was Joseph of Arimathea.*

Some while before God sent the two brothers unto the Earth, He called upon a third one of the Youngest.

And God said unto him: "Behold, your elder brother is distressed, the times are evil, for Darkness rules everywhere upon the Earth. I, your Father, ask of you: will you prepare the way for him? Will you seek to remove some of the stones from his path, that his footsteps shall not falter upon his journeying? My son, will you go with your brother?"

His son answered Him and said: "Father, I am ready; give me Thy blessing, and I shall go with my brothers."

But when he had answered thus, God spoke further.

And He said: "Teach human beings to shun the deeds of Darkness; teach them to turn away from their false gods; teach them to repent of the evil they have done, that they may travel the straight road unto My Kingdom. My son, pray for those who are bound by Darkness. My son, seek to remember your eldest and fallen brother."

And God took away his memory, but He let him keep a faint remembrance of the brother that he loved, and for whom he should prepare the way. God did this so that he should know the eldest of the Youngest, when they met in their journeying through life upon the Earth.

And God sent him unto the Jewish people, and he was called *John,* named *The Baptist.*

10.

Was the Birth of Jesus Supernatural? Was he Conceived by the Holy Ghost?

The *earthly body* of Jesus was conceived and born of the desire and will of man and woman.

And the eldest of the Youngest was bound unto this body, bound with the life-giving cord of the Light; for thus are all spirits of Light bound unto earthly bodies by the Will of God.

But *God Himself* guided and protected him in his arduous journeyings through life upon the Earth.

11.

What were Jesus' own Thoughts Concerning his Mission on Earth?

In evil times he was born unto the Earth.

In evil times he grew up among mankind.

His thoughts were pure. His eye saw and his ear heard more than the feeble eyes and the deaf ears of human beings.

Love and compassion filled his heart. And his hands brought healing unto many.

But his countenance was sorrowful, for he bore the heaviest burden upon his shoulders.

And he was a stranger among human beings.

His eye saw much sin, many sorrows and much suffering.

And he heard people in the synagogue and in their homes cry unto their god to free them from the yoke of bondage and soon, soon to send them *the Messiah,* the promised, the long awaited One.

Slowly, God called to life the thought in the mind of Jesus that he was sent unto the Earth to deliver the people from the yoke of *sin,* and to cleanse their hearts of all impurity; that he was sent unto the Earth to teach the people to love one another, to strengthen their faith in their Heavenly Father.

Slowly the hope awoke in the heart of Jesus that *he* was the promised, the long awaited One.

But he dared not fully trust this hope.

And he pondered much on these thoughts.

Often he sat in the synagogue and studied the ancient Scriptures.

3* C

And he listened to the elders and to the scribes expounding the words.

But he found not the peace that he sought.

Long and deeply he studied the ancient Scriptures. And his heart became heavy, for the god of the Scriptures was often vengeful, and he was in no manner *just*.

But Jesus did not grow weary, he continued to seek until he faintly discerned a fond and gentle countenance – *the God of Truth, of Love and of Compassion.*

But the God of Truth and of the Light, whose countenance he discerned behind the Lord of wrath and vengeance, reminded him of the Father, whose image he bore within his heart.

And unto this Father he prayed fervently for help, for peace and for strength.

And God heard his prayer.

And He granted him *strength, purity and peace of heart.*

But at the moment Jesus knew himself to be strengthened, he went unto the synagogue and stood forth, and he spoke against the elders and against the scribes.

And all who heard his words wondered greatly, for his words were clear, and he spoke with much authority.

But some of the words of Jesus were these: "Behold, I say unto you; the god you fear and worship is not the God of Truth but the God of Falsehood! For I say unto you: should you search with care in the ancient Scriptures, which speak of this your god, then would you see how weak and faltering he is. Now he wields the scourge of vengeance and retribution over the heads of your forefathers and drives his people into exile, then he calls them back. Now he bids their leaders, through the prophets, take arms against their neighbouring peoples to plunder, to pillage and to slay, and when thus he has raged for a time with might and power, then he *repents* of his actions, *repents* of the evil that he has done, and promises to temper his wrath, promises to show greater mercy. Truly, truly I say unto you: this is not the God of Truth, *this is not the God of Justice!*

"And what worship he craves of you!

"How many beasts does he not bid you slaughter before his countenance, that this sacrifice may please him! How much blood is not spilt upon his altar, that the scent thereof may rise unto the heavens and delight his heart!

"Behold, I ask of you: is it not said unto you in the Law of Moses that you should not kill one another? And how often has your god not spoken, through the prophets, unto your forefathers and bid them slay thousands upon thousands of their enemies? And has he not promised your forefathers to reward them for these evil deeds with much glory, many riches and much land! Truly, I say unto you: that God who says, *thou shalt not kill* and that god *who bids you kill* are not the same; *for that god who bids you slay your enemies, he is of the evil, and you should shun him."*

And Jesus continued to speak; for deep silence had fallen upon them all.

And he sought by the words of the Scriptures to show them the God of Love, of Truth and of the Light; the God who with perfect righteousness punishes the transgressions of mankind. He sought to show them the God whose embrace was open unto each repentant sinner, the true, the highest, the only God. He, who was not only the God of the Jewish people, but of all the world – yea, even the God of the heathen.

But when he fell silent, all were dismayed.

And the scribes spoke harsh and condemning words against him.

And the ruler of the temple stood forth and forbade him ever again to speak in the synagogue, yea, forbade him to expound the words of the Scriptures.

But Jesus answered him and said: "None has the power to bid me keep silent in my Father's House."[1]

Then they all became yet more dismayed, and some cried: "Behold, the Evil One has possessed him and speaks through his mouth; hear how he profanes the holy and scorns the exalted."

And they sought to drive him out of the synagogue.

But Jesus answered them not. And he walked of his own accord out of his Father's House.

When the people in the city heard of that which had come to pass they wondered much, and many were angered.

But the parents of Jesus, the carpenter Joseph and his wife Mary, rebuked him sternly for the words that he had spoken in the synagogue against the elders and the scribes.

But Jesus answered them and said: "Know you not that I love you, and have I not sought to do your bidding? How much more, then, should I not seek to do the bidding of *Him,* who sent me? How much more, then, should I not love my Heavenly Father, love Him who reigns over all the Heavens?"

But they understood him not, and they grieved much, for they believed that his thoughts were confused.

---

[1]) Jesus regarded not only the Temple in Jerusalem, but also every synagogue as his "Father's House".

12.

How are we to Understand the Baptism of Jesus?

But some time after Jesus was driven out of the synagogue, he heard much talk of a man John, called "The Baptist", who journeyed from place to place in the region of the river Jordan.

And Jesus heard that he spoke unto the people there, and taught them much about the Kingdom of Heaven; he heard that this man spoke sternly unto the people, for he rebuked them for their lack of faith, rebuked them for their worship of Mammon and of power.

And some of this words were these: "The Kingdom of Heaven is nigh, when you repent of the evil you have done, when you turn away from the false gods of this world, when you shun the deeds of Darkness."

And when men and women came unto him in sorrow and repentance, he took water from the river into his hand and poured it over them.

And he said: "As with water I cleanse your bodies of earthly dust and soil, so will the Lord cleanse your hearts with heavenly fire; cleanse you from the soil of sin and evil."

But, if anyone asked him: "Are you the Messiah, whom we expect?", then he answered, saying: "One who is greater than I shall come. But the Lord has sent me to prepare the way for him."

Many spoke of this unto Jesus.

And God awakened in his heart the desire to see this man and to speak with him; for that which he had heard caused him to wonder.

And Jesus went unto the place where John was.

But when John saw him coming, his spirit knew him.

And he bowed down before Jesus, saying: "Brother, be welcome!" And John turned to the many who were with him, and said: "It is *he*, whom I awaited, unto him I prepared the way."

But Jesus rejoiced greatly in his words.

And he spoke unto John, saying: "Brother, baptize me, as you baptize the people, that cleansed I may go forth unto my work."

Then John bowed down before him and said: "Even as your body is clean, so is your heart clean also."

But Jesus answered him and said: "None is pure but God."

Then John did as Jesus wished.

But when he had baptized Jesus, he turned toward the people who had gathered about them.

And he called in a loud voice: "This is the Son of God, the Beloved! Follow him, and be obedient unto him; for his words are true."

When Jesus rose from the water, the multitude fell back, for he stood before them as a king.

Many bowed down before him, and some sought to kiss the hem of his robe, but Jesus bade them to refrain.

And he abode with John, and they spoke of a great many things.

But after a time they departed from one another.

And they went each his own way.

13.

How should we Interpret the Temptation in the Wilderness?

After his meeting with the Baptist, Jesus often journeyed unto the desert places, so as to search his heart in the stillness, so as to ponder his task and to listen to that which was inspired in him.

But when he was thus alone his eldest brother, the Servant of Darkness, stood at his side and sought to instil impure and sinful thoughts in him.

But Darkness could not defile the mind of Jesus.

Then the Elder sought to instil *pride* in his heart.

But when Jesus perceived these alien thoughts, he heard with his inner ear a distant, a gentle voice which said: "Pray for him who is bound by evil!"

And Jesus, who was able to see with his mind's eye, sought all about him to find the evil spirit which inspired in him the sinful thoughts of pride.

But he saw no one; for Darkness concealed his eldest brother.

And then he believed that the thoughts were his own, that the distant voice sought to warn him against these his evil thoughts. And he prayed humbly and fervently unto his Heavenly Father to forgive him the pride which filled his mind.

But the thoughts were not erased.

And once more the voice said: "Pray for him who is bound by evil!"

Jesus listened to the words, and he sought to interpret them.

But he was not able to do so; for the curses that the Elder had hurled upon him oppressed his mind and obscured the faint remembrance that he bore in his heart of the brother who had fallen to the power of Darkness.

And a great fear filled the heart of Jesus; for he feared that an evil spirit had possessed his body and hindered him in discerning between good and evil.

And he cried: "Depart from me, thou who art of evil!"

But when the thoughts persisted he called in his distress upon his Heavenly Father and cried: "Father, deliver me from the one who threatens me!"

When God drew Darkness away from the Elder, and Jesus beheld his brother's countenance – then he dimly remembered the promise that he had given his Father before he began his journeying upon the Earth.

And he heard a distant, sorrowful voice which said: "My son, the path of your journey will be strewn with stones and filled with dust, and human beings will bring you death – death upon the cross."

But from that moment Jesus knew no joy; for he bore the heaviest burden of sorrow in his heart.

And later, when some time had passed, and he spoke unto his disciples of the Evil One who tempts mankind to sin, some of them asked: "Master, say unto us, did the Evil One ever tempt you?"

Then Jesus answered: "While I walked in the desert places he came and spoke unto me, so as to awaken pride in my heart; but I said: depart from me! For I was not able to *pray* for him; for I forgot the promise that I had given unto my Father."

But they who heard the words understood them not.

And they dared not question him; for they saw that he sorrowed greatly.

14.

Did Jesus Teach of an Eternal Hell? Did he Teach Nothing more of the Kingdom of Heaven than what is already Known through the Gospels?

But about the time that his eldest brother's countenance was revealed to Jesus, some people came unto him; for they had seen him by the river Jordan and heard The Baptist's words concerning him. And they much desired to hear him speak.

And Jesus did according to their wish.

And he expounded much of the Scriptures for them, spoke unto them of the God of Truth and Justice.

But they who heard these words spoke unto others thereof.

After this, great multitudes came to seek Jesus, to see him and to hear his words.

From among these multitudes Jesus chose twelve men, that they might walk with him upon his journeyings and help him speak unto the people; for he faintly remembered the twelve who were with his Father.

Thus he journeyed from town to town, in company with several of his chosen companions.

Jesus spoke in the synagogues, in homes and at the places where people gathered to rest when the labours of the day were done.

And he spoke unto them of God, their Father, spoke of His love and His compassion. And he rebuked them sternly for their intolerance, their hatred and envy of one another.

But some of the words of Jesus were these: "Love one another as brothers and sisters; for even as you love, so will your Heavenly Father love you also.

"Be compassionate toward all who come unto you; for show you compassion, then will your Father show compassion toward you also.

"Forgive your enemies and all those who sin against you, for *in the same measure* as you forgive, so will your Heavenly Father forgive you also, when you repent of what you have sinned against Him. Truly, I say unto you: be converted, repent of your sins and seek to cleanse your hearts of all that is unclean; for then shall you surely behold the glory of Heaven, then shall you surely enter the Kingdom of Heaven. For in my Father's Kingdom are many mansions, and they are all prepared for you; and all joy and glory are there for those who have repented of that which they have sinned. And I say unto you: you shall go forward unto greater bliss, yea, *you shall go forward until you behold our Father's countenance.* Therefore be you all perfect, even as your Heavenly Father is perfect! Be you all pure, for then shall you surely behold the countenance of *Him,* who loves you all.

"But, I say unto you: *never must you demand the Kingdom of Heaven as wages* for the good that you will do. Never must you let trumpets sound for you in streets and market places, that all may know what you have done. Nor ever must you with loud voice proclaim: behold, we have fed the hungry, we have clothed the naked, we have given our gifts unto many; ours is the Kingdom of Heaven! For do you act in this way and do you speak these things, then shall the Kingdom of Heaven *not* be yours. For I say unto you: are you good, then will you do that which is good, *for you will not desire that which is evil!* Are you merciful, then will you show mercy unto all, *for you will not be able to let this be undone!* And have you love in your heart, then will you have compassion for all who suffer, but then will you forgive your enemies also, and all who have sinned against you.

"Truly, I say unto you: do you all this, even as *I* have told you, then shall you surely behold the blessings of Heaven; for then shall the Kingdom of God be yours!"

But some came unto him and said: "Master, tell us, how shall we enter the Kingdom of God?"

Then Jesus looked upon them, and he said; "Heard you not my words? Behold, I say unto you: you shall love your God and Father with all your heart. And you shall love your neighbour as yourself!"

But they who had asked answered and said: "*We* heard what you spoke unto us; but many are they who did not hear the words."

Then Jesus said: "Go forth and proclaim that which you have heard, that all may share in the blessings of Heaven."

And Jesus spoke yet more unto the people.

And some of his words were these: "But will you not be converted and repent of your sins, and will you not cleanse yourselves of your uncleanliness, but continue to walk in disobedience and sin, continue to live in lasciviousness, to rob, plunder and kill, continue to bear false witness against your neighbour, continue to hate, persecute and curse one another; then surely shall you go unto the Evil Place, and there shall you suffer eternal[1] pain. There no sun will shine and no moon bring you light in the darkness; but there a fire[2] will be kindled in your hearts, a fire that will not be put out, but neither will it devour you. There shall you suffer the torments of hunger and thirst; for none will still your hunger, nor will anyone give you to drink. There shall you grieve; for there will be no joy, but only weeping and the gnashing of teeth; for the worm[2] of sin shall gnaw at you and pain you."

But when he spoke in this manner, a great fear came over the multitude.

And some went unto him and said: "Master, tell us, does no one return from that place?"

Then Jesus remembered the countenance of his brother, remembered his broken promise, and he answered: "Truly, I say unto you: be converted and repent of your sins while there is time; for no one

---

[1]) Eternal – an inconceivably long time. Must not be understood as lasting through all eternity, since this is not what Jesus meant.

[2]) Because Jesus often spoke in images, the above expression must be understood as a metaphor describing the painful and gnawing memories of sin. The Evil Place that Jesus describes here is the ravaged Kingdom, the home of the Eldest. During his earthly life, Jesus kept many of his remembrances from his transcendental existence, though not all of them were equally clear and comprehensible to him.

but God knows whether any will return; no one but God knows whether the fire shall be put out; yea, truly, I say unto you: *no one but God knows* whether the worm that gnaws and pains shall die!''

But the people continued to question, and they said: "Master, tell us: how shall we prevent that many must go unto that Evil Place?''

Then Jesus looked upon them and answered: "Heard you not the words I spoke unto you: you must repent and be converted.''

But those who had questioned answered him and said: "*We* heard the words, but many are they who did not hear them.''

Then Jesus said: "Be you the salt; for even as meat is salted, that it shall not be tainted, so must you salt the hearts of human beings also, and proclaim unto all that which you have heard. But I say unto you: you must speak in *my* name; for if the salt lose its power, then shall the meat be tainted and it will reek badly – but then will neither the salt nor the meat be fit any longer, and all shall be cast away. Thus shall it be with you also.''

Then the disciples understood him, understood that they were not to speak in their *own* words, but *proclaim the words of Jesus.*

And they went forth to impart unto others that which they had heard.

Jesus won many from among the multitudes; many followed him, and they who followed him loved him deeply.

But the scribes, and they who were called Pharisees and Sadducees, hated him and persecuted him.

15.

Did Jesus Perform Miracles?
Did Jesus Heal the Sick?

When Jesus journeyed from city to city, he sought out the sick and the poor.

And he shared with the poor the gifts that he received from those who loved him. But unto the sick he spoke words of hope and words of comfort also. And to lessen their sufferings, he often laid his hands upon their bodies; but when he perceived the power and strength of his spirit come upon them, he prayed: "Father, if it be Thy Will, let these be healed!''

Thus he brought healing and strength unto many.

But this is not a miracle; many have done this from the earliest times, and many will be able to do this for as long as the Earth exists.

Was Jesus able to Call the Dead back to Life?

And during one of Jesus' journeyings it came to pass that a man came unto him and pleaded: "Master, heal my daughter, for she suffers much. Follow me and heal her, for she is nigh unto death!"

But when Jesus heard the words, he answered: "It will be of no avail that I come, for I have no power to deliver her from death."

But the girl's father continued to plead, and he said: "Master, help her, for she is the delight of my eye!"

And Jesus took pity on him; for his heart suffered with the suffering.

And he followed him.

But when they were come unto the house, they heard that the girl was dead.

And when Jesus saw the father's grief, he went in with him to strengthen and to comfort him.

And while Jesus stood at the child's bed, he saw with his mind's eye that her spirit had departed somewhat from her body; but the body was not dead, for the cord binding her spirit had not yet severed.

When he had seen this, he turned toward those who were present and said: "She is not dead, she sleeps; but I shall seek to waken her, I shall seek to call back her spirit."

But when he had spoken these words, he took her hand, looked steadily upon her and called her name in a loud voice. And behold, her spirit returned unto the body, and she awoke.

When Jesus saw this he said: "Strengthen her with food and drink, and give her care, for she is very weak."

Then all were stricken with awe, and they wondered much.

And they said unto one another: "His power is great. Truly, he must be the Son of the Most High."

And they bowed down in the dust before him, yea, they would even worship him.

But Jesus drew back from them.

And he said: "Heard you not my words? Heard you not that I said: she is not dead, she *sleeps!*"

The people answered him and said: "Master, we heard your words – but we *saw* that the girl was dead!"

Then Jesus said: "I say unto you: if the spirit has left the body, then life is no more, then the body is dead. But I perceived her spirit; for it stood among us, and when I called upon it, *then* she awoke."

But the people answered: "Master, *we saw that you gave her life.*"

Then Jesus became angered, and he said: "You foolish ones, you see, and yet you do not see, you hear, and yet you do not hear, and you would not believe me, when my words are true; but should I speak lies unto you, then would you believe me, then would you fall down before me and worship me. But I say unto you: you should by no means worship *me,* but worship *Him,* who sent me; for He has given me all, and of myself I can do nothing. Yea, verily, you should pray unto your Heavenly Father that He should enlighten you so as to make you see; for you are surely not able to know right from wrong. And never should you speak unto others of the death of this girl in that way; *for you know not whereof you speak!"*

When Jesus had spoken thus, he left them and journeyed on.

But that which Jesus did was not a miracle. Many have been able to do this before his time and after his time, and it can be done for as long as the Earth exists.

Was Jesus able to Drive out Unclean Spirits?

On his many journeys Jesus came upon human beings to whom were clinging spirits of the dead, people who were possessed. And their sufferings were very great, for the unclean spirits defiled their thoughts and drew much strength from their bodies, so that these became wretched and weak.

But when Jesus, with his mind's eye, saw unclean spirits enveloping the earthly bodies of human beings, he spoke sternly unto them, bade them to leave and thus restore peace to these human beings; and he forbade them to come back.

And unto those he had thus delivered, he said: "Cleanse your hearts and your thoughts of all that is evil, of all that is unclean; for do you abide in sin and in vice, your sufferings will become greater yet; for then will the unclean spirits return to cause you new and yet greater torments."

Some of those who had been possessed did what Jesus bade them to do; but many remained unclean.

Thus Jesus was not able to bring peace unto all whom he sought to help.

But that which Jesus did was not a miracle. Many have done this before him, and many have done it since his time.

16.

How should we Interpret the Transfiguration on the Mount?

Jesus often went unto the desert places, that in the stillness he might search his heart and ponder his thoughts.

But when he dwelt in solitude, he grieved much over the wretchedness of mankind, grieved over their sufferings, grieved over their hatred and wickedness toward one another.

And he prayed unto his Heavenly Father to grant him the power and the strength to guide the sinful and erring human race.

One day as Jesus rested in solitude, oppressed with sorrow, while those who walked with him had fallen asleep, tired from their journeying, God sent two of the Youngest unto him, that they should appear before his earthly eyes and thus bring him comfort and strength.

But when Jesus faintly perceived the forms of the bright and radiant figures, he called out: "Father, I thank Thee!"

Upon hearing this sudden cry, his companions awoke from their slumber, but they kept a faint remembrance of the glory that they had seen. For while their bodies rested, their spirits had seen and known the bright and radiant figures.

17.

What was the Relationship of Jesus to the Apostles?

The twelve chosen by Jesus from among the disciples all had to labour hard to sustain themselves. But Jesus helped them; for he shared with them the gifts which he received from those who loved him.

But a number of those who walked with Jesus had a wife and a home. Therefore could they not always be in the company of Jesus; but he often came unto their dwellings so as to rest a few days, when his body was weary from the many journeyings. And the companions of Jesus welcomed him with much joy, and they took leave of him with sorrow, when he left them once more; for he was much loved by all his disciples, loved by men and women.

Eleven of those who walked with Jesus were of the Youngest. These were good, and their spirits were strong. But they were far beneath Jesus in earthly knowledge and learning; and the remembrance they bore in their hearts of the times that were before mankind was very faint; for their earthly bodies and their eldest brother's curses weighed heavily upon them all.

But the twelfth of those who walked with Jesus was of the Eldest.

And his name was Judas Iscariot.

Often when Jesus spoke unto the disciples, before the time when he had chosen the twelve, he saw Judas among them. And when the spirit of Jesus knew him, he saw that Judas bore the heavy burdens of Darkness.

And after Jesus had chosen the eleven, he went unto Judas and said: "Brother, come unto me and be among my followers."

But Judas turned his countenance away and said: "Master, are you able to give me the peace that I seek?"

Jesus answered him and said: "Not I, only the Most High has the power to do that!"

And he spoke yet further unto him, and he said: "Judas, seek to repent of that which you have sinned, take your burdens unto our Heavenly Father, then will He forgive you, that your heart may be cleansed."

But Judas answered: "Never will my heart be cleansed – *I* must bear my burdens alone; for none can bear them for me."

Then Jesus continued to speak unto him.

And Judas hearkened to the words and promised to go with him. But he said: "Behold, I am not able to help you in your task; for did I this, then would the unclean defile the clean."

From that moment Judas was among the followers of Jesus. And when Jesus spoke unto them he listened to the words; but his countenance was dark, and he did not question, nor did he speak unto the people, and he chose to walk alone; for the eleven followers of Jesus shunned him; for they loved him not.

Jesus often spoke with his followers, and he sought to awaken the full strength of their spirit.

And he taught them how they could heal the weak and drive out the unclean spirits by the will of their thought and by the strength of their spirit.

But he said unto them: "Pray unto the Most High to give you wisdom, that you may know when you are able to help, and when you are not able to do so; for this you cannot know of yourselves."

Jesus often sent them two by two unto the cities of the region, that they might proclaim his words unto many.

He did this so as to strengthen them in their task; he did this so as to try their strength of spirit.

And he spoke much with them of the times that would come,

when they should be alone upon the great mission; spoke much of the time when he should leave them. For he understood that he was not able to overcome the evil will of mankind, and he told his followers that the hour of his death drew near.

But when he spoke thus his followers said: "Master, how shall we fare when you are no longer with us? For we have neither your wisdom nor your power."

But then Jesus answered: "When I am returned unto my Father, then shall I ask Him to give you still more of His strength, to give you still more of His Holy Breath."[1]

When he had spoken thus, some of his followers asked: "Master, tell us, when you have left us, will you then return unto us nevermore? Shall we not see you among us while we are here? Shall we not meet again until also we have left this world?"

But when they had asked this, Jesus was silent a while; for he remembered the fair and radiant figures that he had seen with his earthly eyes.

And he said: "If our Heavenly Father allow me this, then shall you surely see me among you."

Then they all asked: "Master, when shall we await you?"

But to this Jesus answered: "This no one knows but God."

18.

Was Jesus always Ready when he was Called unto the Sick and the Grieving?

And it came to pass that Jesus came unto the house of Simon Peter to rest after many days of arduous journeying. As he entered, he spoke a greeting and said: "Give me water to drink and food to eat; for I thirst and hunger much."

And Simon Peter and his wife bade him be welcome and gave him a cup of water.

And while Jesus washed his body and cleansed his robe, Simon Peter's wife prepared him a meal.

When all was ready she said: "Master, eat, and strengthen your body; for you are sorely in need thereof."

But behold, at the same moment a shepherd entered the room; he went forth unto Simon Peter, greeted him and said: "If you know

---

[1]) God's Breath is identical with God's Spirit or Thought. Here the expression means "greater spiritual life."

where I should seek the Master from Nazareth, then tell me; for I wish to see him and to speak with him."

But Simon Peter pointed toward Jesus, and he said: "The one you seek is here!"

Then the shepherd turned to Jesus, greeted him and said: "Master, my aged mother has sent me unto you; for she has lain still on her bed for many days. For she is sick and palsied and she is not able to come unto you. Master, come with me, for death draws near, and she desires much to hear your words."

When he had spoken thus, Jesus rose and he answered: "Brother, I will come with you."

But the wife of Simon Peter stepped forth and said: "Master, strengthen your body with food and drink, and rest, for you are sorely tired – the old woman can wait a while."

Then Jesus looked upon her, and he answered: "They who grieve and they who suffer shall in no wise call upon me in vain – and neither does death wait."

Then he took his staff and departed with the shepherd.

When they had walked for some time along the stony roads, they came unto a low and humble dwelling. And when Jesus had entered the room, he withdrew in haste; for a vile stench met him. But when he discerned the old woman lying upon the bedstead in the darkness of the hut, he went inside once more, laid his hands upon her head, and said: "The Lord's peace be with you."

The old woman greeted him and thanked him.

And Jesus said: "Behold! I am come; for you desired to speak with me."

The woman answered him and said: "My time is drawing near; but I am in fear of death and of the wrath of the Most High; for I have sinned against His commandments."

Jesus looked kindly upon her and said: "Those whom the Lord loves He forgives much."

But the old woman answered him and said: "I have sinned against the commandments of the Lord; how can He then forgive me?"

Then Jesus was silent for a while; for he spoke with his God and Father, and then he knew in what manner he should form his words.

And after some time had passed he said: "Tell me, where lives your daughter, your youngest child? Is she not with you in your old age to give you comfort? For I only see your son, the one who brought me unto this place."

The woman answered him and said: "My daughter is no longer here; for she hardened her heart; for her mother's home was not worthy, and she walked in ways unknown to her mother."

Jesus looked at her, and he said: "And you have cursed her and driven her away?"

But then came great strength upon the old woman; she raised herself upon the bed and she cried out: "How could a mother curse and banish the child that grew in her tender care? How could a mother curse and banish the child she bore and gave life? Truly, you know not the heart of a mother!"

Gently, Jesus laid her back upon the bed, and he said: "Behold, your daughter has sinned against you, and though she has not repented and has not come back you have already forgiven her in your heart. But this you have done *out of your love for her.* Truly, I say unto you: if you, who are of this world, can find forgiveness in your heart for the child who sinned against you, how much more will not our Heavenly Father forgive *His* children; for though your love be great, His is still greater. Behold, I say unto you: never shall you fear death, neither shall you fear the wrath of the Lord; for you have loved much, and you have forgiven much – *much shall you be forgiven.*"

Then the old woman took the hands of Jesus and said: "Master, your words brought solace to my heart and banished my fear. But I pray of you: find my daughter, lead her back onto the right path; tell her that her mother forgave her, before she departed from this life."

But when the old woman had spoken thus, she closed her eyes.

And Jesus stayed with her until her spirit was returned unto the heavenly dwellings; then he rose up and journeyed back, alone, walking the long and arduous road unto the house of Simon Peter. But when he was come there, behold, he sank unto the ground, for his body was weak and weary from the many and arduous journeyings.

But Simon Peter saw him, and he took him inside and made him to lie down and to rest.

From that time Jesus sought without ceasing, and he inquired about the daughter; but none knew her, nor did anyone know where she lived.

But when some time had passed, and Jesus came unto Jerusalem, he heard that the young woman lived in the city, that she abode with a wealthy merchant; and Jesus was shown unto that place.

Jesus sought her, stood before her and spoke unto her in the name of her mother. And he bade her to follow him away from the ways of sin back unto purity and peace. And he brought her greetings from her aged mother, brought her the old woman's forgiveness.

Then sorrow and remorse awoke in the heart of the daughter. The costly raiment and the glittering jewels tempted her no longer. And she left the merchant's house; for she was not his wife; and she departed with Jesus.

And he brought her unto the house of Simon Peter. And Simon Peter and his wife received her with much kindness, and they gave her care, and she abode with them.

But this young woman was Mary Magdalene.[1]

19.

Did Jesus Speak on the Significance of Baptism with the Words Ascribed to him by Tradition?

People often came unto Jesus to be baptized.

But Jesus did not baptize.

And it came to pass that some came unto him, and they asked: "Master, baptize us, that we may be cleansed of our sins!"

Jesus looked upon them, and he said: "Tell me, how often do you cleanse your body?"

The people wondered at his words. But they answered him and said: "We cleanse ourselves each day; for each day our labour, the dust of the road and our sweat defile our bodies."

Again, Jesus asked: "Tell me, do you cleanse yourselves today for the mire which will cling unto your body tomorrow?"

Then they answered: "This we do not do; we cleanse ourselves today of what has defiled us today, and tomorrow of that which will defile us tomorrow."

Then answered Jesus: "Yea, this you do, for the other cannot be done. Therefore, I say unto you: *each day* shall you repent of your sins and *each day* pray unto the Lord that He forgive you. For He does not forgive today your sins of tomorrow. Truly, I say unto you: that which is *has being,* and this the Lord our God is able to forgive; but that which *is not,*[2] neither can it be forgiven. Yea, I say unto you: repent and ask for forgiveness each day, then on the day of your judgment shall you surely be shining and pure; for then will no evil thought bear witness against you, and no false words judge you."

But when he had spoken thus, the people answered: "John

---

[1]) The old woman's hovel lay in the mountains about four kilometres from the town of Magdala.

[2]) Many of the apostles and followers of Jesus thought that baptism not only cleansed one of sins already committed, but also of future sins. Jesus tried to remove this misconception, for which reason he always explained that baptism was merely a symbol. See chapter 20.

4* C

baptizes all who come unto him."

Then Jesus looked upon them and he said: "John has shown you the way; go and do even as he has shown you, and as I have told you."

But they wondered greatly at his words.

And they went from him unto John. And they let themselves be baptized by him; for they understood not the words of Jesus.[1]

20.

Why did Jesus Refuse to Baptize the People who Sought him?

After his baptism, Jesus spoke with many who had been baptized by John, and he saw that not all were able to interpret baptism in the proper way; for the people often put greater meaning in this act than was intended by John; yea, some even believed that through baptism they were cleansed for ever of the impurities of sin.

For this reason Jesus refused to baptize; but he sought to guide all who came unto him, sought to teach them that baptism was merely a *symbol*, and nothing more.

21.

Why did Jesus then Allow the Apostles to Baptize, when he himself Refused to do this?

When Jesus sent his followers upon journeys from place to place to proclaim his word, they were met with much opposition and distrust when, after the desire of Jesus, they refused to baptize those who sought them.

And when the followers of Jesus had returned from their first journey, they said: "Master, suffer us to baptize in the way that John does; for often the people turn from us when we will not baptize them, for they believe that this would make them worthy to be received in our community."

But Jesus answered them and said: "Baptize not, when it is not *required* of you; for many are they who do not understand the true

---

[1]) Because Ardor, in the telling of the above episode from the life of Jesus, only very indirectly has answered the questions posed, further reference should be made to the Commentary to chapter 19.

meaning of baptism, and we should not confuse their thoughts still further."

But they continued to pray for sufferance.

Then Jesus answered: "Are you met with opposition and distrust, and is it required of you, so baptize all who desire it; but then shall you teach those you baptize to repent each day and pray unto their Heavenly Father to forgive that which they have sinned; yea, teach them that they will sin each day, even *after* baptism."

And the followers of Jesus promised to do as he bade them.

22.

How did the High Priests and the Scribes Look upon the Works of Jesus?

But when the enemies of Jesus heard of all that had come to pass, a great anger came upon them. And they took counsel with one another as to how they should hinder the people from going unto Jesus, and how they should hinder them from following him; for they much desired to harm him.

And one of the high priests said: "Let us go unto Jesus of Nazareth ourselves and call him to account; let us seek to beguile him, that we may turn his words against him; for then could we accuse him before the Council; for then could we bear witness to that which we had heard."

And some of the scribes went unto Jesus.

And one of them said: "We have heard that you have much power, and that through this power you heal the sick and drive out the unclean spirits. Tell us, in whose name do you this?"

But Jesus knew their evil purpose.

And he said: "Tell me, in whose name did your forefathers drive out unclean spirits? And in whose name do you this?"

The scribes answered him and said: "In the name of the *Most High*."

Then Jesus looked upon them, and he said: "Truly, I say unto you: that which I do, this I do in the name of the Almighty, in the name of my God and Father; for He sent me unto the Earth that I should be His witness, that I should reveal His power, reveal the glory of His Kingdom."

But when he had spoken thus, the scribes cried: "Hear how he profanes the holy!"

Jesus answered them and said: "It is not *I* but *you* who blaspheme; for you profane Him who sent me; for you are evil in your thoughts, you are arrogant and proud, and you *pretend* to righteousness before your god, though your hearts are hard as stone. Verily, I say unto you: you close your eyes, for you will not see; and you stop your ears, for you will not hear. And this you do because you will not receive me, I who am sent to you. Verily, I say unto you: the hour shall come when you shall see me with the hosts of Heaven, and then shall you know my power and my glory. Yea, I say unto you: the hour shall come when you shall bow down before him you denied, bow down before him you would not receive when he was among you.''

But when Jesus had said this, the ruler stood forth before them.

And he said unto all who were with him: "Heard you not his ungodly speech! Heard you not how he profaned the Lord? For he said that he was the Son of the Almighty, of the Most High!"

And they all answered, and they cried: "We heard the words, and we shall bear witness against him."

Then the ruler turned to Jesus, and he said: "We forbid you to spread your false teachings among the people; for it is our place to guide them, that they shall not go astray."

But Jesus looked upon him and he answered: "The blind cannot lead the blind; for can none of them see, then will they all fall into the pit, and they will perish wretchedly."

Then the ruler was yet more angered.

And he said: "Cease you not your ungodly speech, then shall we accuse you before the Council, and we shall all testify against you; for now that we have heard how you profane the holy and scorn the exalted, we know whence your power springs, and we know by whose help you drive out unclean spirits; for this you do with the help of Satan, with the help of him who is the most evil."

And when he had said this, they all cried: "We know that you do this with Satan's help."

But Jesus looked upon them, and he said: "If you say that I drive out evil with the help of evil, then it is but good that I do so; for I say unto you: if I do this, then are Satan and all his brood in discord with one another. Yea, I say unto you, are the servants in conflict with one another, and in discord with their master, and if he drives all of them out of his house, then is the door open, and any who wish may enter and bind up the master of the house; for then has he none to give help. Truly, I say unto you: if I, through Satan, drive out all his brood, then have *I* prepared the way for *you,* then have *I* opened the door for *you,* and then may you enter and bind up the Hated One - *if you possess such power!*"

"But I say unto you: if your words are false, and if you do not mean what you say, then beware the Day of Judgment; for on that day shall you be called to account for each false word that you have spoken, yea, you shall be called to account for much."

And Jesus spoke further.

And he said: "That which you have sinned against me, that I forgive you, for you are blinded and you know me not. But that which you have sinned against the holy[1] within you, that shall you not be forgiven until you have suffered for it and repented of the evil you have done. Yea, I say unto you: beware the Day of Judgment; *for then shall your words bear witness against you, then shall your words judge you.*"

When Jesus had spoken, he rose from the stone upon which he sat and walked away from them.

But he continued to heal the sick, continued to drive out the unclean spirits. And he continued to speak unto the people of God's love and compassion; continued to interpret the Scriptures as his spirit moved him.

But the enemies of Jesus were yet more embittered.

23.

Was Joseph of Arimathea able to Assist Jesus in his Work?

And behold, it came to pass, when Jesus was near Jerusalem, that a scribe came unto him and walked with him along the road, while they spoke with one another.

But the scribe was Joseph of Arimathea, a man of much learning, of much esteem.

And he was among those who yearned for the coming of the Messiah; and daily he prayed unto God that He would grant him the joy of beholding the long-awaited One.

And when God saw his heart's yearning, He awakened in his mind the hope that *Jesus of Nazareth* was the Messiah, the promised One, the long-awaited One.

But Joseph dared not fully trust in this hope; for he had heard much evil talk among the scribes of this man named Jesus, and he knew that many of the elders and the rulers had complained to the Council in Jerusalem, had complained of the blasphemous speech of the Nazarene.

---

[1]) The divine element that every human being receives from God. See Commentary to chapter 7.

And when he heard that Jesus was near, he decided to see him and to speak with him.

And Joseph went forth from Jerusalem to meet Jesus.

But the Elder, the Servant of Darkness, followed him unseen upon this journey.

And the Elder sought to blot out the faint remembrance Joseph bore in his heart of the times that were before mankind; and when he stood before Jesus, his spirit knew him not.

But the spirit of Jesus knew his brother.

And Jesus said: "Brother, be welcome! Be with me and strive not against me."

Joseph wondered greatly at these words.

And after a pause, he said: "Truly, I am not against you, but you are against me. Yea, you strive against all of us, who are the true leaders of the people, and you stir the people against us. Tell me, by what right do you this?"

Jesus looked upon him, but he answered him not.

Then Joseph continued to speak.

And he said: "Many say that you are the Messiah; and are you the One we all await, then should you not strive against us. Then should you gather the people about you, that together we may break the heavy yoke of bondage. Then should you gather all the people about you, that together we may cast off the heavy burdens that the heathen have placed upon our shoulders. Yea, are you the Messiah, then should you come unto us, for then should we make you the leader of all the people, then should we array you with the purple robe and place you upon the Throne of David, that we might thus fulfil the words that were spoken unto us of the Messiah. And then should *all* the people bow down before you, and they should *all* obey your words."

But Jesus answered him and said: "Truly, I say unto you: I was not born unto the Earth to rule over mankind; for my Kingdom is not of this world. Truly, I say unto you: I have not come to gather the multitudes about me by force, I have not come to kill, nor have I come to cast out the strangers, nor to rob, nor to plunder. But I was sent unto the Earth to teach human beings to *love one another,* so as to bear witness to our Father's Justice and to lead them all unto His Kingdom."

While Jesus spoke thus, Joseph heard with his mind's ear a faint and distant voice.

And the voice said: "Sustain one another, bear each other's burden, do not fail!"

And Joseph listened to the words; his heart softened, and he said:

"Are you the Messiah, then tell me, and I shall speak for your cause before all the people; then shall the elders and the rulers receive you upon my word."

But Jesus answered and said: "Are you to speak for my cause, then must you walk with me, then must you give your great wealth unto the poor, then must you renounce all power, honour and esteem. Yea, truly, I say unto you: would you speak for my cause, then must you forsake all that is yours and walk with me upon the stony and dusty roads. Then should we sustain one another, then should we bear each other's burden, and together should we lead humanity unto our Father."

While Jesus spoke thus, Joseph heard the distant voice, once more.

And the voice said: "Follow your brother, do not fail!"

Then Joseph faltered, but again doubt arose in his mind, for the Elder, the Servant of Darkness, stood at his side and sought to confuse his thoughts.

And Joseph said: "Are you the Messiah, then tell me, then give me a sign, that I may know that your words are true."

Once more Jesus looked upon him.

And he said: "Does your heart not tell you that my words are true, then can a sign help but little; *for they who doubt and they who waver demand ever more signs, demand ever greater signs.* Truly I say unto you: outward signs will never decide the doubts that are yours, they will but make them grow stronger, and then will hope and faith never turn to assurance."

When Jesus had answered thus, he departed in anger; yea, his anger was so great that he did not turn to take leave of the scribe.

But from that time, there was no peace for Joseph of Arimathea; for the worm of doubt gnawed ever at his mind, and often his inner voice whispered unto him these words: *"Follow your brother, do not fail!"*

But at these times, and in those places where Jesus spoke unto the disciples and unto the many who gathered about him, Joseph was often among the people, listening to his words.

And they saw one another, but they could not draw nigh unto each other; for their elder brother, and the curses that he had uttered, stood between them and bound their hearts.

And they both grieved deeply.

24.

Did Jesus Foretell the End of the World and his "Second Coming" in the Manner Handed down by Tradition?

And it came to pass, when Jesus went out from the temple in Jerusalem, that one of his followers said: "Master, behold this temple. How magnificent it is, and glorious. Surely, no other is more richly adorned!"

But Jesus answered and said: "Truly, this temple is beautiful to behold, yet I say unto you: the time shall come when the abomination of destruction shall pass over it and stone shall not be left upon stone."

When his followers heard these words, some said: "This temple shall surely stand until the end of time, for the stones are closely fitted."

But Jesus answered them and said: "Know you not that the prophets have cried out: woe, woe betide Jerusalem, woe betide all people, yea, woe betide all the Earth?"

And Jesus continued to speak.

And he said: "Know you not that the day will come when Jerusalem shall be laid waste, when all that human hands have built shall crumble and be destroyed? Have you not heard that the day will come when nation shall rise against nation, when brother shall stand against brother and father against son? Yea, have you not heard that the day will come when the mountains shall fall upon you and crush you, when the rivers shall be dried up and the seas shall flood the lands, flooding away all that lives? Verily, this the prophets have prophesied unto you – and you know it not! Behold, I say unto you: when that day comes, then shall the Earth shake to its very foundation, then shall all things be laid waste, then shall the sun not shine, nor the moon. Yea, all the stars shall be extinguished. But then will you see the Heavens open, then will you see me in my Father's Kingdom with the heavenly hosts, and then shall you know my power and my glory. And you shall hear a mighty voice everywhere, yea, you shall hear it throughout all the Earth. For the Lord God will call upon the dead and He will call upon the living. Then shall He send His Angels to gather those who were, and those who are in that hour. And when all are gathered together, then shall I go forth and lead the just and the good unto our Father's Kingdom, and there shall be great joy. But the unjust and the evil shall go unto that place which has been prepared for them, and there shall they suffer much."

But when Jesus had spoken thus, some of his disciples said: "Master, tell us, when shall all this come to pass?"

Then Jesus looked upon them, and he said: "Say unto me: have the prophets proclaimed the day and the hour?"

But those who knew the ancient Scriptures answered: "No, this they have not done."

Jesus answered them and said: "I say unto you: the prophets have not made this known unto you, for no one knows the day, nor the hour, but *God* alone.

"But *I* say unto you: you shall turn from all sin, from all evil, and from all misdeeds, that such days shall never come. Yea, truly, I say unto you: pray daily of your Heavenly Father that never the time shall come when men shall curse their offspring and women bewail the children they have borne; for when men and women do this, then shall the end be near."

Thus spoke Jesus unto his followers and his disciples of all that *the prophets* had foretold about the destruction of Jerusalem, of the nations, and of the Earth.

Thus he spoke unto his followers and his disciples of the time when all the generations of the Earth should see him in his Father's Kingdom, and know his power and his glory.

But *never* did Jesus speak unto his followers, nor his disciples, of a time when he should once more walk upon the Earth among mankind.

25.

Was it Predetermined that Judas should Betray Jesus? With what Purpose and with what Words did Jesus Institute the Holy Communion?

And behold, when the time for the Passover drew near, Jesus resolved to journey unto Jerusalem and to keep the feast there.

But when he felt that the hour was at hand when mankind would bring him death, he sent word unto his twelve followers and bade them to meet him in Jerusalem at the house of his disciple Samuel the Water Bearer, that together they might hold the Feast of the Passover there.

The followers of Jesus promised to attend, but some went ahead to make preparations.

When the hour was come and they were met in the house of Samuel the Water Bearer, Judas was not with them.

But Jesus said: "Let us wait a while, that we may all be gathered."

When a time had passed, Judas came in to them, and Jesus went to meet him and he said: "Judas, we have missed you, be welcome among us."

But Judas' countenance was dark.

And he answered not; but he went straight unto the place that had been prepared for him at the table.

When all were seated, Jesus prayed unto God that He should bless their supper. Then he poured the wine into their cups, took the unleavened bread and gave them all thereof, and bade them to eat the Passover.

When Jesus had done this he looked upon Judas, and he said: "Behold, I bade you be with us in this hour, that I might bid all of you farewell before I leave you."

But when the followers of Jesus heard these words they said: "Master, stay with us, depart not from us!"

Jesus answered them and said: "Truly, I say unto you: it is not according to my wish that I leave you, but the people *demand* my life."

Then Jesus spoke further unto Judas.

And he said: "None shall say to me that I fear mine enemies, and none shall say that I hide from them; for when our supper is ended, then shall I go to meet them; for I know that they seek after me.

"Judas, I say this unto you, that you shall not listen to your evil thoughts, that you shall not turn your evil thoughts to deed."

But when Jesus spoke these words, great fear and anger fell upon the eleven of the followers of Jesus, and they cried out: "Master, tell us, what has he done unto you; for we understand not your words?"

Jesus answered them and said: "Be not dismayed, for I spoke unto Judas alone – and I saw that *he* understood my words."

But when they had all eaten and the supper was ended, Jesus took his cup and said: "Brethren, at this hour must we take leave of one another; for soon must I depart to suffer that which is prepared for me."

Some of his followers said: "Master, if you go then shall we go with you; if you suffer death for the sake of your teachings, then shall we share your sufferings."

But Jesus answered them and said: "I go, for it is required of me; I go that through my death I may confirm the truth of the words that I have spoken unto you. But you shall stay and proclaim unto all the people that which I have taught you. Yea, you shall go even unto the gentiles and seek to draw them unto you. But I say unto you: never shall you fear for the words that you shall speak; for when I am returned unto our Father, then, as I have promised you, shall I ask of Him to send you of His Holy Breath, send you yet more of His power and strength. And then shall you at all times know the words that you shall speak."

Jesus spoke further unto them.

And he said: "Brethren, I ask of you: *remember me in times to come, when you are gathered together at this supper; for then shall I surely be among you!*"

And Jesus spoke unto each singly, and he took leave of each one.

And he passed them his cup, and they drank thereof. But when he came unto Judas, who was the last of them all, Jesus offered him the cup and he said: "Judas, drink of my cup, and betray me not!"

But Judas turned the cup away.

And he rose hastily, and he left them without taking leave.

Some of the followers of Jesus would hasten after him, but Jesus held them back, and he said: "Judge not your brother; for truly is he tempted by the Evil One, and he does ill unto himself."

When Jesus had spoken these words he left the house of Samuel the Water Bearer.[1]

And he went unto the Garden of Gethsemane to ponder in stillness that which was to come.

Some of his followers went with him, for they wished to be near him until the last.

But Judas let his evil thoughts turn to deed.

26.

What were the Words Spoken by Jesus when he Stood Accused before the Council?

And behold, it came to pass, when Jesus and his companions left the Garden of Gethsemane, that they saw a band of men who were servants of some of the scribes and of the chief priests.

The men came to meet them, and with them was Judas Iscariot.

But when Judas saw Jesus, he pointed unto him, and he said: "He is the one you seek."

And when he had said this he left them hastily, for he dared not stand before the countenance of the one he had betrayed.

When the followers of Jesus heard the words they stood forth to

---

[1] The Feast of the Passover was observed in strict accordance with Jewish custom. Only those words and actions of Jesus which have general interest are included here, in order to show that Jesus took leave of his apostles at the Feast of the Passover without using the words which have since been ascribed to him. See chapter 33 and Commentary, p. 232.

protect the one they loved. And in his anger Simon Peter struck one of the servants.

But Jesus restrained them and bade them to stand back, and he said: "Defend me not, nor follow me, lest more lives be taken than the one that is demanded."

Then the servants surrounded him, bound his hands, and they led him unto the house of Caiaphas, where the Council was assembled.

But among those that should sit in judgment on Jesus was Joseph of Arimathea.

And Caiaphas was chief of the Council.

All the scribes, the elders and the chief priests spoke much with one another on how they should ensnare Jesus; for they were in no wise of one mind.

But when Jesus was led before them, deep silence fell upon them all; for he stood before them as a king.

Caiaphas had summoned many people whom he knew to be enemies of Jesus.

This he had done, that their words should bear witness against him.

But the witnesses were all divided among themselves, and their testimony was at great variance. Yea, not even two of them spoke the same words; yet they all had many complaints against him.

Then Caiaphas became impatient, and he said: "Jesus of Nazareth, clear yourself of that which the people speak of you! Defend yourself, that we should hear your own words and judge you rightly thereafter."

Jesus answered him and said: "The people have accused me. Judge me according to their witness."

But Caiaphas answered him and said: "We cannot judge you by the words of the people, for their testimony is divided."

Jesus looked upon him, and he said: "If the witnesses quarrel, if their testimony is divided, if not even two of them speak the same, then surely is it not difficult for you to judge rightly."

But when he had spoken thus, Caiaphas became angered, for he understood the words of Jesus; and he pondered how best to ensnare him.

And Caiaphas said: "Many of the elders and the chief priests have heard you say that you are the Son of the Most High. Answer us: have you spoken thus?"

Jesus answered him and said: "That which you say is true. Those were my words. And I say unto you: the day will come when you shall all see me in my Father's Kingdom, and then shall you all bow down before me."

When Jesus had answered thus, Caiaphas turned toward the Council, and he cried: "Truly, we need not seek witness among the people; for from his own mouth have you now heard the blasphemous words, heard him speak falsely of the Most High. Let us judge him thereafter!"

When Joseph of Arimathea heard the words spoken by Caiaphas, he rose and silently departed from the chamber of the Council, for he dared not sit in judgment on Jesus.

But those who were present judged him guilty – guilty unto the death of the cross.

When Jesus heard their judgment, he said: "That which you have sinned against me, that I forgive you; for you know not what you do. But when we meet in our Father's Kingdom, then shall you know that my words were true; *for there will the judgment you pronounced upon me accuse you and judge you.*"

But when he had spoken these words, he was taken from the chamber.

And in that same night Caiaphas placed guards over him, that his friends should not help him to flee the city.

But the following day, in the early morning, he was brought before Pontius Pilate, and he affirmed the judgment.

27.

What were the Words Spoken by Jesus before he Died on the Cross?

But when Jesus was led through the city, large multitudes followed him, and they shouted at him, scorned him and derided him; but Jesus answered them not.

And he was led by the guards unto the place which was called Calvary, where the condemned were crucified.

When Jesus passed through the gate of the city, he saw some women weeping. And he said: "Weep not over me, for my sufferings will soon be ended; weep for yourselves and the unborn generations, for many sorrows and great sufferings await them."

But when they were come unto the place, the soldiers took from him his robe, and they bound him unto the cross, placing a piece of wood beneath his feet; this they did so as to prolong his sufferings.

But when the cross had been raised, the multitudes broke forth and gathered about him; and the people continued to deride and to mock Jesus; yea, many took stones and cast them upon his body.

And the guards sought to drive away the multitudes, but time and again they returned.

And behold, it came to pass that the sun was darkened; for slowly a heavy, black veil was drawn across the heavens, covering the radiant circle of the sun; and close darkness fell everywhere, while the Earth was shaken to its very foundation.

Then, great fear and terror came upon them all; for many remembered the words of the prophets foretelling the destruction of the Earth, and they thought that the end was nigh. And terrified, they fled into the city, where they hid themselves in their houses for as long as the darkness prevailed.

But some of the followers of Jesus and some of the women remained at the foot of the cross.

And among the women was the mother of Jesus.

When darkness fell upon the Earth, in great fear she stretched her hands toward her son and she cried out: "My son, my son! Why did you not abide in the faith of your fathers? Behold, the Most High has forsaken you!"

But when Jesus heard the words, he said unto those who were with her: "Sustain her and comfort her, for her sufferings are very great."

When he had said this, he felt his body weaken, and he prayed unto his Heavenly Father to forgive all who had sinned against him, who had sinned by condemning him unjustly.

And he prayed unto his Father for greater strength, that he might bear his sufferings with patience.

And God heard the prayer of Jesus.

And He sent unto him some of the Youngest, and Jesus felt his sufferings no more.

But when a time had passed, he lowered his head, and he said: *"Father, receive my spirit."*

And behold, then his spirit was delivered from the earthly body; and the Youngest who were with him brought him unto their Father's Kingdom.

And God took him in His embrace, and He forgave him all in which he had failed in his life upon the Earth.

But they grieved with one another over the son and brother who still walked upon the Earth, grieved over the son and brother who had failed in the promise that he had given.

28.

Was the Resurrection of Jesus Bodily or Spiritual?

When Jesus had died, some of his followers went unto Joseph of Arimathea; for they had often seen him among the people when Jesus spoke. And they besought him to seek leave for them from the Council to take the body of Jesus and to bury it.

And Joseph promised to speak to Caiaphas thereof.

But when he came unto them with the leave of the Council, he questioned them whether they had a place in which to lay the body of Jesus. But they answered him that they had no place. Then said Joseph: "Bring his body unto my garden, which I shall show you; for there in the rock is hewn a grave where I myself should be laid to rest. This place shall I give unto you, that the Master's body may rest in peace!"

The followers and disciples of Jesus thanked him much for this gift.

But Joseph spoke not these words for the sake of Jesus, nor for the sake of the disciples, but for his own; for he had often heard it spoken that Jesus would rise from the dead and appear before them; therefore would he hold watch, that none should steal the body and thus be able to say: behold, he is risen from the dead!

But the disciples carried the body of Jesus unto the tomb, and the women anointed his body, wrapping it in white linen, and they laid it in the tomb and rolled a great stone to the door of the sepulchre.

When all this was done they left the garden, that together they might mourn over him who had departed from them.

Only Joseph remained, watching over the tomb until the light of day broke forth. Then he went back unto his home; for he knew that upon that day of rest, while the sun was high, none would remove the body.

And he pondered all day on how he might hinder that anyone should take the body of Jesus.

While he pondered, the Elder, the Servant of Darkness stood at his side and gave him evil counsel.

And when the last hour of the day of rest had passed, Joseph summoned an old servant and bade him to go with him unto the garden. And they took implements with them, that with these they might dig in the ground.

But when they were come unto the place they rolled away the stone and they laid upon the ground the white linen which had been spread upon the body of Jesus. Then they bore his body unto a distant corner of the garden and buried it in the earth. And they covered the place with branches, that none should see what they had done.

When they had accomplished this the dawn began to break, and they hastened back unto the tomb so as to return the stone to its place before the entrance.

But when they reached the place, Joseph heard a faint and distant-voice that said: "Brother, why did you this?" And when he turned he saw the insubstantial form of the radiant figure of Jesus. And in great fear he fell unto the ground.

But when the old servant hastened to help his master, behold, he stood before the man whose body he had lately buried in the earth. And great fear and terror came upon him, and he fled from the garden.

When Joseph awoke to his senses the vision was gone, and he was alone. But he heard a distant voice which said: "Return the body of Jesus unto the place whence you took it; for should you not do this, then will your evil act bring much confusion upon mankind."

But the Elder, the Servant of Darkness, stood at his side. And Darkness descended upon Joseph, while his heart was filled with fear, so that he dared not go back unto that place where he had laid the body of Jesus.

And he fled out of the garden unto his house.

But when he was come there, behold, there sat the old servant, wailing and lamenting upon the threshold, while many confused words issued from his mouth.

Then Joseph knew that this man was not able to keep silent upon that which he had seen.

And the Elder, the Servant of Darkness, whispered evil counsel unto him; and Joseph said: "Behold, I shall bring you a cup of wine, that you may be strengthened thereby, for that which you have seen has made you exceeding weak."

Joseph brought him the wine, but in the cup was death.

And a while after the old man had drunk thereof, he fell back upon the ground, and his spirit departed from his body.

But Joseph went into his house, so as to be alone with his terror and with his remorse.

And when the day broke, the servants of the house found the old man. Some of the servants bore him inside, while others told their master of what had come to pass; and they all believed that the old man had died of infirmity, and none came to know that his master had taken his life.

But a while after Joseph had fled from the garden, some women came to mourn by the tomb and in stillness to talk of the one who had left them.

When they were come unto the place they saw that the stone was taken away from the sepulchre. And they wondered much and dared not enter therein; for they feared that someone lay hiding in the darkness.

But when they had spoken with one another on this, the woman who was Mary Magdalene said: "I will go therein, for I fear not."

And when she stood by the hewn grave, she saw that it was empty, and she found the white shroud in disarray upon the ground.

And she returned in haste unto the waiting women, and she said: "He is gone! Perchance unto his Heavenly Father, as so often he said that he would? Or has someone taken away his body? Let us go unto the city and tell of what has come to pass!"

But as she turned to leave the garden, she saw before her the insubstantial form of a radiant figure, Jesus of Nazareth.

He smiled and stretched his hands toward her.

When Mary Magdalene saw him she cried out with joy: "Master, have you come back to us?" And she ran forward to greet him.

But when she reached the place, he was no longer there.

And with sorrow she called unto the other two women and said: "I saw him, he was here; but he is gone once more. Stay in this place, that he shall not be alone, should he return to us again. I shall make haste unto the city and call upon Simon Peter and some of the others."

And she hastened away.

The women who remained wondered at her words, for they had not seen Jesus of Nazareth. They saw only Mary Magdalene run forth, and they heard her cry out; but him they did not see.

And they said unto each other: "Let us seek him in the garden, for surely has he not gone far away."

While they wandered about they searched everywhere, but they found him not.

Then one of the women said: "Let us look in the tomb; perchance he is hiding there."

And they went therein.

But they saw only the empty grave, saw only the white shroud upon the ground. And disappointed they returned.

And they agreed to go to meet the friends who were on their way.

When they had walked along the road in silence for some time, the woman who was Salome said: "Behold, I had a vision in the dark tomb; for I saw an angel in a radiant garb. He sat by the hewn grave, but a great fear tied my tongue so that until now I was afraid to speak thereof."

The other woman, Mary, who was the mother of Jacob, one of the followers of Jesus, answered and said: "Surely, I had the same vision, but there were two angels; for I saw another behind the one sitting by the grave. His hand pointed upward and he spoke some words, but I could not distinguish them clearly."

Salome, the woman who had spoken first, maintained that but one angel had sat by the grave. And they quarrelled heatedly and at length over something neither one had seen. For each had knowingly spoken falsely unto the other of her vision; for not all people are equally truthful, and these women would not be second to Mary Magdalene.

And later when Simon Peter, followed by certain of the disciples, came unto the place where the women awaited them, they both spoke of what they had seen in the darkness of the tomb. And they all wondered much.

Simon Peter and the others hastened unto the garden, and they searched everywhere; but they found him not.

And they saw that the tomb was empty, but him they did not see.

29.

How many Times did Jesus Appear before the Apostles? Did he Speak to them?

But Simon Peter sent for the followers of Jesus – though not Judas Iscariot – and he asked them to meet him that evening at the house of Samuel the Water Bearer, that they might speak together of that which had come to pass.

When the hour was come and they were all assembled, Simon Peter said: "You have all heard that our beloved Brother and Master has appeared before Mary Magdalene. And I, and others with me, have searched the tomb, searched the garden, but we found him not. And we have sought him in many places in the city, but still we did not find him, none has seen him. I believe that he is ascended unto the Kingdom of Heaven, unto his Father, as often he said he would. Therefore, let us pray of the Lord God that He may grant us the joy once more to behold our beloved Master among us, so that from our heart's conviction and our sure faith we may proclaim unto all that he was the Messiah, the Son of God."

When Simon Peter had spoken thus, he prayed on behalf of them all.

And when his prayer was ended, behold, visible to all, Jesus of

Nazareth stood by the upper end of the table and a bright radiance emanated from his body. And he raised his hands toward them, and he smiled and said: "Peace be with you!"

The followers of Jesus knew their Master's countenance and they knew his voice, though it sounded faint and distant.

And they rose so as to embrace him and to greet him; but he vanished before their eyes.

And they all grieved that he had left them in such haste.

And it became known to the people in the city that the Nazarene had risen from the dead and had ascended unto the Kingdom of Heaven, that he had appeared before his followers, and that a woman had seen him.

Then they all wondered much. Many believed the words, and many were converted from their life of sin and vice.

But Pilate and Caiaphas caused a search to be made everywhere for the body of Jesus, for they believed that his disciples had removed and hidden it.

But it was never found.

And in the following days Jesus was seen in diverse places by many; some saw him on the roads near Jerusalem, others saw him on the Mount of Olives, where he was wont to linger; some saw him at Bethesda, yea, he was even seen by the Sea of Galilee, and many had heard him speak.

But it was the same with these visions as with the visions of the angels that the women had seen at the tomb. Many false words were spoken of the resurrection of Jesus, *for only few are entirely truthful.*

The many reports of the Nazarene also reached Joseph of Arimathea.

And again the distant voice sounded unto him. And it spoke: "Go unto the Council and tell of that which you did; for *you know* that the spirit of Jesus lives; for *you know* that his body is dead, and *you know* where it is to be found."

But Joseph dared not reveal his evil deed, for he feared to lose his dignity, feared to lose his esteem.

And he remained silent.

Thus was it on account of the doubter and murderer Joseph of Arimathea that the *false belief* in the *bodily resurrection* of Jesus of Nazareth spread abroad among the people.

30.

How should we Interpret the "Miracle of Pentecost"?

And it came pass on the day of Pentecost, when the followers of Jesus and some of his disciples and others were gathered in a house in the city, that a thunderstorm broke over the region; heavy clouds darkened the skies, and violent gusts of wind shook the house.

But the twelve[1] took no heed of the weather; and unto the people who were gathered they continued to speak of Jesus of Nazareth, the One crucified and risen, who was the Messiah, the Son of God.

And behold, it came to pass while Simon Peter spoke, that a blinding bolt of lightning crossed the sky, and for a short instant the twelve were brightly illuminated by a flaming glare – for they stood in front of the high window – and a great rumbling was heard.

Great fear and terror came upon all who were present, for they remembered all that they had heard and seen in the latter days.

And they feared that the Lord God was calling them unto judgment.

But the Eldest, the Servant of Darkness, stood unseen among them.

It was he who awakened the fear in their hearts. It was he who confused their thoughts, so that they called and cried out, praying unto the Lord God to forgive them of all that they had sinned, that they should not be cast out into darkness. And many words were spoken that could not be understood, and there arose much disorder and much confusion.

And one of the disciples called out unto the twelve. "Behold, surely the Lord has brought His holy, flaming Breath upon you, in the manner promised you by the Nazarene!"

Many believed the words and they cried: "His words are true, for we saw a flaming fire upon you!"

Then there arose among them yet greater confusion.

But the followers of Jesus sought to calm the people, and they exhorted them to quiet and to orderliness; and after much toil and much trouble, silence fell upon them all.

Then the twelve stretched out their hands toward Heaven and thanked the Almighty for the gift that he had given them.

And the simple faith of their hearts gave their spirits ever greater power and ever greater strength.

But none of those who were present understood that they had seen

---

[1] A twelfth apostle had replaced Judas Iscariot.

the lightning of a storm; for it was the dry season, and not the time in which the clouds of heaven send lightning and thunder.

Some days thereafter, there came unto Simon Peter messengers from the scribes and the chief priests. These reproached him in harsh words for the unseemly conduct by all at the meeting on the day of Pentecost; reproached him that they had tasted overmuch of the sweet wine.

Then Simon Peter became angered, and he rejected their evil accusations; for he said that the meeting had been early in the day, and that none had touched the wine.

And he continued to speak, saying: "But you shall know, that what had come to pass was promised us of the Nazarene and foretold by the prophets, and on the day of Pentecost the Lord God fulfilled that which was promised and foretold!"

And he spoke unto them yet further, saying: "For you shall know that Jesus of Nazareth is he of whom the Most High spoke unto David in his day; for you shall know that Jesus was the promised Messiah; but in your blindness have you scorned him, mocked him and crucified him."

And they parted in great anger.

But Simon Peter never doubted that his words were true; for some of the disciples had told him that strangers had been present at the meeting on the day of Pentecost, and these had said that the cries and words sounded to them as if in their native tongue. But this the disciples said unto him because they were ashamed of their fearfulness; for thereby they meant to prove that they had received some of the heavenly power and strength also.

And Simon Peter believed that which they told him.

But after that time it often came to pass that one or more of the disciples came forward at the meetings, beat themselves upon the breast, stretched their hands toward heaven, and cried and spoke many and sundry words which were not understood. Later, they had all to interpret the meaning of that which they had spoken.

However, the followers of Jesus always sought to hinder these utterances; but they were not able to do so, and it spread to more and more of the disciples.

In this way the speaking in tongues came into being, born of the fear and confusion of the day of Pentecost.

31.

Were the Apostles able to Proclaim the Teaching of Jesus as Truly as they had Received it?

When the eldest of the Youngest – Jesus of Nazareth – was returned from his life upon the Earth, he resumed the leadership of mankind's many earthly journeyings. Then he also sought to lead his inheritors along the path that he had shown them while he walked among them upon the Earth.

But despite their promises and despite their good intentions, they were not able to proclaim the teachings of Jesus purely and simply, in the words that had come to them from his own lips; for the Elder, the Servant of Darkness, fought against them, and he sought to instil false words and alien thoughts in their speeches to the people.

Thus, as they proclaimed the words of Jesus, they often used their own; for all that they had seen and experienced since they parted with their beloved Brother and Master overshadowed in their remembrance the time when he had walked with them.

And they spoke unto the people of the imminent return of Jesus, when he should be the judge and ruler of mankind; for they thought that the time was at hand when he would return and show himself unto all the world in his splendour and glory and thus confirm his words; confirm that he was in truth the Son of God.

With these utterances they gained many followers; for the people were much afraid for the future, and many thought to escape judgment and punishment for their unclean and sinful lives by being a disciple of Jesus.

In this way the new teaching was brought from place to place; many were converted and many were baptized, so that, cleansed of the impurities of the heart, they could be received into the community of the followers of Jesus.

32.

How was Saul Converted from Persecutor to Preacher of the Teachings of Jesus?

But the Elder, the Servant of Darkness, stirred the scribes against the disciples of Jesus.

And the chief priests persecuted them, scorned and mocked them, imprisoned and punished them; yea, some of the friends and disciples of Jesus were put to death; for they would not deny their faith; for they would not fail their Brother and Master.

But among the scribes there was a learned man, and his name was Saul.

This man was greatly God-fearing, highly learned in the law, and in his heart he was sorely vexed over the new teaching. He despised all the apostates, persecuting them and casting many stones in their paths.

When the chief priests saw his great zeal, they chose him as an envoy; for they had much faith in him.

And they bade him to go unto the distant city of Damascus, for the new teaching had reached there also.

And they sent with him greetings and a letter from the Council in Jerusalem unto all the chief priests in Damascus, and they instructed him to ensure that the disciples of Jesus in that city should be imprisoned and punished; for in this manner they thought to halt the further spread of the new teaching.

Saul promised to do their bidding. And he chose some companions, and they set forth upon their journey.

But the way was long and arduous, and he had much time to think upon that which he had heard of the Nazarene. And often in his thoughts he repeated many of the fine and tender words of Jesus.

Slowly anger and hatred receded from his heart.

Slowly the thought arose in his mind that the Nazarene's words were true, *that he was indeed the Son of God, the Messiah that they had all awaited.*

But he dared not put his trust in these thoughts, and he sought to drive them away; but they always returned, and they much tormented him. And he pondered much and deeply on all that he had heard. But his companions wondered at his silence.

When they were come near to the city he was much fatigued, and he felt exceedingly weak; for the sun glowed upon their heads and the white dust of the road burned in their eyes.

Saul and his companions sought to rest a while by the wayside, and sleep fell upon his weary body; but his spirit kept vigil.

And behold, Jesus of Nazareth stood before him in all his radiant glory.

But his countenance was sorrowful. And he said: "Saul, Saul, why do you persecute me?"

For while Saul's body slept, Jesus came thus unto his spirit so as to stay his evil conduct if this were possible; for Saul was of the Youngest.

But when Saul's spirit saw his brother and knew him, he was dismayed at the evil that he had done.

And his fear awakened his slumbering body.

And at the sudden awakening he kept a faint remembrance of the glory that he had seen, while the words of Jesus sounded in his ear.

But when he arose, he was dismayed yet more; for his eyes were blinded, and all was dark about him.

In his fear he cried unto his companions, and he told them that the radiant lustre of Jesus of Nazareth had blinded his eyes; but they understood him not.

But when they saw that he was sick and weak they led him into the city, to a place where he might in stillness rest himself. And when they had tended him for some days his eyes grew stronger, and he was able once again to see; for it was the sun and the dust of the road that for a time had blinded his eyes.

But Saul understood that God, through Jesus of Nazareth, had called upon him, so as to keep him from going astray. And in his heart he promised both of them that in times to come, he would *himself* proclaim the teachings that he had formerly opposed.

And Saul became a mighty warrior for Jesus of Nazareth.

33.

In what Manner did the Doctrine of Atonement Arise?

Fearful of the anger of the Council, Saul dared not return unto Jerusalem; for he had destroyed the letter which he should have presented unto the high priests in Damascus. Nor dared he present himself before the followers of Jesus, for he was afraid that they would not believe the truth of his conversion. Therefore he decided to withdraw for a time and stay with distant kin.

And he fulfilled that which he had decided.

And there, while abroad, far removed from all clamour and strife, he searched his heart, and he pondered much on that which he had heard and seen.

And he sought to find the hidden meaning of the human embodiment of Jesus.

But the Elder, the Servant of Darkness, stood at his side, and slowly the thought arose in Saul's mind that Jesus, the Son of God, was sent unto the Earth to reconcile God with his earthly children, the wicked and ungodly human beings. For the human being Saul was a scribe and highly learned in the law, and he was not fully able to reject all the ancient Jewish teachings. And to him the Most High was and remained a god of wrath, whose righteous anger must be appeased with unceasing sacrifice of blood and sweet incense.

In Saul's interpretation of that which had come to pass, Jesus therefore became the Sacrificial Lamb, who through death of his own accord redeemed humanity from judgment, retribution and damnation; yea, he became the Lamb, whose blood washed away all human sin and impurity.

But Saul understood not that the Elder, the Servant of Darkness, had implanted this false interpretation in his mind; for Saul was a highly *self-righteous* man, and the self-righteous are never fully able to discern whether the thoughts implanted in them are of Darkness or of the Light; for they often neglect to seek counsel of God in the *greatest* though they will seek counsel of Him in the *least*.

And thus Saul's teaching of the embodiment of Jesus of Nazareth became a mixture of Darkness and of the Light.

When Saul returned unto Damascus, having lived in foreign parts for some years, he began to proclaim *his* teaching of Jesus there; and he preached it unto many – to the Jews and to the so-called gentiles. Many heard his words and believed his interpretation, yea, many who were formerly disciples of the followers of Jesus turned from them and followed him.

And when later he reasoned with Simon Peter and other followers and disciples of Jesus, these were still not able to change his perception of Jesus: *that he was the Saviour and Conciliator of humanity.* And Saul continued to proclaim his teaching after those words and thoughts that he believed he had received from God and from Jesus.

Later, when the so-called Communion, or the Lord's Supper, was adopted by the congregations founded by Saul, he tried in the usual manner to explore and to clarify the intent with which Jesus had gathered his followers for a meal on the Day of Unleavened Bread.

And he interpreted the act in this way: when Jesus meted out the bread to his disciples, he thereby made known unto them that as now he satisfied them with his bread, that they should not hunger and die, so would he give up his body for their sake also, that through his death he would fill them with eternal life. And when Jesus gave his disciples wine from his cup, he thereby made known that he would shed his blood for them, and thus blot out their guilt of sin.

And in the mind and thought of Saul these words were conceived and born: my body and my blood I submit unto you as a new covenant between you and the Lord.[1]

And he taught his disciples this interpretation of that which had come to pass, and they received the words and they used them at their Communions, and they spread far and wide from congregation to congregation.

And people kept these words in their hearts, for they believed that they were spoken by Jesus. And when the time came that men wrote down the accounts of the earthly life of Jesus, they ascribed to *him* these words which *the Elder* had treacherously implanted in the mind and in the thought of Saul.

Thus Saul founded Christianity with his teaching.

Many congregations were founded among the gentiles, many people were won and Christianity spread far and wide; for Saul never grew tired, but travelled far on perilous and arduous voyages. And wherever he went he proclaimed his teaching on Jesus of Nazareth, who was the Son of God, a Saviour and Conciliator of humanity.

But none of the spiritual heirs of Jesus – neither his followers nor Saul – were able to gather all the people into one congregation, which in deep humility and childlike love would in unison bow down before their Heavenly Father; a congregation, in which love of one's neighbour would defeat sinfulness, the lust for power and human selfishness.

And thus became overshadowed by Darkness the commandment that by Jesus was stated to be the greatest: *love for God, love for one's neighbour;* for from the time of the earliest Christian Church, anger and hatred toward one another were known in the congregations, as were the lust for power and self-righteousness.

Thus was Jesus' simple and beautiful teaching of love neglected, and thus it failed to thrive.

---

[1]) Originally, without any later distortions, the explanation which Paul gave his disciples after having thought out the matter in the above fashion was the following: "As Jesus gave the apostles of his bread and wine, so he gave his body and his blood to his followers as spiritual food and drink; yea, he gave himself as a sacrifice for sin, a sign of a new covenant between the Lord and us."

34.

Did the Light Make no Advance against Darkness with the further Spread of Christianity?

Slowly, Christianity spread from place to place, from nation to nation. Thousands upon thousands chose to follow the Christian teaching. But only few found their way unto their Heavenly Father. Guided by the inner Light, guided by their profound repentance, these few sought and won forgiveness for their sins and for their evil deeds.

But many continued to walk in the Darkness of sin.

Unseen by human beings, many of the Youngest laboured to bring the Light unto the Earth; and they drew the purifying streams of the Light unto those human beings who truly sought to live in purity and in mutual forbearance; they drew the purifying streams of the Light unto those brothers and sisters who, bound unto earthly bodies and thus visible to human beings, sought to break the power of Darkness.

But Darkness and the Eldest hindered the progress of the Light; for the Elder, the Servant of Darkness, *sowed the evil seed of wrath, the evil seed of hatred in the hearts of mankind.*

Troubled times arose for the Christians in the mighty Roman Empire; for the highest ruler of the realm, the Emperor, decreed that all people should bow down before him, decreed that all people should honour him as a deity. And the governors persecuted all who hailed not in worship the image of the Emperor.

But not all Christians would renounce the teaching which had brought peace and purity unto their minds and thoughts. And those who would not worship the Emperor were tormented and slain. But they bore their sufferings with much patience; for their conviction of God's mercy and compassion and their firm belief in the victory of truth strengthened their spirit and strengthened their earthly bodies. Numerous Christians went to their death with songs of praise upon their lips, and their courage and steadfast faith won ever more followers unto the new teaching.

And as the years passed, as century was added to century, more and more people embraced the Christian faith. But only few found their way unto their Heavenly Father, while many who bore the name of Christians continued to live in sin, in vice and ungodliness; for the evil seed of Darkness thwarted without cease the progress of the Light.

And the Elder, the Servant of Darkness, continued to corrupt the

Christian teaching, so as to call forth strife within the churches and to separate them ever further from one another.

And he instilled his evil poison into the minds of the leaders, into the minds of the learned and those versed in the Scriptures, so that their thoughts conceived and gave birth to new and yet more obscure interpretations of the human embodiment of Jesus, of his word and of his works. Further doctrines were devised and were developed, and there arose much controversy and much dispute; for the learned were divided; for the one would not yield unto the other, and each would acknowledge only *his own opinion, his own thoughts.*

And they continued to dispute about a great many things.

Some of the learned held that, contrary to the many gods of the heathen, there was but One God, that all power in Heaven and on Earth was rightly His alone. But their adversaries believed that God indeed was One, but yet strangely was He also three; for they made Christ, the Son of God, One with the Father; and they made God's Thought, His creating and life-giving Breath, an independent, divine Being. Thus were they three: the Father, the Son, and the Holy Ghost; but together they formed that entity which was God.[1]

Some of the learned maintained that God had bestowed upon human beings a free will; held that these, by virtue of this will, could rise toward the Light and struggle free from sin and Darkness. But their adversaries believed that human beings were blind, weak-willed beings in the hand of the Most High. They believed that God, before He created them, had pre-ordained some to eternal life in heavenly glory and joy, and others to eternal perdition, to an everlasting life of suffering in the misery of Darkness.

Some of the learned maintained that the bread and the wine that were offered at the Lord's Supper changed into the flesh and blood of Jesus when blessed or when eaten. They believed that by partaking of this they shared in his suffering and death and thereby received the forgiveness of sin. But their adversaries thought that the Lord's Supper was established as but a remembrance of Jesus.

Some of the learned held that human beings, through baptism, received inheritance and part in the life and the blessedness of Heaven; maintained that all those not baptized were doomed to eternal perdition. But their opponents thought that baptism was but a symbol of the cleansing of mankind from the impurities of sin.

Thus the learned continued to dispute, for they would not yield to

---

[1]) Several other versions of the unity of the Son and the Father are not included by Ardor, as any one who so desires can make private studies of the controversies of those times.

one another. And they hurled hateful and condemning words at one another.

But they *all* forgot to seek counsel, strength and guidance from God the Almighty, forgot to turn unto *Him* who alone could guide them.

And thus pride infested their minds, thus hatred and lust for power bound their hearts, while Darkness prospered ever more among them.

But Christ, the eldest of the Youngest, grieved for mankind's intolerance, and he faltered under the heavy burdens that mankind heaped upon his shoulders.

Despite the strife among the Christian congregations, better times arose; for succeeding rulers of the Roman Empire saw that they were not able to thwart the victorious advance of Christian teaching. And when all persecution ceased, Christianity spread wider yet.

At many places in Christendom splendid and magnificent buildings were raised, richly adorned to the honour of God. And in these buildings the congregations gathered to worship and to bow down before God and Christ in the expounding of the Scriptures and the singing of songs of praise.

But some pious men and women withdrew from the large congregations to worship the Most High in solitude, in prayer and in self-torment. And in many congregations they began to honour those men and women who had been put to death when they would not renounce their faith. Yea, some even besought these so-called holy men and women for help, support and intercession with God and Christ.

Inspired by Darkness, conceived and born of the thoughts of unknowing people, numerous accounts appeared of the great piety and wondrous deeds of these martyrs. In the same way arose confused and incomprehensible stories of Mary, the Mother of Jesus: the chosen, the immaculate virgin who bore the Son of God, conceived by the Holy Ghost. And many Christians honoured her and bowed down before her.

But they who heard these stories believed them.

And the words were passed from mouth to mouth, and they were spread far and wide.

Slowly, Christianity spread to ever more distant lands, and when the time came that one of the Roman Emperors took the Christians into his protection, then Christianity grew into a power before which mankind was compelled to submit.

More and more of those learned in the Scriptures were joined to the numerous and mighty congregations, but over these – the priests – were the bishops, and they took unto themselves ever greater power, ever greater riches; *for their lust for power was insatiable.*

Some of the bishops sought, with great authority, to settle the never-ending disputes; but though certain interpretations and doctrines concerning the embodiment of Jesus and his words and deeds were chosen before all others, so as to form a solid foundation for Christian teaching, they could not procure universal accord.

But slowly, from the strife and discord there arose the "Holy Catholic Church", which sought by *force* to gather the divided congregations into a single community. And the bishop in the city of Rome was made the highest ruling and governing authority.

But when Christianity was grown strong, the Christians ceased to be *the persecuted* and became *the persecutors*; and they persecuted the so-called heathen, and they who would not renounce their gods and their beliefs were put to death.

And thus Christianity, even as it spread, departed more and more from Christ's teachings of love, purity and compassion.

35.

Did the Youngest not seek to Counter the False Teaching that the Elder had Instilled in the Minds of Human Beings?

But when the Youngest saw their elder brother's profound sorrow for mankind's blindness, intolerance and lack of understanding, they agreed for a time to unite their efforts upon a *single task*: to destroy the false doctrines of Darkness and bring forth *the pure teachings of Christ.*

For this purpose several of the Youngest let themselves be bound anew to human bodies, and they let themselves be born unto the Earth in diverse lands and in diverse places.

And when their bodies and their spirits were become ready, they set forth and strove mightily to destroy the false teachings and to make the truth be known.

But only few understood them, and only few followed them, while many scorned and derided them – yea, some of them were persecuted unto death.

And among these was a man known to the people by the earthly name of *Mani.*

This man brought unto mankind some of the truths of the Light;

and he spoke wise and eloquent words on that which lay beyond the earthly world.

But the Elder also was able to instil false teachings into his preaching of the spiritual truths; and neither full light nor full clarity was shed upon the teachings of Mani.

Many were they who listened to his words; some followed him, but still more derided and persecuted him; and these rewarded him with death for the truths that he sought to bring them.

Thus the Youngest continued in manifold ways to strive for the true teachings.

But Darkness and the Elder hindered the advance of the Light; Darkness blinded human beings and bound their thoughts.

Thus the Youngest strove from century to century, while Christianity, *the false teachings of Saul,* spread to distant lands.

Then came the century in which one of the Youngest, known by his earthly name of *Mohammed,* succeeded in proclaiming the teaching to humanity that God is One, that none is over Him, that none is under Him, and none is at His side. And he taught that God alone was the source of all creation, was the Creator of the Universe.

When Mohammed appeared before the people of his native land with these teachings, he was met with *scorn, anger and contempt.*

Few only listened to his words, few only followed him.

But as the years passed, he gained more and ever more followers. And as his enemies feared his ever-growing power, they sought to put him to death. When Mohammed learnt of their evil intentions, he left his house in the city of Mecca and fled unto the city that was later named Medina.

Mohammed's dominion over the people became ever greater; an ever larger number of people gathered about him, and his words spread far and wide.

But the Elder, the Servant of Darkness, sought to confuse his thoughts, sought to defile his mind.

And the Elder awakened pride and the lust for power in his heart, awakened the passion and desires of his body, and his lust for beautiful women became insatiable.

Darkness descended upon him and he stumbled time and again; for his foot was caught in the snares that were laid for him.

And Mohammed summoned certain from among the highest in the land, and he spoke unto them and bade them to wage war upon their enemies, so as to propagate his teachings by force; for he proclaimed, falsely, that to God this would be a pleasing act. And he promised that God would reward those valiant men who died in battle; he promised that God would reward them for their victories with the most lavish and the most glorious pleasures of Paradise.

And with a mighty troop he went unto the city of Mecca, made himself the master of it and the ruler of the people, and all who refused to follow him were slain or were banished.

But from that time, Darkness gained yet greater power over him. His thoughts grew yet more confused, his teachings became less and less lucid, and often he would be at variance with his own words.

But Mohammed's dominion over the people was not diminished, and he was honoured greatly; though he himself found no peace and no rest; for Darkness was upon him; for the Elder strove against him.

And when his body succumbed to earthly death, his spirit grieved that while he was a human being he had not been able to proclaim the *whole truth;* grieved that he had not been able to break the power of Darkness.

But some time after Mohammed's death people began to collect and to write down his teachings. Numerous sayings and doctrines appeared and were ascribed to Mohammed, sayings and doctrines that he had never spoken nor considered; and therefore arose much disagreement and multifarious disputes.

Thus became also the Holy Scriptures of the Mohammedans a mixture of good and evil, a mixture of the teachings of Mohammed, of the work of human beings, and of the false teachings of Darkness.

After the death of Mohammed, the Elder incited his followers and they waged war upon the neighbouring peoples, seized much land, much power and untold riches, and they forced numerous of the conquered nations to submit to the teachings of Mohammed.

But the Christians saw with anger that the teachings of the Prophet spread further and ever further; and they were astonished to hear that many even followed his teachings of their own free will.

And when it became known among Christians that the Arabian people had made themselves masters of Jerusalem, the Holy City, then they felt yet more anger, and they grieved deeply when they came to the city to worship and to linger at the holy places. And from this arose, over the following years, much strife between the Christians and the followers of Mohammed, the Prophet.

And yet later, when the tidings reached far across the lands that a warlike, Mohammedan people[1] had conquered Jerusalem, then

---

[1] The Selukians. – Publisher's note.

hatred and the desire for revenge burned deep in Christian hearts. Many swore upon the Cross of Christ that they would drive out the strangers and recapture the city; yea, they even promised to crush and to destroy *all* who were enemies of the teachings of Christ.

Then began the cruel wars and battles between the Christians and the Mohammedans.

Now the followers of the Prophet won, now the Christians. Thousands upon thousands were slain, for one power would not submit to the other. And while century followed century, *violence, murder and gruesome misdeeds were perpetrated in the name of God and Christ.*

But as time passed and the Christians saw that the Sign of the Holy Cross by which they fought did not bring them the victory they expected, they became more and more disheartened. And when two centuries had passed, the Christians had to yield; for the followers of the Prophet were the stronger.

But during these numerous and protracted wars, Darkness gained ever greater power over mankind.

Bound to earthly bodies, the Youngest sought without cease to advance the truth and the Light; but time and again they had to give way to Darkness, for it had many and powerful helpers among the embodied Eldest.

Nor were the Youngest able to halt the endless disputes among the Christians.

New doctrines were devised, giving rise to new quarrels. Bishops and priests gathered unto themselves more and more power, greater and greater wealth. And raised high above them all, over nations, princes, kings and emperors, stood the highest of bishops, the so-called pope in the city of Rome. And against all who would not acknowledge his might and his power, he hurled his mighty curses; for the Vicar of God and Christ forgot the words of Christ: **Forgive your enemies!**

And with implacable hatred, the Christians persecuted all who would not profess the Christian faith. In many a place and country, the pyres blazed, where Mohammedans and Jews, the so-called heretics, were tortured and burnt to the honour of God and Christ. Many Christians even, who sought to protect the persecuted, were to follow the condemned unto the stake and suffer the same tortures, the same horrible death; for mankind forgot the tender words of Christ: *Love one another as brothers and sisters!*

Truly, the power of Darkness was awesome!

Deeper and heavier sank Darkness over the Earth, blinding mankind, dulling and binding their thoughts.

Numerous Christians bowed down in worship before painted and sculptured images of Mary, the mother of Jesus, bowed down in worship before numerous images of holy men[1] and women.

But in all this idolatry,[1] they often forgot to pray unto God the Almighty, forgot to pray unto their God and Father, forgot to pray unto *Him, who alone* was able to grant their prayers.

More and more pious men and women – monks and nuns – withdrew from the world and lived in their own retreats, under the laws of their own communities. But though these men and women vowed to live in chastity, not all of them were able to keep their vows. Only few were pure of mind, only few found their way unto their Heavenly Father, only few sustained the poor out of love and compassion; and only few ministered to the sick out of pity for their suffering.

Deeper and heavier, Darkness laid itself upon the Earth, and only few of the Youngest dared in human form to fight against the evil.

Then came the time when many of the Youngest were gathered once more with their elder brother, in the outermost sphere about the Earth.

And they spoke much with one another of that which came to pass at that time in the world on Earth, spoke with one another of the ways that they should follow to lead mankind out of Darkness.

But they were all faint of heart.

And one of them said: "Let us cease our work among mankind; for we are not able to lead them unto our Father's Kingdom. Again and again have we let ourselves be bound unto earthly bodies; but none of us, while we were human beings, has yet been able to break the curses our eldest brother has hurled out. But not one of us, while we were human beings, has been able to pray for our brother and thus deliver him from the binding power of Darkness. We have brought only grief and suffering upon *ourselves* with our work

---

[1]) Many Christians prayed directly to the Virgin Mary and to the holy men and women, rather than asking them to intercede with God on their behalf. Saint-worshipping thus became idolatry. And since the mother of Jesus, and *all* "saints" – despite their good deeds – are subject to the Law of Reincarnation, any prayer to them is in vain, and is, indeed, often senseless; for the worshipped saints live on Earth from time to time as human beings, and consequently are unable to hear any calls for intercession or help from their fellow human beings.

Among the spirits who were bound to the earthly bodies of the so-called saints can be found both the Youngest, the Eldest, and human spirits. In the latter case, the law of rebirth has been established by God so that they can go forward and upward. The Eldest brought themselves under this law because of their first, unlawful self-incarnation. The Youngest have submitted voluntarily to this law while working for the advancement of mankind. Thus, when human beings call upon holy men and women, they pray to beings whose existence as saints is imaginary.

among mankind; let us therefore return unto our Father's Kingdom, that the children of the Earth may walk in their own ways."

But when he fell silent, Christ, the eldest of the Youngest, stood forth.

And he said: "Though all of you turn from mankind, so shall I not forsake them; though there be none among you who will help me bear the burdens that mankind has laid upon my shoulders, so shall *I* never lay down these burdens, but pray unto our Father to help me *that I may bear them all.*

"Truly, I say unto you: break not your promise; for be the power of Darkness great, *so is the power of the Light still greater;* and our Father's words to us were these: if we *will,* then *can* we lead mankind unto His Kingdom of Glory and overcome Darkness. *And the words of our Father are immutable!* But would you follow me, then let us pray unto our Father to show us the way, for once more is the way lost in the mists."

When he had spoken they all were silent, for they searched their hearts.

But in the stillness, God let His voice be heard.

And God said: "My children, be patient! *For only they who have patience will be victorious!* Fail not one another, nor fail your elder brother, nor ever break the promise you have given Me, your Father; for you must remember *that My blessings are upon you, My thoughts follow you and My hand sustains you while you strive for the Light, for that which is true and for that which is good.*

"My children, hear My words, and I shall guide you.

"Behold, I say unto you: once more must you bring the Light of the spirit and clarity of thought unto mankind; for they are no longer able to reason clearly; for they are not able to sift falsehood from the truth, the clean from the unclean. Teach mankind this! And you must gradually teach them to discover some of the eternal laws, teach them to release and to make use of some of the many hidden powers. You must teach them to look out into the vastnesses of space, teach them to discover and to measure the paths and orbits of the heavenly bodies. You must open the eyes of human beings unto the pure lines of earthly forms, unto the splendour and diversity of colour. You must teach them to listen to the fulness and beauty of music.

"And when you have taught mankind all this, then will they themselves begin with wakened eyes and clear thoughts to perceive the web of lies that Darkness has spun about them; then will they themselves begin to search the ancient Scriptures, themselves sift out the grains of gold and cast away the dross of Darkness.

"My children, I, your Father, have shown you the way. Follow it! For do you this, then shall My blessing be with you."

But when God's voice fell silent, they all answered: "Father, we shall follow the way that Thou hast shown us! Help us, that we may never fail!"

Once more many of the Youngest let themselves be bound unto earthly bodies, that once again they might bring the Light of the spirit and clarity of thought unto those human beings who were led astray by the Eldest and by Darkness.

But when they had brought greater knowledge and learning unto mankind, and dispersed some of the Darkness about them, would others of the Youngest follow, and seek to overturn some of the false teachings of the Elder, and thus prepare the way for mankind's own study of the Holy Scriptures that were inherited from their forefathers.

The first who ventured forth to speak unto the children of the Earth on those matters that were as yet beyond their understanding were ill received and met with scorn, anger and contempt.

But more and more of them came forward with that which they had promised to bring.

Some of the Youngest taught people to cut alphabetic characters in wood and in metal, to use these to manifold the written words, and thus bring them into the possession of many. Others brought them greater knowledge of the world they lived in; and through perilous voyages new lands were discovered, and hidden riches won from the bosom of the Earth.[1]

Some of the Youngest brought unto mankind new and useful implements, whereby daily life became easier to live. Others sought to retrieve the wise and profound writings of times gone by from the depths of oblivion.

Some of the Youngest brought joy to people by renderings of graceful images in clay, in wood and in hard marble.

Others portrayed the men and women of the Holy Scriptures and the earthly life of Christ in fine pictures, rendered the life and endeavours of mankind – all in the profusion, splendour and beauty of colour.

Once more mankind began to awaken; eyes were opened, thoughts became more free and more lucid. But only slowly did the Light advance, for the Elder, the Servant of Darkness, sought always to hinder its progress.

---

[1] The spirits bound to explorers of those times were not all of the Youngest – several were of the Eldest.

Closer and closer he drew Darkness over the Earth, and sowed yet more of his evil seed. *And hatred, anger, violence, murder and iniquity thrived among human beings.*

And the Elder strengthened the Christians in their worship of the Virgin Mary, strengthened their faith in the help and intercession of holy men and women, so as to hinder them in praying to *God alone.* And he strengthened them in their belief in the torments and sufferings of Hell, that the fear and terror thus awakened in their feeble hearts should give him greater power over them. And in their fear of Hell, many Christians sought to buy dispensation from future punishment with gold and with silver and precious gifts, sought to *buy absolution* from the mighty popes.

But the Youngest continued to strive for the advance of the Light; for God strengthened them, and God sustained them.

And again they taught human beings to build magnificent temples to the honour of God, taught them to build fine palaces for their princes, kings and emperors, taught them to embellish temples and palaces with vaulted domes, lofty towers and soaring spires.

And human beings were filled with joy for the splendour they beheld.

But Darkness lay heavily upon the Earth.

War and strife reigned everywhere.

The princes of the nations warred among themselves; the popes fought with the prelates beneath them, fought among themselves,[1] fought with emperors, kings and princes, while mighty curses were hurled against all who would not yield.

And the Elder, the Servant of Darkness, continued to strengthen humanity's belief in the power held by the Prince of Hell over all sinners. And he implanted in the fearful the thought that a great many men and women were able to bring harm upon their enemies and opponents by summoning the help of the Evil One, and the so-called sorcerers and witches were persecuted with much severity. Many were tortured and burned for misdeeds which they had never committed, for people believed they saw evil spirits and demons wherever they turned.

But the Youngest continued with patience to work for the progress of the Light, for God strengthened them, and God sustained them.

And once more they taught human beings to look out into the

---

[1] At times the disputes between the prelates were so severe that they resulted in the election of several popes, who fought among themselves for the Holy See in Rome. – Publisher's note.

vastnesses of space, taught them to follow the paths and orbits of the glittering stars. But for a long time this knowledge remained very incomplete; for human beings as yet possessed but few and imperfect means whereby they could observe the celestial bodies, whereby they could measure and reckon their positions and paths.

Some of the Youngest conveyed the thoughts and longings of their spirit in beauteous, resounding and melodious stanzas; and many human beings rejoiced at these new and beautiful things that they had received.

And the time came when the Youngest who had promised to prepare the way for humanity's own study of the Scriptures came forth and sought to separate some grain of gold from the heavy dross of Darkness.

But among them were two men, who are known by the names of *Luther* and *Zwingli*.

These two grieved much over the blindness of human beings, grieved much over their profound debasement; and they both sought to break the yoke of bondage which Darkness had laid upon humanity.

And in their great zeal they both turned against the highest authorities of the Church, they showed how small and insignificant the popes were, despite their power and might; they showed how wretched they were in their anger, hatred and lust for power, and they both proclaimed that the popes, the Vicars of God and Christ, were by no means *infallible.*

And they sought to show the so-called Christians that they had become idolaters by worshipping the numerous images of holy men and women; for many knelt *only* before these saints, while they forgot to bow down before *Almighty God.*

Luther and Zwingli won many followers by their lucid writings and by their masterful speeches, for they awakened human beings to reflection.

But the Elder, the Servant of Darkness, sought to estrange them from one another. And these two, who before their earthly lives began had promised their Heavenly Father to walk together, became bitter foes; for the Elder stood between them, and he drew Darkness closer about them so that they were not able to agree upon a common teaching. For they were not agreed upon a great many things, for they fought against each other on many of the ancient doctrines.

And as the years passed, they also acquired many enemies and many adversaries.

But Luther was a mighty warrior, and he met all attacks with harsh words, with fiery and severe speeches; for none was able to subdue his proud spirit.

But although Luther *himself* at times erred, he continued to lead humanity toward the Light; thus he caused certain of the ancient Scriptures to be published, that human beings might seek consolation and sustenance from the study of the words and doctrines, which had been handed down from their forefathers.

Though Luther's power and authority were great, though he was hard and unyielding toward his foes, he still remained *faint* of heart when alone; for he perceived that God's full strength was not upon him. At times, he was seized by fear and terror of the Darkness that streamed toward him, and he felt that he was bound by the hatred that emanated from the Elder, the Servant of Darkness; so that at times he did not heed the voice which sought to guide him.

And Darkness gathered yet closer about him. Harsh and condemning words sounded from his lips. And when some of the people who laboured hard and suffered much united to secure more and greater rights for themselves, he angrily turned against them, and in his anger he cried out that these unworthy should be *put to death,* that their evil intentions should be destroyed.

But despite the many and grave faults of Luther as a man, he was able to reject certain of the false teachings of the Elder, and he and Zwingli together were able to bring humanity a few steps further toward the goal.

But neither of them was able to carry out that great work, which had been laid down before they were born unto the Earth, the great work that together they should have performed among human beings.

When Luther and Zwingli met once more in the heavenly abodes, after death had broken their earthly bodies, they both grieved much over the enmity which the Elder had called forth between them while they lived upon the Earth.

But yet more of the Youngest sought to sustain their brothers in the struggle against the papacy, and one of them is known by the name of *Calvin.*

His thoughts were lucid and keen, and with wise words he formed the new teaching.

But he was not in full agreement with Luther, nor was he fully agreed with Zwingli. For influenced by the Elder, he revived some of the ancient, rejected doctrines; he worded them anew and defended them with much authority.

Many followed him, and he was much honoured.

But Calvin was a stern man, and he demanded much of his followers, demanded purity, piety and obedience. And he was unbending in his sternness, for the Elder, the Servant of Darkness, stood at his side and hardened his heart, so that he pronounced harsh judgments on all who were against him; indeed, in the hardness of his heart, he even let one of his adversaries suffer death at the stake; for he had forgotten the words of Christ: **Forgive your enemies!**

Thus neither was Calvin able to break the power of Darkness, nor to overcome the curse of the Elder.

But even though Luther, Zwingli, and Calvin could not present the full truth, they were nevertheless able to bring forth some of the grains of gold in the ancient Scriptures, and were able to teach the Christians to study for *themselves* and reject several of the false teachings. And thus was some of the Darkness enshrouding mankind dispelled.

But with the attacks that those fearless men aimed at the papacy and the numerous fallacies of the Christian teaching, lengthy and fearsome conflicts and struggles broke out anew in many places. For as the years went by, and more and more people joined the new forms of the Christian faith, certain of the followers of the old faith sought to uphold the faltering papacy.

Further and more severe monastic orders were founded, some of the old fallacies were abandoned, and new, more stringent laws enacted, demanding greater purity, greater piety and greater obedience.

And the followers of the Papal Church sought to punish the apostates with fearsome persecution, torture, and death, seeking to halt the progress of the new Christian teachings.

Once again, Darkness descended more closely and more heavily upon the Earth.

Again, the pyres blazed to the honour of Almighty God. Thousands upon thousands were put to death. And in their blind hatred and lust for revenge, certain of the followers of the papacy had several thousand adversaries slain in a single night.

Truly, the power of Darkness was awesome!

And the time returned when nation rose against nation, brother against brother, ruler against ruler.

And while songs of praise rang out in the churches to the honour of God, murders, plunderings, and frightful misdeeds were perpetrated *in His name!*

Closer and heavier, Darkness descended upon the Earth. Poverty and misery abounded in the lands.

The fear of human beings grew greater yet, and they feared yet more the Prince of Hell and all his helpers. And sorcerers and witches were tortured and burned.

Darkness was everywhere and sufferings were everywhere; for the evil seed of the Elder sprouted and bore fruit.

But no longer were the Youngest faint of heart; for they trusted in God, their Father; for He strengthened them, and He guided them.

Amid suffering, violence, death and misery, they strove to advance the Light, strove to bring more knowledge and more learning unto human beings.

And when after each completed life upon the Earth they returned unto the heavenly abodes, many of them did not accept the rest that was rightfully theirs; *for they all yearned to break the power of Darkness, for they all yearned to overcome the curses of the Elder;* and they hastened to be bound unto new earthly bodies, that they might lead mankind forward toward the goal.

As century was added to century, the Youngest sought in numerous ways to augment the knowledge that they had already brought unto mankind.

And they gave unto humanity yet more of the splendid and colourful paintings, with which they adorned churches, palaces and the mansions of princes.

Slowly the Youngest taught mankind to study the structure of the human body, its tissues and cells; taught them to discover healing for some of the body's many ills. Taught them to capture the winding ways of fleeting thoughts; taught them to form, clarify and preserve their thoughts in wise sayings.

And they taught them to listen to the beauty and fulness of sound. They taught them to fashion instruments, large and small, with which they could bring forth an abundance of pure and resonant tones, a diversity of beautiful and harmonious sounds.

They taught them to fashion instruments with which better to unravel the paths and positions of the glittering stars in distant space.

And they taught mankind to unleash some of the hidden powers of nature and how to draw benefit from such knowledge; taught them to study the many forms of life; taught them to discover some of those laws which govern creation – the least as well as the greatest.

As centuries receded, human beings learned to improve the routes and the highways between the many kingdoms and continents of the Earth; learned to locate and to unearth some of the beautiful cities, mighty temples and proud mansions of olden times; numerous hidden treasures were brought to the light of day from the bosom of the

Earth, treasures which told of the life and customs of their fore-
bears.

In this manner the Youngest brought ever more knowledge and yet
greater learning unto mankind.

And as the years passed, *the Light began slowly to spread once
more across the Earth.*

But there was still fighting and dissension; as yet, murder, killing
and misdeeds still flourished. Princes, kings, and emperors were still
able to rouse nation against nation in battle and destructive warfare.

Numerous Christians still kneeled in worship and prayer before
the lifeless images of the holy men and women. Many still debated
old and new doctrines with masterful words and fiery speeches; and
numerous forms of Christianity arose.

But the Light continued to spread throughout the Earth – *and
slowly Darkness began to yield.*

But the Elder, the Servant of Darkness, continued to instil his
poison into the hearts of human beings. And in the minds of some
he implanted the thought *that God did not exist.* And those who believed him stood forth, and in their folly they defended this blasphemous thought with great authority.

But Darkness continued to recede, and the Elder knew that he
could no longer halt the advance of the Light; and he knew that the
hour drew near when the power of Darkness should be broken.

Then fear and terror were born in his heart. For he knew that
should the Light overcome him, then must he himself reap the evil
seed that he had sown among human beings, he knew that all the
curses that he had hurled out must turn against himself. And he
feared that retribution would crush him and destroy him for all
eternity. For he thought that for his sins there could be no forgiveness; *for he forgot his Father's infinite love, forgot His omnipotence, forgot His compassion.*

36.

Did the Spirits of the Dead Continue to Walk among Human Beings, or did God Gradually Succeed in Calling back all of them?

A little more than eight decades before the eldest of the Youngest
was born unto the Earth as Jesus of Nazareth, God called for the
first time upon the earthbound spirits. But from that time, at the last
hour of each passing century, God let His voice be heard by them to
awaken remorse in their hearts. But fewer and fewer returned unto

the spheres, for only few were able to repent of their sins and misdeeds, for Darkness lay heavily over the Earth.

And as the centuries passed, Darkness bound ever more human spirits after their death to walk upon the Earth among the living.

And the time came when the spirits of the dead became a mighty host – legion upon legion. They wandered everywhere and brought much discord wherever they went, for they inspired mankind to many sinful lusts, many evil and unclean thoughts.

Some people could see the spirits as shadow-like beings, some heard their speech as faintly whispered words; and this strengthened their belief that they were surrounded by devils, evil spirits and ghosts.

And human beings feared the dead.

Some of the Youngest who were not bound unto earthly bodies often went unto the Earth, where with kind and gentle words they called these wretched beings back unto life and to the Light. But the Youngest were able for but a short time to dwell among the spirits of the dead; for the close Darkness and evil vapours made them weak and faint of heart.

But after they had rested for a time in their dwellings, unseen by human beings they went forth again unto the Earth to bring help once more unto the children of Darkness. And God, their Father, strengthened them, and He sustained them in their arduous task.

But the eldest of the Youngest, Christ, did not tire. Despite Darkness, despite evil vapours, he persevered. Kindly and tenderly he sought to awaken remorse in the hearts of the earthbound spirits, and he carried home many of the fallen unto their empty dwellings.

And upon his journeyings he was wont to find a brother[1] or a sister[1] who had stumbled over the stones cast in their path by the Elder, while they fought for the progress of mankind. But Christ brought them back unto the outermost sphere about the Earth, and he helped them to cleanse themselves of the Darkness which had defiled them.

But wherever Christ ventured, there was he followed by God's watchful eye. And God saw his deep sorrow over the wretchedness of human beings, saw the patience with which he sought to bring help unto the fallen – unto the living and the dead.

And God granted him yet greater power, yet greater strength.

---

[1] The Youngest who, tempted by the Elder, committed misdeeds during their lives on Earth were often, because of their consciousness of sin, bound to an existence without rest among the earthbound human spirits, after their earthly lives had ended.

But behold, then Christ ventured into the ravaged Kingdom, to seek his elder brothers and sisters there.

And he spoke with them and he tenderly bade them to return unto their Father, bade them to return Home. Many scorned him and mocked him; but some were drawn by the pure and radiant Light which surrounded him, were drawn by his tender words; and remorse awoke in their hearts. And he carried them unto a distant place, where they could rest in peace until remembrance of all that was awoke in their memory.

And Christ walked among the living human beings. Unseen and unknown, he came unto the sinner and the breaker of law. With his tender love, with his unending patience, he often drew them back from the abyss which threatened to swallow them. By his warning call, he forestalled many a sinful and impure thought, so that it never turned to deed. Many evil and wicked deeds were thus averted by his purity, they were forestalled by his call and by his warning.

And no longer did Christ tire, neither did he falter; but he carried with patience the heavy burdens that mankind continued to lay upon his shoulders; for God strengthened him; for God gave him ever greater power, ever greater patience.

And when the time came that the Light again began to spread slowly across the Earth, a faint joy, a faint hope awoke in the mind of Christ. But when he saw that the Light spread still more, he understood that the time was drawing near when the power of Darkness should be broken; *and he fervently rejoiced.*

———————

And it came to pass, eighteen and a half centuries[1] after the time when the eldest of the Youngest was born to live among human beings as Jesus of Nazareth, that God called him unto His Kingdom of Glory.

When Christ heard God's calling voice, he hastened unto his Father, greeted him and said: "Father, Thou didst call! Behold, I am come."

But when he had spoken thus, God fondly bade him be welcome.

And He said: "My son, I, your Father, have followed you in all your works. I saw your deep sorrow over the misery of humanity. I saw your longing to lead your eldest brother back unto his rightful Home. I followed you, while, unseen by the children of the Earth,

———————

[1] 1857.

you walked among them to draw them away from sin and impurity. I followed you, while you walked in the ravaged Kingdom to call back your elder brothers and sisters. Truly, for all this *I thank you!*

"And behold, I have followed the work of your brothers and sisters for the progress of humanity, followed your guiding of mankind's many journeyings in life upon the Earth, and I have rejoiced over the good fruits which your love, which your patience have borne. *For by your work has the Light made Darkness to recede.* Truly, for all this I thank each of you. But unto you I say: would you continue to follow the way that I have shown you, then shall you surely reach unto your goal, though centuries may lie before you."

And God spoke further.

And He said: "My son, I bade you to come; for I desired to show you a shorter road by which you may reach your goal more quickly. But I say unto you: would you follow this shorter road, then must you walk through thorns and thistles, over chasms and through streaming waters, then must you bend again and again to remove the stones which hinder your progress; then must you never grow weary – and you must bear your burdens with yet greater patience."

When God had spoken thus, He was silent a while.

But Christ answered Him and said: *"Father, show me the road of which Thou didst speak; for can it lead us sooner unto the goal, then should we surely follow it."*

Then God spoke further.

And He said: "From you and through you have human beings learnt much; but they have no complete knowledge of our world, they know nothing of the world that remains hidden from their mist-veiled earthly eyes. My son, I say unto you: give you the children of the Earth knowledge of some of the laws whereby life is lived; My son, *speak unto humanity!"*

And God spoke further.

And He said: "Some of the many human spirits who are bound by Darkness, bound unto the Earth by their sins and misdeeds, have from the earliest times when they began to walk among the living sought often and in manifold ways to make themselves known unto human beings; many have seen them, many have heard them, and many could receive messages from them. Turn this to good account! For you know that also you can in manifold ways make yourselves known unto human beings. My son, I say unto you: from the Light shall you build a bridge across the chasm which separates our world from the Earth. You shall lift a corner of the veil which covers the entrance to that life which is for ever! But I say unto you, seek those human beings who are able to see through the earthly veil of mist with their spirit's eye! Seek those human beings who are able, with their spiritual ear, to perceive the high vibrations that arise from the sound of your voices. Seek those human beings who can withhold their earthly selves, that they might receive and render the thoughts that you think and inspire in them! And when you perceive that they have complete trust in you and in your words, then shall you speak unto them of your brothers and sisters, who are theirs also, and who, concealed by Darkness, wander across the Earth without home and without rest. And do they understand you, then make you them your helpers, make them your intermediaries. *For the thought and speech of human beings is more easily perceived by the spirits of the dead.* Indeed, you shall teach human beings to *pray* for those who are bound by Darkness, teach them that the loving thoughts of their prayer can draw the Light unto all for whom they pray; and when *repentance* awakes in the hearts of the earthbound spirits, then can you lead them back unto the dwellings that stand empty. My son, I say unto you: will you follow *this shorter road,* with human beings as intermediaries and helpers, then within a century can you draw all spirits of the dead away from the Earth and back unto life and the Light – and then will purer and brighter times soon come unto all of you. But I say unto you: would you do this, then shall you know that for a long time must you leave your fine abodes, then for long periods must you remain in the Darkness, fog and evil vapours upon the Earth; for you must without cease protect the human beings that you choose for your helpers, that Darkness shall not descend upon them and shall not lead them astray."

When God had spoken thus, He remained silent for a time.

But Christ answered Him and said: "Father, art Thou with us, then shall we surely overcome; but Father, I ask of Thee, how may we in this manner win back our eldest brother?"

Then God looked upon him with favour.

And He said: "My son, *your brother is among those who are bound by Darkness, bound by sin; teach mankind to take pity upon him and his sufferings also! Teach them to forgive that which he has sinned against them. Teach them to pray for him also, teach them to pray for his salvation!* For do they this, then will the loving thoughts of their prayers break for ever the power of Darkness over him. Then shall the bonds that bind your brother be broken, and then can we draw him unto us."

But when God had spoken thus, Christ bowed down his head. And his voice was sorrowful when he said: "Father, mankind loves not Thine eldest son as *we* do; human beings hate him, fear him and curse him. *Verily, no one will pray for him.*"

But God answered him and said: "My son, seek among those that *love you;* for upon *your word* and by *your intercession* will they surely pray for your eldest brother. My son, I say unto you: find you but *a single human being* who with trust in your word and with compassion of heart will pray for him who created a world of sin, sorrow, and misery, then will the power of Darkness be broken, then will your brother be free, and then shall we, who know him and love him, forgive him and receive him in our midst."

Then Christ looked steadfastly upon his Father, and he said: "Father, say that Thou art with us; for then shall I know that we shall be victorious."

But God embraced him, and He said: "My blessing shall be upon you in all that you do."

Then Christ returned unto his dwelling in the outermost sphere about the Earth. And he called upon all of the brothers and sisters who at that time were not bound unto earthly bodies.

And when they were gathered together, he stood forth and spoke unto them of the road that their God and Father had shown him.

But when he had spoken, deep silence fell upon them all; for they understood that this would be a sorely trying, an exceedingly burdensome journey.

And when none answered him, Christ continued to speak, and he said: "Fear you to follow me, then shall I walk alone; but I say unto you: *forget not that our Father has promised to be with us!*"

Then they answered: "Brother, brother, we shall go with you and help you to bear these new burdens. Truly, you shall not walk alone. And be our Father with us, then shall we surely be victorious."

Christ thanked them, and he said: "Not all can follow me; for some of you must remain in these our dwelling places to make straight and to lead, that all shall not become disorder and confusion."

And he chose certain of his brothers and sisters, and they promised to lead and to make straight all in accord with his spirit.

But when all was prepared God let His voice be heard by them.

And God said: "My children, I, your Father, thank you all. But ere you journey unto the Earth, would I speak unto you these words: *sustain one another, never fail one another! For should you fail, and should you falter, and should you tire, then will the shorter road become for you the longer.*"

Then they cried out: "Father, be with us, that we may never fail!"

And God answered them.

And He said: "I, your Father, shall give you the strength that you need; *for My Thought shall lead you, My hand shall sustain you and My blessing shall be upon you!*"

7 C

When God's voice ceased, a host of the children of the Light went forth unto the Earth, that without human embodiment they might begin their difficult journey.

And they went unto those places where people gathered to receive messages from the spirits of the dead.

And with kind and tender thoughts, the Youngest sought to influence the men and women who were intermediaries between the living and the dead. But this was exceedingly difficult; for their thoughts could hardly pierce the Darkness that shrouded the earthbound spirits; for these thronged in great multitudes about the so-called mediums, those people who in various ways sought to interpret the thoughts and the words of these wretched beings.

But as time passed, the Youngest became ever more skilful in leading the mediums with the help of the Light. And the messages that were received became clearer, easier to understand and less filled with error.

But when the Youngest in their talks with human beings dared question the venerated faith, then were they met with harsh words and stern judgment. Many were angered, many were vexed; for in their unwisdom these thought they were in discourse with evil spirits or devils. And Christ and those who were with him had to journey on to seek other and better helpers. And they grieved sorely over the great blindness of humanity.

But as the years passed, they found greater understanding and greater trust. Then they spoke unto mankind of the life that follows earthly death.

Many listened to the thoughts and to the words, and some believed that which was imparted.

And in numerous places of the kingdoms and the continents of the Earth, more and ever more men and women sought to communicate with the dead, while knowledge of the messages from the spirits spread more and more.

The learned then began to listen, indeed, some of them pondered, searched, and studied to discover the laws that governed all these things. But from this there arose much discord and much strife; for, as was their custom, the learned were by no means in agreement. Some spoke for, and others spoke against the truth of that which came to pass.

But, without growing weary of the scorn, anger and intolerance of human beings toward one another, the Youngest continued along the road that their Father had shown them; but wherever they went, they were pursued by the Elder, the Servant of Darkness. And he drew Darkness still closer about the men and women who were mediums, seeking to confuse their thoughts, seeking to falsify the words that they received. *And in the hearts of many he awakened pride, self-righteousness, and the lust for power.*

But the Youngest sought to protect their mediums, sought to warn them of Darkness and of falsehood, that they should not listen to the thoughts and to the words of the Elder.

But in spite of all warnings, against all admonitions, many mediums followed the Elder's alluring thoughts and sayings – and many fell. Indeed, some rose up at large gatherings to exhibit their accomplishments *for their own gain;* and did they not succeed in making the desired contact, then would they often make pretences. But this led to great confusion and much falsehood. But when the Youngest saw that despite the given warnings their helpers and intermediaries succumbed to the temptations of Darkness, they turned away from them and went on to seek other, more perceiving helpers.

And they grieved over the people's blindness, grieved over their feeble trust.

But despite the power of Darkness, the Youngest continued to meet with ever greater understanding. And then they began to tell about the many spirits who, bound by sin and evil and without earthly embodiment, walked among human beings without home and without rest.

People listened and many believed the words, and they who believed that which was said began to help these wretched beings, and they prayed unto Almighty God for peace and salvation for the spirits of the dead.

And behold: it came to pass even as God had spoken, that the compassionate thoughts of human beings awakened remorse in the hearts of many of the earthbound spirits, and the streaming waves of the Light drew the repentant spirits back unto the dwellings that once they had left.

And the Youngest who were in the spheres received them tenderly, and they gave them all care.

Slowly, the Youngest advanced further toward their goal; and they found more and still more helpers. But when Christ spoke unto them of the many false teachings of the Christian faith and told them who he was, only few dared listen to his words, only few dared trust him; for they believed that he was the *Evil One who sought to lead them astray with kind and tender words.* And many turned away from him, and from those who were with him.

And Christ sorrowed greatly.

But the years passed; and a new earthly century[1] began. A multitude of the spirits of the dead was still bound unto the Earth, the power of Darkness was still not broken, and invisible to human beings, Christ and those who were with him still journeyed from place to place, striving to obtain the help that they desired.

And as the years passed, they found more and better helpers. More and more people prayed unto God the Almighty for peace and for salvation for those who were bound by Darkness.

And upon his journey across the Earth from place unto place, from country unto country, Christ found a few people who came to trust him fully, came to trust his word. And Christ rejoiced greatly; for then he knew that they were drawing near unto their goal.

But wherever they went, God's ever wakeful eye followed them. He sustained them and He strengthened them.

God saw their untiring love, saw their great patience, their many sorrows, their few joys. And He resolved to sustain them still more.

And when little more than a decade[2] of the new earthly century had passed, God let His mighty voice be heard over all the Earth to call back the spirits of the dead.

But this came to pass a few earthly years before a century had passed since the time when God had last let His voice be heard by all the dead.

Behold, they all ceased in what they were about, and they all listened; for God called upon each one, He called each one by name, and He spoke unto each one, He spoke unto them all.

And He said: "My children, I, your Father, ask of you: will you for ever be slaves unto your evil lusts and impure desires? Will you continue to walk in Darkness and in sin? Truly, you shall know *that no sufferings, no curses, no impurity and no Darkness can endure for all eternity.* My children, hear Me! Seek to repent of that which you have sinned! For then will the bonds that bind you be broken, then will the Light draw you back unto peace and to rest. My children, answer Me, your Father, *will you not return unto life and to the Light?"*

When God had spoken thus, He fell silent for a time.

But the stillness oppressed the spirits that were bound in sin. And they called upon their Father, they cried out and they answered Him.

All who walked in Darkness upon the Earth and the Eldest in the ravaged Kingdom cried out and answered Him – *only the Elder made no answer.*

---

[1] 1900.
[2] 1911.

And the answers sounded as a mighty cry: "Father, forgive us that which we have sinned; deliver us from the power of Darkness!"

And God spoke unto them.

And He said: "My children, that which you have sinned against Me, and that which you have sinned against the eternal laws, that shall you be forgiven, and it shall be blotted out! *But that which you have sinned against one another, that must you also forgive one another!*

"My children, *be you all welcome back unto life and to the Light.*"

But when the voice of God fell silent, behold, the Light welled forth. Borne by its eternal, streaming waves, thousands upon thousands of the fallen spirits were drawn away from Darkness, away from the Earth, back unto the dwellings that stood empty.

And the Youngest who were in the spheres received them with love and they gave care unto them all.

And God sent unto the Earth a multitude of the Youngest so as to sustain and to guide those who were fallen the deepest, those who could no longer rise, those who were blinded by Darkness. Borne by the Youngest, the deepest fallen were brought back unto their dwellings.

And soon they were all returned unto peace and to rest.

In fear and in terror the Elder saw the Light well forth, saw its clear, pure waves flood and wash away the ravaged Kingdom, saw it absorb the evil vapours and dispel the heavy Darkness.

And he fled from that place in terror, fled across the Earth.

But the ever-streaming waves of the Light pursued him and enfolded all the Earth as a glowing dawn.

But for the Elder there was no peace, there was no rest; *for he was still bound by Darkness, still bound unto his creatures, and he was still the Servant of Darkness.*

And without home, without rest, he continued to flee across the Earth.

But when a time had passed, a voice sounded unto him, a gentle, loving voice that said: "Brother, why do you flee?"

And he ceased his frenzied flight; and behold, Christ stood before him in all his radiant glory, and the Elder bowed down his head; for the brilliant light blinded his eyes.

But Christ embraced him, and he said: "Brother, I am come to bring you rest, to bring you peace!"

But the Elder answered him and said: *"The wrath of our Father will crush me and destroy me."*

Then Christ said: *"Our Father's love, His tenderness, His compassion will draw you away from Darkness, away from your sufferings."*

And Christ spoke yet further.

And he said: "Brother, follow me for I will lead you unto human beings who trust me, who trust my words; surely will they take pity upon you, surely, at *my intercession,* will they pray for your peace and salvation; *for this is the wish of our Father.* Brother, seek to repent of that which you have sinned, for then will the bonds which bind you be broken, then will the Light carry you unto our Father's embrace."

But the Elder answered him and said: *"Humanity hates me, fears me and curses me - no human being will pray for the one who created a world of sin, of sorrow and of suffering."*

Then Christ said: "Brother, I say unto you, the power of prayer is great when it is borne by thoughts of love. Follow me and trust me; *for on my word will human beings pray for you."*

When Christ fell silent, the Elder stood for a time, answering no word.

Then *hope* awoke in his heart, and he answered: "Brother, I will follow you!"

And Christ led him unto an earthly dwelling, where people were gathered; for they spoke with some of the Youngest, who were there unseen to sustain and to guide them in their work.

But Christ called unto the people who were there; and they listened, for neither could they see *him.* And he said: "I, Christ, your elder brother, speak unto you - hear me! Help me pray unto our Father that He may grant peace and salvation to the brother I have brought unto you. Have compassion for him; *for so deep has he fallen that none can fall deeper; for so much has he sinned that none can sin more, and his sufferings are very great!"*

When he had spoken thus, he turned toward the Elder, and he said: "Tell them who you are, tell them that which you have sinned, and they will help you; for they fear you not - our Father is with them!"

And the Elder spoke unto them, he told them who he was, told them that which he had sinned.

The human beings listened, and they understood that his words were true; for they perceived the evil streams of Darkness that emanated from him.

But when he fell silent, then they prayed from the compassion of their hearts unto God the Almighty, prayed that He should grant peace and salvation unto *him* who was the cause of all sin, all sorrow and all suffering.

And God heard their prayer.

Then awoke the full memory of the Elder, then he remembered vividly the blessed times that were before mankind. And he faltered beneath the mighty burden of remembrance.

But some of the Youngest sustained him, that he should not fall.

Behold, then *grief and remorse* awoke in his heart, and he cried out: "Father, Father, help me to break the power of Darkness, to break the bond of Darkness! Help me to remove sin and suffering from the human beings, my creatures! Father, forgive that which I have sinned against Thee and that which I have sinned against all!"

And God heard his cry.

And He sounded His voice unto him.

And God said: "My son, that which you have sinned against Me, your Father, and that which you have sinned against the eternal laws, that shall you be forgiven, and it shall be blotted out! And that which you have sinned against your brothers and sisters, that I surely know they will all forgive you. *But that which you have sinned against human beings, your creatures, that must they themselves forgive you!*"

"My son, I, your Father, bid you welcome back unto the Light, bid you welcome unto your Home."

When God was silent, the Youngest carried their brother, whom they all loved, back unto their Home, back unto their Father's embrace.

And God received His repentant son with tenderness and with fervent joy.

And God spoke unto Christ and unto those among the Youngest who had been with their brother, *thanking them all* for the work they had done, *thanking each one* for the great patience, for the great love that they all had evinced.

And there was great joy and they all shouted in jubilation; for they knew that thenceforth would there arise brighter and happier times for them all. Yet they knew that much time would pass *before mankind became purer and less sinful;* yet they understood that aeons must pass *before the Light had fully absorbed all Darkness and removed it from the Earth.*

And the Youngest led their eldest brother unto a place, where in stillness he might rest and ponder all that had come to pass.

Then they went unto the outermost sphere about the Earth so as to rest for a short while in the beautiful dwellings for which they had yearned so long.

But, when one earthly year had passed, God let His voice be heard by the Elder.

And God said: "My son, your time of rest has ended. Go unto the Earth, unto the human beings. *Say unto them that they are no longer to fear you, to hate you, or to curse you. Bow down before them, seek to obtain their forgiveness for all you have sinned against them; for do they forgive you, then will the bond break asunder, the bond that binds them unto the curses you have hurled upon them. Then will they with greater ease overcome the Darkness that enshrouds them, and then will the Light shine with greater purity and brightness upon the Earth."*

The Elder listened to the words. And he said: "Father, then shouldst *Thou* surely be with me; for I fear that human beings will have no trust in me; for I fear that they will turn from me, that they will not hear my words."

But God answered him and said: "Follow your younger brother; for he has promised to sustain you and to guide you! *My blessing shall be upon you!"*

Then the Elder bowed down his head.

And he said: "Father, I thank Thee; Thy will be done!"

But when he had spoken thus, Christ and some of the Youngest stood with him.

And Christ said: "Brother, in the year that has passed we sought to prepare the way for you. Follow us; for we will lead you unto human beings through whose help you may form your thoughts in earthly language and in earthly signs."

The Elder thanked them, and he followed them.

And they went unto the Earth. And with the help of human beings they built a bridge over the chasm that separates the world of Darkness from the world of the Light, and they lifted a corner of the veil that conceals the entrance unto eternal life.

For God, their Father, was with them.

Behold, I, Ardor, the Elder, once the Servant of Darkness, obeyed our Father's command and I spoke unto you; spoke of the Darkness, the sufferings, and the wretchedness that *my fall* and *my sin* brought upon the human beings, my creation. *And through you I speak unto all mankind, unto all generations that are, and unto all generations to come.*

And I say unto you all: *fear me not, hate me not, curse me not! For I am no longer the Prince of Hell, and Hell is no more!*

And I pray you from the depth of my heart – if you can overcome your hatred, if you can overcome your anger – to forgive me that which I have sinned against you all!

Forgive me, that the peace of our Father and His blessing may be with you now and for all eternity!

Amen.

———————

LOVE ONE ANOTHER!

Love One Another!

"Again I say unto you, That if two of you shall agree on earth as touching any thing that they shall ask, it shall be done for them of my Father which is in heaven. For where two or three are gathered together in my name, there am I in the midst of them."[1]

Matthew 18: 19,20.

I Christ, the eldest of the Youngest, speak unto you. Hear me, for I speak in the name of our God and Father!

He sent me unto you so as to teach you and all mankind some of the laws which are given for your journeying toward the distant goal; and He bade me likewise to show you how you may all live in forbearance, peace and love with one another.

My words shall sound unto all the peoples of the Earth. All shall hear them, and they shall reach unto the farthest regions of the Earth. Generation after generation shall be born, shall live and shall die, but my words shall live through all eternity. Yea, truly I say unto you: *as a blazing torch shall my words shine before you, that you may not ever go astray!*

For all of you, for you who suffer, who doubt and who seek, I raise my torch high over all the Earth, that its clear radiance may fall upon the ways that lead unto our Father's Kingdom.

Through all eternity shall my torch shine for you and disperse the Darkness which is about you; *and never shall it be quenched;* for it is nourished by an eternal and holy fire, the fire that was kindled by our Father's flaming Divinity, *lit by His deep, unending love and compassion.*

High over your heads I raise my torch, and I walk before you. Follow me, all who suffer, all who labour with toil and trouble, all who sigh and groan under heavy burdens! Follow me all! *For I shall lead you unto our Father, I shall give you rest in His embrace!*

---

[1]) These words were spoken by Jesus not only to the Apostles, but to *all* the disciples who were present on that occasion, and thus apply in a wider sense to *all* the followers of Jesus. He is only present in person when this is necessary for one reason or another; in all other circumstances in which he is called upon, Jesus answers through his thought. Those who apply to him in spirit, in truth and with their whole heart feel his help as a deep spiritual peace and repose.

Yea, truly I say unto you: will you walk in the paths that I show you, will you follow me without fear and without doubt, will you hold your head high and harden your will, then shall you surely overcome the evil within you, then will your burdens not weigh down upon you, then with abhorrence will you turn from all misdeed, from all sin – yea, will you follow me, then shall the peace and blessedness of Heaven come upon you; for then will the hope in your hearts for eternal life become joyous certainty; then will you know with immutable certitude that death separates you only for a while from those you love, *that you shall meet again in the heavenly*[1] *dwellings.*

Yea, follow me all! For I have promised to lead and to guide you unto our Father's Home! But hear my words, for I say unto you: do you let anger and hatred, do you let doubt and fear rule over you, do you continue to walk in sin and in Darkness, even then shall you not walk alone *for I shall be beside you!*

Do you stumble upon the many stones in your path, then shall I support you, that you shall not fall; does your foot slip on the steep verges of the abyss, then shall my hand steady you, then shall I lead you back onto the level paths; yea, do you go astray among the bottomless sloughs of Darkness, then shall I lift you up, then shall I cleanse you of all soil and mire. Yea, though you hate me and curse me, though you flee from me and conceal yourselves, even then shall I know how to find you and bring you back onto the straight and proper paths. For our Father's words to me were these: "My son, your earthly brothers and sisters are all equal before My Fatherly heart, all are welcome in My Kingdom, all shall I receive in My embrace! My son, none shall be turned away, none shall be condemned, none shall be cast out, and none shall perish in the outer Darkness!" And I, your brother, once more say unto you: *none shall be turned away, none shall be condemned, yea, not one of you shall be cast out, nor one devoured by the outer Darkness!* For I have promised to lead and to guide you, and I shall not leave you nor forsake you until I have brought the last of you to rest in our Father's embrace.

---

[1]) See Commentary, p. 191.

I.

I Speak unto you of some of Our Father's Laws!

All have you been endowed with eternal life from our God and Father; unto all of you has He given a spark of His flaming Being, that through *many lives upon the Earth,* and with the help of your free will, you can make your way out of Darkness and go forward unto purity and Light.

But our Father *compels* none among you to accept the gift which He has given. This I say unto those who in their doubt of God's perfect justice have hurled curses against Him, *have cursed the One who out of His entire love and compassion has made you all His children.* And you who have uttered curses should know that your curses are powerless and dead, for they cannot reach their high goal. When conceived or when uttered, at the selfsame moment are they blotted out by our Father's strong Will; for were the curses not blotted out, *then would they crush and destroy the one who uttered them.* And you who curse and do not give thanks, you shall know that after your life upon the Earth has ended you can choose whether to fulfil your journey toward the distant goal, or whether to return unto your Father's bosom whence you came. But should you choose – despite suffering, grief and adversity – to fulfil your journey, then shall our Father's *blessing* be with you, that you may never again go astray. But I say unto you: never have any chosen to return unto their Father's bosom; for *who among you would of their free will allow their living selves to be extinguished for all eternity,* when each of you by hardening your will, by asking our Father for power and strength, can reach His Kingdom of Glory.

Hear my words! For I say unto you: *do you not possess the will to live, then neither shall you fear the gift of eternal life! For no one compels you!*

Slowly, each life upon the Earth brings you forward along the path, save you go astray; for then must you live through many lives upon the Earth to atone for your errors and sins, before you go forward toward greater perfection once more. This I say unto those who resist not and fall into the many temptations of Darkness. And this I say unto all who let themselves be guided by the lust for power, by hatred and envy, unto all who forget to strengthen their will for the good, who forget to ask for our Father's help. For do you not strive *against* evil, but follow you lusts and unclean desires, *then surely can you never be victorious.*

Yea, hear my words! For I say unto you: do you not strive against evil, against the temptations of Darkness, then will you bring much needless suffering upon yourselves, for that which you sin each one of you must atone for in full. But do you refuse to restore what you have destroyed – for no one compels you to do that which is right – then you cease your progress toward the Light and the Kingdom, then through many lives upon the Earth will you remain at the same place. For no progress can there be for those who of their free will turn away from truth, from purity and from justice. This I say unto those who in their vanity and foolish pride will not yield, and will not acknowledge that they have erred and that they have sinned.

Yea, verily: all must you fully atone for that which you have transgressed; *for my death upon the cross as Jesus of Nazareth in no wise lessens your guilt of sin; my death was no atonement for your sins, and my sufferings cannot deliver you, nor can they save you from sin and from Darkness;* for had I, as Jesus of Nazareth, been able to pray for help for our eldest brother, then would death upon the cross never have been mine. This I say unto you all, that you should not listen to *false interpretations* nor cling to *false hopes.*

Yea, hear my words and never forget them! For *I* say: *each of you shall reap the good or the evil seed which you have sown.*

But you shall know that the knowledge and the powers that your spirit has gained through the many lives upon the Earth shall by no means be taken from you, no matter how often you go astray, no matter how much you may sin. For the goal of your journey lies *ahead* and no road leads *back.* Yea, though the knowledge and the powers that you have gained do not reach your earthly consciousness, you may be certain that all that your spirit has gained *remains in its full possession when it is delivered from the earthly body.*

Be you the masters of your thoughts! For every thought, howewer fleeting, is recorded by the high vibrations of Darkness or of the Light, and you must all bear full responsibility for the sin and the evil that your thoughts create.

This I say unto you all. For you shall know that by thought you influence one another to commit evil deeds or to do good; and you shall know that each thought, after a shorter or after a longer time will return unto its source: *the good thoughts draw the Light toward you,* bringing you peace and joy; *the evil thoughts draw Darkness toward you,* causing you many sufferings, much sorrow; for all the evil that you have wished upon others *will turn without fail against yourself.*

Yea, hear my words! Be mindful of your thoughts and be you the masters of them! For each thought bears its good or its evil fruit; *and when it is ripe, then must your own selves reap the fruit that your thoughts have borne.*

Never let your evil thoughts turn to deed! For you must all account in full for each of your deeds. Have you sinned against the earthly laws, then must you submit and acknowledge your errors and your sins, then most you accept and suffer the penalties allotted to you under the laws of your society, for do you this, *then have you fully atoned for that which you have transgressed.*

But would you flee from the responsibility which rests upon you, would you deny the evil that you have done, would you accuse *another* of being guilty of *your own* sins, then shall you know that though you may evade *justice upon the Earth,* then shall you by no means evade *the justice of Heaven.* For our Father follows you, His Eye sees all, His Thought knows all. And when your life upon the Earth is ended, then will He demand of you to give account of the evil you have done. Then must you answer to the full His question: why you let your evil thoughts turn to deed. Yea, verily, He will not release you before all is considered and answered. For there shall be no progress for you, nor shall you be able to begin a new life upon the Earth *before you have acknowledged your errors, before you have repented of your sins.*

Yea, hear my words and never forget them! For *I* say unto you: you shall all give full account of your deeds, and each of you in your lives to come upon the Earth must *yourself* endure those sufferings, sorrows and miseries that you have brought upon *others. For each evil and sinful act you have committed must surely turn against you.*

Furthermore, you shall know that do you good unto others thereby to gain advantage for *yourselves* in this or in future lives upon the Earth, then you deceive yourselves; for selfishness is of the evil! *Only the good deeds that are born of the merciful love and compassion of your hearts will draw the Light toward you, will disperse the Darkness and lighten your journey.*

Guard your tongue and weigh your words! For I say unto you: you must all fully account for each improper word you have spoken. Never allow hard, condemning, unjust or false words to pass your lips; for they will accuse you and reveal the hardness and deceit in your heart.

Truly, I say unto you: *you must at all times be fully honest, truthful and just; for then will you harm no one, but do good unto others and unto yourselves.*

8 C

Do not harbour anger in your hearts! For out of anger arises hatred and out of hatred curses, and you must never curse one another; for the curses you utter will only bind *you,* and for long times will they stay your progress toward the Home and toward the Light. For have you cursed others, then must you live through many lives upon the Earth, until you have learned to *bless* those whom formerly you cursed.

Yea, hear my words and never forget them. For *I* say unto you: *curse not, but love one another as brothers and sisters, that peace and love may dwell among you for all eternity!*

Do not wilfully shorten the days of your life upon the Earth! For thereby you create far more and far greater sufferings than had you borne the burdens of your earthly life with patience. Yea, should you seek to free your spirit by a death of your own choosing, then must you without cease suffer in your thoughts the agony, sorrow and dishonour that you desired to escape. In Darkness and loneliness, far from those you love, again and again must you then in your thoughts live through that which you sought to escape; for by the taking of your own life[1] can you never release your spirit and your thought. By your evil deed you bind the spirit for long times, and the thought neither ceases nor is released *until the day and the hour is reached that was pre-ordained for the death of your earthly bodies.*

This I say unto those human beings who are fearful, weak and faint of heart, and unto those human beings who hope, by the taking of their own lives, to escape the consequences of their evil transgressions or foolish deeds. And this I say unto you, that you may know what agonizing sufferings you create for yourselves by the taking of your own lives.

Yea, hear my words and never forget them! *Be not fearful, weak nor faint of heart, but place your trust in our Father, then in His love and compassion will He sustain you and strengthen you.*

Do not murder nor kill one another! For do you this, then for long times you stay your progress toward the Home and the Light; indeed, often must you then remain at the same place through several hundred lives upon the Earth. For you cannot journey onward *until you have saved from sudden death as many human beings as you have slain or sent unto their deaths.*

Yea, hear me, human beings! Give ear and be not heedless of my words! For *I* say that nothing is as evil or sinful as is *murder* and

---

[1] Regarding suicide, see Commentary, p. 185.

killing; nothing destroys your progress as do the *spoiling and disgraceful wars* that are waged among you; there is no greater abomination than that nation should rise against nation, that brother should slay brother. For you must remember that you have *all* the same Father, remember that He loves you *all* with the same deep and boundless love. But do you wage war and kill one another, then He turns from you, then He grieves for you.

This I say unto you, that in your wars you should not call upon our Father for help and support; *for He does not hear you.* And pray not unto Him to bless you or your armaments, that you may conquer your enemies; for never does He bestow His blessing upon you, that you may rob, plunder, desecrate and kill with greater gain.

Yea, verily: do you wage war upon one another, then shall you not thank Him for your victories, nor reproach Him for your defeats.[1] For our God and Father is not a god of wrath and vengeance, neither is He inconstant; for He does not say unto some of you: *"Thou shalt not kill",* and to others: *"Go forth and kill".* His message is for all of you, before Him are you all equal. And through me He cries unto you: **"Take heed and beware of murder and of killing, beware of hatred and of envy, of strife, of war and of enmity, beware of all the evil and sinfulness that is about you and among you!"**

Yea, hear me, you human beings! Engrave my words upon your hearts, that you shall never forget them! Neither forget to pray unto our Heavenly Father to enlighten you, that you may fully understand what guilt *they* bear who awaken strife and enmity among you; what blame *they* bear who send thousands upon thousands of your brothers unto wars and battles, unto sufferings and death!

Yea, hear me, for I say: *live in peace and forbearance with one another, befriend one another and extend unto one another the hand of brotherly concord, that everlasting peace may reign everywhere upon the Earth! For if all act upon these my words, then will our Father be with you, then will His Thought guide you, His hand support you, His strength and His blessing be with you in all your works.*

I have spoken unto you of some of the laws which are given for your journeying, laws that pertain to all of you, whichever doctrine

---

[1] See Summary, pp. 330–32.

you profess, whichever faith you embrace. Hear me, all Christians,[1] Mohammedans and Buddhists, yea, hear me *all* by whatever name you profess your faith: for that of which I have spoken concerns you all. For you shall know: *that no faith has rights or advantages before the others. No doctrine is the one and only way to salvation;* for our Father asks you not which faith you embrace, but whether you have sought to strive forward toward the Light, whether you have overcome evil and the many temptations; He asks you whether you have supported the weak, comforted the sorrowing, fed the hungry, clothed the naked, helped the poor, the sick and the suffering; and He asks you whether you have done your good works out of love and compassion, or whether you did them *for your own gain.*

Yea, truly, our Father asks not your faith, *but whether you have fully lived and acted in accordance with that which to you was truth and justice.*

Therefore, would you advance, then must you submit and abide by our Father's laws. But you shall know that never will He let you walk alone, for then would you unceasingly sin against these laws, but you shall know that He surrounds you with good and benevolent beings, your guardian spirits, who seek constantly to lead and to guide you. Their warnings, counsel and admonitions will sound to you as a faint, inner voice: your *conscience.* Therefore, never act against your conscience, but obey it in every way, *for then will you never be mistaken, then will you never go astray.*

And you shall know: that your guardian spirits keep watch over you and walk with you until your spiritual selves at death are loosed from their earthly bodies; then will they lead you by the paths of the Light back unto the dwellings from which you departed at the time when you were born[2] unto the Earth. In these dwellings, which were made for you by our Father, must you in peace and in stillness ponder deeply upon the earthly life just ended, render a full account of your thoughts and your deeds. *Nothing* can remain hidden; for *everything* stands clearly before you. And it profits you nothing that you thrust it from you; for it will remain until you have understood and acknowledged your sins, faults and shortcomings. When you have grieved for yourselves, grieved over your sins and follies, when you are ready to atone for your transgressions, when you have unfalteringly answered our Father's questions, then will He pronounce

---

[1]) Catholics, Protestants, and all Christian sects are included.

[2]) Spirits count their earthly birth from the moment they are brought to Earth to be bound to future human children. From that moment they lose all recollection of their former existence.

how long or how short a time for rest and learning[1] will be granted unto you, before you may once again begin a new life upon the Earth.

This I say unto you, that you shall not in fear and trembling dread some distant day of a common judgment, a day when God the Almighty, to the horror and dread of many, will summon all the dead and all the living to judgment and retribution, a day when some of you shall go forward unto everlasting bliss and others unto everlasting damnation; *for such a day of judgment will never dawn!*

Yea, hear me, human beings: *it will come to pass even as I have said: after each earthly life will come the reckoning and the judgment for each of you; your good and evil thoughts and deeds will accuse, defend and judge you – and our Father will seal the judgment.*

I speak unto you of prayer and of the power of prayer.

Have you erred in your life, have you sinned against the earthly or against the Heavenly laws, then shall you not straightway lose courage, nor shall you despair, for by despairing will you draw Darkness but closer about you. But seek to correct yourselves and strengthen your will for the good, yea, seek to repent of that which you have done. But do you think that you are not yourselves able to overcome the evil or that which tempts you, then must you as children turn unto our Father for greater help and greater strength. Yea, speak in full trust unto Him of all that causes you grief and concern! For never does He grow weary of your complaints and your worries, for ever is He ready to grant you all the help you may need.

But when you pray unto our Heavenly Father, then shall you not *demand* His help, then shall you not recite one prayer after another nor say: do we pray so many times for this, so many times for that, then shall our prayers surely be granted! Nor need you recite prescribed prayers at various hours of the day or the night; *for nothing that is outward or according to habit will ever reach unto our Father.*

Would you pray, then must the prayer be born in your hearts and carried by your thoughts, then will even the faintest call reach unto our Father. And never shall you fear that the words that you utter sound poor and weak; for do you pray from the affliction and longing of your hearts, do you pray with sincerity and in full trust, then will our Father hear you and then will He *grant your prayer.*

Truly, I say unto you: the more fervent your prayer, the stronger your thought, the greater will be the strength that you receive from our Father. *For in prayer your thoughts meet with His Thought; in*

---

[1]) See Commentary, p. 186.

prayer your will for the Light and for the good meets with His Will, which is all Light, all purity, all love.

But hear me, you human beings who suffer, who are sorrowful, who are weak and in despair: are you yourselves unable to pray from the depths of your heart, are you unable to gather and to contain your thoughts, then shall *I* be your advocate, then shall *I* carry your prayer unto our Father.

This I *shall* do for all who know me and love me. This I *shall* do for the many who have never heard my name; *this I shall do for the many who need me, who are in need of my help.*

And hear me, you who have not ever prayed, you who have not the will, you who have never learnt this, you who have neither hope nor belief in the granting of prayers, and all of you who believe that there is no God. You shall know that when you grieve over the evil and the sin that is in this world and within your own selves, when you rejoice at that which is beautiful and good, then will your thoughts meet with the Thought of our Father. And He who sees all and knows all, He receives your glad and loving thoughts as your *gratitude* for the good which He has bestowed upon you, and He receives your sorrowful thoughts as a *prayer* for help, a prayer for greater power and strength, and He grants you that of which you are in need.

Yea, truly: *be they joyous or sorrowful, your thoughts often weigh more heavily with our Father than even the most beautifully formed prayer.*

Be not selfish in your prayer! Pray not for your own selves alone, but pray for *all* human beings upon the Earth. And forget not those who at death are delivered from their earthly bodies! Yea, pray for all who are returned unto the heavenly dwellings; for your prayers and your loving thoughts will gladden and strengthen them in their hard time of self-searching. Seek lovingly to remember those who are departed from you; for nothing is more painful and bitter to them than to see how soon remembrance fades and passes into oblivion; nothing is more painful and bitter to them than to see how soon the empty places are filled once more. Therefore, do not forget those whom once you loved, but keep them in your memory; and did they offend you and did they sin against you while they walked upon the Earth, then should you forgive them with all your heart! *For this will relieve them of many a heavy burden.*

Remember with sadness and love those you have lost, but do not wail nor lament! For your sighs and selfish tears[1] will bind them and hinder that they fulfil the account which they must render. Nor must you call upon them to speak of foolish and trivial matters. *And never must you inquire into your future weal and woe; for such questions they are not permitted to answer, and thus it serves neither them nor you.* But do *they* call upon you, and do they speak unto you in the name of our Father, then must you hear them; for then surely have they come to warn you or to ask for your help or intercession.

Yea, human beings, hear me! Be not selfish in your prayer, but pray for every human being upon the Earth; pray for those who walk with you and for those who are departed from you. For with your prayer you disperse Darkness and draw the Light toward you and toward those for whom you pray. Truly, I say unto you: *the power of prayer is great, when it is borne by loving thoughts; for you must remember: in prayer shall you meet with our Father!*

Even now I say unto you who love the "Lord's Prayer": do you feel you are better able to gather in this prayer rather than form your own thoughts, then pray simply and in trust:

> Father, who art in Heaven,
> Hallowed be Thy name,
> Lead us, till we enter Thy Kingdom;
> Thy Will be done on Earth, as it is in Heaven;
> Give us this day our daily bread;
> Forgive us our trespasses,
> and help us to forgive those who trespass against us;
> Guide us, when we are tempted,
> and deliver us from evil;
> Take the dead into Thy care;[2]
> Protect and keep us all.
>   Amen.

---

[1]) See Commentary, pp. 247–250, on the disturbances which selfish sorrow over the dead can cause.

[2]) This is how Jesus taught the Lord's Prayer to his disciples. The prayer for the dead was omitted by Paul because of the consideration that the dead, who were resurrected and saved through faith in the death of atonement of Jesus, were not in need of intercession, and they who died without such faith could in any case not be saved by intercession.

II

I would speak unto you on how you should lead your lives, on how you may best fulfil the tasks that are entrusted to you, and on how you should carry out the labour, the work which is yours, that you may all live in love, in peace and in harmony with one another.

I speak unto you who are called the Vicar of God and Christ upon the Earth, I speak unto you in the name of God the Almighty.

Hear me! For you shall know that the office and the power that is held by you and by those who went before you rest upon false words! Never did I give unto Simon Peter "the Keys of the Kingdom of Heaven". Never did I suffer him to loose, much less to bind, according to his own judgment and will.

This I say unto you, that you shall know that *you are not the heir of Simon Peter,* no more than were any of those who went before you.

Further you shall know that you cannot grant the forgiveness of sin in the name of our Father; for that which mankind has sinned against Almighty God, *He alone can forgive;* and that which human beings have sinned against one another, that they must themselves seek to forgive one another.[1] *Your absolutions are therefore dead and without power.*

Furthermore, you shall know *that our Father has never cursed, nor will He ever curse, any human being,* no matter how much human beings have sinned against the divine and the earthly laws. And if God cannot and will not curse, how then can they who are called His Vicars do this?

Nay, never must you curse, neither in the name of God, nor in the name of Simon Peter. For do you this, then must you share the fate of many of those who went before you, for they have suffered much under the mighty curses which they have uttered.

Truly, I say unto you: you shall not *curse* but rather shall you *bless in the name of our Father.* And when you bestow your blessing, never forget to pray from deep in your heart unto our Father to confirm the blessing, that it may become a benefit unto those who are in need thereof. For you are not able to separate the worthy from the unworthy.

Be a father unto your congregation! Conduct yourself in such manner that all may love, honour and esteem you. Not as the heir of Simon Peter, nor even as the Vicar of God and Christ, but as the

---

[1] See Ardor's Account, p. 101.

highest and most exalted authority of your Church.

And at the feasts of the Church, surround not yourself with an over-abundance of splendour and glory, as long as there are men, women and children in your congregation who must for ever beg for their daily bread, and whose clothes are soil and rags. But seek with the abundant means of the Church to make less some of the deep poverty and misery.

Be a teacher and a guide to the many servants of your Church and to each single member of your congregation; teach them, with the love of a child, in hope and in trust, to direct themselves in prayer unto *God alone.* Teach them that the many prayers unto the Virgin Mary and to the holy men and women for help, for intercession and protection do not benefit, nor have they ever been of benefit to humanity; for all the so-called saints must continue their journey through the many lives upon the Earth, as must all human beings, until at last they reach the goal: *the Kingdom of God our Father.*

You must also teach the servants of your Church and all those in your congregation that it will profit none to withdraw into austere cloisters behind forbidding walls, removed from the temptations, the struggle and the toil of life. Teach them that all who live as monks and nuns, that all who seclude themselves and that all who seek solitude for some years or for their lifetime, are *breakers of the law.* For all who conduct themselves in this manner *follow* not, but *break* the law which our Father has given for the progress of humanity toward the Light. For human beings are not sent unto the Earth to *escape from Darkness,* but to *meet the evil in the numerous forms that it takes in life, to overcome sin and iniquity and to* **gain victory** *over the many temptations.*

Teach them that God does not demand, nor has He ever demanded, that either men or women shall live and not be married; *for our Father does not demand of human beings vows that deny human nature.*

Teach them that the many penances and severe self-torments profit them nothing, that they only draw Darkness unto all who torment and maltreat their bodies. Teach them that those who would wilfully exhaust or weaken themselves in diverse painful ways, either according to the dictates of a cloister or of their free will, are not fully able to defend their spiritual selves against the treacherous onslaughts of Darkness. Teach that all who torment themselves *are for ever afflicted by sinful and depraving thoughts because of the body's exceeding weakness.*

Teach them also that the many good deeds that are done by the rule of church or cloister have no spiritual value, save that the doers are able to let these acts spring from the need of their own hearts to show love and compassion.

Further shall you teach them that the many sacraments of your church are *needless and of no avail;* teach them *that only in the profound and fervent devotion of prayer do human beings meet with divine Thought and Will.*

Yea, be you truly a father, a teacher and a guide for all who join with you; and be you of help to me in leading them all unto our common goal: our Father's Kingdom of Glory!

That which I have spoken unto you with these words I bid you carefully to consider; and for your own sake I bid you to seek counsel of your God and of your conscience. And when you have understood that my words are true, then must you do as I have said, *then must you follow the way that I have hereby shown you!*

Do my words not reach you who at this time[1] hold office as the Vicar of God and Christ, *then are you without blame,* then shall my words concern your successor, then is he your heir. Yea, my words concern not you alone, but *all* who come after you.

I speak unto you who are called the servants of the Most High or servants of the Church, to whichever nation, to whichever faith you may belong and whatever office, high or lowly, you may hold within your holy community. I speak unto you all, by whichever name you know your deity, and whether you submit to one god or to many gods. Hear me! For my words concern you all.

Would you be *servants of the Most High,* then must you strive to keep His commandments, strive to abide by His laws. Then must you teach all who join with you and heed your preachings *that God is One,* that there are not two, nor three, nor many gods. Then shall you teach that God the Almighty is the *Creator and Father of the immortal spirits of human beings, but that He did not create their mortal bodies.*

Yea, truly I say unto you: would you be the servants of God, then must you all serve Him in spirit and in truth; *then shall you speak gentle, loving and simple words to all* who in doubt, despair and remorse turn to you for help and guidance; then shall you with tireless constancy comfort and strengthen the weak, the despondent and the faltering; never shall you speak hard, condemning words to the living, and even less shall you speak ill of the dead; never, so as to assert your authority and your power, shall you *threaten with eternal*

---

[1] 1914.

damnation, nor menace with the punishments and torments of Hell.
Never must you teach that the human spirit after life upon the
Earth will live again in the bodies of beasts, nor that the spiritual self
after many burdensome but gainful journeyings will be engulfed by
the great nothingness – will sink into a state of eternal impassivity.

Neither shall you teach that self-torments and penances are pleasing unto God. And never must you perform blood sacrifice[1] to the
honour of the Most High; no human being,[1] no beast of the field nor
bird of the air shall you sacrifice; *for all such deeds are the dreadful
inventions of Darkness.*

*Be helpful and compassionate toward all who are poor or sick or
wretched;* let your churches, temples and meeting houses be open
unto all, that every grieving and every suffering person may at all
times, on days of work or on days of rest, kneel before the altar to
seek strength and comfort in fervent prayer unto their God and
Father; and that all who so desire may walk in peace and tranquillity
within the places of beauty that are hallowed and consecrated unto
our Father.

And when on days of rest or holy celebration you are gathered
with your congregation, then must you teach them to *submit unto
the guiding hand of our Father with the trust, hope and love of a
child,* then must you teach them that songs of praise and thanksgiving shall stem from the deepest depths of their hearts. Then shall you
teach them that all outward and empty forms of worship are of no
avail, *that all sacraments are needless.*

Further, I say unto you all: would you be God's servants, then
shall you not unceasingly quarrel and dispute with one another over
the ancient words and doctrines of faith that are received from the
many writings of your forefathers. Then shall you not constantly
maintain *that your own church and your own faith is the only true
one and the only way unto salvation.* And never must you by the
sword or by decree compel others to accept your faith and your
opinion.

Seek rather that all shall meet in common yearning for the pure,
the exalted and the divine. *Yea, seek you all to meet in your common
yearning for the love of a Father and the righteousness of a God.*

What I have said unto you with these words I ask you all carefully
to consider; seek counsel of God and of your conscience, and never

---

[1]) When human beings make God their highest war-lord, every loss of life in battle becomes a blood sacrifice to His honour; and when the clergy consecrate soldiers prior to com-
bat they become participants in, and accessories to, the human sacrifice of war.

act against your inner conviction! *When you have then understood that my words are true, then be of help to me in guiding your brothers and sisters unto the common goal: our Father's Kingdom of Glory.*

I speak unto you who are the rulers of the many nations, whether you be rulers by inheritance or election, and whichever title you may bear. Hear me, for I speak unto you all!

Make it your common goal that each of you shall become the best and most worthy person of your nation. Demand much of yourselves, that you may demand much of others. Be beyond reproach in your dealings, that all may respect, honour and love you. Choose your counsellors with great care and wisdom, and choose them from among those who are unselfish, truthful, wise and just. Protect the weak, the poor and the oppressed. Be unselfish in your care for the welfare of the nations and the peoples. Never act against that which *your conscience tells you to be truth and justice.*

Do not gain dominion over the realms of others by force or by cunning, and never compel the people of other nations to submit in humility to your rule; *for all this is of the evil!*

Be understanding and patient toward the people whose native countries have been seized by your forefathers, by your predecessors or by yourselves. Seek to rectify and to assuage some of the injustice that has been brought upon those who have been compelled by force and through hatred and envy to live under foreign rule, *and who against their will have been separated from those states to which they rightfully belong.*

Be as brethren toward one another. With good will abolish all strife and dispute, and never disturb the peace which prevails among the realms and the nations.

Yea, truly I say unto you: *be you the first to establish an enduring, brotherly concord; and pray unto our Father to bless you and the pact which you agree upon, that you and your successors may be able to keep the promises that you have given one another. Yea, pray unto our Father to bless you, that you and those who come after you may never, never again break the peace upon the Earth!*

Pray unto our Father to enlighten you upon the truth of my words. Pray unto Him for help and guidance, that each of you may truly fill the position that is yours.

I speak unto you who are the givers of laws, unto you who in numerous ways take part in the various kinds of governance in the

nations and the states. Hear me, for I speak unto you all!

Make it your common goal fully and with all your might to serve the country and the people to which you belong. Prepare your laws *as though you yourselves should be judged by each and every statute,* for then will your laws be just.

Do not by guile or with deceit force yourselves into high positions that are not rightfully yours and which you cannot properly fill. Be truthful to the utmost and be sincere in all your speech. *Never act against your conscience, indeed, never act upon selfish thoughts of personal gain!* Cease all your disgraceful strife and quarrelling. Never hurl bitter or hateful words against those who share not your beliefs. Do not besmirch the name and honour of your adversaries by false accusations, by untrue and wicked slander. Be meek toward one another. Go to meet one another, seek to work in mutual peace and understanding, that you may best further the interests of the nations and the peoples.

Abolish all condemning unto death; for no human being has the right to take the life of another, no matter how many crimes have been committed. Do not prepare laws that compel your brethren to murder and to slay one another in warfare; *for all this is of the evil!* Let all bearing of arms be of the free will, until all the nations and lands upon the Earth are united in a lasting, unbreakable pact of peace.

Give proper care unto the poor, unto the sick and to the wretched of all ages – men as well as women – unto all abandoned wives, unto all needy widows and unto all orphans among you. For I say unto you: however vast your nation may be, *there shall not be one single human being in distress – man, woman or child – who must beg for their daily bread.* Nor must anyone able and willing to labour[1] drift about without home and without work. Therefore, provide shelter, food, clothing and work without delay for all who cannot obtain these for themselves.

Support not and help not in any manner by which it becomes demeaning charity, but in such manner that those who receive the help and support from your society can with gladness and gratitude[2]

---

[1]) Society holds no responsibility toward those who are unwilling to work.

[2]) Anyone employed by the state, the municipality or any private employer is entitled to a suitable yearly compensation from the state or the municipality, once their years of service have ended, thereby enabling them to face old age without financial worries. Society must also fully care for all who become crippled while performing their work or who become unfit for work through illness. Likewise is it the duty of society to maintain homes for the aged and the sick who are alone, and for employees and servants who are unable to work, etc. The state or the municipality must also, when help is needed, provide sufficient support for widows with children under age until these have reached the age of majority.

accept the help that is offered them.

Yea, truly, I say unto you: *your obligations are many, and your responsibility is great;* I ask you therefore carefully to consider that which I have said unto you. For you shall know that if out of selfishness or faintness of heart you give not care unto the poor, unto the suffering and to the unfortunate, then shall you surely taste the want and misery of the homeless and the poor in your coming lives upon the Earth *until you have learnt to take pity on your unfortunate fellow human beings.*

Pray unto our Father to open your eyes, that you may see the truth of my words. Pray unto our Father to sustain and to guide you; *for is He with you, then shall your laws surely be fully just.*

I speak unto you men who are fathers, and unto you who are husbands also. I speak unto you women who are mothers and unto you who are wives also. Hear me, for I speak unto you all, to whatever nation, community or people you may belong!

You men and women: bring not children into this world until you are able to give them care; for you shall know that you have the same responsibilities, the same duties toward all your children, *whether or not they are begotten and born in your society's lawful wedlock.*

Thrust not your children thoughtlessly out into the world without giving them the means to go forward in life. Never let them stand alone, without help and without protection; for do you not care for them and do they fall into the temptations of Darkness, are they drawn downward by sin and iniquity, do they become lawbreakers and evil-doers, *then will the blame be upon you, then will you bear the responsibility,* then must you help them in coming lives upon the Earth to atone for what they have transgressed, *before you yourselves can journey onward.*

Hear me, *you fathers:* have you thus denied any of your children, have you let them stand alone and without knowledge of who gave them life, then make haste to search them out and to make amends for that which you have sinned against them. Yea, truly, I say unto you: you must fully provide for their upbringing and for their every need; and you must give them *equal inheritance and portion* with those children who were born unto you in lawful wedlock; *for such is theirs by right.*

And unto you, *the unwedded mothers,* I say: *neglect not your motherly duties.* Cause not your children to suffer at the hands of strangers from the lack of a mother's loving care and affection. Take care that the fathers of your children do not fail in their fatherly duties. Yea, guard and protect your children against all that is evil and impure in life.

You men and women: do you bring into this world so many children, in or out of lawful wedlock, that you cannot provide all of them with food, clothing, shelter and good and abundant knowledge, then must you never claim that this was *in accordance with God's Will;* for I say unto you: even as your Father does not compel you to make vows in conflict with nature, *neither does He command you to beget and give birth to so many children that their numbers grow beyond, or far beyond, your ability to support them.* Therefore, never allow your children to suffer from hunger, cold or the lack of knowledge, because you have not the full control over your body's lusts and desires.

You fathers and mothers! Love all of your children with a deep and abiding love. Be kind and self-sacrificing toward those to whom you gave life. Seek to create for them a bright and happy childhood, that for all time they may remember you and their home with fervent joy.

Be understanding but not weak, foolish or indulgent, when you see that they err and sin. Never torment or maltreat them, neither spiritually nor bodily. Bring them up with loving patience, support them with a firm hand, lead them with calm authority. Teach your children to love their neighbour as themselves. Teach them to turn with the trust of a child to their Heavenly Father, that He may sustain and help them where you are not able. Bring up your children to become good, truthful, diligent and just human beings, rich in knowledge. Teach them to be pure and chaste in mind and in thought. Help them to strengthen their will, that they may readily overcome the unclean desires of the body.

Teach your sons to become faithful, considerate husbands and loving, dutiful fathers; and teach your daughters to become wise and faithful wives, and to become loving, dutiful mothers.

Yea, hear me: bring up your children in such manner that you may truly say unto them: *if you fall into the temptations of Darkness, into sin and iniquity, then is the guilt your own; then must you yourselves bear the full responsibility.*

You husbands and wives, love one another with all your heart! Bear with one another's faults and weaknesses, guide and help one another with patience and loving kindness. Share the many burdens and sorrows of daily life; share your longings and your joys. Never embitter the minds of your children with disgraceful quarrels or violent deeds. Allow not passion for other men or for other women to estrange you or to separate you. Be faithful toward one another, though the fulness of years may stoop your bodies and silver your hair.

Yea, journey faithfully hand in hand, until death loosens the bond of your marriage; and then seek to keep lovingly all the many remembrances, that with joy you may meet again in the Heavenly dwellings.

You men and women, consider with care that which I have said unto you. Pray that our Father be with you to sustain you and to help you, *that you may never act against that which your conscience bids you to do.*

I speak unto you, the young men, and unto you, the young women. Hear me, for I speak unto you all, to whichever nation, society or people you may belong!

Love, honour and esteem those who gave you life. Follow the counsel and the admonitions that you are given, until the time is come when you yourselves must bear the responsibility for all your deeds.

Bear with the aged among you and honour them, that the generation which comes after you may bear with you and honour you, when you draw near unto the grave.

Abandon not yourselves to sinful and impure desires. Nor ever shall you sell your bodies to fornication.

You men, never shall you violate and seduce women!

You women, slay not the children to whom you gave birth! Nor shall you ever wilfully destroy the life that you have conceived; for I say unto you: *all this is of the evil! And by such acts will you bring much suffering upon yourselves.*

Be merciful toward animals; never torment them, never hunt and exterminate them when there is no need of this.

Be prudent with all strong drink and dulling drugs; for you shall know that you yourselves must bear the full responsibility for the foolish, evil and wicked deeds that you commit when you lose control of your senses and of your will through carelessness or evil habits.

Seek at all times to enrich your spirit with gainful and instructive learning. And when, in time, you make your own way in life, *break not ever the laws of truth and justice, whatever position is yours, whatever work you may do, whether you be counted among the givers of laws, among those who govern, among those who judge, or whether your work be in other areas; and never act against that which your conscience bids you to do.*

Place not any heavier burden[1] upon those who are under you than they are able to bear; and reward[1] their labour with the wages that *you yourselves would demand,* were you in their place.

Be faithful and trustworthy in all that you do. If you become discontented with the work that is yours, and if you leave the work which you have taken upon yourselves, *then never compel your companions to follow you; for thereby you transgress against the right of the free will and take upon yourselves a heavy responsibility.*[2]

Should you gain riches by the thoughts of your spirit, by the work of your hands, by inherited fortune, or should you gain riches in any other *honest way,* then are these riches rightfully yours; but I ask you to think of those who have little or nothing, and to support them.

And I say unto you who have few or none of the blessings of this world: envy not those who are in better circumstances, for their responsibility is far greater than yours; *and never demand to share in the rightful possessions of others; for you have no right to make such claims.* Enjoy that which is yours and that which is given unto you, but never demand that which is not yours.

Should you gather riches by usury or by fraudulence, by theft or by robbery, then shall you surely in your lives to come upon the Earth return all such gains unto their rightful owners – yea, verily, *you shall give back all with interest, and interest upon interest!*

Delight in all that is glorious and beautiful in this world, put to manifold use the many gifts which our Father has bestowed upon you, and gather yourselves together toward this goal: *in unison and*

---

[1]) It is the duty of every employer to ensure that the employees and assistants under his supervision are not faced with any work that is too strenuous for them to manage; likewise must every employer reward employees or assistants with such wages as fully cover the work that is done, and which allow them such conditions of life as befit their place in society.

(The above pertains to states and municipalities as well as to companies and to private employers).

[2]) People who because of their own discontent with the prevailing conditions seek to invoke similar feelings among their fellow workers, that through joint action they may enforce compliance with their own requests and demands in various areas, are therefore acting against the words of Christ and are likewise acting against the divine laws of order, forbearance and justice. Whatever is gained in any one incarnation by such improper conduct must be given back in full in the following incarnations. Anything of material value that is destroyed, each individual must compensate for with interest and compound interest, just as these individuals must endure the same spiritual suffering which by their actions they have brought upon their fellow human beings.

harmony to prepare the way for an everlasting, unbreakable peace among the many realms and nations of the Earth.

Yea, hear me, you young men and women! Consider with the utmost care the words which I have spoken unto you; for you must remember: *you are the creators and the bearers of the time to come.*

Pray unto our Father that He may support you and help you, that under His guidance you may lay down the first stones for the new building of the world. Yea, pray that our Father be with you, that future generations may look back upon the time that was yours with fervent joy, *and thank you for the good that you have done.*

———————

Even now shall I speak unto those who hate and in many ways persecute the people in whose midst I was born as Jesus of Nazareth. Hear me, for I say unto you: *you have no right to hate and to persecute a people because of the sins and misdeeds of its forefathers! Therefore, cease your persecutions and quell your hatred; for do you not this, then shall the Jewish people surely be closest to my heart.*

Indeed, never allow racial hatred to blind you and to divide you; for you must remember that before our Father are you all equal. He loves all peoples and all races, no matter what colour their skin may be, the least as well as the greatest, with the same profound and boundless love. He shows the same patience and compassion unto you all; *and in time will He welcome you all in His Kingdom.*

Lastly, I appeal *to all human beings* upon the Earth and I pray of you all: *seek to have compassion for our eldest brother, seek to forgive that which he has sinned against you, that the many curses which he has uttered may be broken and blotted out!*

Yea, forgive him with all your heart, then in his deep gratitude will he stand at my side and with all his strength help me to lead you unto our Father.

I have raised my torch high over your heads that its clear radiance may shine upon the roads that lead unto our Father's Kingdom. Follow me, all you suffering, searching and doubting human beings! Follow me; for I have promised to lead you, and I shall not let you go until I have brought the last of you to rest in our Father's embrace!

Father! I pray unto Thee, bless my words that they may reach the ears and the hearts of human beings. Father, be with us all!

Amen.

AS YOU SOW, SO YOU SHALL REAP!

The Lord God the Almighty has sent me, His Servant and Harbinger, unto you, that my words, expounded by you, may reach all the peoples of the Earth.

Human beings! *Your God, the Father of your spirit, bade me to speak unto you:*

At the dawn of earthly time, God's youngest children promised their Father to restore that which their elder brothers and sisters had destroyed.

After many ages of suffering, grief and disappointment, they have now progressed so far by the power of their will, by the power of their love and with their Father's help, that they have overcome Darkness, have delivered their eldest brother and won him back unto the Home and to the Light. But many aeons shall still pass, before they can fully redeem their pledge: *to lead you, God's very youngest children, unto His Kingdom of Glory.* For not until the last among you is received into the Fatherly Home will the work of love of the Youngest be fulfilled.

Human beings! Many aeons must still pass, before you can meet with your Heavenly Father, before you can meet with Him who out of His profound compassion for those created by His fallen children bestowed eternal life upon the human spirit. Many aeons must still pass before your journeying is ended, for you are as young children who can see but cannot comprehend, who can hear but cannot fathom. As children you rejoice over the pretty-coloured fruits, but little are you concerned that the worm has destroyed the flesh and the core. As children you are not able to discern between tinsel and gold, with eagerness and desire you reach for the gaudy tinsel that is of no use, while you spurn the pure and precious ore.

Yea, *you are less and worse than young children;* for in your blind desire for earthly treasure, for power and honour, in your hatred and envy of one another you unceasingly quarrel and wage war upon one another, you murder, rob and ravage and refuse to understand that the sufferings and the sorrows which you thereby bring upon others, *you also bring upon yourselves.* Hard but just retribution will fall upon you, so long as you continue to abuse and disdain the gift which your Father has bestowed upon you – the will to *seek* the good, the will to *seek* victory over evil; and so long as your will is for sin and misdeeds, for lies and for strife, then can *the Will of your Father* not prosper among you.

Hear, all human beings! Your Father calls upon you, and through His Servant He asks of you:

When will you pass over the threshold of childhood?

When will you open your eyes and behold your imperfection?

When will you understand that you must be born unto the Earth again and again, that each earthly life can bring you nearer unto your God and Father?

When will you learn to follow your conscience and to heed the voice of truth, of love and of justice which speaks unto you?

When will you cease to deride those who are further advanced in knowledge?

When will you with understanding receive the children of the Light who suffer themselves to be born among you to draw you out of Darkness?

When will you learn to rejoice in that which is yours without envying your neighbour or taking his possessions from him?

When will you cease taking your own or your neighbour's earthly life by force or by negligence[1] before that death and that hour is come that is pre-ordained for each of you by the Lord God?

When will you cease the gruesome, bloody and blasphemous wars that are constantly waged among you?

When will you banish all racial hatred and learn to esteem and to love one another?

When will you let your own will meet with the Will of your Father?

And when, when will you – of whatever race you may be – all unite to bid a lasting peace welcome among you?

These questions your Father bade me to ask of you. *What will be your answer?* For the future rests in your own hand; even as you desire it, even as you will it to be, so do you create your future and that of those who come after you.

If you continue to walk in the ways of Darkness, if you will not cease to hate and persecute one another; if you continue to suffer

---

[1]) Murder, killings and deaths that are due to war or individual violence, dereliction of duty, thoughtlessness, etc.

thousands upon thousands of your brothers, husbands, fathers and sons to be slain in deadly warfare, so as to satiate your hatred and lust for power; if you continue to murder, rob, plunder, ravage and burn, for ever tearing down what has been built up, and scattering that which has been gathered; *then will your Father grieve over you; then will sorrows, sufferings and disappointments hinder the Youngest in their work of love for you; then will your journey toward the distant goal become endlessly long and endlessly troubled.*

But would you walk in the way of the Light that the eldest of the Youngest, your leader and guide, of his own free will has hereby shown you; would you lean upon the hand which he offers you in love; would you receive with trust the message that is hereby presented unto you in the name of your Father, so as to bring you the clarity and peace which you all desire; *then will your Father rejoice in you; then will the children of the Light with greater joy suffer themselves to be born among you, to lead you out of Darkness; then will your journey, though it become arduous and long, be shortened by many aeons of time. For then will the seeds which your Father has planted in your hearts sprout in victory over Darkness, they will blossom and bear fruit: not ten, not twenty, nor even sixtyfold,* **but a thousand times a thousandfold!**

Human beings! Choose now the ways that you and those after you shall walk in the time to come! Choose without constraint! *For Almighty God compels no one, and none shall compel his neighbour.* But pray you all unto your Father to strengthen your will, that it may overcome evil and bring you forward toward the Light!

Human beings! *Your Father yearns for you;* He follows you through good and evil. He follows you through sorrow and joy, whether you walk in the deepest Darkness or in the brightest Light. *His love for you is beyond measure and His patience is without bound.*

Human beings! Your Father yearns for you!
He bade me, His Servant, to bring unto all of you His
Fatherly Greeting.
His Peace be with you for ever and ever!
Amen.

ADDENDUM

The Two Brothers

Two men, two brothers, walked together along a stony path. The burning rays of the sun blinded their eyes and whitened the dust upon the ground.

The one man was short and slight of stature.

Upon his shoulders he bore a large and heavy burden. His pace was steady and sure, for he leaned upon a staff. He held his head high, and his countenance shone with gladness.

The other was tall and strong.

Upon his broad shoulders he bore a small burden. His pace was unsteady and unsure, for he did not lean upon a staff.

His head was held low, and though the burden was small he sighed and moaned under its weight.

The first brother sought to encourage him with words of good cheer, and he said:

"The road unto our Father's Home is long and arduous; my brother, how will you fare, when at the road's beginning you heave and sigh beneath your burden?"

The other answered, cursing the long road and its stones that wounded his feet.

The first brother became saddened, and side by side they journeyed on in silence.

From by-ways large multitudes of people joined the road that the brothers followed.

Some journeyed in groups together, others walked in pairs, many walked alone.

Some of the people journeyed briskly and surely along the road, though they all carried burdens upon their shoulders.

Some bore large and heavy burdens, while those of others were small and light.

Those who leaned upon a staff walked speedily past the brothers, greeted them and called out:

"Behold, we go unto our Father's Home. We shall greet Him and say that you are soon to follow." And they disappeared into the distance.

Many poor unfortunates came staggering along the road, sighing under the weight of their burdens. They moaned for the burning rays of the sun and for the thirst that plagued them.

The first brother went unto them and spoke with kind and gentle words.

He saw they had no cups to fill with water from the well by the road.

He took his own cup from his girdle, filled it with water and gave them to drink.

He saw they had no staff upon which to lean; he gave them his own, that they should not fall.

He saw they faltered under their burdens. He took their burdens, laid them upon his own shoulders, and he went calmly and steadily upon his way. And they all marvelled greatly.

Then they spoke among themselves of this and said:

"Behold, this man gave us to drink, he lent us his staff, he took from us our burdens and laid them upon the heavy burden of his own – and yet he walks steadily and calmly along the road. *How is this possible?*

But he answered them and said:

"I journey unto my Father's Home. *The hope of beholding my Father's loving countenance lightens unto me my burdens; my Father's tender thoughts shorten unto me the length of the road.*"

And, turning toward the multitude, he said:

"Follow me, all you who falter and sigh under the toil and trouble of the road. I shall lead you unto my Father's Kingdom; for He has many mansions. And I shall ask of Him to prepare for you a place where you may rest after the toil of the journey."

And they all rejoiced greatly, and they all followed him.

When the son came unto the Father's Kingdom, the servants threw open the mighty portals and they rejoiced as they saw the son enter through the gate, followed by the multitude.

And the son went unto his Father's mansion, laid his burdens at His feet, kissed the hem of His robe and said:

"Father, behold: All these poor wretches I bring unto Thy Home. I saw how they faltered under their burdens and I gave them my staff, that they should not fall. I saw how they thirsted, and I gave them my cup filled with water from the well by the road. I heard how they sighed, I took their burdens and I bore these burdens for them. Father, I promised them that Thou wouldst prepare a place for them where they might rest after the toil and trouble of their journey."

The Father looked gently upon his son and answered:

"Unto your Father's heart have you brought great gladness." And

He turned toward the multitude and said:

"Be you all welcome in My Kingdom; for this shall you know, that you are all My children; for in the heart of your Father are you all equal – high or low, rich or poor. Be you all welcome; for this shall you know, that I, your Father, sent you upon the journey from which you are now returned.

"My servants will lead you unto the abodes which are prepared for My children; there shall you in solitude ponder your life's journey. When all is become clear to you, then shall you answer Me, your Father, these questions: answer Me, why has the burden which I gave you to bear weighed you down even unto the ground? Answer Me, why have the stones in your path wounded your feet, and the radiance of the sun blinded your eyes?

"Unto some of you I gave a great burden to bear and but small tasks to perform; unto others I gave small burdens to carry and greater tasks to accomplish. Many of you came before I called, many of you long after I called.

"My servants will now lead you unto your abodes.

"When all is considered, when all questions are answered, then will you become seeing, then shall the tears of remorse wash you clean, and then shall I, your Father, give unto you the white robe which is the forgiveness of sin."

And He raised His hands and pronounced His blessing over their lowered heads.

And the servants led them away.

But the Father turned toward the son and said:

"My son, many poor wretches have you brought unto My Home, but one is missing. Mine eyes have sought and sought, *but they found him not!*

"My son, speak unto your Father and answer me: *where is the brother who was with you at the beginning of the road?*"

But the son answered Him and said:

"Father, my brother will soon arrive. My brother was tall and strong, and his burden was light, he had no need of my help."

Then the Father's countenance darkened, and He said:

"My son, when your brother no longer kept pace with you, did you not turn and call to him? Otherwise, how can you know that he needed not your help?

"My son, saw you not that your brother faltered, saw you not that the stones in his path wounded his feet? Saw you not that the blazing radiance of the sun blinded his eyes? Heard you not that he sighed and groaned under the weight of his burden?"

Then the son bowed his head in shame, and he answered and said:

"Father, when my brother no longer kept pace with me, I turned not about nor did I call to him. Father, I see that I have done a great wrong; Father, *I forgot my brother!"*

Then the Father looked sorrowfully upon His son and said:

"Take up your staff and turn back; seek until you find the brother who fell behind you upon the way!"

The son bowed his head, and he said:

"Father, I will go forth and seek my brother – I will not return, except that I bring him with me."

He took his cup and filled it with water from the well, he took up his staff and he turned back upon the road that he had just left.

He bore no burden upon his shoulders, but his Father's sorrow lay heavy upon his heart.

He searched and searched, his eye sought and sought – but he did not find his brother.

He journeyed back more than half of the way.

Then he saw his brother!

He lay by the side of the road. The burden had fallen from his shoulders. The flaming radiance of the sun had blinded his eyes. The sharp stones of the road had cut his feet. His robe was torn in shreds and tatters, his body covered with wounds and soiled with the filth and dirt of the road.

The brother knelt by his side and gave him to drink of the water from the well of their Father's Home; and he raised him up, and he took his own girdle and bound it about his loins, that the tattered robe should not fall to the ground. He gave him his staff to support him, he took his burden and laid it upon his own shoulders.

He laid his arm tenderly about him and guided him along the road unto their Father's Home.

When the servants saw the brothers come, they threw open the mighty portals and bowed their heads in silence for them both.

And the brothers made their way to their Father's mansion, and the son brought the new-found brother unto their Father.

The Father opened his arms and pressed the new-found brother to His heart and said:

"My son, My son, why did you make your Father wait so long? *Heard you not My calling voice?*

"My son, the spirit I gave unto you was strong and beautiful – but behold, how you have besoiled your body!

"My servants will now take you unto the abode that has so long stood prepared for you. There shall you in solitude ponder the long journeying of your life.

"When all has been considered, when all things are clear to you, then shall you answer Me, your Father, why you did not perform the task that you promised Me to fulfil; answer Me why you let the stones in your path wound your feet; and you shall answer Me why you fell down under the small burden that I gave you to bear, wherefore the filth and dirt of the road bespattered your body and besoiled your robe! And you shall say unto Me wherefore you did not answer to My calling voice, *wherefore you let your Father wait so long.*

"When you have answered, then shall your blind eyes become seeing, then shall the tears of remorse wash away the mire from your body, and then will I, your Father, give unto you the white robe which is the forgiveness of sin."

And He laid His hands upon His son's lowered head, and the servants came and led him unto the abode which had long stood empty.

But the Father turned toward the other son, lovingly took his hand, and said:

"My son, you have brought great joy unto My heart; for this you shall know: *no joy is greater than the joy in the heart of a Father when the son who has fallen is brought back unto the Home. Truly, you shall know this: no joy is greater than the joy of a Father, when the son that He believed had perished is returned unto the Home!*

"My son, unto you much was given, unto you shall more be given – go unto the abode which My Fatherly heart has prepared for you, and there accept the reward that awaits you."

7th March, 1911.

The above parable applies first and foremost to the relationship between Jesus of Nazareth and Joseph of Arimathea in that earthly life during which they were to have supported and complemented one another, according to their promise to God. Since Jesus, after his conversation with Joseph,[1] did not attempt to win him over, but continued on his way without worrying about him, the Father's reproach in the parable is rightfully aimed at Jesus. And as the son in the parable was to search for his brother, so was Jesus (the eldest of the Youngest) to search for Joseph of Arimathea, when Joseph's spirit upon the death of his body did not return to the Heavenly abodes.

By murdering his old servant, by fearing to lose his wealth and his prestige among the people and by keeping silent about his part in the disappearance of the body of Jesus, Joseph brought himself under the power of Darkness. Because of this guilt of sin, his spirit had to lead a long earthbound existence after the death of his body, until the eldest of the Youngest, after centuries of searching, found him sunk in deep spiritual darkness.

---

[1] See Ardor's Account, p. 55.

10 C

The parable also applies to humanity at large. When anyone during life on Earth sees a relative or a friend sink under his burdens and shows no concern nor offers a helping hand, he or she must invariably, after the life on Earth has ended, answer God's question: *where is that brother or sister who accompanied you?* The same holds true for those human beings who prior to their incarnation have promised to support each other in a particularly difficult mission in order to bring it to a favourable conclusion. Although it is a thing of the past to search the astral counterpart of the Earth, or the Hell-Sphere, for spirits who fall under the burdens of their earthly life, it can still be difficult enough for such negligent human beings to make the required amends in the future for their failure. This penance might for long periods of time prevent those who have been neglectful of their duties, or who have broken their promise, from advancing spiritually. Therefore: *never forget your relative or your friend, and never ignore that inner voice, which prompts you to offer your help – spiritual or material – in cases where your assistance can be of value, whether your fellow human being is faltering under the heavy burdens, or whether by your word, authority or prestige you can help a brother out of a difficult situation or support him in the struggle for truth and justice.*

In other respects the symbolism of the parable can be interpreted according to one's own thoughts and feelings.[1]

The Woodland Pond

A man and a woman stood together at the edge of a calm woodland pond. The woman delighted in the reflection that the crystalline water gave of the sky with the white clouds, the greensward, the blossoms and the trees; she greatly rejoiced; for the reflection was serene and beautiful with its clear and bright colours.

But the man laughed at her joy, and he said: "A painted picture is far more beautiful, this is but a fleeting image; for the colours are neither true, nor will they endure; I can easily spoil the whole of it." And he bent down, took a stone and cast it into the pond. The fall of the stone muddied the water, while bubbles and rings rippled the surface.

Sadly, the woman looked at him and said: "Why did you destroy this beautiful reflection? Do you believe *that we should rejoice more in the work of human beings than in the work of God?* Indeed, you

---

[1] The interpretation of this parable was given by the intermediary's spiritual guide in the spring of 1916. – Publisher's note.

shall know: *this image is true;* for no matter how many stones you cast into the pond, no matter how much you muddy the water, when the mud has settled again, when the pond is still and God's sun shines over it, the clear water will reflect once more *the self-same image.*"

In stillness they waited at the edge until the mud had settled. And behold, the clear water reflected anew, as beauteous as before, the same image of the sky with the white clouds, the greensward, the blossoms and the trees.

Then said the woman: "See, I was right! For the deep, crystalline water under the radiance of God's sun will always reflect calmly and precisely all that is about it, and the pure water will mirror all that it receives far more clearly and precisely than any picture painted by human hands."

Then the man fell silent, for he saw that the woman was right.

14th November, 1911.

The Roads

A man on his journey through life upon the Earth came to a place whence many roads led in various directions.

He halted and said: "Which road shall I choose? Which is the right road?" And searchingly his eye followed the many roads to find the right one.

He chose a path which led over green fields and past flower-filled gardens, and prepared to continue on his journey.

Behold, there then arrived at that same place another man; he also halted, looked about him, and called upon him who had first arrived: "Friend and brother, tell me, which road shall I follow? By which road shall I most quickly reach the goal?"

The first man answered him and said: "By this one; *for this is the one that I have chosen.*"

But then said he who had last arrived: "Do you not see the high mountains in the distance? That path leads over them, and it is dangerous to journey among the deep chasms and along the steep precipice, nay, then this one is better. This is the one that I shall choose." And he pointed to a broad, straight road lined with tall trees.

Then became the first man angered and he said: "But do you not see yonder river? There are strong whirlpools which will drag you down, and surely you will perish miserably."

Then became the other angered also, and he cried out: "Say you that I have chosen a bad road?"

And they quarrelled at length, without being agreed.

In this manner, each delayed the other in his journeying.

But lo! A third man came unto the same place.

He halted, and listened to their quarrel; he called to them and said: "Friends and brothers! Why are you quarrelling? Why do you not choose the path that leads through the forest? There is the journey cool, for the leaves of the trees will shade you from the burning rays of the sun, there is it quiet and peaceful; come, let us all journey together in peace and in concord. *I* believe that along this path we shall arrive most quickly at our goal."

But then cried the two others: "You foolish one, know you not that the forest is filled with wild beasts? Even if these do not tear you asunder, you will still not be able to find your way out of the darkness."

But he did not answer them.

And he journeyed on toward the forest.

Then the two looked upon one another, and the first one said: "Friend and brother, let us part in peace and each travel his own road, the road that leads most quickly to the goal is the right one."

And they shook hands and they parted in peace and reconciliation.

Along these different roads, the three men were led through many trials, across mighty seas and churning rivers, over steep mountains and through dark and wild forests. But they overcame all tribulations.

When, weary from their journeying they reached unto the goal, behold, then they stood *at the same time* before the entrance to their Father's Kingdom.

They marvelled greatly, and they said: "Friends and brothers! How is this possible? We chose each our own road, and behold *we stand before the goal at the same time!*"

But then the Father's servant came unto them, and he said: "The ways of your Father are many, and His ways are past finding out."

And he bade them to enter.

Then stood the three men and brothers, hand in hand, before their Father's countenance.

And their Father received them fondly; He took them unto His heart, blessed them and said: "When you follow the calling of My voice, when you journey forth along that path which in hope and trust you have chosen, then will you come most quickly unto My Kingdom!

"My ways are unsearchable, and My ways are many – but they all lead unto My Kingdom, unto My Abode."

23rd November, 1911.

The Prince and the Poor Men

One day a rich man, a prince, stood outside his palace. Then a man came by, clad in rags; he stopped and asked for a pittance.

The prince answered him and said: "Bread and water shall I give you, for none shall go hungry and thirsty from my door; and you may labour in my vineyard and in my garden; *but your wages will be according to your work."*

The poor man bowed deeply before the prince and said: "My Lord, you are mighty and you possess much estate and great riches. Give unto me the least precious of the rings that you wear upon your hand, that with it I may buy a booth in the marketplace, *for such is my wish."*

Then the prince looked sternly upon him and said: "Then truly must you labour much when you demand such wages! For you shall know that I will give you no wages until you have done the work!" And the prince offered him a piece of bread and a cup of water.

The poor man threw the bread upon the ground and struck the cup from the prince's hand and cried: "Lord, you are evil and hard-hearted, for you will not give of your rich abundance. For all eternity shall you be accursed!"

But the prince answered him and said: *"Your curses will all turn against yourself, for you would not receive what I would give you!"*

But the poor man turned away from the prince and went his way to beg elsewhere – and the prince sighed for the badness of mankind.

Then another poor man came by; he stopped and asked for a pittance.

The prince answered him and said: "Bread and water shall I give you, and you may labour in my vineyard and in my garden; *but the wages shall be according to your work."*

The poor man took the bread, laid it in his sack and placed the cup by his side, bowed deeply to the prince and said: "Lord, the work you would give me *does not befit me,* for it is most arduous; *make me your cup bearer or your gatekeeper, and I shall serve you faithfully.*"

The prince looked upon him and said: "If you do the work that I would give you to my contentment, then shall your wages be increased twofold and I shall make you my gatekeeper."

Then the poor man went into the vineyard and began to labour; but he soon grew weary, for the work did not befit him. And he went unto the prince and said: "Lord, would you have me labour for you, then must you increase my wages twofold, for the work is most arduous."

The prince looked upon him and said: "You foolish one, *how can I increase your wages for the work that you have not yet done?* Go back and be faithful."

Then the poor man became angry and cried: "Lord, you are evil and hard-hearted, for you will not give of your rich abundance!" And he left the prince's palace and went his way to beg elsewhere – but the prince sighed for the badness of mankind.

Behold, a third man in rags then came by, he stopped, and likewise asked for a pittance.

The prince answered him and said: "Bread and water shall I give you, and you may labour in my vineyard and in my garden; *but your wages shall be according to your work.*" And he offered him bread and water.

The poor man ate the bread and drank the water, bowed deeply to the prince, thanked him and said: "I will gladly take the work you would give me, for I have long sought work, but found none." And he went into the vineyard and began to labour.

The poor man kept everything in the best of order. The plants blossomed with fine flowers and the trees bore good fruit, for he had cast out all the weeds from the garden.

Then the prince went unto him and said: "My faithful servant, I am content with your work; I shall increase your wages twofold and make you my master gardener."

The poor man kissed the hem of the prince's robe and thanked him. And he continued to labour with great diligence.

One day the prince went unto the gardener to look upon his works; but then the gardener stood sorrowfully before a withering plant,[1] and he said: "Lord, behold, this plant withers away and I cannot find the cause; what shall I do with it?"

But the prince answered him and said: "Dig it up and cast it away,

---

[1]) Symbolizes a poorly performed task among the many good works that he had done.

it is worth no more; for there must be no withered plants in my garden."

When some time had passed, the prince stood once more with the gardener to look upon his works; but then the gardener said unto him: "Lord, behold this green and sturdy plant, see how many blossoms it bears; Lord, this is the plant you bade me to cast out."

The prince rejoiced over its vigorous appearance and fine blossoms, and he said: "Say unto me, how did you keep it from withering?"

The gardener answered him and said: "Lord, I found a worm at its roots. I cast the worm out, for it had already gnawed several roots asunder; but I planted the plant again, nourished and watered it well, and cut away all the withered leaves and branches. Then once again it began to sprout green and sturdy buds."

Then said the prince: "My faithful servant, I shall not increase your wages twofold, nay nor even tenfold, but I shall give you a thousand times a thousandfold more than I have given you before; *for I shall make you my son, and you shall inherit all my riches."*

But the gardener threw himself down before the prince's feet and exclaimed: "Lord, I am not worthy to be called your son." But the prince raised him up and said: *"My son, you were faithful in that which was least, you will be faithful also in much,"* and he led him unto his palace.

The prince's servants bowed deeply before him, greeted him and received him as their master's son.

2nd January, 1912.

The Fruit Seeds

A man was in possession of some precious fruit seeds; with great care he planted them in the richest soil in his garden. But it happened that he lost one of the seeds while he was working. Patiently he searched everywhere to find the missing seed, but he found it not, and he was deeply grieved.

Much time passed and the fruit seeds were all sprouted from the soil; some were but frail and slender plants, others had sturdy leaves and some bore blossoms.

One day as the man tended his plants he came upon a tiny shoot at the outer edge of the garden, and he remembered the missing seed.

Carefully, he unearthed it, and behold, he wondered much! For it had fallen with the seed sprout facing downward; with great difficulty the sprout had grown upward along one side of the seed until, frail and crooked, it had reached above the ground.

Truly, I say unto you: *all life will go forward and upward toward the Light, even along dark and tortuous paths!*

19th March, 1912.

The above parable refers to the downfall and return of the Elder (Ardor).

Uni and Esar

A realm[1] was divided among many princes and kings,[2] but one of them[3] was the mightiest, and he was high above them all. This prince saw with grief that many of his people turned to other lords. Then he chose two men from among his many servants, called them Uni and Esar, and he said unto them: "Go forth into the land, and seek to win many people for my kingdom and call upon all of them to return; for many have turned away from me."

Uni and Esar promised to carry out the task that the prince had placed upon them.

The prince blessed them and bestowed his royal emblem upon them both, and he promised to reward them according to their work.

Uni and Esar went to their dwellings to prepare for their journey. Uni chose to garb himself in a robe of camel's hair, he bound wooden sandals under his feet and draped a black cape over his head and his shoulders.

Esar chose to clothe himself in splendid raiment; he bound sandals of kidskin under his feet, anointed his hair and laid a scarlet cape about his shoulders.

Thus attired, they walked together along the road, but when they were come through the gates of the city, each went his own way.

Uni kept the royal emblem of his lord near his heart.

---

[1]) The Earth.
[2]) The many different religions and sects of human beings are like princes and kings.
[3]) God, as representing the religion of love and compassion.

He walked about in the city, searched out the sick and the grieving, tended to their bodies and spoke words of encouragement, and he built for himself a dwelling among the poor. He spoke unto them gently and forgave many of the poor the taxes that they owed the prince. And many flocked about him, indeed, many journeyed from afar unto the city to seek comfort and counsel through his words.

Uni spoke kindly and gently unto all, and thus he won many people unto the kingdom of his lord.

Esar bound the royal emblem of his lord over his brow, and he then went into the market place to be seen by all. He summoned the people with the flourish of trumpets. He spoke unto them sternly and admonished them to serve the mightiest of all in humility; for great riches should then be their reward. But those who would not follow should be cast into the darkness of prisons and delivered unto death.

When the people heard these words, they were stricken with much fear, and many brought Esar the taxes that they owed to the prince. But many would not follow, and Esar cast them into prison.

Then the people spoke loudly against him, but Esar went unto the temple of the city, searched the ancient laws and expounded them in all their severity. And the people dared no longer oppose this stern servant of their lord, and they made him their high priest.

But when Uni heard of Esar's hard judgments, he went unto him and pleaded with him to show mercy. But Esar answered him and said: "I do but my lord's bidding, and I judge the people according to his own laws."

Then Uni answered him and said: "All laws can be interpreted with much severity, and *all laws can be observed with kindness and compassion.*"

But Esar would not listen, and Uni departed with a heavy heart.

But when much time had passed, the prince sent messages to Uni and Esar, that they should return and render their accounts.

Uni rejoiced, for he longed to see his lord again. And he summoned the people once more, admonished them to live in love, peace and forbearance with one another, and once more he forgave a great many of the poor the taxes that they owed to the prince, and he promised to intercede on behalf of the transgressors.

Thereupon he quietly took leave of them.

But the people grieved much and deeply; for they had learned to love and honour Uni for his kind words and good works.

When Esar received the message from the prince, he sighed deeply; for he wished not yet to leave his splendid mansion and his many riches.

He went unto his treasure chamber, he counted his gold and said: "All this have I gathered in the name of my lord; *truly, my reward shall be royal."*

Once more he called the people together, he spoke unto them sternly and admonished them to serve obediently the mightiest of all lords, and he warned that he would bring accusations against those who had not yet brought unto him the taxes that they owed to the prince.

Thereupon he clothed himself in splendid raiment, anointed his hair and laid a scarlet cape about his shoulders. And in splendid procession his servants followed him. But when they were come unto the gate of the city they turned back, *and Esar was alone!*

The people rejoiced greatly in Esar's departure; for they had learned to fear his cold heart and stern judgments. Many soon turned to other lords, and they forgot the mightiest of them all.

But it came to pass that Uni and Esar left the city at the same time, and they met within the portal. Uni spoke kind words of greeting, but Esar turned his countenance away; for he did not wish to acknowledge Uni.

And they walked in silence until they reached the princely palace.

The prince summoned both of them, and Esar stepped forth before the prince – but *the prince* bade Uni speak first.

Uni bowed deeply and said: "My lord, I kept your royal emblem close to my heart, I searched out the sick and the grieving, nursed their bodies and cheered their spirits; I forgave many of the poor the taxes that they owed to you; for I taught them that you were a forbearing and compassionate lord. And when I departed from them, I promised to intercede on behalf of the transgressors. Lord, if I have done wrong, then let the punishment fall upon me, but spare the people."

Kindly, the prince looked upon him and said: "You have spoken kindly and wisely to the people. Truly, *your deeds shall be my deeds, your words shall be my words, and I shall surely honour the promises that you have given in my name.* Truly, you have been a faithful servant unto me and your reward shall be in accordance therewith."

He called upon the elders of his council, and he said: "Take this man within your midst; for from this day forth shall he be the greatest among you."

The elders of the council greeted Uni, and they took him within their midst, and behold, *he was the greatest[1] among them.*

---

[1] Greatest in the spiritual sense.

But the prince turned toward Esar and bade him to render his account.

Proudly, Esar bowed to the prince and said: "My lord, I bound your royal emblem upon my brow, that all could see which lord I served. I summoned the people and admonished them to serve you, the mightiest of all lords, to serve you in obedience and in fear; and all those who did not bring unto me the taxes that they owed to you I cast into the darkness of prison, and many I delivered to be put to death.

"I searched through the ancient laws and interpreted them with great severity, and I judged the people according to these, your stern laws.

"Lord, in this manner I won many people for your kingdom. Lord, I await the reward that you promised unto me!"

Then the prince looked sadly upon Esar and said: *"My royal emblem shall not be bound upon the brow nor borne to be seen by all the world. My royal emblem shall be kept in the heart, but it shall be seen in every deed.*

"You admonished the people to serve me, the mightiest of lords, in obedience and in fear; *but you neglected to speak to them of my forbearance and my compassion.* You interpreted the ancient laws in all their severity and you judged the people accordingly; *but you neglected to speak to them of the law of love and compassion, the law that stands above all laws.* You warned that you would accuse all who did not bring unto you the taxes that were owed to me, your lord; *but you neglected to teach the people to live together in love and forbearance.* You say that you won many unto my Kingdom; but *I* say that *many have turned from me, and many others will turn from me, when they remember your stern and cruel words.* Truly, you were unto me an *unfaithful servant,* and your reward shall be in accordance therewith."

And the prince called upon the youngest of the council and he said: "Take this man into your midst and teach him, for he is the least among you all. And when his learning is complete, *then shall he be sent again into the city, that he may raise up that which he has torn down."*

Yea, verily, I say unto you that this man became the least among all, for he was an unfaithful servant unto his lord! Thus weighs the Lord, our Father, the self-righteous against the just of heart. *And thus, as you judge others, so will our Father some day judge you.*

4th April, 1912.

SEEK AND YOU SHALL FIND!

The Wisdom of Jesus Sirach, Chapter 1:1,
All wisdom cometh from the Lord, and is
with him for ever. – 1:5, The fountain of
wisdom is God's word on high, and her
ways are the eternal commandments.

1.

Light and Darkness, in a transcendental sense, are abstractions to human beings, but to God and to all spiritual beings they are realities – powerful, magnetically acting forces.

Through all eternity, primal Light and primal Darkness each had two opposite poles that rested in a state of complete latency. Although Light existed only as a faintly sparkling core, surrounded everywhere by Darkness, the radiations of the two primal forces were of *exactly equal strength*.

Between[1] the two primal forces, on the boundary between Light and Darkness, rested Thought and Will; although passive themselves, they were through all eternity subject to the equal influence of the radiations of Light and of Darkness.

After eternities of absolute inactivity, a change occurred in the static balance of the primal state, in that Thought and Will reacted with a slight agitation to the radiations of Darkness. This weak agitation was the first sign of the transition of Thought and Will from a state of passivity to a state of awakening activity, since this vibration brought the primal state out of balance.

Gradually, through aeons of time, Thought and Will moved further and further away from the radiations of Darkness and in toward the Light, whose radiations assisted them with a steadily increasing attraction that drew them toward the poles of the Light. Every time Thought and Will followed the attraction of the Light, the Light gained in strength and in volume. After unknown aeons of continued attraction, Thought and Will reached the poles of the Light, which at the moment of contact were awakened from their latent state. At the same time Thought and Will awoke to a fully *conscious* and *willed* activity and developed a mutual attraction, so that through countless aeons they slowly drew closer to each other. As the distance between them grew less the Light gained still more in strength, volume and radiation.

---

[1]) It will be seen that Ardor's Account omits the period of time during which Thought and Will were inert with respect to Light and Darkness. When Ardor related this part of his Account he was unable to give the intermediary a clear understanding of this state. This period was therefore deferred for further explanation in the Commentary.

Attracted and guided by the Will, the Thought strove onward, but in each advance lay a temptation for the Thought to cease the struggle before full victory over Darkness had been won. But due to the attraction of the all-powerful Will, the Thought did not cease its struggle forward toward the steadily approaching Will, and for this reason the Light constantly increased in strength and in brightness, until after further eternities – with the meeting and harmonious union of Thought and Will – the Light wrested itself free from Darkness, raised itself victoriously out of and over it, so that the Light surrounded and enveloped the Darkness, which then slowly contracted, became denser and formed a dark core in the sea of Light.

By the perfect and harmonious merging with each other of Thought (the female) and Will (the male), God arose as a personal Being, as the centre of the universe.

This picture of the inert state and the struggle of Light, Darkness, Thought and Will must be understood as abstractions and not interpreted in terms of factual, earthly concepts of space, measure and time, nor in terms of known forms of radiation, inertia and motion. No explanation beyond the foregoing can be given regarding the presence through all eternity of primal Light, primal Darkness, Thought and Will; no further explanation can be given that could be understood by human thought at this time. Only this can be said: that Light, Darkness, Thought and Will were not *created,* but *existed* through all eternity – a problem that cannot and will not be solved or comprehended by human thought in the present state of human intelligence.

An earthly scientist could no more lecture on philosophy to a young child in the expectation of being understood than a transcendental being could advance a detailed explanation of the existence through all eternity of these entities in the hope of being understood by mankind. But when human beings have attained greater spiritual maturity, there is a possibility that one of God's emissaries will undertake during an earthly life to explain the riddle of eternity and the mystery of the uncreated.

If Thought and Will had not succeeded in uniting with each other, and if Thought-Will as a united power had not triumphed, so that the divine Being could arise, then the energy and brightness of the Light, at the moment when Thought and Will were no longer able to attract and retain each other, would once more have begun to diminish, while Darkness would have gained in strength and in radiative power until slowly but inevitably it would have absorbed the Light. Forced by Darkness, Thought and Will would then have drawn forth the latent poles of Darkness. These activated poles would then – through eternities – have slowly attracted each other until, at the moment of their merging, a being would have arisen who would *in every respect* have been the antithesis of God.

But since the poles of the Light, fused with Thought and Will, continued unceasingly to approach each other, the Light gained greater and greater dominance over Darkness, and with the emergence of God the possibility was eliminated for ever *that the poles of Darkness would evolve into a being that would be the antithesis of God in thought and action.*

Primal Darkness (i.e., chaos, or *disorder and confusion*) thus *lacks its own guiding Will and creative Thought.* It therefore acts at random and has become destructible as a result of the victory of the Light. The Light, on the other hand, is governed by divine Thought and Will.

By Thought (i.e., logos) an infinite diversity of changeable forms of power and life are radiated. Above Thought, as the highest concentration of the Light, stands the Will – the supreme, fructifying and life-giving energy – for so long as the thought of creating or of acting is *only* thought, it has only the potential for life, it is coming to life. But the moment the Will begins to fructify, Thought unites with Will and changes from a state of *becoming* to a state of *being*; it becomes concrete. However, the Will is *nothing,* so long as it does not have Thought as a constant basis for its activity.

Thought is thus the primary abstract female concept: intuitive, formative and creative; and Will is the primary abstract male concept: fructifying, productive and dominant.

The twelve Helpers, or Servants, who emerged from the Light simultaneously with the personified Divinity, were emanated by God through the power of Thought-Will.

These twelve Helpers were in God's Thought from the very moment Thought and Will fused with the poles of the Light. As thoughts within the divine Thought – united with it, yet independently conscious – they experienced the struggle out of Darkness and therefore knew its awesome power.

Since the Helpers emerged by God's Will, He stands above them as the only perfect One, who alone has the full knowledge of life's eternal energy.

The moment that God emerged as a personal Being, He drew the Light by His Will into an eternal and unbreakable circulation and let it flow through His flaming Self; at the same time He drew Darkness into the circulation of the waves of the Light in order thus to purify and eliminate it.

Both Darkness and the Light consist of extremely fine particles which were in a state of *absolute inactivity* for as long as primal Darkness and primal Light were at rest and in equilibrium. But when the thought of eliminating Darkness arose in God, the realization of this thought made it necessary for Him to bring the ether (i.e., the Light, and the Darkness enclosed by the Light) into a vibrating, circulatory wave motion. By the strength of His Thought and Will God thus brought the particles both of Darkness and of the Light into a rotating motion about each other. The smaller or the larger the particles, the faster or the less rapid became their vibrations or oscillations, just as the capacity determined by God for mutual attraction, cohesion and adhesion became the greater and stronger, the smaller the particles.[1]

Since the particles of Darkness, even the smallest, are larger than the largest particles of the Light, the oscillations of Darkness became slower than those of the Light, which caused Darkness to precipitate in the streams of the Light during the great, purifying circulation through God's flaming Self, for which reason the purification and elimination of Darkness – by absorption into the Light – advances at such an inconceivably slow pace. *Only God* knows when the power of Darkness will be destroyed by its total absorption into the Light.

And *only God* knows why Thought and Will, after eternities of exactly equal influence from the radiations of primal Light and primal Darkness, were drawn toward the Light, which was thus made victorious.

Within His all-encompassing Thought, God embraces time and space, both in a limited and in an unlimited sense. Since space (i.e., the universe) is unlimited to the human mind, and therefore has no identifiable stable centre, *God must be regarded as the centre of all existence, of all creation.* Wherever God, by the power of His Will, may be present as a personal – limited – Being, He still remains, by virtue of His unlimited Thought, for all time and at all places the centre of creation, so that the eternal circulation of the Light is *never* broken.

---

[1]) As soon as the particles escape human sense perception, they take the forms of the four-dimensional world. Transitional forms nevertheless exist between the three- and four-dimensional states, in which the particles can be sensed at one moment and escape human sense perception the next, depending on whether a material or an immaterial influence predominates at the given moment. Similarly, there exist forms in which the presence of particles can be recognized but not perceived. The particles are in this case located on the boundary between the three- and four-dimensional worlds, and may manifest themselves on either side of the boundary.

The eternities that passed before the emanation of God are known only to God; all other spiritual beings regard His emergence as a personal Being as the beginning of time. However, for the sake of accuracy it should be noted that time, as a term for the progression of events, began with the first faint attraction of Thought and Will toward the poles of the Light; *in other words, with the transition from a state of rest to a state of struggle.*

When time began, *being* became *existence.* Time, in the transcendental as well as in the earthly sense, is an expression of the progression of events. Spiritual beings measure time in terms of time-periods and not in terms of earthly years.

When spiritual beings communicate with human beings in messages concerning time, they normally make use of earthly terms.

By the power of God's Will, time, having once begun, will never cease to be.

The terms Darkness and the Light, describing the two primal forces, were chosen because these forces do in fact exist in the same relationship and contrast to each other as do earthly daylight and the darkness of the night, with which human beings are so familiar on Earth. And, as the earthly night and day display numerous transitions from dusk to deep darkness and from dawn to bright sunlight, so do the two primal forces display a wealth of transitions and degrees of strength; however, these cannot be more accurately clarified or defined here. But in order to achieve at least a partial understanding of the primal forces, one should imagine both Darkness and the Light divided into three main categories, according to the size of the particles. The classifications are the following: 1) material, or molecular Darkness (small particles); 2) astral Darkness (smaller particles); 3) spiritual Darkness (still smaller particles).

1) Astral-material Light (very fine particles); 2) ethereal-astral Light (still finer particles); 3) ethereal Light (much finer particles still). The size of the particles is thus constantly decreasing. In relation to God's Kingdom or to God, the scale of ethereal-material, spiritual and spiritual-ethereal Light is used. However, it should be remembered that *all* these designations, whether they relate to Darkness or to the Light, *should be regarded only as a means of identification.*

It is impossible to give a description of God's Kingdom (landscapes, dwellings, etc.) or of life as it is lived there, since all this is so inconceivably far beyond human comprehension, and because no earthly language contains words that can even approximately convey a graphic description of these things.

2.

When God still had His uncreated first children in His Thought and was considering everything that might pertain to them, He knew that some day they would inevitably have to be confronted with Darkness in order to learn how to let the will exercise complete control over the thought, so that each individual, of his or her *own* will, could limit or halt the desires of his or her thoughts.

The wish to become manifold did not arise in God until *after* His emergence. Thus, in contrast to the twelve Helpers, God's children had not existed in His Thought until He emerged as a personal Being. For this reason they had not *consciously* taken part in the struggle out of Darkness, and consequently they could have no knowledge of its power. Therefore, if God did not at some point confront them directly with Darkness, they would never become *contributing*, but only *receiving* beings, and for all eternity they would continue to be as dependent, protected children, rather than personalities of independent thought and action – and the gulf between them and God would have become immeasurable.

In His omniscience God saw that there were several possibilities from which His yet uncreated children could choose. Thus they could *all* overcome Darkness and thereby rise infinitely high; or they could *all* meet with downfall, and by their fall create a temporary life in sin and in suffering; or a larger or a smaller number of them might rise infinitely high – or they might fall.

When God had considered this, He also knew that the moment He had created His children He would by His omniscience *know beforehand the choice of every individual*.

Thus, to render equal justice toward all of them, God decided to *limit His omniscience* before He created them, that they could remain free and independent in every case, without being in the least influenced by His prescience.

If God had not limited His knowledge, then those of His children who would later succumb to Darkness could rightfully have reproached Him, that possessing the full knowledge of their choice He had created some to be defeated and others to be victorious – in which case God would not be what He is: *a loving and just Father*.

In order to bestow upon each one a sovereign free will, God therefore limited His omniscience by the power of *His Will*, so that He would have *no knowledge* of the future choices[1] that His children would make.

---

[1] See also Commentary, pp. 171–72.

Thus: *God created His many children in perfect justice; He gave them all an equal inner nature, gave them equal fulness of love, equal wisdom, equal ability to will and equal ability to grow spiritually. All were equal.*

God created them two and two, a male and a female being, destined for all eternity to complement and supplement each other.

As a result of the perfect union of divine Thought and divine Will that culminated in the emergence of God and His twelve Helpers, both God and His Helpers embody a male as well as a female principle within their nature. But God created His children as man and as woman, so as to maintain the dualistic attraction for all eternity. Each individual embodies both Thought and Will. However, *Will* prevails in the male part, and *Thought* prevails in the female part.

The female's thoughts and emotions are richer, deeper and more intuitive than the male's; but her thought structure is not as stringent as his, since she possesses only to a small extent the ability of the male will to formulate, retain and make fruitful the constantly changing images of thought. (This holds true also for the spiritual individuality of human beings).

The Thought and the Will of God, and of each of His Helpers, are balanced – they are of uniform strength; but God's Thought and Will are, of course, infinitely greater than those of His Helpers.

The emotional lives of the duals resemble each other, their thought and their will supplement each other.

Life partnership, in the earthly sense, does not exist for these male and female beings, even though through thought and will they may be united from time to time in a higher sense.

Under the instruction of God's Helpers they all advanced far in the development of thought and will, and in knowledge of the creative power of thought and will, but they did not attain any understanding of the *everlasting energy* of the life-principle. For this reason they were able only to create, or rather to fashion, lifeless objects by the power of thought and will and from the radiations of the Light (e.g., building their dwellings and fashioning objects, artistic ornamentation, etc. They were similarly capable of creating mental images in the likeness of living beings, but these were phantoms of an ephemeral nature).

The fact that God's children developed in different ways, although created with equal potential, is due to the strange, individual and mysterious (i.e., hidden) nature of the free will.

The free will, a gift that God has given each of His children, *is a reflection of His own Will* – an abstraction whose true and innermost nature is known only to God.

On account of this free will some of God's children pursued a more intellectual development of thought, tried to investigate the cosmic laws and to perfect their knowledge of the endless abstractions of thought, while others devoted themselves more to the world of beauty and emotion – to the world of form and colour, of music and poetry, etc.

Thus: *although equally endowed from the beginning, God's children have through the exercise of the free will become essentially different, they have become individualities.*

3.

When God's children through countless aeons had lived a life of beauty, splendour and joy in their Father's Kingdom, He saw that they had advanced so far in their understanding of the dominance of Will over Thought, and in their understanding of the need to limit the desires of the thought according to the ability of the will to make fruitful and implement, that there was a possibility for them *all* to emerge victoriously from a confrontation with Darkness. He then decided to set them a difficult task – that of leading spiritually immature beings forward to full equality with themselves.

The beings whom God thought to create He would create from the weaker and more material radiations of the Light combined with some of His own divine Self.

Through higher or lower frequencies of oscillation both Darkness and the Light can produce greater or lesser ethereal effects, and similarly lesser or greater material manifestations, both in the transcendental and in the purely earthly sense. In Darkness as well as in the Light there exist, as stated earlier, extremely fine particles; the higher the frequency of oscillation, the smaller are the particles and the greater their capacity for cohesion and adhesion.

Propagation and death were not intended for these beings; once created through God's Thought and Will they should continue to live in a development of constant progress. This development should not only take place spiritually but also physically, since their bodies through spiritual progress should at the same time gain in radiance and beauty as the various stages on the road to

God's Kingdom were attained. All sin, all impure thoughts would clearly be entirely unknown to these children of the Light; for sin, as well as propagation and death, exist only in Darkness and in all that it produces. But when they had attained a certain degree of maturity they should be confronted with Darkness in the same way as God's first-created children, that they might learn to overcome its power.

God, His Helpers and the first-created children would make themselves known to them through revelations. All guidance should take place by the help of thought, that is to say, through inspiration and intuition.

In order to carry out this intention, God first had to provide dwelling places for the beings He had thought to create. Since these beings would be spiritually much weaker than God's first-created children, they would not be able to sustain an existence in the radiant Light of God's own Kingdom until through a long process of maturing they became capable of maintaining their individuality, so that on their entry into their Father's Home they would be in no danger of merging again with their paternal origin.

For this reason God conceived and developed the plan for the four star universes or star systems.

The mother suns were formed by God by the power of His Will, setting the ether – the Light and the Darkness precipitated in it – in a rotating motion around four centres of force, which were borne and held by and in His Thought.

Since the Darkness that is precipitated in the ether has a lower oscillation frequency than the Light, the rotation around the centres of force caused it to collect as a core. This core was surrounded by the Light, which spread outward in oscillations of ever-increasing frequency, until there was created about each centre a well defined globe, consisting of a darker core[1] surrounded by a corona of Light. The outermost layer of this corona, formed by the more rapid and more ethereal-astral oscillations of the Light, is not visible to earthly eyes, whereas the radiations from the precipitated Darkness,[2] together with the radiations from the more rapid molecular oscillations of Darkness, can be detected and reflected by the human eye.[2]

---

[1]) This core is formed of Darkness.

[2]) It must always be borne in mind that the term "Darkness" should be understood by human beings only as a designation for a power that manifests itself in many different ways in the earthly world. This power can therefore also manifest itself as radiations that are luminous to the human eye.

The radiations and the concentration of the Light thus increase with rising frequency of oscillation. But only in God's Kingdom does the Light unfold its greatest energy of concentration and radiation, just as the particles here are very much finer than in the other forms of the Light. Spiritual beings are able to see the cores of Darkness of the globes, as well as the brighter, more radiant corona of the Light. Only one of the mother globes will at some future time become visible from the Earth.

The mother globes contain *all* the elementary substances and *all* possibilities for life[1] – seeds from which God by the strength of His Thought and Will can call forth life. And since the four star systems, directly or indirectly, stem from the mother globes, this applies also to all suns (i.e., stars) and planets within these four systems, with the exceptions due to the incursions of Darkness[2] on the globes in that star system to which the Earth belongs.

In order to understand the motions of the mother globes one should visualize the universe as a picture projected onto paper.

God's Kingdom, an enormous sun formed from the high ethereal-material vibrations of the Light, supports and maintains the four star systems as their Central Sun.

The mother suns are positioned in pairs directly across from each other on either side of the Central Sun; when the Central Sun and the four mother suns are all in opposition, an imaginary line passes through the centres of the four suns and the Central Sun.

The mother suns are of exactly equal weight. Each sun revolves on its own axis.

The distance between the mother suns comprising each pair (measured from the centre of each sun) is equal to the radius of the Central Sun (God's Kingdom). The composite orbit of the pairs around the Central Sun describes a perfect circle, whose radius equals seven times the radius of the Central Sun. The circumference of this great circle passes through the midpoint of the distance between each pair of mother suns. The mutual orbits described by the mother suns thus lie halfway outside and halfway inside the circumference of the great circle.

The mother suns balance each other in pairs by equal attraction and equal repulsion. The distance once established will therefore always remain constant.

---

[1]) Contained in the Light-corona of the globes, in the global layers that are invisible to the human eye.

[2]) See Ardor's Account, p. 9, and Summary, pp. 296–97.

The individual movement of each sun following its partner around the Central Sun describes an open circular orbit (a spiral orbit) so that the midpoint of the distance between each sun within a pair moves along the circumference of the great circle.

The pairs turn in opposite directions.

If a diagram shows the pair of mother suns *(a–b)* to the left of the Central Sun and the other pair *(c–d)* to the right, and with all the five suns in opposition so that *a* and *c* lie nearest to, and *b* and *d* farthest from, the Central Sun, and assuming that this position is the starting point for the orbits of the mother suns, then *a* and *c* will turn away from and *b* and *d* toward the Central Sun. The spiral-orbit of the one pair *(a–b)* thus turns from the left side of the Central Sun to the right side, and the other pair *(c–d)* at the right turns to the left side. After about three million years, the pair *(a–b)* will occupy the place of the pair *(c–d)* on the right side of the Central Sun, and vice versa for *(c–d)*. The complete revolution of both pairs along their common orbit round the Central Sun takes two aeons, which corresponds to about six million years.

Once established, the speed of rotation of both pairs will always remain constant, since they all counterbalance one another at any given moment. The equilibrium between these pairs, with God's Kingdom as the centre, will therefore never be disturbed.

A star system (a "Milky Way") shaped as an elliptical ring moves along with and rotates around each mother sun. Each star system was directly or indirectly spun off or ejected by eruption from its mother sun. (The globes and suns that originated directly from the mother sun have then again, through spin-offs or eruptions, subdivided into smaller globes – and so on). Centrifugal force has caused the globes of the star systems to move in elliptical rather than circular orbits around their mother sun at one focus and an immaterial centre of force (invisible to the human eye) at the other focus.

If the orbit of a globe is to describe a perfect circle around its sun, the following three factors must be of exactly equal strength: the speed of axial rotation of the sun in question, its forward thrust through space and the combined forces of spin-off and attraction that interact at the time of the formation of the daughter globe. If the formation of a new globe comes about through an ejection produced by inner explosive eruptions in the sun globe, the force of ejection in most cases will exceed the force of a normal spin-off process (drop spin-off). The globes that come into being through eruption-ejections therefore move in a more or less elliptical orbit. If the orbit does become elliptical, then an immaterial centre of force will automatically arise in juxtaposition to the material sun. Depending on the shape of the orbit, this immaterial centre of force will be nearer to or farther from the material sun.

The irregular orbit of a globe can also be caused by attraction from other suns.

Similar conditions prevail in the numerous solar systems within the four main systems. Because of the centrifugal force, the suns and the planets[1] have similarly deviated from the circular orbit to a greater or lesser elliptical orbit around their centre sun at one focus and a centre of force,[2] equally invisible to the human eye, at the other focus.

If one visualizes each of the four star systems in the shape of an ellipsoid, then one axis will equal 1/7 of the radius of the open circle (the spiral-circle), which the mother suns describe in their specific orbits; the second axis will equal 1/28 of the arc length of that same spiral-circle, and the third axis equal 3/7 of the longest axis.

Since the size of the second axis, i.e., 1/28 of the arc length of the spiral-circle, cannot be given exactly in terms of human calculations, then neither can the third axis (3/7 of the second, the longest axis) show exactly the indicated size of 3/7.

The combined volume of the four mother suns and their related star systems represent 1/7000 of the Central Sun, God's Kingdom.

The number of globes is *limited* at any given moment – the opposite would be in conflict with the law of balance – but in the course of time their number will become *unlimited*. New globes will come into being again and again, while older globes disappear and decompose into their constituents, but so long as the four mother sun systems by the power of God's Will orbit in space, the combined weight will always balance with zero. The number of globes thus becomes finite in terms of the concept of *being*, but infinite in terms of the concept of *becoming*.

All suns, even the most distant nebulae, that can be observed from the Earth belong to the same system, whose mother sun – one of the four – will some day be seen from the Earth, though probably not until the instruments of observation have undergone certain alterations and improvements. At that time the mother sun will be visible low in the southwestern sky.

The system of suns and planets to which the Earth belongs is located in the inner part of the elliptical ring of the "Milky Way",

---

[1]) In that system of which the Earth forms a part, not all suns and planets are ejected or erupted parts of their Central Suns; several are globes that through collision with floating accumulations of Darkness have first been expelled from their orbits, and have since been attracted to and held captive by a larger sun. (See Summary, p. 297). In the other three systems there are no drifting accumulations of Darkness; the Darkness there precipitates to the core of the globes and is slowly eliminated through the great circulation of the Light-ether.

[2]) The immaterial centres come into being automatically under established laws.

and it moves toward the immaterial centre of force.[1]

4.

Aeons were to pass, while the universe was formed, before the time came when God chose the Earth as the first dwelling place for the uncreated beings who were as yet in His Thought.

When God informed His children that He would give them the difficult task of leading primitive beings forward to greater spiritual maturity, He confronted *all* of them with Darkness the moment that He spoke to them and said: "In the fulness of time shall I choose from among you some ..."

God does not reveal to whom or to how many He will assign this task. He leaves it undecided, in order to observe the reaction of His children to the possibility that some might be chosen in preference to others. Since God at the creation of His children had limited His foreknowledge of their future choice between good and evil, He could know nothing of the impression that His words would have on the individual until they had all carefully considered the proposed task. When He had disclosed to them the new-formed world that irradiated and made fruitful by the Light slowly ripened to life, He therefore allotted them a certain time, that they might all become familiar with the contemplated work.

In Ardor's Account, reference is made to the Eldest and the Youngest. However, these names serve merely to distinguish between them, since they were all created at the same time - i.e., they emerged simultaneously as visible individualities. But some time elapsed between their creation and their emergence, since God created one after the other in His Thought, and not until His Thought had created the last one did they *all* - by the power of His Will - *simultaneously* emerge as visible beings.

Those of God's children who are called the Eldest had mainly been interested in abstractions of thought and the cosmic laws, while the Youngest are those who had been most interested in the arts of colour, form and music, etc.

---

[1]) Upon further inquiry, the following has been stated and confirmed from the transcendental world: all the globes of the galactic system move in their orbits around the mother sun and the invisible, i.e., immaterial, centre of force. As the globes approach the mother sun or the centre, their speed increases, and it decreases proportionately as they recede. The velocity around the immaterial centre, however, is much lower than that around the material mother sun. The same holds true for the comets and the planets; their velocity is likewise much lower around the immaterial centres than it is around the material, i.e., visible, centres. In the cases where the form of the orbit approximates a circle, the increased velocity round the immaterial centre is so low that it can scarcely be detected. - Publisher's note.

The Eldest very soon formed the opinion that they must be the best qualified to assume the leadership of immature beings. God then knew that their lust for power – a result of the influence of Darkness – had begun to awaken, and that their will was not strong enough to limit or to contain the desires of their thought. And God warned them; but when they ignored God's warning and remained in the Light-world that irradiated the Earth, Darkness began gradually and unnoticed by them to emerge and separate from the circulation of the Light.

As time passed, Darkness gained greater and greater influence over the Eldest and manifested itself in self-righteousness, impatience and lust for power.

When Darkness through the disregard of God's warning by the Eldest began to separate from the Light, it also began its work of destruction on the Earth itself, millions of years before this became known to the Eldest. Slowly – inconceivably slowly – the Earth's core of Darkness[1] absorbed the Darkness that was flowing in, and slowly – inconceivably slowly – the Earth was transformed in the course of millions of years from a world of Light to a *world of Darkness*.

The Darkness that took the Earth into its possession and transformed it was of the astral and the molecular forms. The astral Darkness, which is a lower form of spiritual Darkness, has smaller particles with somewhat greater capacity for cohesion and adhesion than the molecular form of Darkness.

When God saw the incipient destruction of His work, He knew that His eldest children would suffer a downfall; but although the Eldest in their impatience and lust for power were themselves intent on creating living beings, God would not abandon them and He warned them once again – though with the same negative result. Each time the Eldest ignored God's warning, Darkness gained greater and greater power over them, so that by the time they had in full agreement resolved to create beings from Darkness, they had departed so far from God and from the influence of the Light that their will for the good had been completely broken.

Through the combined strength of the conscious thought and will of the Eldest, large amounts of the precipitated Darkness were drawn out from the concealing waves – or streams – of the Light and completed the destruction long since begun; and since the Eldest in their powerlessness were incapable of stemming the onrush of Dark-

---

[1] See Sumary, pp. 260–61.

ness,[1] they had to stand by as helpless and bewildered spectators to the dreadful catastrophe that overwhelmed their beautiful world. In their horror at what had happened they forgot for long periods of time the true cause of the destruction: their desire to create living beings themselves, and therefore they all devoted themselves to vain attempts once more to come into contact with the Light; but despite their many exertions they did not succeed and were therefore incapable of rebuilding or re-creating the world of Light that Darkness had destroyed. Since they had all *voluntarily* allied themselves with Darkness its magnetic power bound them, and in the same way that the Light streams through God Darkness streamed through the Eldest. In this way, through the thought and will for evil of the Eldest, the poles of Darkness were awakened from their latent state – even though the Eldest themselves did not understand the cause of this.

Having thus of their own free will been brought under the binding influence of Darkness, the Eldest could not be redeemed before they had fully repented of their sinful actions. If God through His own power[2] had broken the stream of Darkness, they would immediately have lost all possibility of ever returning to their Father. Such action would have doomed them to everlasting, irrevocable perdition, which could never be reconciled with God's fatherly love. The Darkness that streamed through them would have to be neutralised by the free will for the Light of the Eldest themselves, before the Light could once more absorb it.

Neutral Darkness – in this case the neutral spiritual Darkness that is produced by the fastest oscillations of Darkness – is Darkness that in one way or another has become depolarized. This depolarization can occur, for example, when the spiritual sufferings of an individual evoke grief and thereby remorse over sinful thoughts or sinful actions.

The spiritual Darkness that influenced the Eldest – and is identical to the Darkness that afflicts humanity – can be depolarized in two ways[3].

1) Through the corrupt, sinful or criminal act that is committed at the moment the corresponding thought is realized through the individual's will for evil. The action results from the meeting of thought and will and with this result, or action, Darkness is depolarized, losing for a time its capacity for attraction. But it is only the particular

---

[1]) The Darkness that destroyed the world of Light of the Eldest and infused their spiritual bodies was astral and spiritual Darkness.

[2]) See also Summary, pp. 267–68.

[3]) A third way exists, but is known only to God.

grain of Darkness that impels the individual to action which is depolarized. A moment later a new wave of Darkness may influence
the same person to the same thought and action, or to another act of
Darkness.

2) Through the individual's grief over the impure or sinful
thoughts, thought and will lose their reciprocal power of attraction
toward evil, since there now occurs a first movement toward the
Light, whereby Darkness is depolarized. The evil thought and the
evil will are eliminated through remorse, since the Light gains full
victory over Darkness[1] with the remorse of the individual.

In order to evoke grief and remorse sooner among the Eldest, if
this were possible, God promised his youngest children to call upon
their fallen brothers and sisters; for if the sound of God's voice
could awaken memories in the thoughts of the Eldest, and if these
memories could in turn awaken grief over that which had been lost
through their arbitrary actions, then remorse would quickly follow
and break the stream of Darkness, enabling the Light to carry them
back to the glorious world of their Father's Home.

The supplication of the Youngest to their Father first occurred several million
years after the precipitation of Darkness had begun. The Youngest had gradually
become accustomed to the thought that their elder brothers and sisters would be
chosen, and since the Eldest so often visited the new, radiant world of Light around
the Earth, unaccompanied by the Youngest and without informing them of their excursions, the Youngest had grown accustomed to the prolonged absence of their
brothers and sisters. But as time passed and the Eldest failed to return, the Youngest
grew apprehensive and sought the counsel of God's Helpers, who then informed
them of what had happened. And their grief became boundless.

Despite their continuous communion with God, *He* had not mentioned anything
to the Youngest about the fall of the others. In His infinite love, He did not wish
them to know of the sorrow and painful separation until they themselves inquired
about their absent brothers and sisters.

Through the millions of years that passed while the Eldest sought
in vain to cleanse Darkness from their Kingdom and to re-create it,
Darkness flowed closer and closer about the Earth, united with the
Earth's core of Darkness and brought to life some of the germs of
life[2] that God had given. These germs of life, both those intended to
become animal forms and those intended to become plant forms,
would not have been subject to death and decay if they had been

---

[1] See Summary, pp. 297–301, regarding depolarization of Darkness.
[2] See Summary, pp. 261–63.

called forth under the direct radiance of the Light. For it had been God's intention that they should retain their original forms for the joy and the benefit of the beings of the Light that He had thought to create. Once the Earth had served its purpose as the first dwelling place for these beings, the animal and plant worlds would then by the power of God's Will be dissolved again and absorbed by the Light.

However, since it was Darkness that made the latent seed fruitful and vitalized it, *nothing* developed in the way that God in His Thought had decided at the beginning. Everything became grotesque, hideous and without meaning; and because of the low capacity of Darkness for cohesion, adhesion[1] and regeneration, all animal and plant forms became subject to a limited life span of longer or shorter duration.

When their many attempts at reconstructing the ravaged Kingdom had failed to give the Eldest any positive result, they decided to descend to the Earth to investigate the destruction that had occurred there.

Besides the monstrous beasts mentioned in Ardor's Account there were also certain micro-organisms, such as decay-causing bacteria. But most of the disease-causing spores came into existence after this time, called forth by Darkness and often planned and created by the Eldest. Numerous species have thus appeared, degenerated or become extinct, while new ones have come into existence. And this will continue through countless ages, but in decreasing measure as Darkness is eliminated. Nevertheless, some individual micro-organisms, such as the aforementioned decay-causing bacteria, or similar species, will exist as long as there is life on Earth.

In the millions of years that passed since the time Darkness began spreading over the Earth, there gradually developed the numerous forms of plant and animal life that were extant at the time when the Eldest discovered the destruction that had taken place on the Earth. The development progressed very slowly through many and diverse stages, from single-celled[2] to multi-celled,[2] to more and more complex organisms and forms. And as Darkness concentrated further on and about the Globe the gruesome, gigantic and fantastic animal figures appeared.

Some of these animal creatures that dismayed the Eldest with their horrifying appearance became progenitors of many of the later

---

[1]) See Summary, pp. 266–67.
[2]) See Summary, pp. 260–63.

animal species; but many of these later animal forms developed through the continued vitalization of the still dormant germs of life. This development also progressed slowly from the primitive to the higher organisms. The earthly material effect of Darkness was not reduced until the connection between the Light and the Earth that had been interrupted by the fall of the Eldest was re-established.[1]

Until the Globe was once again drawn into the cycle of the Light, the beasts mated at random. Innumerable species resulted from these cross-breedings. Only gradually, as the Light later gained a greater organizing influence, were conditions for a more regular reproduction of the existing species improved, whereby the animal kingdom – as well as the plant kingdom – became in many ways enriched and refined.

The molecular oscillations of Darkness (the oscillations of its largest particles), which then produced – and which still produce – the earthly forms and figures visible to the human eye, are held together and stabilized by the somewhat faster oscillations of the astral Darkness.

If the molecules of Darkness were not stabilized by astral[2] Darkness, then the molecules would easily loosen and dissociate because of their lower frequency. Therefore, all earthly forms of plant and animal, all organic and inorganic matter and all that is issued from or made thereof have an astral counterpart, invisible to the human eye, consisting of the faster oscillations of astral Darkness, i.e., smaller particles with greater capacity for cohesion and adhesion.[3] These astral counterparts are interwoven with the earthly substance in such a way that even from the transcendental world it can be difficult to determine where one ends and the other begins.

The frequency of astral Darkness lies about midway between the highest and the lowest frequencies of Darkness. Spiritual Darkness has the highest frequency and is the Darkness that influences the thought and the will to sin. In Ardor's Account no distinction is made between spiritual and astral Darkness.

When the earthly creatures and forms are attacked by disease – i.e., accumulations of Darkness, microbes, malnutrition, heat, drought, cold, and the like – then the connection between the astral counterparts and the earthly molecular formations is loosened, since

---

[1]) See Ardor's Account, pp. 15-19.
[2]) See Summary, pp. 266-67.
[3]) See Summary, pp. 266-67.

the frequency of oscillation of the molecules is reduced. If the various states of weakness, disease, etc., cannot be eliminated so that the loosened connection may again be tightened and resume a normal function, then the living organism passes away, it becomes lifeless. The astral counterparts of the soft substances of the dead bodies and plants will be released and separated out, and after a shorter or a longer period of time they are absorbed by Darkness, only to be transformed into or to reappear in other forms.

By the separation of the astral counterparts and their earthly forms, the molecular oscillations of Darkness again become considerably reduced, with the result that the molecules entirely lose their resistance to attack by micro-organisms. The soft substances of the dead bodies and the withered plants will then decompose unless they are preserved artificially by drying, freezing or by chemical treatment, and they will be absorbed into the ground and the atmospheric layers. Later they are transformed again, partly into earthly and partly into astral forms.

The astral counterparts of the more solid substances of the dead bodies and plants such as bones, cornual tissue, teeth, bark and wood[1] are not released until these substances in one way or another are destroyed by mouldering, attack by fungus, burning or the like; but the connection between the counterparts and the earthly forms continues to be loose, i.e., the somewhat lower frequency is maintained. As these counterparts are gradually released, they are also absorbed by the astral Darkness.[2]

Even though the former Light-world of the Eldest had been completely saturated by the influx of Darkness, the Eldest were still able to distinguish and differentiate in the Darkness because of their divine origin, just as all the structures in the ravaged Kingdom were real and tangible to them, whereas everything on Earth which had been produced by the molecular oscillations of Darkness appeared to them as hazy and unreal forms of life.

When the Eldest on their journey across the Earth had seen that the plant and animal life of Darkness was destructible, they realized that they were unable to create immortal beings in their own like-

---

[1]) If leaves, flowers and stems are cut while they are still alive, and then shortly after subjected to dehydration or any similar process, the astral counterparts are not released until the forms, or anything manufactured from them, are destroyed in one way or another. If fresh twigs, shoots or branches are cut and then grafted or planted, the counterparts are not released; the connection that is loosened after the cutting is tightened by the renewed supply of nourishment.

[2]) See also Summary, p. 295.

ness; but in spite of this knowledge they decided nevertheless to create. However, their attempts invariably failed until they agreed upon taking the animals for a model,[1] especially concerning questions of propagation and nutrition.

For about two million years – a long time according to human perception – the Eldest worked at shaping their thoughts in the astral as well as in the earthly material.[2] Finally they succeeded in creating the first individual beings of the human race that were capable of surviving – animal-like creatures. But since many were involved in this work, and since their sense of form and beauty had been confused and distorted by the influence of Darkness and was no longer on a level with the capability of each individual's will, many very different types were created that were all only slightly superior to the animals.

Thus: *the human race did not descend through various evolutionary stages from the animals, but evolved from created beings.*

The manner in which the Eldest accomplished this act of creation will *never* be divulged to mankind.

5.

When the Eldest decided to create intelligent beings, having become convinced of the impossibility of leading the beasts that the vitalizing influence of Darkness had produced on Earth, it was rather with the intention that these, their own creatures, should assist them in the struggle against the gigantic monsters. Thus it was neither pure selfishness nor pure lust for power that motivated the Eldest during their attempts at creation. The spiritual counterparts of the first human beings were for this reason endowed with a faint element of spiritual life through that element of the Light that was in the thought that had formed the basis for their creation. Once given, this faint life-spark of spiritual Light could *not be taken back,* and it therefore had to be passed on from the first-created human beings to the progeny that they bore and bred. While new human bodies are formed during pregnancies, the astral counterparts are formed concurrently. They are given a faint element of spiritual life through the stream of Light that is carried by the waves of Darkness that constantly stream out from the Eldest, and which is transferred from them to human beings, who are infused by it. This heritage is thus given and received from generation to generation, and it will continue for as long as the Eldest by the circulation of Darkness through

---

[1]) See also Summary, pp. 267–70.
[2]) See also Summary, p. 269.

them are bound[1] to the human race.

Since the spiritual life element of the Light did not stem directly from God, but was given by beings who acted against His Will, it was not strong enough to impart conscious, independent thought and will to the creatures of the Eldest, neither in the earthly nor in the transcendental world. The "human shadows"[2] – the astral counterparts – were therefore condemned in advance, after the cessation of earthly life, to *exist for all eternity* without ever gaining *conscious knowledge* or *conscious understanding of* their own or their fellow creatures' existence.

Some of the oldest races of human beings have *in the apes* left a visible reminder of the primitive stage of development in which they languished for many millennia, until the Light was brought to the Earth and ennobled mankind.

Through many ages of time human beings remained, bodily as well as spiritually, at about the same level as the animals, and since Darkness had reigned practically everywhere on Earth at the time of their creation, they also became related by blood to all the mammals extant at that time. By mating with several different animal species[3] the first apes came into existence.

Since no element of the Light was present during the matings that were responsible for the emergence of the apes, and which took place only to satisfy the mating instincts of human beings, the astral counterparts of these creatures received none of the spiritual element of Light of their human ancestors; for which reason the apes, like all other beasts, are not endowed with spiritual life. After death, the astral counterparts of the apes are absorbed and converted into other forms in the same way as with all other astral counterparts.

Through the inter-breeding of the early apes and their own and their offspring's cross-breeding, partly with human beings and partly with other mammals, there gradually developed the profusion of ape species that are now found spread throughout the Earth, and of which certain species are more or less directly descended from human beings. Other species have through countless cross-breedings diverged radically from their human ancestors.

The regulating and Darkness-separating influence of the Light has removed human beings as well as most mammals far from their

---

[1]) See Summary, p. 322.

[2]) See Commentary, p. 189

[3]) Through frequent and very diverse cross-breeding, several of the animal species used in this way degenerated and became extinct. People with the requisite ability and interest can through careful research discover which prehistoric and contemporary animal species are related to some of the known apes.

12* C

former common blood relationship. As is well known, however, some such relationship can still be shown between human beings and the so-called anthropoid apes, just as a similar relationship can be shown to exist between certain mammals that superfically appear to be unrelated. However, these traces of a common blood relationship will gradually disappear completely.

The primitive state of the original human beings can be judged by the fact that even the most primitive contemporary races *can no longer* produce viable offspring through matings with animals.

When somewhat over a million years had passed since the creation of the first human beings, God called a second time upon the Eldest in order if possible to awaken their remorse. Some of the Eldest had long grieved over the dreadful life endured by their creatures on Earth, and through the deep desperation they felt for what had happened, they had come to understand the extent of the evil that they had done.

Their grief over their sin was so great and sincere that the moment they heard God's calling voice their *first* request for help was for their hapless creatures, before they thought of obtaining any betterment of their own miserable existence.

When God saw that their grief and remorse was genuine and deeply felt, He forgave them in His inifinite love and compassion all they had sinned against Him and promised at the same time to make their imperfect creatures His own children. Through the power of His Will God fulfilled His promise partly by sending a stream of His own divine Being to each human creature – to the "shadows" as well as to those who lived on Earth – and partly by adopting these newly formed human spirits into His Thought, and thus imparting *eternal life to the entire human race.* And from the moment God thus established a connection with mankind, the divine stream has flowed through *all* in an unbreakable cycle *and is imparted to every new creature at the time of conception.*[1]

When God informed His youngest children of His adoption of the creatures of the Eldest and asked them if they would be of help in leading these wretched beings out of Darkness, they all fell silent – they shrank before the enormous task they would have to take upon themselves if real help were to be afforded. And although they knew that no one would exert pressure upon them, even if they should give up before the work was completed, they dared not immediately accede to their Father's request.

---

[1]) See Commentary, pp. 188–90.

The thought of helping humanity according to God's wish awoke *first* in the female dual of the eldest of the Youngest. But the very moment she conceived compassion for mankind, this thought was seized by the male dual and with *his will* he turned her thought to action and came forward with the offer to support and to lead mankind. Through this voluntary act he gave life to the thought of his dual, but thereby *he* also assumed responsibility for its further execution.

If the eldest of the Youngest had not heeded the thought of his female helpmate her thought would *never* have come to life – to action – since the male power to act – *the will* – was required for the realization of such an overwhelming task, *for which reason he may rightfully be called the saviour and leader of mankind.*

From one of his incarnations, his last one, the eldest of the Youngest is known to human beings by the name *Jesus of Nazareth – Christ.*

As a reward for his voluntary offer, God not only placed in his hands the leadership of mankind, but He made him also the uppermost among the Youngest – the male as well as the female.

The eldest of the Youngest's dual has contributed her help in various ways through repeated incarnations, as have all of her younger brothers and sisters.

At the downfall of the Eldest – when God had confronted His children with Darkness – the thought that God's choice must fall upon them arose first among the female Eldest; but through the will of the male, the female thought of lust for power brought all of them to downfall. The thought of creating living beings also first arose within the Elder's female dual, but it was brought into action by *his* will. *The Elder consequently became the uppermost among the Eldest and rightfully bears the responsibility for the creation of the human race.*

It was thus a female *thought of lust for power* that brought sin and downfall, and a female *thought of compassion* that brought *the necessary help for regeneration.*

6.

When God had promised His remorseful children to take their spiritually and bodily malformed creatures into His care, and when all the Youngest had promised to help lead them out of Darkness, He decided to create habitats and dwellings, both for the Youngest and for the spirits of human beings, where they could abide whenever they were not incarnated on Earth.

If the Youngest had permanently resided in God's Kingdom during the time of their leadership of mankind, it would have become very difficult for them to subject themselves to the earthly order of time.

From the astral-material and the ethereal-astral Light that generates the material forms in the transcendental world God formed six habitats, or spheres, which together with the Kingdom created previously but ravaged by Darkness – i.e., "Hell" – constituted seven worlds of astral Light that surrounded the Earth.

In order that all of them, the Youngest as well as the spirits of human beings, could have access to the Earth in the future without having to pass through the Darkness of the ravaged Kingdom, God opened a pathway through the habitat of the Eldest by the power of His Will. He extended this pathway through all the spheres to the outermost one and let it be pervaded by the Light. This provided a pathway, a Passage of Light, directly to the Earth, so that all[1] of them could readily journey back and forth.

The transcendental dwelling places are as visible and material to spiritual beings as everything on Earth is to human beings. The higher the spirits advance in their struggle out of Darkness, the higher will be the ether-oscillations that produce the material from which these, their limited worlds, are formed. The farther the dwelling places are located from the Earth, the brighter, the more splendid, the more harmonious everything becomes, both dwellings and nature, e.g., seas, rivers, lakes, lands, flowers, etc. So long as the spirit stays in the sphere which it has reached by purification through its reincarnations – i.e., earthly rebirths – its body moves about in the same way as one moves about on Earth, i.e., by walking, running, etc. However, the movements of the released spirit are quicker and easier, just as the thoughts are more lucid and more precise than when the spirit is bound to the heavy earthly body that imposes so many restrictions upon it.

The means of transportation in the spheres are similar to those on Earth; however, they are all better, faster and more comfortable than those on Earth. All innovations and improvements that in the course of time have been brought to humanity have first been proved in the spheres, before they have become a reality on Earth.

If the Youngest do not wish to make use of the Passage of Light when communicating with inhabitants of the various spheres and of the Earth, they apply the energy of thought and will that lets the

---

[1]) However, the human spirits were only allowed to use this Passage of Light when accompanied by their guardian spirit, i.e., with the permission of God.

spiritual body be transported by the ether, which by virtue of the fourth dimension penetrates everything.

The fourth dimension cannot be explained in greater detail, since humanity as yet lacks the basis for an understanding of this concept.

The higher spheres are invisible to the inhabitants of the lower ones. The lower spheres are partly invisible to the inhabitants of the higher, and even the Youngest have only a moderately clear view of them, when, borne by the oscillations of the ether, they move from sphere to sphere, or from place to place within the various spheres.

The inhabitants of the lower spheres cannot on their own, either by thought and will or by the Passage of Light, ascend to worlds that are above their own sphere. They can descend only to the Earth[1] or to the lower spheres that lie in between, and only through the Passage of Light. However, within their home sphere and the sphere of the Earth, they are able to move about by thought and will, but only to a limited extent. They are thus unable to penetrate strong concentrations of Light or ethereal Light-radiations.

God's Servants and the Youngest can move about everywhere by the power of their thought and will, and therefore do not always make use of the Passage of Light. If they so desire, they can even make their way through the Earth's numerous accumulations of Darkness.

In the course of time God has created a number of animal figures for the enjoyment of human beings, for example birds, horses, dogs, cats, etc., so that they should not miss the purely earthly surroundings too much. However, these animals are not astral counterparts of earthly animals, but thought-forms without everlasting life. When the spheres have served their purpose as temporary habitations for the spirits, these animal figures, i.e., thought-images – creatures and objects – that are only temporarily contained in and by the Thought of God, can therefore have no eternal life and will disappear. By the Will of God they are then retracted into the substance from which He created them, they will dissolve and revert to their original state – the Light-ether. But so long as the spheres exist, human spirits will always be able to find reproductions there of the animals that they most cherished during life on Earth. And since God creates these animal figures to conform exactly to their earthly prototypes, everyone will be able to find his or her favourite horse, dog, cat, bird, and so on.

---

[1] See also Commentary, pp. 247–50.

In several of the accounts that departed human beings have conveyed to their earthly connections about life in the spheres, it is often stressed that the animals are endowed with everlasting life. This refers to the aforementioned thought-forms. However, there is some justification for such erroneous information that is given by deceased relatives and friends, since even the more advanced human spirits find it difficult to realize that these animals, which are apparently as alive as they themselves are, have only been endowed with temporary life. In a few cases where such messages have apparently been given by higher spirits, this erroneous information about the eternal life of animals must be ascribed to the Elder, who implanted these false thoughts while the communicating spirit was in contact with a medium. This has occurred quite often and cannot really be held against the mediums, since the Elder would of course avail himself of every opportunity to falsify any information given by the spirits of the Light.

But these and other false assertions could have been rectified in time if the mediums or the séance leaders had always analysed the various passages of every message and demanded verification that *all* was in exact agreement with the truth; *for where the truth was demanded in the name of God, the Elder would have had to yield.*

Through the eldest of the Youngest, God gives a broad outline of the life of each human being on Earth[1] and also determines its duration, all in agreement with that which can be allotted each individual on the basis of that person's thoughts, actions and progress in the preceding incarnation, as well as all that has not been atoned for from previous earthly lives. Before entering upon a new incarnation the spirit receives a message specifying how the forthcoming earthly life shall be lived, what demands will be made upon it, and for which deeds it shall atone. Not until the spirit has closely considered what is to come, has understood why the new incarnation must take the exact form specified and has accepted what has been proposed, will it be incarnated in that place and in those surroundings that are best suited to that particular purpose.

But since everything must take place on a voluntary basis, and as the human spirits, especially the undeveloped ones, do not always immediately understand the purpose to be served by a new incarnation and therefore often refuse to undertake such a venture, they must remain in their dwellings with no possibility of further progress open to them until, after the elapse of a shorter or longer period of time, they come to acknowledge and comprehend the advantages that they will achieve through a further incarnation. Once this recognition is achieved they can continue the temporarily interrupted

[1]) See Summary, pp. 307-10.

journey toward their Father's Home.

However, it is not left entirely to human beings themselves to overcome all earthly difficulties. In order to render effective help, guardian spirits[1] watch over them and try by influencing their thoughts – i.e., "stirring their conscience" – to guide every human being into the ways of life given by God. But since human beings are endowed with a free will, in the same way as the Eldest and the Youngest, and since they very seldom pay full attention to the admonitions of their conscience, the incarnation often becomes a sad departure from the specified plan; and as human beings frequently take their own lives instead of awaiting the time and manner of death appointed by God, they very often create much needless suffering for themselves.

A human being who commits suicide while in a delirium (i.e., unpremeditated suicide) will be reincarnated immediately after an account of the earthly life just ended has been given. These immediate reincarnations, without time for rest and learning, are given by God partly as a continuation of the abruptly terminated life, and partly so that the individual can move beyond the spiritual sufferings recently endured on Earth. Even if the new incarnation should be of short duration, the spirit will be able to look back upon the mental or physical anguish of the previous Earthly life with greater calm when it is again released. (Regarding premeditated suicide, see Speech of Christ, p. 114).

A guardian spirit is normally in charge of many human beings, sometimes several hundred, and is in direct thought-communication with all of them. The older the human spirit, the clearer and the more emphatic does the voice of conscience sound to that human being. The younger the human spirit, the more closely does Darkness surround the human being, and the fainter and more uncertain does the voice of conscience sound. Many human beings often hear two voices that contradict each other, one of which constantly opposes the admonitions of the conscience to follow the ways of truth and of the Light. *At the present time*[2] this argumentative voice is that of the human being's own selfish and undeveloped spirit, giving its own opinions on the questions or situations under consideration; but clearly nothing is gained by overriding the conscience in order to yield to the human being's own desire to sin and to commit evil deeds.

---

[1]) Guardian Angels.

[2]) During the time when the sin-bound spirits lived on the astral counterpart of the Earth (the Earth's astral plane) this opposing voice often stemmed from these wicked and evil beings, and in many cases it also stemmed from the Elder, who in that way tried to lead human beings astray. See also Ardor's Account, p. 29, Commentary, pp. 203–04, and Summary, pp. 307–09.

When the spirit at death is released once more from its earthly body, the guardian spirit brings it in a state resembling sleep[1] to the sphere and the dwelling that it left upon its incarnation.

Upon awakening, the spirit must carefully consider the earthly life just ended, must review *all thoughts and all actions* – the evil as well as the good – and account for *all* the occasions when, as a human being, it was in disagreement with its conscience. God Himself poses the questions to which He requires more detailed answers by letting His voice sound to all spirits who have completed the rendering of their accounts.

God speaks through His Thought, and by His Will he transforms the vibrations produced by His Thoughts into waves of sound. God normally "speaks" to thousands of spirits at a time; but each individual hears only the questions addressed to that spirit alone, and the words sound as though God spoke in the earthly language used in the spirit's latest incarnation. When all questions have been answered in accordance with the truth, the spirit is given once more into the care of the guardian spirit for protection during the time of rest.

When the allotted time of rest[2] is over the spirit is transferred to a better dwelling or to a higher sphere, if the spirit has become worthy of this through its life on Earth. If this is not the case it will remain in its former dwelling, for however much the human being has sinned, the spirit will never be relegated to a lower sphere or to a poorer dwelling. In the world of Light there is only progress or for a time standstill, *but there is never retrogression.*

After the time of rest, whether the spirit is transferred to another place or remains in its dwelling, it receives instruction[2] in the special matters that will be of use during the next incarnation.

In all the spheres there are numerous institutions of learning, corresponding to the schools and universities of the Earth. All scientific and literary works that exist, or have existed, on Earth are available there, reproduced in the earthly languages, except for the most primitive ones. Each institution of learning has its own large libraries with appropriate reading and study halls. All public buildings, churches, assembly halls, universities, observatories, museums, etc., display great architectural beauty and are adorned with many works of sculpture. Many of these buildings have been designed and built by human spirits during their time of learning and thus were not created by God by the power of His Thought and Will, but were constructed from the materials of the spheres, similar to those on Earth (stone, wood, etc.).

---

[1]) See Commentary, p. 204.
[2]) See section in small type, p. 185.

From the moment God endowed the human souls with life, He created them in the likeness of His first children, two by two, man and woman, so that when they had completed all the stages of their journeying and reached God's Kingdom, they would belong to each other for all eternity. Each retains his or her individuality. They are two, yet as one, *since one will always be a reflection of the other.*

Wherever possible, the human male and female duals accompany each other in their existence on Earth as man and wife, brother and sister or as other close relatives. But they do not always succeed in finding or understanding each other under earthly conditions.

Like God's other children, each human spirit is endowed by Him with the characteristic of its spirit-body, but this is not seen in its full beauty until the goal – God's Kingdom – is reached.

A description in broad outline is hereby given of the bodily appearance of the spirits.

The spirit-body, like the human body, consists of an outer form that encloses various internal organs. The outer form has the appearance of the most beautiful human body, many times idealized, but without sexual organs. (The female spirit-body is softer and more rounded than that of the male, but the actual difference in the outward appearance of the male and female cannot be explained, since human beings lack any basis for understanding this difference). The internal structure of the body bears only a remote resemblance to that of the earthly body. The physical digestive system consisting of the stomach, intestines, kidneys, etc., and all reproductive organs are non-existent, but the vascular and nervous systems are far more extensively and finely developed. By breathing in through the nose, the windpipe and lung-like organs, the body is supplied with the necessary ether currents, which then circulate through a finely and extensively ramified "vascular network" and back to the respiratory organs, where the currents are renewed. The vascular system is a double one. The network of vessels leading from the organ on the right side terminates on the left side, and vice versa. There are no blood-carrying vessels. If a spirit of the Light stays in or passes through accumulations of Darkness, a sensation is experienced similar to that of a human being breathing air of low oxygen content.

The spirit-body has no bone structure, but is nevertheless entirely firm in its construction, since it is supported everywhere by a strong musculature.

Instead of the human brain, but in the same place, there is a nerve centre from which an extremely fine network of nerves spreads from the head along the back and through the entire body. All the nerve fibres lead back to the brain-centre through a lesser centre that corresponds most closely to the human heart and is situated at approximately the same place; here the nerve-ends converge and lead through two cords, one on either side of the neck, back to the point of origin, the brain-centre.

Beings in the transcendental world need not take nourishment, if they do not wish to do so.

Nourishment, if taken, consists mainly of fruit,[1] which is consumed in the natural state or prepared in various ways. This nourishment is taken by mouth (the tooth structure of which is similar to that of the human body), is distributed through a finely ramified tubular system to the entire body, and is then imperceptibly secreted through miniscule pores of the skin by interaction between the tubular and vascular systems of the body and the surrounding ether of Light or of Darkness. The pores of the skin are not unlike those of the human body's pores for prespiration, but are much finer and are all connected directly with the tubular and vascular systems.

The spirit-body as it has been described here is alike for *all* spirits; but because the human spirit in the transcendental world is always an exact copy (see pp. 188–91) of the human embodiment of its previous incarnation, the spirit-body also contains duplicates of all the organs, etc. of the human body. In the transcendental world everything human remains completely latent – rests in a state of dormancy. On the other hand, for as long as the spirit is incarnated the organs of the spirit-body are at rest, since these can be used only when the spirit is released. But the nervous system of the spirit-body functions at all times, although to a lesser degree during life on Earth.

When the spirit has completed all its incarnations and is released from life on Earth, God removes by the power of His Will all the rudimentary organs that stem from its human existence, and the spirit-body then appears exactly as God created it.

7.

The moment the first frail seed of a new human body is formed at conception, it is endowed with its share of the divine stream of Light that binds humanity to God. Gradually, as the embryo develops, the divine element absorbs the faint spiritual Light given by the Eldest, which through the streams of Darkness is also received by every human embryo at the moment of conception, and thereby faintly brings to spiritual life, or animates, the astral counterpart of that human being. However, the counterpart itself[2] is not absorbed, since it is completely interwoven with the earthly body. The astral counterpart of Darkness is not loosened and separated until *after* the death of the earthly body has taken place.

---

[1]) All of the spheres abound in flowering and fruit-bearing trees and plants that are unknown on Earth. According to laws given by God, the fruits and flowers develop without pollination and have a flavour and fragrance far superior to those of the fruits on Earth.

[2]) See also Summary, pp. 274–75 and p. 289, regarding astral counterparts and dwellings in a state of disrepair.

When death has occurred, the astral connection to the soft substances[1] of the body is loosened, and the counterpart[2] is released and separated. The moment it is released it has the outward form and appearance of the dead body, but this likeness is only retained for a brief period of time – from five to twenty minutes. It then dissolves, becomes misty, is absorbed and disappears. The time of absorption differs, since it depends on various circumstances. If a person dies in the open air the counterpart is quickly absorbed, whereas the absorption is retarded in closed rooms.

If a person meets with sudden, violent death, with no preceding illness, it then takes longer before separation of the counterpart and the earthly body is completed. This span of time can vary from about two hours to about twenty-four hours.

At the birth of a child, the element of Light received from the Eldest is completely eliminated by the divine element that enshrouds the child's body as a faintly luminous cloud of mist, in which the frail human form can barely be' discerned from the transcendental world. As the child grows bodily, so in the same measure does the spiritual shroud of Light, but it still retains its misty appearance. When the physical body dies, whether at a tender age, in old age or in the years in between, the spiritual shroud of Light is released and at the same time condenses into an exact copy of the dead body. A new human spirit has thus been created, and in the earthly life that has just ended it has taken the first step on the difficult journey toward the Father's distant Home.

What has been stated here about the binding of a divine element to the human body holds true for every human embryo.[3] But in those cases where one of the Youngest is to be bound to a new human body, or a previously created human spirit is to continue its incarnations, the binding takes place during the fourth or fifth month of pregnancy. The spirit that is to be incarnated is brought to the Earth and bound to the foetus with the "life-giving"[4] cord – a resilient cord, fashioned from the finer substances of the Light and interwoven with the vascular and nervous systems of the human brain[4] in

---

[1]) What has been stated earlier – on page 177 – about the counterparts of the more solid substances of animal bodies also applies to the human body.

[2]) As stated earlier, the astral counterparts of the first human beings could not dissolve, because they were held together by the faint spiritual Light that had been brought to them from the Eldest. These counterparts – "shadows" – retained to some extent the outer form of the human body, but without any real firmness. Thus, at one moment they would dissolve into a mass of mist, and the next they would again assume a human form. In his Account, Ardor states that the shadows "wandered about", but undulated or floated would more aptly describe the movements of these counterparts.

[3]) Human foetus.

[4]) Ardor describes the cord as life-giving, because the spirit is connected by this cord to the brain of its physical body, thereby giving "spiritual life", i.e., thought and will to the human being. See also Summary, pp. 278–79.

such a way that only death can dissolve the bond.

Once bound to the foetus, the spirit remains in close proximity to the pregnant woman. As the formation of the foetus progresses the outer contours of the spiritual body gradually fade away, until the moment of birth when it merges with the child's body, enshrouds it like a mantle and takes on the appearance of a more or less luminous formation of mist, in which the human form of the child can be perceived from the transcendental world as a darker body.

When the spirit becomes united with the human body at the birth of the child, it slowly fuses, through absorption, with the divine element that the embryo received at the moment of conception. This divine element thus enriches the spirit with an ever greater spiritual strength at each new incarnation, if it is a human spirit. But if one of the Youngest is bound to the child, the divine element merges with the spirit without adding further spiritual strength, since each of the Youngest is on an infinitely higher level than even the most advanced human spirit.

If the foetus dies before it is fully developed the spirit that is bound to it is released, and within a very short time it has resumed the appearance it had before it was bound to the foetus – the incarnation will thus not be completed. If the spirit is united with the child during birth – has taken on its appearance – and the child dies soon after birth, the spirit, in the form of the child, is brought back to the spheres and grows up there in foster homes until the age of maturity is reached, upon which it enters a new incarnation. These periods during which spirits grow up like children in the spheres are regarded as times of rest and learning.

The foregoing holds true for *all human spirits* whose earthly bodies die during childhood.

When the Youngest are released at death from their earthly existence, their spiritual bodies retain the forms of the human body until, after the elapse of a shorter or a longer period of time, they have rendered a careful account of what they have accomplished among human beings; the spirit then assumes once more the appearance that it received from God. If the Youngest are bound to human bodies that die during childhood, they do not grow up in the foster homes of the spheres as do human spirits, but are brought by their guardian spirit to their home in the last sphere where, after a short rest and by the power of God's Will, they assume their original form. Much unnecessary delay would otherwise be caused to the work of the Youngest for the progress of mankind.

The Youngest can assume any of the forms of their previous incarnations whenever they so wish or whenever it may for some reason or another become necessary. They often avail themselves of this capability when they visit human spirits in the various spheres, so that these may recognize the relative or friend who became dear to them during a contemporary incarnation.

Since the younger and undeveloped spirits normally stay only for a short time in the spheres (from five to thirty years), human beings cannot expect after every incarnation to meet *all* their departed relatives and friends. However, it is always ensured that human beings who loved each other or were friends during an earthly incarnation can meet each other from time to time during their sojourn in the spheres.

Human spirits who have had common spiritual interests, sympathetic connections and the like during their earthly existence often form larger or smaller circles. The various members of these circles will then meet sometimes in the earthly and sometimes in the transcendental existence; and when they have all overcome the power of Darkness through the strength of their will for the Light, and have thus completed their many reincarnations, those who have come together will *all simultaneously* be transferred to one of the globes in the distant star universes, so that they may there complete their spiritual development.

When released, the human spirits retain the characteristics of their earthly body until a new incarnation is begun. Then, as stated earlier, they assume the appearance of the new-born human child and develop accordingly as it grows up and lives its life.

If the human being dies at an older or at a very old age, the released spirit retains the characteristics of this age until it has rendered the account of its life on Earth. It then assumes the appearance that the human body had between thirty and forty years of age.

The spirit remains connected to the body by the life-giving cord during spontaneous release, which may arise during serious illness when the body is unconscious under the attack of fever, or through an accident that causes the body to faint, or under narcosis or the like. Human beings sometimes retain vague memories from this separation of the spirit and the body.

The spirit remains bound to the physical body by the life-giving cord also during sleep release[1], even though the spirit may be in the spheres while the body is asleep. Such nocturnal release is permitted in cases where the spirit has undertaken some mission to be carried out in a human existence. When necessary it can from time to time return to its dwelling in the transcendental world, where it can gain strength for the earthly task through consultation with its spiritual leaders.

---

[1]) See also Summary, pp. 292–93.

So that the Youngest and the human spirits may be capable of eliminating the Darkness that unceasingly pervades the human body, an absorption layer is automatically formed by the power of God's Will at the time of birth. This absorption layer is formed from the finer substance of Light and surrounds the entire body as a closely fitted casing about 1/8 millimetre in thickness. The casing is itself enclosed by the spirit, which, after being united with the child and absorbing the divine element, constantly absorbs and to a greater or lesser extent eliminates the Darkness that unceasingly streams through the astral body from the Eldest. This Darkness was originally depolarized by the spiritual element of Light that formed the basis for the creation of mankind.

Seen from the transcendental world the human being resembles an egg-shaped, more or less strongly luminous misty formation, in which the human contours can only vaguely be discerned. The first to be seen in the misty formation is the spirit in human form, somewhat more faintly luminous than the enshrouding Light. Within the contours of the spirit-body can be seen a darker body. This is the human body itself together with its astral counterpart, framed by a luminous line – the casing. The higher and purer the spirit that is bound to the human being, the more strongly luminous are the misty formation and the radiations of the spirit-body – the aura.

The absorption layer serves also as an insulation layer, since the side of the casing that is turned toward the spirit is such that it can normally exclude the knowledge, characteristics, memories and experiences that are possessed by the spirit bound to the body, and which must not be conveyed through the life-giving cord to the human (i.e., physical) brain. The connection between the spirit and the earthly body is arranged in such a way[1] that only as much of the intelligence of the spirit can flow through it *as is necessary to produce the human personality in the forthcoming life on Earth.* Through the brain[2] the human being maintains communication with the spirit, so that all the knowledge and experience acquired by the human being during the many lives on Earth *become the permanent possession of the spirit.*

If the spirit, while it is bound to a human body, were not protected by an insulation layer it would be brought too closely into contact with the physical brain. This would cause the sufferings associated with residing in the earthly environment to become unendurable, especially where the Youngest are concerned. The memory of life in

---

[1]) See also Summary, pp. 278–79.
[2]) See also Summary, pp. 277–89.

God's Kingdom and the yearning to return there would then inevitably become so crushing and depressing *that the Youngest would be incapable of carrying out their work for humanity's journey toward the Light.*

At the time of death, the insulation layer is loosened and absorbed by the Light in the course of three to six hours. However, there have been instances where, because of accumulations of Darkness, the Light has not been strong enough to absorb the insulation layer within the allotted time. These casings have as a result often lingered for years in the place where the corresponding earthly body had expired. Because the casings bear an unmistakable resemblance to the body they once enclosed, clairvoyants have on occasion incorrectly assumed them to be the spirits of the deceased[1] – i.e., ghosts.

Thus: *a human being is composed primarily of an earthly body and its astral counterpart, with the addition of an absorption and insulation layer that enables the spirit to eliminate the streams of Darkness from the Eldest and prevents the memories of experiences from previous incarnations from exerting a disturbing influence on the individual's conduct of life. In addition there is the spiritual self (thought, will and spirit-body) which is represented either by a newborn or by a more advanced spirit, which is bound to the human body by a cord, or bond, that severs and is dissolved at the time of death of the human body.*

In the earthly three-dimensional world, the casing, spirit-body, cord and the spiritual shroud of Light have no space-filling properties.

Since animals are not endowed with everlasting spiritual life – no spirit being bound to animal bodies – animals, in contrast to human beings, have no absorption and insulation layer.

The "intelligence", or instinct, of animals is retained from individual to individual in the brain of the astral counterpart, which so affects the animals' earthly brain that they live their earthly lives entirely by instinct and impulse. (A further explanation is given in the Summary, pp. 295–96).

8.

The civilized realms[2] that were destroyed in the remote past by mighty natural catastrophes varied greatly in size and in the level

---

[1]) See Commentary, p. 255.
[2]) In order to achieve a better survey, the accounts of the three vanished empires have been amalgamated. See also Ardor's Account, pp. 22, 26 & 28.

of civilization of their peoples.

The oldest empire, located in the Pacific Ocean, was the largest in size. In the very remote past it was geographically attached to the northern part of South America, but was separated by volcanic eruptions and subsidence of the ocean floor. The numerous island groups of Polynesia still show evidence of this land's existence and in part of its location. In about 30,000 B. C. this realm perished. It was split up into larger and smaller islands, which also came about through volcanic eruptions and subsidence of the ocean floor. The devastation continued for about eight centuries. The realm was completely destroyed, all plant and animal life vanished and only the highest-lying areas remained. Later, because of shifts in the ocean floor, some of the submerged parts reappeared as islands.

This empire's inhabitants were the ancestors of the Malayan people. However, the Malays of today are no longer of pure descent, but have been greatly intermingled through association with other people and are spiritually much less advanced than were their prehistoric forefathers.

In the most ancient times, during the many earliest millennia after the Youngest had begun their educational work among mankind, the peoples of the Pacific empire were predominantly sun and fire worshippers. Though the empire stretched over vast areas, it was only sparsely populated. The people lived in tribes or families of various sizes under the leadership of a chief. They were all at about the same cultural level.

The eldest of the Youngest underwent his first two incarnations[1] in this Pacific empire. In his first incarnation he was the chief, or leader, of the empire's largest and most important tribe, which at this time was still at a rather low cultural level. For this reason his work among these people had no lasting significance.

In his second incarnation, about two thousand years before the destruction of the empire, his rank and mission can best be described as that of high priest. By his authoritative yet gentle manner, he succeeded in calling to life among his people the belief in a Deity of Love. However, by that time the Eldest had already tried for millennia, and by every possible means, to undermine the work of the Youngest among humanity. And as the spiritual influence of the Eldest became ever greater, polytheism prevailed and the "new" God, the God of Kindness and Love to whom the sun was dedicated as a symbol, became more stern and cruel in the minds of the people. He was elevated to highest god, and under the constant influence of the Eldest was made into a terrifying monster of cruelty. The symbol of this highest god was the all-consuming, all-destructive fire; and to satisfy the ever-rising demands for atrocities that the priests in the name of this "divine" monster imposed upon the

---

[1] Not mentioned directly in Ardor's Account, since it was deemed unnecessary by the transcendental world. – Publisher's note.

people the first human sacrifices took place, and over the years they became more frequent and gruesome. A much favoured punishment for religious transgressions was to hurl the transgressors into a deep extinct crater.[1] If the victims were not crushed to death by the fall they died from starvation, because anyone caught offering help was liable to suffer the same punishment.

The Teotihuacans, or the Mlawayans, lived mostly by hunting, fishing and barter. Agriculture was known only to a few tribes and was not organized. The first primitive boat originated here and was made from dried animal hides. The bow and the stern were held together by plant fibres. The middle of the boat was distended by pointed sticks, it was steered by a forked branch and drifted with the current along the rivers; oars were unknown.

During the destruction of the empire large numbers of the population fled toward the west. The flight took place in boats that were better constructed and better equipped than the type mentioned above, and which bore a strong resemblance to the boats of the Eskimo people. The refugees and their descendants arrived by way of the intervening islands at the eastern and southern shores of Asia.[2]

Other inhabitants fled toward the east and reached – also by way of the intervening islands – South, Central and North America where they became the ancestors of the Indians, the so-called indigenous peoples of America. Some of the many types of Indian evolved from the union between the Teotihuacans and a primitive, animal-like people – the true aborigines – whom they encountered upon arrival in America. The inhabitants of Tierra del Fuego and the Eskimos are the most direct descendants of the aborigines of America. None of the Youngest had been incarnated among these beings, and consequently the level of their development was extremely low, but they still ranked somewhat above the first human beings in intelligence. This slight spiritual progress was due to the divine element that every human embryo has been given since God endowed humanity with spiritual life.

The second empire that perished was a large island in the Atlantic Ocean, the so-called Atlantis. In the remote past this island was connected with the southern part of North America, but through volcanic activity it became separated from the mainland.

The shape of the island can reasonably well be compared to a diagonally elongated, inverted Latin "S" – the upper curve at the right, and the lower at the left. The island's northernmost point extended to about latitude 40 degrees North, longitude 34 degrees West. The island extended south to about latitude 25½ degrees North, and west to longitude 47 degrees West, latitude 27½ degrees North, and eastward to about longitude 28 degrees West. An imaginary line from the town of Plymouth in England to the centre

---

[1]) See Ardor's Account, p. 22.
[2]) Any indication of locality is given by present-day geographical names.

of the island of Trinidad would cut through the length of the island and touch its easternmost and southernmost points. Thus, the larger half of the island would lie west of this line. The position given is only an approximate one, since the coastline of the sunken island is constantly changing due to major or minor upheaval and subsidence in the ocean floor; investigations that might be undertaken would show it to be within the indicated area.

The area of the island was 5/6 that of the Iberian peninsula. The Azores, located North North East and East of the island, were uninhabited at that time, but they had been connected with it in a more remote past.

Some minor groups of islands were situated between the Azores and the Iberian peninsula; there were also some small islands South West and South East of the Atlantic island, but all of these have now disappeared.

This island empire was destroyed about 12,000 B.C. by subsidence of the ocean floor in conjunction with violent volcanic eruptions.

Earthquakes and volcanic activity ravaged the entire island for about ten months until the final catastrophe completely destroyed and obliterated the rich and cultured empire within a few hours. The final eruption created a flood, the effect of which reached far and wide. The memory of this flood is still retained in the ancient legends of many peoples.

Polytheism predominated here also, but at that time without human sacrifice. However, animals were sacrificed throughout the island. The inhabitants were sun and fire worshippers. The people were generally at a high cultural level. The priests had quite an advanced knowledge of astronomy – several were astrologers[1] or magi – and were able to distinguish between the planets and the fixed stars and to calculate approximately the eclipses of the sun and the moon; however, they attributed these phenomena to the intervention of an evil spirit.

The art of printing made its first primitive appearance on this island, the priests having managed, by a form of hectography, to produce multiple copies of the written accounts. For this purpose an extract of crushed animal and fish bones was used, which after careful distillation was poured into flat earthenware moulds. Closely woven fabrics of plant fibres were used, since neither papyrus nor parchment was known at the time. Impressions were made with a printing ink consisting mainly of burnt bone mixed with some adhesive substance. Pictographic text was mostly used, though ideographs were used in some places.

Agriculture, hunting, fishing and a certain amount of animal husbandry were known. Several of the merchants traded with the surrounding islands and the nearest mainland coasts. The production by hand of clay utensils was widespread.

---

[1]) See Summary, p. 317.

Basins, bowls and vases were often engraved with ornamental animals and leaves, whose outlines were filled in with brilliant colours. Gold, copper and to some extent silver were all known and used for jewelry and finer utensils, as well as for inlays in the carved wooden images of the gods. Many such images were hewn in stone or formed out of various metallic alloys. The art of building was especially highly developed. Lyrical poetry was coming into being, especially in the form of religious hymns that were intoned by the priests to the accompaniment of the beating of cymbal-like copper plates at the sacrificial rites. The cult of death was known over the entire island.

The island was divided into three realms that had a common sovereign ruler. In one of the realms the succession to the rulership descended by both the male and the female lines. The supreme ruler was in addition the chief servant of the temple.

On this island the eldest of the Youngest was incarnated for the third time, as prince and high priest.

He was greatly loved by the people for his humane and gentle rule, he made several religious and ethical laws, but his attempts to abolish polytheism did not succeed. His incarnation on this island left few traces upon the culture of the people, since he died in the same year that the island disappeared into the sea. His memory lived with those who escaped the destruction by fleeing and was preserved through many generations. He was regarded as a divine emissary.

Some of the islanders who survived the catastrophe fled via the intervening islands to the coast of North Africa and slowly, through several generations, migrated as nomads eastward to the valley of the Nile, where they settled. Legendary accounts can be found in ancient Egyptian scriptures telling of a God of the Light who for a time assumed human form. These accounts refer to the incarnation of the eldest of the Youngest on the vanished island.

A few individual islanders fled to the Iberian peninsula and were assimilated by the people living there; others reached Central America, where they encountered descendants of the Teotihuacans (or Mlawayans). After long and bloody conflicts they succeeded in seizing territories extending from the peninsula now known as the Yucatan,[1] over the Isthmus of Panama[1] to the northwestern coast of South America. From there they spread northward to large areas of Mexico and southward and south westward along the coast to the lands that are now known as Peru and the upper part of Chile.

The culture that they brought with them became greatly influenced by that of the Teotihuacans, especially with respect to idolatry and the associated human sacrifice. The people from the island kingdom gradually merged with the Teotihuacans, their culture degenerated and their descendants, the Nahuacans, Aztecs, Incas, Toltecs and several other tribes whose names are only remembered in ancient Indian legends, never attained the high cultural level of the Island people.

---

[1] Large stretches of the coasts of Central America, where the Island people settled, have since perished through volcanic upheavals.

The smallest of the three vanished empires lay in the eastern part of Central Africa, just below the Abyssinian mountains (South South West and South South East of the mountains).

The religious cult in this realm was rather more highly developed, it was very simple and beautiful. The highest god, Ra, god of the sun and god of creation was also the deity of peace and love. Under him ranged a number of gods and goddesses, among whom Shunut, the god of fire, ranked highest as protector and guardian of the land. Human sacrifice all but ceased in the last centuries before the country perished. The people were extremely warlike; their ruler had subjugated many of the neighbouring tribes and his dominion reached to the head waters of the Nile. The last ruler of the empire was called Kharu – the dark prince, or more literally, he who is dark and tall, he who towers above all others. The name of the realm was Khuum, i.e., valley, depression or lowland. The largest city was called 'Lukna-Tee-Ra,[2] i.e., the property of the god Ra, the city consecrated to Ra. The inhabitants were culturally less advanced than the Islanders, but hunting and river fishing were known, as were to some extent agriculture and mining. Material for the great palaces of stone was quarried from the mountains and decorated with bright ornaments of lava in many different colours.

Despite the warlike tendencies of the people in relation to their cultural level, they had achieved a deep and sincere belief in a just and gentle deity, and their form of religious worship was superior to that of other civilized countries. The eldest of the Youngest was therefore not incarnated there, since the people would have been incapable of accepting and comprehending more than had already been given them by the many of the Youngest who were or had been incarnated among them.

The priests had some knowledge of astronomy, knew of the moon's orbiting around the Earth, but did not understand how to calculate precisely the eclipses of the sun and the moon. The priests were also magi, and no important undertakings were begun before they had pronounced the consent of the gods. The dead were laid to rest in rock tombs; rulers, priests, warlords, and the members of the more prominent families were honoured by special death rites.

The land was destroyed by a volcanic eruption about 10,000 B.C., and was buried completely under lava and huge boulders. In several places the Earth opened in broad, gaping fissures.

Large numbers of inhabitants survived the catastrophe and fled northward along the Nile, and there in its valley – the later Egypt – they found a young, highly civilized kingdom created by the people whose forefathers had survived the destruction of the Island Empire.

---

[1] The apostrophe in "'Lukna . . ." denotes a sound almost like the vowel "e". The word 'Lukna was represented by one of the two symbols of Ra: 1) Several triangles, together describing a star, symbolizing the many, all-seeing eyes of Ra; or 2) a ring – the sun disk – symbolizing Ra, the creator. Sometimes these symbols were bordered by flaming tongues or rays.

The refugees[1] intermingled with the inhabitants of the Nile valley, but although the Khuummi people were in the minority they succeeded in retaining some of their culture and imprinting upon the people of the Nile some elements of their form of worship, which gradually merged into the cult prevailing there that was based upon the memories and traditions from the peoples of the vanished Atlantic island.

Other refugees migrated southward, lived as nomads, wandered from place to place, intermingled with much inferior tribes and finally met with extinction.

9.

When the Elder of the Eldest stepped forward and defended the common desire for incarnation, after God had warned the Eldest against letting themselves be incarnated, he spoke of the beauty of the Earth and the joy of mankind as seen with human eyes – not of the Earth and all that was in it as seen from the transcendental world.

Whenever they wish, and by the power of their will, both the Eldest and the Youngest are able for short periods of time to utilize human organs of sight, in much the same way as human beings use binoculars. The spirit who wishes to "see" with earthly eyes stands behind a human being, thrusts aside the spirit that is bound to the human body by so much that, for an instant, the upper part of the body is deprived of the enshrouding spiritual light, and the spirit wishing to see leans forward until its organs of sight are aligned with those of the human being – and the purpose is achieved.

When employed by the Eldest this procedure often had a harmful effect on the human being used in this way, since the Eldest invariably enshrouded their victims in a cloud of Darkness, thus dragging them spiritually downward. In those cases where the spirits of the Light have used this procedure, no harmful effect resulted of course, since the spirits of the Light *never* impart any Darkness whatsoever to their-mediums.

The disembodied *human spirits* can only dimly and indistinctly see in this way, since their will is not so strong that by the strength of it they can with their spiritual sight break the resistance that is offered by the – to all spiritual beings – more solid substance of the casing and the astral counterpart. Thus, whatever is seen in this way appears to the human spirits as grey, hazy images, without light or shadow.

When the Eldest had disregarded God's warning and had all agreed to incarnate themselves as human beings, they attempted to

---

[1] After the migration of the Khuummi peoples into Egypt, two further immigrations from the south took place, with centuries between, by tribes related to the initial immigrants.

bind themselves to human foetuses by means of Darkness, on the supposition that if their younger brothers and sisters could be bound to human bodies, so could they likewise be bound. But they forgot *that God's Thought and Will guided and directed the action of the Youngest;* and the many attempts by the Eldest on their own invariably failed. Not one of them was able to fashion from Darkness an insulation layer that was sufficiently dense to prevent their spiritual selves from establishing too close a contact with the human brain, for which reason they failed to achieve their objective, namely, to forget their fearful experiences in the Kingdom of Darkness.

The Elder nevertheless continued to experiment with Darkness until he succeeded at last in creating an insulation layer[1] that to some extent prevented the spirit from manifesting itself too strongly in the human personality, and he then promised to incarnate his brothers and sisters.

The first appearance of the Eldest as human beings occurred about half a century before the destruction of the Atlantic island, for which reason many of those who were incarnated there experienced this dreadful catastrophe.

When the Elder, after helping his fellow sufferers, wished to incarnate himself he was unable to prevent his own strong personality from breaking through the protecting layer; and since he did not possess the ability of God for limitation of the self he understood that although bound to a human body he would have to remain the being he was. An earthly life under such conditions was unthinkable, since instead of bringing him oblivion it would create intolerable suffering for him. He therefore had to abandon his contemplated incarnation as a human being.

In contrast to the spirits of the Light, who are bound to the human foetus between the fourth and fifth month of pregnancy, the spirits of Darkness, the Eldest, were already bound in the third month.

God's Helpers and the Youngest, who direct the incarnations of human beings, always make certain that a male spirit is bound to a male body, and a female spirit to a female body. The reverse has *never* occurred, neither in respect of human spirits nor of the Youngest.

The Elder, on the other hand, incarnated the spirits of Darkness at random. Often a male spirit would be bound to a female body[2] – or

---

[1] By earthly measurement, this insulation layer of Darkness is approximately ½ millimetre in thickness.

[2] See also Commentary, p. 201.

vice versa – whereby the incarnations of these wretched beings became *a succession of indescribable sufferings.*

When the Elder realized that he alone (having also incarnated his female dual) had to remain as his own self in the Darkness without being able to achieve the desired oblivion, his *hatred of everything and everyone* awoke; and with the mighty curses that he hurled against humanity and against those who had fallen with him, *hatred* was brought into the world, and Darkness gained yet greater power over the inhabitants of the Earth.

The curses that he hurled against the Youngest also had a strongly adverse effect upon their work for the progress of humanity, since only the deepest love, the most profound compassion and the greatest patience are able to destroy and eliminate hatred, and thereby overcome and resolve its curses. The greater the love of the Youngest for their fallen brother, the better they understood his anger and hatred, and the easier it became for them to overcome the Darkness that by the power of his curses he had gathered about them during their incarnations. But although everyone among the Youngest loved their elder brother when they were not incarnated and would do everything within their power to win him back, it became extremely difficult for them during their human existence to escape the human fear and terror *of him who was the highest representative of evil.* However, with each incarnation lived in compassion for humanity, out of love for the Elder and with the desire to deliver him from Darkness, the power of his curses gradually diminished, bringing the Youngest closer and closer to their goal.

The curses that the Elder had hurled against those brothers and sisters who had shared his downfall caused them to fight incessantly among themselves and to oppose the Elder's plans and proposals. In order to punish those who defied him, the Elder often refused their request to be incarnated. But forced by the absolute will of his brothers and sisters to be incarnated, he would in most cases be compelled to do so. He then avenged himself by incarnating them under the worst possible conditions. For instance, he often incarnated them among primitive tribes or bound a male spirit to a female human body, or vice versa, and so forth.

The curses that the Elder hurled against God were blotted out by the power of God's Will the moment they were uttered; otherwise they would have rebounded and destroyed the Elder himself.

God immediately obliterates all curses that are thought or uttered against Him. Because of His infinite love and compassion, *He will not allow* His children to forfeit the gift of eternal life, no matter how much they sin, no matter how deep they fall. *Nothing can shake God's deep, infinite love and compassion for all fallen beings.*

The thoughts of the Eldest, both the incarnated and the disincarnated, are so strong that the evil they call down upon the person who is the object of their hatred can become reality. However, the power of the curses is weakened or diminished in the same measure as the person against whom they have been uttered is aware of God's omnipotence. And if curses are directed at human beings who have completely and unreservedly submitted to God's guidance with faith and trust in His love and justice, then those curses will completely lose their power, *since no evil can harm human beings who know that they are under God's protection.*

This holds true for all human beings, regardless of the religion or the sect within the various religions to which they belong. Even people of primitive religious beliefs (polytheism, fetishism or the like) are fully protected against the onslaughts of Darkness if they turn to their deity in childlike trust, because God at all times extends His help to whoever calls upon Him sincerely and with absolute trust in His omnipotence, *regardless of the name by which He is invoked, and regardless of the form which this invocation takes.*

Even though the curses of the Eldest *can strike* their objective, the repercussions will sooner or later turn against *the Eldest themselves* and cause them the same suffering, grief and misfortune that they have called down upon others.[1] This is the Law of Retribution.

Persons to whose bodies human spirits are bound have, on the other hand, no power to bring the miseries of Darkness upon the heads of their fellow human beings by uttering curses.[2] But since every thought – good as well as evil – returns to its originator after the elapse of a shorter or a longer period of time, the curses thus turn exclusively upon the person who uttered them *and bring upon the individual the same misfortunes and sufferings that were intended for others.*

When the Eldest against God's Will incarnated themselves on Earth their ability to draw Darkness closely about human beings was enhanced, since all the evil of Darkness and all base passions were concentrated in the spiritual selves of these Eldest, and their lust for power drove them to seek the most prominent positions in all walks

---

[1]) See Speech of Christ, pp. 111 & 113.

[2]) Since human beings influence one another through their thoughts, those who utter curses are in danger of inciting by way of thought their fellow human beings to utter similar curses in hate and anger, which will then bring fresh consequences upon the originator. See Summary, pp. 309-10.

of life, even though they attained their objectives through countless crimes, through the breaking of both divine and human laws.

As far back as history can be traced one can find accounts from all the countries on Earth of such figures, men as well as women, who in hatred, evil, crime and lust for pomp and power infinitely exceed the average human being.

By thus knowingly bringing immeasurable sufferings upon their own creatures – the human beings – the Eldest brought themselves under the Law of Retribution, the law under which every human being lives the many lives on Earth.

However, when some of the Eldest after a few incarnations realized what sufferings they had brought upon themselves through their embodiment as human beings, some of them decided to remain in the ravaged Kingdom rather than face as human beings the harsh repercussions of the Law of Retribution. But despite his many attempts to do so the Elder was incapable of restoring to the Eldest their full spiritual personality, so that they could all become "themselves" from the time before their first appearance as human beings. Those who chose to remain in the ravaged Kingdom therefore appeared as exact copies, both spiritually and bodily, of the earthly beings to whom they had been bound during their most recent human embodiment. These beings then tried to create in the world ravaged by Darkness an existence for themselves resembling life on Earth. Through the power of their thought and their will they fashioned from the astral substance of Darkness shadow-dwellings and shadow-realms in the likeness of those on Earth; but these imitations were colourless and they more resembled cities and dwellings in a state of disrepair.

In order to render existence there more pleasant they used their strong will to force weak and sinful human spirits to populate this world of Darkness after the death of their earthly bodies and to serve them as their slaves. In this way great multitudes of human spirits were prevented from returning to the spheres about the Earth.

The Eldest who continued their incarnations gathered large accumulations of Darkness about themselves while they were embodied on Earth. These accumulations of Darkness that were attracted by the strong radiations of Darkness from their spirit-bodies similarly bound thousands upon thousands of human spirits to wander about on the Earth after the death of their earthly bodies, instead of ascending to their appointed dwellings in the spheres. However, Darkness and the evil will of the Eldest had power only over sinful and dissolute human beings and human spirits; but since these have always been predominant in number, the astral plane of the Earth soon became overcrowded with the spirits of the dead, who wandered restlessly and uncomprehendingly about among the living, keeping mainly to the places where they had lived their last lives on Earth. And since the human being after death is an exact copy, both spiritually and bodily, of the person before death, these sinful and depraved beings caused a great deal of harm and disturbance among the living, often through their thoughts inciting susceptible people to wicked and criminal action.

The disincarnated Youngest tried unceasingly to help these restless spirits, who by staying on the astral plane of the Earth broke the laws that God had given for the life of human spirits in the spheres; but their efforts stranded more often than not upon the will for evil of the spirits themselves – and their numbers increased rather than diminished. *At times there were more "dead" than living upon the Earth.*

Authentic accounts from the earliest historical times and from all the peoples of the Earth tell of these apparitions,[1] which were often seen and heard by clairvoyant[2] and clairaudient human beings.

During the millennia in which the earthbound spirits wandered about on the astral plane of the Earth, many of the laws that God had given for the human spirit's binding to and release from the human body were broken by these wicked and sinful beings, who tried in every way to bring sin, grief and suffering upon mankind.

Among the laws thus violated was the so-called "Law of Sleep", which will be further explained in the following.

According to this law, the spirit of a human being was normally lulled to sleep by the guardian spirit, when death of the physical body had occurred. This was done in order to facilitate the release of the spirit from the lifeless body, and in order that the spirit should not acquire any gruesome memories of the deceased body to which it had been bound. But if, for instance, the dying person had many *unrepented* sins on his or her conscience, or if the cause of death was suicide, a great many of the earthbound spirits would gather around the dying or deceased body. These beings of Darkness would then hamper the guardian spirit in rendering assistance at the critical moment, and consequently the released spirit would be exposed to the risk of witnessing the dead body, the grief of the bereaved, the cremation or interment of the body,[3] its decomposition, and so forth.

---

[1] See Commentary, pp. 234–36 and p. 255. See also Summary, p. 319.
[2] See Commentary, p. 255.
[3] Since the cord by which the spirit is bound severs at the time of death of the physical body, it is entirely out of the question that the spirit can feel any suffering at all by cremation of the remains. Any accounts to the contrary are due to undeveloped and therefore ignorant spirits, or to imagination on the part of mediums.

However, since the astral plane of the Earth has now been cleansed of all earth-bound spirits and of all spirits bound in sin,[1] there is no longer any hindrance to the guardian spirit in extending the aforementioned help to each of the dying. Even the most sinful person (a murderer, suicide or the like) *will now and in the future always be lulled to sleep on the death of the physical body and will not awaken to consciousness until the spirit has been brought by the guardian spirit to that sphere in which the dwelling of the spirit is located.*

The spirits of the Light will always be present to extend their aid at major catastrophes or during wars, when many people lose their lives at the same time.

The Law of Sleep is applied only in few of the cases in which the Youngest are released from their deceased physical bodies, since these exalted spirits experience as a rule only a deep and intense joy over their deliverance.

With the accumulations of Darkness that in various ways were drawn across the Earth by the spirits bound in sin, new difficulties were created for the Youngest, who at the time of the first incarnations[2] of the Eldest had achieved many good results among human beings.

The strenuous spiritual struggle against the incarnated Eldest came almost to the point of breaking the courage of the Youngest and of crushing their hopes of leading the Light to a final victory over Darkness. *Only the never-failing love of the eldest of the Youngest for his fallen brothers and sisters and for suffering humanity prevented them from abandoning the struggle.*

When the Youngest at the request of their elder brother turned to their Father to ask Him for greater help in the difficult struggle against Darkness, God renewed His promise to support them, partly by giving them still greater spiritual strength, and partly by calling upon the earthbound spirits at the last hour of each passing century, in order if possible to awaken their memory and their remorse.

Having comforted and strengthened them all, God sent a host of them to be incarnated among the Jewish people, where at that time there were the best prospects that a large and concerted effort by the powers of the Light might bear fruit.

Those who were sent to the Jewish people were also to prepare the way for the incarnation of the eldest of the Youngest as Jesus of Nazareth.

Before the Youngest leave the spheres to let themselves be born as

---

[1] See Ardor's Account, pp. 100-01, and Commentary, pp. 234-39.
[2] About 12,000 B.C.

human beings, God speaks with them and gives them guidance in broad outline for their work on Earth; but God names only the main points and the limits for the conduct of their lives. Within this framework given by God they must themselves under the leadership of their guardian spirit find the ways and means most suitable to the fulfilment of the task with which they are entrusted.

In His discussion with the eldest of the Youngest prior to his incarnation as Jesus of Nazareth, God pointed out to him that the times on Earth were evil, and that human beings were in dire need. This was said so that he should be fully aware of *the difficulty of the task that was assigned to him,* a task that he might still not be able to fulfil.

Since it was the Gospel of Love that the eldest of the Youngest was to bring suffering and struggling humanity, it was necessary for him, in his life on Earth as Jesus of Nazareth, to bring his deep and fervent love to his earthly brothers and sisters. But in order to bring the full truth he *first* had to overcome Darkness, and as the human being Jesus he *first* had to remember his promise to pray for the fallen brother. If he were able to carry out this part of his mission, then with his victory over Darkness he would be fully able to win mankind for his teachings of love. God therefore assigned him *the task of praying for the brother who was bound by Darkness.*

But since *love, kindness, and compassion* were to characterize Jesus as a man, he could not at the same time be endowed with the authority that he possessed as a released spiritual personality, since such an absolute authority in the earthly world could easily lead to self-righteousness because of the power of Darkness. As a human being he might in that case forget to ask for help and guidance from God, the Supreme Leader, at the crucial moment when difficulties presented themselves, and thus easily be tempted to misuse his earthly authority.

God thus knew that if the eldest of the Youngest did not succeed in the first part of his assigned task – to pray for his fallen brother – he would hardly be able to assert himself with sufficient authority when human beings, led astray by Darkness and the Elder, turned against him in their doubt, anger and contempt. God therefore said to him: "If you forget to pray for your brother, *human beings* will bring you death – death upon the cross." Jesus' death on the cross was thus determined by earthly, human conditions (and not by God), and neither was it a demand nor a wish on the part of God *that the son with his death should atone for the sins of human beings in order to bring about a reconciliation between God and humanity.*

In His discourse[1] with the son, God showed him his life on Earth

---

[1]) See Ardor's Account, pp. 32–33.

as the victorious one as well as the one *conquered by Darkness and by human beings.*

The eldest of the Youngest was to lead his earthly life between these two extremes. Because of His self-limitation not even God knew at this point whether Jesus would be able to accomplish the contemplated mission. It was left to him as a human being, guided by his guardian spirit (in this case God), to make the best of the given situation.[1]

All accounts of the personality and conduct of Jesus handed down to posterity through the Gospels are marked by his love of humanity, by his kindness and compassion. Only in glimpses does his authority become apparent.

10.

About eighteen centuries before the eldest of the Youngest was incarnated as Jesus of Nazareth, he was embodied as a human being for the fourth time as a priest in northern India.

In this human embodiment he became the true founder of Brahmanism, although not in the form that is known today.

Only a fraction of his original teaching has survived in the old myths and songs. A few highly distorted remnants of his ethical tenets can still be found in the scripture called "The Code of Manu".

Jesus was born in *Nazareth* – at the home of his parents – and not, as tradition has it, in Bethlehem. The year of his birth has been established about five years later than the actual event. Since the 24th December has come to be honoured as the birthday of Jesus, the eldest of the Youngest does not wish this date to be changed. The correct date of his birth will therefore not be disclosed.

The accounts of the three wise men and the flight into Egypt are legend. Neither in a dream nor as a vision was the birth of Jesus announced to Mary or to Joseph. Everything on this subject is legend. None of God's Servants (see the legend of Gabriel) has ever appeared before human beings, since no human being would be able to perceive these radiant beings of the Light, neither with the eye of the human body nor with the spirit's eye.

However, God's Servants have often *spoken* to human beings as an intensified voice of conscience, when the thoughts of the Young-

---

[1]) See also Commentary, pp. 212–13.

est were unable to penetrate the Darkness.

The Angels mentioned in the ancient Scriptures have mostly been the Youngest, who with God's permission and for some specific reason have appeared before human beings. But not all these accounts and legends are in accordance with the truth. In several cases what has been handed down is no more than fiction – figments of the human imagination.

Also the Eldest have appeared before human beings with the purpose of gaining greater credence or gaining greater power over them.

No human being has seen God, and no human being, incarnated or disincarnated, will ever be able to see Him until the journey to His Kingdom has been completed.[1]

In the incarnations through which the eldest of the Youngest lived, God was his personal guardian spirit and guide, or conscience; He was in other words in constant thought-connection with the son. No one else has ever had God as guardian spirit from the moment they were born to life on Earth. But because of their unshakeable trust in God many of the incarnated Youngest have placed themselves under His guidance and protection and thereby rendered the guardian spirit superfluous, since God always takes into His care anyone who trusts Him implicitly. Only very few human spirits have ever become one with God's Thought and Will during their life on Earth, and thus made Him their guardian spirit. But God watches over everyone and follows their earthly lives, just as through His Thought He often intervenes if the guardian spirits or His Servants fail in their attempts to guide human beings. However, God does this in such a way *that He never applies any pressure on human free will.*

11.

To the great sorrow of his parents Jesus had no interest in the trade of carpentry, in which his father wished to train him.

At an early age he sought instruction from the priests and the scribes and learnt to form his own opinions, which were often at variance with received tradition. He read the ancient Scriptures eagerly and was well versed in Egyptian religious cults. He also had some knowledge of Persian, Indian and Assyrian forms of religious worship. He often went to Jerusalem and studied there under the eldest and most learned of the scribes and scholars of the time. Jesus also visited other places where there were major synagogues in order to investigate and to study the an-

---

[1]) See Summary, pp. 334–35.

cient writings[1] that existed there. His knowledge of languages was quite extensive for his time, and he had some acquaintance with Greek philosophy.

Jesus went about a great deal before his emergence as a religious founder and conversed at length with well-travelled people such as merchants and itinerant philosophers, but he himself never travelled beyond the borders of his homeland.

At the age of twenty-three he appeared in public for the first time, at the synagogue of his native town of Nazareth. Accounts of this event can be found in the Gospels, but they are *all* inaccurately reported (Matthew 13:54-57; Mark 6:2-3; Luke 2:42-50 and 4:16-30; John 7:14-20).

The fragments of Jesus' speech in the synagogue at Nazareth quoted in Ardor's Account are fully correct. On the whole the words of Jesus as they were spoken at the time are quoted by Ardor as accurately as possible, though allowance must be made for the fact that they are quoted in another language. For this reason it was not always possible, through the medium, to find words that fully expressed the Aramaic speech – but *nothing* has been changed or distorted in the thoughts that underlay the words used at that time.

The speech in the synagogue at Nazareth gave the scribes and high priests their first grounds for anger and hatred toward Jesus. Up to that time he had been regarded as a disciple and prospective Rabbi, but his words concerning their incorrect understanding of Yahweh, or Jehovah, put an immediate end to such hopes.

12.

The meeting with John took place about four years after the first dispute between Jesus and the scribes. (The speech at Nazareth).

No dove was sent down from heaven at the baptism of Jesus, and neither did *God* speak to the people gathered there. It was John who called out the words: "This is the Son of God![2] ..." (See Ardor's Account, p. 38).

When Jesus let himself be baptized he regarded his baptism as an initiation into his forthcoming work among the people. It was not until his talk with John that he fully understood the symbolic significance of baptism: *the cleansing of mankind from the defilement of sin.*

---

[1]) Although teaching by oral tradition was common practice at the time of Jesus there were many written accounts, though several of these were only fragmentary.

[2]) Quoted with complete accuracy, John's words were: "This is the divine son! ..."

Baptism as an expression of cleansing and initiation was known long before John's time.

It was first practised on the vanished Atlantic island as a symbolic initiation of the priests into the service of the temple.

13.[1]

Since Darkness streams constantly through all human beings *none* can be free of sin. However pure and exalted a spirit Jesus was in the transcendental world, he had to suffer, like all the Youngest when bound to human bodies, under the sins, impurities and base desires that cling to the human race. But since God was his guardian spirit, his conscience, Jesus transcended *all* human beings in purity as only he can *who has "God's Thought and God's voice" for his conscience.*

When the Youngest have reached a certain degree of spiritual and bodily maturity in their earthly lives, their guardian spirit seeks by every means at its command to guide its charge toward the appointed task. Only in a few individual cases have the Youngest, during their incarnation as human beings, been guided into an understanding of intercession for the Elder, their fallen brother. Where a definite promise was made before incarnation to attempt to render such help to the Elder, the task of the guardian spirit has first and foremost been, as a prelude to the charge's work among human beings, to awaken the memory of the pledge that was given before the earthly existence began.

The moment has always been chosen in consultation with God, but not until the guardian spirit has made the best possible preparations, and not until the charge has reached the culmination of spiritual development in the human existence. The moment this point is reached the guardian spirit intervenes to give support and guidance. Under the onslaughts or temptations of the Elder, the guardian spirit has then usually tried to awaken the charge's memory of the prayer for the fallen brother; but if the charge has not been able to remember the given promise or to understand the prompting, the favourable moment – for that particular incarnation – is forfeited and any new attempt will be in vain. Such a further attempt cannot possibly succeed if the charge was not able to accomplish it having reached the culmination point *in the particular spiritual area that formed the necessary basis for the successful accomplishment of the promised mission.*

---

[1] See also Commentary, p. 221, regarding The Temptation in the Wilderness.

The reason why no new attempt is made is that when Darkness has gained the advantage in the instance first chosen, human beings cannot attain further spiritual growth during their present incarnation in *the area* where Darkness gained victory. Growth ceases, human beings stagnate, often with respect to *all* spiritual insights, and in most cases Darkness gains more and more influence and becomes more easily able to confuse and corrupt *all perception and all concepts.* The moment in which the human being was to remember the given promise by being confronted with the Elder or with the assumed task therefore often becomes the *absolute* peak of spiritual maturity.

However, if the human being at the appropriate moment can recall the promise given prior to incarnation, this first great victory over Darkness will result in the acquisition of a spiritual strength even greater than the one already possessed; and if the victory that has been gained leads to further victories over Darkness, the human being will grow still further in spiritual strength, firmness and authority. This kind of ever-increasing growth – increasing in the same measure as Darkness is overcome – can then continue, if this is necessary for the fulfilment of the promised mission, up to the point when the spirit, having completed the task, is absolved through physical death from all further obligations.

Though Jesus was a man in every respect – though he felt, suffered and desired as a man – *his thoughts were nevertheless pure.* The Elder's attempt to instil unclean and sinful lusts in him stranded on the purity of his being. But the Elder sought relentlessly to make Jesus unfit for the mission that he had taken upon himself; and even though the love of the eldest of the Youngest for his fallen brother and for suffering humanity was deep and sincere, he was as the person Jesus not yet able with love and compassion to repel the Darkness that the Elder had gathered about him, for which reason he misunderstood the urgent voice of God, his conscience, at the crucial moment. And the moment was forfeited when Jesus, through prayer for help not *for himself,* but for the Elder, the Tempter, could have evoked remorse in him, and thereby delivered him from the constraint of Darkness.

God chose to remind Jesus of the prayer for the fallen brother the moment the Elder tempted Jesus the most severely by trying to instil in him prideful thoughts about the work among mankind with which he had been entrusted. At the same time, the love and compassion of Jesus toward humanity had also reached its culmination. At the commencement of his task he thus stood at the point of fulness of his love and compassion, trusting in God's help and in his *firm belief* that by his testimony of God's infinite love and compassion he could teach human beings to love one another, to live in peace and in understanding under the leadership of the Most High. Filled with joyful expectations, Jesus had sought a place of solitude to consider how he could best proceed with that which weighed upon his mind.

But the Tempter pursued him, and when *human* fear and *human* selfishness caused Jesus to call upon God on his own behalf, God by the power of His Will withdrew the Darkness from the countenance of the Elder, and Jesus recognized him. At the same instant he remembered his given promise - the prayer for the fallen brother - but then it was too late, Darkness had gained victory over him.

In order to remind Jesus of the possibility that the Elder could gain further victories over him by leading people astray and by turning them against him, God repeated the words He had spoken to him during their discourse before his incarnation: "Human beings will bring you death - death upon the cross." With these words Jesus should always be reminded that it was not God, but the Elder and human beings who would inflict upon him the sufferings and the possible death that awaited him.

With each incarnation lived by the Youngest out of love for the Elder and compassion for mankind, a portion of the power of Darkness is broken, so that with each new incarnation they are ever better able to repel the onslaughts of Darkness. The eldest of the Youngest - who by his voluntary action and pledge in response to God's request for help for the creatures of the Eldest made the first and greatest contribution toward the redemption of his fallen brothers and sisters and the salvation of humanity - proved himself by this act to be *the noblest, purest and most sublime reflection* of God's own fulness of love. He thus became the one most likely to succeed some day in redeeming the Elder and all who had fallen with him.

Through the position of leadership among his brothers and sisters that he thus came to occupy, a possibility was created that with his unique feelings of love[1] and compassion[1] and after living through but a few incarnations[1] he could achieve victory over Darkness. There was hence a possibility, although it was remote, that as early as the fifth incarnation - his incarnation as Jesus of Nazareth - he might be able to fulfil his promise: as a human being to have compassion for his fallen brother and through fervent prayer for his salvation to evoke his remorse and to win him back. But it has already

---

[1] See Commentary, pp. 201–02.

been stated that Jesus as a human being was not fully able to free himself from the oppression of Darkness, and even though his love, compassion and pity for the suffering human beings never waned, his trust and faith that his mission would bear visible fruit gradually diminished. And it was at this vulnerable point that the Elder levelled his attacks, with the result that Jesus was not always able to act with sufficient authority, especially when confronted with opponents and scoffers. He often remained silent without engaging in any argument, either for himself or against the others. Because of this despondency on his part, the Elder, being the Servant of Darkness, could continue to exert his power over the people in order to oppose the mission of Jesus; this opposition grew in direct proportion to the despondency of Jesus, it finally broke his spiritual authority, and it brought him death upon the cross.[1]

Jesus was clairvoyant, and was thus at times able to see with his "mind's eye". Since the spirit envelops the earthly body, the expression is in a way misleading. However, since this figure of speech has gained acceptance in everyday language as meaning "psychic sight", it has been used in Ardor's Account, where other expressions and forms would have broken the rhythm of the style.

14.

Jesus' ideas and thoughts of "Hell" (the Kingdom of the Dead, the Underworld, Purgatory, the Evil Place) were very unclear. He intermingled his own vague memories of the ravaged Kingdom partly with the Jewish conception of the Kingdom of the Dead, and partly with the Egyptian, Greek and Persian ideas of life after death. At one moment the stay in "Hell" appeared to him as the sum of all suffering and misery – a state of torment and punishment – and at another as a state of contemplation or improvement, an idea which originated from his vague recollection of the life of the human spirits in the spheres. Jesus himself was thus utterly confused regarding this point. Consequently, he was not always able to maintain a clear and explicitly formulated line of thought in his speeches on the fate that awaited sinful human beings after death. And as on numerous occasions he remembered his broken promise, he often thought with deep and sincere grief of the dreadful sufferings that would befall those human beings who persisted in sin and in vice. Jesus therefore described life after death as starkly as possible to such sinners. But

---

[1]) See also Commentary, pp. 225–26.

when he beheld his listeners' terror of "the Evil Place", his own hope was strengthened that the stay there was possibly only temporary and was not meant to last "for all eternity".[1] He therefore always referred questions about definite time-periods to God alone, at the same time urging them all to overcome the power of evil on Earth by fervent prayer for help and strength.

The parable of the salt is rendered here exactly as it was spoken by Jesus.

The parables of the Gospels are often very incomplete. Several of them do not originate with Jesus, but since it was common practice in his time to speak in parables, it is quite understandable that some of the contemporary parables were attributed to him.

15.

Wonders – "miracles"[2] – *do not exist*. All phenomena for which human beings can find no apparent explanation invariably occur *according to spiritual or material laws,* i.e., psychic or physical laws. But that which uninformed and undeveloped people cannot immediately understand or explain themselves is often proclaimed as being "supernatural".

A sharp distinction should be made between the true and the false miraculous events referred to in the Gospels, since much of what is related there has *never* taken place, while other events described have been interpreted from a wrong point of view.

The three forms of wonder described in Ardor's Account all refer to actual events, but without any intervention that was supranatural or contrary to nature.

1) The incarnated Youngest and the more advanced human spirits have a capacity for curing certain ailments of the human body. By the power of their will for the Light they can exert the power of suggestion[3] over ailing persons – especially persons with nervous disorders – or persons whose ailments have already been cured, but who appear to be in a state of weakness because they lack the will to recover.

By passing the palms of the hands, one to two inches from the body, from head to foot – not the reverse – or by laying the hands crosswise over the ailing part of the body, good results can be ob-

---

[1]) See Ardor's Account, p.42, regarding eternity, i.e., an inconceivably long period of time.
[2]) See Summary, pp. 302–03.
[3]) See Commentary, p. 246, regarding suggestion.

tained and sometimes even a complete cure. Under treatment, during which the person treated must lie outstretched in a comfortable position, some of the Light that radiates from the practitioner is transmitted to the patient. The radiations are absorbed by the body and pervade it completely, whereby the sufferings are alleviated or terminated. But it is self-evident that the majority of the diseases of the body *cannot* and *never will* be cured in this way. And since God, through the work of the Youngest on Earth, has given mankind such great knowledge and so many means whereby various sufferings can be cured, or at least alleviated, it is most indefensible if the sick do not in the *first* instance turn to those who through special study of the diseases of the body have become qualified to give medical or surgical assistance, or to those who have knowledge of the healing powers of sunlight, air and water. These must then decide whether it would be efficacious to treat the patient with so-called mesmeric passes.

Only very few human beings are as yet capable of treating the sick with mesmeric passes, or by suggestion, with any prospect of beneficial or lasting results.

2) When after a long and severe illness the body is weak and exhausted, it sometimes happens that the patient, although cured of the disease, remains in an apparent state of death that often lapses unnoticed into actual death. In such cases a loud shout can awaken the body to renewed consciousness because the spirit, although separated from the body and held only by the "cord", involuntarily obeys a stronger will and therefore immediately returns when it is firmly commanded to do so. If the spirit that fled has returned and again united itself with the weakened body, this return to a body on the brink of death can bring it a strengthening stream of Light, whereby the loosening bond between the astral counterpart and the molecular oscillations of the body is once again secured. But if this momentary improvement is to be sustained the re-awakening body must be strengthened by strongly stimulating means.

If, on the other hand, the bond between the astral counterpart and the physical body is so slack that the death of the body occurs, the cord that binds the spirit to the body severs at the same instant – *but once the cord is severed, no shout and no act of will can call the spirit to a revival of the dead body.*

3) Clairvoyants have usually been able to see whether people were possessed or, in other words, whether one or more earthbound spirits were clinging to the person's body in order to participate in vari-

ous ways in earthly pleasures. Persons of strong will have always been able to free themselves easily from these uninvited guests. It was different for people whose will was weak, since the parasites very quickly gained control over them and, in the course of a longer or shorter period of time, left the stamp of sin, vice and evil upon their victims.

Jesus, who was clairvoyant to an unusually high degree, often tried through his strong will to chase away the parasitic spirits, but not always with the same favourable result, since in cases where the people did not improve themselves the spirits would return and regain control.

Possessions[1] by spirits have been known ever since the times when the human spirits were not all capable of rising to their homes in the spheres after the death of the body, because of the increasingly dominant power of Darkness after the incarnation of the Eldest.

The other miracles described in the Gospels are all more or less fictitious. Among the completely untruthful are the following: The Water Turned to Wine (John 2:6-10), The Healing of the Palsied (Matthew 8:5-13; 9:2-7),[2] The Curing of the Blind (Matthew 9:27-30; 20:29-34), The Resurrection of Lazarus (John 11:1-46), The Healing of the Leper (Matthew 8:2-4), and several others, for example The Healing of the Withered Hand, The Mute, The Sick Man at the Pool of Bethesda, and so on. The Son of the Widow of Nain is a version of The Daughter of Jairus.

Several of the "miracles" of the Old Testament form the basis for some of these events.

All accounts of these miracles appeared *after* the death of Jesus, invented by fanatical believers (disciples of Jesus or the apostles) in order to prove the divine origin of Jesus. As the years passed and the stories were passed by word of mouth they grew in exaggeration and improbability until they assumed the form in which they are known from the Gospels.

To the miracles that refer to real events, but which are related in a distorted form, belong The Feeding of the Multitude, The Walking on Water and The Stilling of the Tempest on the Sea of Galilee, for which episodes a more accurate explanation will be given in the following.

---

[1] See Summary, pp. 312-13.
[2] Only the Gospel According to St. Matthew is quoted where the other Gospel versions are similar.

1) *The Feeding of the Multitude* took place in the following manner: about a hundred people were gathered about Jesus to hear him speak. Since it was late and only a few of them had brought anything to eat, Jesus had some of the apostles catch fish from the lake nearby, while others went to the nearest inn where they bought some of the flat loaves of bread then known. While the apostles were thus occupied, Jesus continued speaking to the gathering.

When the apostles returned, the fish and the loaves of bread were handed out, a fire was kindled and the fish were grilled or boiled. Jesus began this meal in the same way that he had always done, by thanking God and asking Him to bestow His blessing on that which they had received.

Many children were present on this occasion, and when these children had become adults the Evangelists received information from them about this mistakenly perceived episode. The children had kept an indelible impression of Jesus as he raised his hands in prayer, and in their young minds they had seen this action *as if it were he who had multiplied the loaves and the fishes by his prayer.*

2) *The Walking on Water.* One evening, as certain of the apostles were out fishing on the Sea of Galilee, or the Lake of Tiberias, Jesus came walking along the steeply sloping banks. He called upon them to be ferried across to the opposite shore. It was a foggy night, and to the apostles it looked for a moment as if he were floating toward them. However, they quickly discovered their error and rowed in toward the shore. Before they had quite reached it, Peter jumped overboard in order to pull the boat ashore.

The apostles often spoke of this incident which, having passed by word of mouth, eventually assumed the distorted form in which it was included in the Gospels.

3) *The Stilling of the Tempest.* One evening as Jesus, tired of the day's journeying, had lain down to sleep in the boat, while some of the apostles sailed it across to the opposite shore, there arose one of the sudden storms so well known on the Sea of Galilee. After they had fought a long and futile battle against the storm, they abandoned sail and helm. In their fear they awakened Jesus, since they believed that they were all doomed. Jesus, who was very skilled in seamanship, chided them, gave his orders, took the helm himself and brought the boat in, while at the same time he reproached them for their lack of trust in God.

This incident was misconstrued by the apostles themselves, who in their worshipful adoration of Jesus believed that he had saved them from disaster with the help of "supernatural" powers.

16.

The Youngest who with God's permission appeared before the earthly eyes of Jesus were materialized.[1] By the power of their will, both the Youngest and the Eldest can render themselves visible to human beings; but the Eldest lack the radiance of light that shines about the Youngest. No human spirits, not even those who have advanced the furthest, are in possession of such a strong will that through this alone they can render themselves visible on the plane of the Earth; they must therefore always employ one or more intermediaries (i.e., mediums), whose earthly material radiations they "borrow" in order to make themselves visible.

Impelled by their longing, many departed ones have appeared before relatives and friends at the moment of death or shortly afterwards. In the case of spirits such appearances have invariably occurred via ordinary materializations through mediums. The one who has seen the apparition has then been the medium, though often unaware of possessing this ability; or else a medium has been present in the vicinity of the person before whom the spirit longed to appear.

No exhaustive explanation of this can be given, since human beings lack the ability to understand the laws that form the basis for this phenomenon. However, in the state of disincarnation it is easily understood by all, even by lesser developed human spirits.

17.

When Jesus promised the apostles to ask his Father to send them more of "His Breath", he was only using the ancient biblical expression. (Compare: "And the Lord God... breathed into his nostrils the breath of life" – Genesis 2:7). This breath, or breath of life, is equivalent to life, or spiritual strength.

It was never in the thought of Jesus that this "Breath" was an independent personal Being that could be merged with God. The word "Breath" was therefore used in Ardor's Account with the same meaning in which Jesus used it, namely, *that at his intercession, God*

---

[1]) Since the apostles were sleeping, they saw the Youngest not with their physical but with their spiritual vision; however, they did retain a memory of what they had seen.

would guide the apostles with His Thought and thereby give them greater spiritual strength.

The Breath of God (i.e., God's Thought) is also identical with eternal life. All who are received into God's Thought, and who by the power of His Will are sustained by it, thereby partake of eternal life. (See Commentary, p. 180).

19.

The words on baptism attributed to Jesus in the Gospel *have never been spoken by him.*

Baptism has no significance as a sacramental act. However, if Christians wish to retain the baptismal ceremony it should be regarded as a symbol for human purification from sin.[1]

Baptism could also be implemented as an initiation ceremony into the Church and would as such be a beautiful and commendable custom. The parents could then bring their children to the church where, at the baptism, these would be incorporated into the congregation in question. But it must be clearly understood by all: *that God in no way gives preference or privileges to those who are baptized before those who are not, whether this be in respect of remission of sin, of eternal life, or of other things;* for God does not look upon outward ceremonies. He considers only *whether that human being in spirit and in truth lives life on Earth strictly in accordance with its conscience; only according to this does God judge the individual.*

22.

The discussion between Jesus and the scribes is rendered exactly as it occurred on that occasion. Some of the words he spoke then have been preserved in the Gospels, but in distorted form.

Since Jesus had many disputes with the chief priests and the scribes, Ardor has selected the one discussion that most clearly shows the deep conflict in their relationship.

Jesus associated only reluctantly with the Sadducees and did so only if they sought him out. He found it very difficult to enter into discussion with them, as they were very quarrelsome and particularly stubborn.

Whenever Jesus felt as though he were speaking to stones, he

---

[1]) See Commentary, p. 209.

seldom pursued any defence of his opinions, especially when he saw that there was no hope of gaining any understanding from among those to whom he was speaking.

Where the Sadducees are mentioned in the Gospels there are several quite well preserved sentences referring to actual events and conversations.

His relationship with the Pharisees is clearly illustrated; but the accounts of Jesus' conversations with them are not accurately reported.

23.

Human beings would have possessed a more complete and truthful account of the earthly life and acts of Jesus if Joseph of Arimathea had fulfilled the mission that he had taken upon himself; for *he* had been chosen to write down the speeches of Jesus to the people. But doubt – one of the worst enemies of humanity – constantly influenced him, until finally he completely ignored the urgings of his conscience.

It goes without saying that in those cases where the Youngest were incarnated with the mission of bringing mankind the full truth, the Elder would make a special effort to prevent the Youngest from cooperating during their lives on Earth.

Since the Elder did not entirely succeed in leading Jesus away from the task he had taken upon himself, he tried in many ways and by every possible means to draw Joseph under his power and the power of Darkness – and in this he succeeded only too well.

Jesus is not entirely without blame in his relationship with Joseph. Later on, if he had tried gently and kindly to develop a closer relationship, he might have succeeded in making him acknowledge the task that had been placed upon him. But Jesus was unable to overcome his human anger toward Joseph.

The profound grief of the eldest of the Youngest over the wickedness, vice and misery of the people inevitably turned into anger in his human incarnation, but it was an anger of brief duration, flaring up when he saw all the sin and impurity about him. Only with respect to Joseph did he lose all self-control, because he fully perceived how much *this man's support* meant to him, and he was unable to make any concession toward him. But the heavier burden of guilt lies with the Elder, as he was the one who tried to sow dissension between them in order to prevent the victory of the Light over Darkness.

The conversation between Jesus and Joseph is partially reflected in the Gospels (Matthew 19:16–22), but in completely distorted and unrecognizable form.

The accounts in the Gospels of Jesus' "Temptation in the Wilderness" are also based on this conversation with the scribe.

Several of the apostles and the disciples were present at the meeting with Joseph, and later, long after Jesus had died, when his friends commemorated him and in various ways tried to explain what they had experienced together with him, some of them stated that Satan, in the figure of Joseph, had tempted Jesus to assume the kingship so as to lead him away from his true mission among the people, but that Jesus had repudiated him with strong and harsh words. This interpretation of what had happened passed by word of mouth, as did so much about the life of Jesus, until it finally appeared in the Gospels in a distorted form, partly as The Temptation in the Wilderness, and partly as the account of The Rich Young Man in Matthew 19:16–22 previously referred to.

The one of the Youngest who was incarnated as Joseph of Arimathea has now fully atoned for the sins he committed as the man Joseph. Among other things, as a disincarnated being he has helped and supported Ardor in the preparation of that part of this work in which Ardor confesses his guilt of sin toward mankind. (See Ardor's Account).

24.

As related in Ardor's Account, Jesus speaks of the destruction of Jerusalem and the end of the world in a somewhat free rendering of what the prophets had foretold. His conception of the last things was very human in this passage. His speech was influenced partly by his knowledge of the teachings of Zarathustra, and partly by his vague memories from his disincarnated existence. Thus when he said that on the last day God would call upon all the dead he had some recollection of the time, about eighty years before his birth on Earth as Jesus of Nazareth, when God first called upon the earthbound[1] spirits. In the thoughts of Jesus as a human being this past experience became a kind of prescience. Since he could not explain to himself where these ideas originated, he believed that God had given him knowledge of the future. His thoughts then led naturally from the dead to the living, and in his speech he therefore let God summon all the living to judgment as well.

---

[1]) See Ardor's Account, p. 31.

When Jesus said: "The evil shall go unto that place which has been prepared for them", he had in his spiritual memory a vague recollection of the fallen spirits (the Eldest) who were brought to distant worlds to be cleansed of the Darkness that had pervaded them at the time of their downfall.

Jesus remembered nothing definite about reincarnation; he knew of it, especially from the Indian teachings, but as he was himself uncertain on that point he *taught* nothing specific about it; but from certain sayings that have been preserved in the Gospels it can be seen that the thought was not unfamiliar to him.

25.

The entry into Jerusalem, which in the Gospels is a prelude to the Feast of the Passover,[1] is a legend deriving from an occurrence at an earlier celebration of the Passover.

Two years before his death Jesus injured his foot by stumbling upon a stone when he was walking along the road to Jerusalem a few days before the "Feast of the Unleavened Bread". As the foot was of great pain to him and he could not put his weight upon it, he asked some of the apostles who were with him to find him a donkey.

This human mishap thus gave rise to the legend of the triumphant entry. (See John 12:12–16).

At the Feast of the Passover Jesus and his apostles were seated at small, low tables that were placed together to form one long table. Although Jesus often took part in meals where the guests lay on couches this was never the case when he himself was the host; everyone then sat on a type of high stool, or hassock, as was the custom in his native town of Nazareth.

Of Jesus' talk with his apostles during the supper only the parts of general interest are included in Ardor's Account, which thus gives only a fragmentary report of all that was said.

In his parting speech to the apostles, when he had bid them proclaim his teaching, he also bid them preach to the heathen; *but he did not exhort them to baptize the converted, as stated in the Gospels.*

The bidding to evangelize among the heathen was thus given at the time of leave-taking and not, as incorrectly stated in the Gospels, at the time of his appearance *after death*.

But when Jesus gave the apostles this command he had in mind

---

[1]) See Commentary, pp. 231–33, regarding The Lord's Supper.

only the neighbouring non-Jewish peoples and the Greeks and Romans, whose worship of many gods was well known to him.

At that time the world was *very small,* and Jesus could therefore only have in mind the human beings whose existence was known to him. Evangelizing among the heathen, as it has been and still is practised, cannot harmonize with Jesus' intentions, since he did not have the slightest knowledge of the more primitive races of mankind among whom attempts have been made in the last few centuries to introduce Christianity through extensive and frequently perilous missionary work.

Still less does this work, carried out among primitive heathen peoples, conform with the manner in which God seeks to educate mankind: *one step forward through each incarnation* from undeveloped beings to lucid, more independently thinking individualities, by which procedure they will better and better be able to conceive of a perfect and exalted divinity as the spiritual self gradually grows and matures and attains conscious recognition of its divine origin and everlasting existence. Seen from a transcendental point of view, religious missionary work among the primitive heathen becomes quite superfluous – just as superfluous as a mother's words to her new-born child of its divine origin and its Heavenly Father. The human spirits who animate these peoples are usually so young and uncomprehending that any attempt at giving them insight into a religion such as Christianity will in most cases *come to naught.* A conversion from heathenism to Christianity, or to other more highly cultivated religions, will therefore not benefit these human beings in the least. *So long as religious and ethical ideas have not become a part of their spiritual consciousness as a matter of course, and so long as these ideas have not become an integral part of their inner being, thus uplifting their ethical standards,* they will in a state of disincarnation reap as little benefit from these thoughts and ideas as would a child in later years from the mother's religious words spoken at a time when the child had not yet awoken to clear consciousness of its own existence in the earthly world.

But as the young human spirits gradually advance through their incarnations, and as their spirits gradually mature to greater insight and greater clarity, also *they* will be initiated into the truths that still lie far beyond their ability to comprehend, either as human beings or as disincarnated beings.

As practised, missionary work among the primitive peoples will therefore *never* give results commensurate with the amount of self-sacrificing work that has been done and still is being done from all sides and in countless ways, in terms of both spiritual and material values. Since only God, not human beings, can decide how deeply a conversion is rooted, the few really good results *can never justify the many human lives that in the course of time have been sacrificed on the altar of missionary work among the heathen.* Usually the missionaries themselves are the ones who benefit most from religious missionary work, since this work often enriches the one who performs it with great spiritual values (e. g., patience, compassion, self-sacrifice, etc.).

On the other hand, *work of general education* among the less primitive peoples may possibly be beneficial in a cultural sense and thereby improve the general conditions of life for these often unfortunate beings and their descendants. Much can be gained if a simple and easily understood teaching of the transcendental is then added. It is sufficient for these spiritually undeveloped people that they should learn that a loving God and Father watches over them, and that in prayer, however childlike and simple, they can always turn to Him for help and protection against the evil in their earthly existence.

As indicated in Ardor's Account, Judas Iscariot was not predestined to betray Jesus. Any *such* predestination is absolutely irreconcilable with God's fatherly and all-embracing love.

Judas *alone* bears the guilt, since he acted of his own free will; the Elder did not tempt him to do it, as Jesus supposed.

Judas hated the eleven apostles of Jesus, who all avoided him as much as possible, and none of them understood the love and care that Jesus showed him, since his behaviour was in every way of a sinister, unpleasant, and repulsive nature. The contempt and ill will that constantly met Judas from the eleven apostles finally aroused his anger, not only against his fellow apostles, but also against Jesus.

Jesus, who was deeply concerned over the more and more seclusive behaviour of Judas, feared that he would act as informer and accuser, for which reason Jesus at the last supper warned him against the evil thoughts that threatened to overcome him. The result was exactly the opposite of what Jesus intended. Judas became still more embittered, and he went away to inform the Council of where Jesus could be found.

However, the condemnation and death of Jesus were in no way dependent on the betrayal by Judas. At that time several members of the Council had already decided to destroy the Nazarene.

In desperation over his treachery, Judas killed himself.

The eleven apostles are all to blame for the manner of Judas' action; if they had tried to emulate Jesus' kindness and love in a sincere attempt to make Judas one of their own, instead of constantly rejecting him, he would hardly have become what he was: a traitor and a suicide.

The story of the thirty pieces of silver is legend.
The vision in the Garden of Gethsemane is also legend.
Jesus was saddened by the thought of that which awaited him, but he was entirely calm. He knelt while he prayed a fervent prayer *for strength to meet what was to come.* The apostles who accompanied him there slept or rested while Jesus was deep in prayer.

The words of Jesus in Gethsemane: "My Father, if it be possible, let this cup pass from me: nevertheless not as I will, but as thou wilt", were later attributed to Jesus in order to explain why God did not save His son from death on the cross. The words: "Not as I will, but as thou wilt" were supposed to prove that Jesus voluntarily submitted to God's Will and that the death of Jesus on the cross was pre-ordained by God. But Jesus *never* expressed himself in this way; it did not even occur to him *to pray to God for help in evading the impending sufferings or the approaching death.*

From the moment when Jesus failed to pray for his fallen brother and thus failed to conquer Darkness, he carried the deep sorrow of defeat in his heart. Although he was convinced that he was God's emissary, he was not certain of being the awaited Messiah,[1] and this deep sorrow and doubt characterized his relationship to human beings as well as to God. And although Jesus during his earthly life had often spoken about the manner in which hope and trust can be undermined by doubt,[2] he was himself in doubt regarding that crucial point. His conduct and his words thus became less steadfast than expected, and his own relationship to God also suffered. For that very reason it became impossible for him to find a way between the two extremes that had been established for his earthly life, even though God, as his guardian spirit and leader, in many ways tried to support and to guide him. The grief of Jesus over not having fulfilled the intentions preyed more and more on his mind and so discouraged him that finally he saw only one way of opposing the doubt, hatred and persecution of mankind: *by his death to confirm the truth of his teachings.* And he walked to his death without fear and without hesitation; he saw clearly that his strength, his spiritual authority, was too weak *to overcome human blindness.*

Thus the eldest of the Youngest was sent to Earth as Jesus of

---

[1]) See Ardor's Account, p. 35.
[2]) See Ardor's Account, p. 57.

15 C

Nazareth in order to fulfil a task that consisted of two parts. The first: *to pray for his eldest fallen brother,* and the second: *to bring the Gospel of Love to humanity.*

Even though he failed in the first part of his mission, he might possibly have succeeded in the second if he had dared fully trust his inner voice – the voice of God – the voice that continually whispered to him *that he was the Messiah.* Through this, his fervent belief in the true and the exalted nature of his innermost being, he would have been able to achieve complete harmony and unison with God and God's Will and gradually, as he had familiarized himself with the thought of being the Messiah, his conduct would have been marked by such divine strength and determination that during the execution of the second part of his mission he would have overcome the influence of Darkness and thereby avoided death on the cross, even though Darkness had earlier prevented him from remembering the prayer for his fallen brother.

Jesus' firm belief that *he* and no one else was the Messiah was to have been the basis for the second part of his mission, and the culmination of his spiritual maturity as a reformer and religious founder would have been reached the moment he fully and completely gave himself up to belief in the truth of the thought that he was the Messiah.

But Jesus' profound grief over the defeat that he had suffered overshadowed the thought of being the Messiah and prevented him from reaching the spiritual maturity that was required for his emergence as a reformer. Thus, he did not succeed in winning over the *leaders* and the *rulers* to his teaching of love, and hence he could also not entirely fulfil the second part of the task that he had undertaken.

Jesus never dared ask others to pray for the Evil One. He knew that *no one* would understand him, since in his earthly existence he was unable to explain the purpose of such a prayer, and as he even had a distinct feeling that intercession would be in vain if the prayer *did not come from deep in the heart, as an expression of the understanding of and compassion for the sufferings of the Evil One* on the part of the person praying, he therefore remained silent, because he knew that everyone about him had only feelings of hatred and terror toward Satan, and also because he felt that *as a human being* he himself did not have the necessary compassion for the fallen brother.

As it happened to the eldest of the Youngest in that incarnation, so has it often happened to the Youngest in the various missions that they have undertaken among mankind. Doubt as to their personal strength, doubt as to the truth of their words or doubt of God's absolute help at the crucial moment has made them falter, whereby they were slowly brought under the influence of Darkness, *and the people have then thanked them for their spirit of self-sacrifice by torturing them in various ways spiritually or bodily - or by giving them death.*

The slightest trace of doubt, the least hint of faltering, invariably diminishes the strength of that wave of Light that streams from God through the Passage of Light to every human being on Earth, whether the embodied personality is one of the Youngest, is a human spirit or one of the Eldest incarnated under the Law of Retribution.

Therefore: *the greater trust the individual places in the divine within the self the greater will be the strength and help from God, and the easier will be the victory over human prejudice, distrust and scorn, indeed, over all that belongs to Darkness.*

26.

Judas did not kiss Jesus when he betrayed him.

Peter, who was impulsive and quick-tempered, struck one of the servants in the face in order to protect Jesus. The account of the sword and the severed ear is all legend.

Peter's denial of Jesus is not included in Ardor's Account, since it in no way plays the part ascribed to it by the Evangelists.

Jesus had often told the apostles that Simon Peter was appointed to be their leader when he himself had left them. Since Peter was of a quick temper, Jesus forbade him to accompany him when he was led to the house of the high priest, lest he should endanger himself or the other apostles by some impetuous action.

Peter's grief over the imprisonment of Jesus was so great that he was unable to comply with this instruction and, unseen by Jesus, he stole after him and hid himself in the courtyard around Caiaphas' house, so as to be as near as possible to his beloved master.

But at the moment he was questioned as to whether he was one of the Nazarene's followers he remembered his pledge to be the apostles' leader, and so as not to act against the wish of Jesus he saw no other course than to deny his acquaintance and relationship with him. Peter thus acted not out of fear for his own life, but out of fear of Jesus' disapproval of his high-handed action.

Jesus' prediction of Peter's denial is fictitious, as is the account of Jesus' subsequent thrice-repeated question: "Simon, son of Jonas, lovest thou me?" (John 21:15–18).

Only excerpts from the high priest's questioning of Jesus are given

15* C

in Ardor's Account, since the Gospels have preserved much of the proceedings more or less correctly.

The examination of Jesus by Pilate was essentially a repetition of the questioning by the high priest. Jesus answered him in the same way that he had answered Caiaphas.

The story about Barabbas is correct; he was set free in place of Jesus.

The account of the dream of Pilate's wife is fictitious.

27.

Two robbers were crucified at the same time as Jesus; they were bound to the cross without a footrest, for which reason they died several hours before Jesus did. As both thieves were deeply stupefied by the drink they were given before their crucifixion any talk between them and Jesus would have been impossible. The Gospel's account of the words of Jesus to the robber is fictitious.

Jesus refused the drug because he wished to endure fully the sufferings that he had been allotted.

The earthquake that was felt immediately after the crucifixion was associated with a volcanic eruption in northeastern Palestine (the ancient Bashan). The effects of the earthquake extended to Jerusalem and to some towns lying to the south of the city, where the tremor was not especially severe. At the same time dark, heavy storm clouds gathered in the sky and transformed the clear light of day into a dark twilight. The clouds dispersed after a few hours without any resulting rainfall. The darkness, the oppressive calm and the earthquake were enough to strike such terror in the hearts of the superstitious people that they all fled in panic into the city.

The statements in the Gospel According to St. Matthew regarding the events that took place after the crucifixion are exaggerated and untrue. (Compare Matthew 27:51–54 with the foregoing explanation).

28.

In the days of Jesus the wall about Jerusalem lay in ruins in several places, and in other places repairs and rebuilding were being carried out. For this reason it was easy for anyone who so wished to slip into or out of the city unobserved, despite the sentries that had been posted.

No Roman soldiers watched over the tomb.

Since Jesus' body was anointed and swathed in linen prior to its interment, the account of the women who came the following morning to anoint his body is incorrect – the women came to mourn at the grave of Jesus.

When the human body dies it must inevitably decompose and disintegrate.[1] Since Darkness has become *destructible* through the victory of God and of the Light *everything* that is produced and created from Darkness must in consequence also be destructible. The resurrection of Jesus' earthly body thus conflicts both with the *temporal*[2] laws of physics and chemistry and with the *eternal* laws of the Light that are never broken by God.

Mary Magdalene was clairvoyant; thus she alone saw the spiritual body of Jesus, which was invisible to the others. Jesus' spirit was thus in this instance not materialized.
Mary Magdalene[3] was the woman who was closest to Jesus during the last years of his life on Earth. Her deep grief and her yearning for Jesus called his released spirit back, and when he stood before her she saw him with her spiritual vision.

29.

In his Account Ardor points out that when Jesus appeared before the apostles he was standing at the upper end of the table. Jesus chose this place so that all should know that he had not come to them through the entrance door in the customary way.
Jesus appeared before the apostles with God's permission and by the power of his own will, thus without the intervention of a medium, although still materialized according to his will.
The ascension of Jesus is legend.

30.

The legend of the wonder of Pentecost must be ascribed to the fear and terror that a sudden, unseasonal thunderstorm wrought

---

[1]) See Commentary, pp. 176–77.
[2]) See Summary, p. 305.
[3]) Mary Magdalene was one of the Eldest. Through Jesus' care for her she was brought under the guidance of God, so that through new incarnations she could atone for her transgressions against humanity.

among the frightened, superstitious and fanatically aroused people.

God, who at all times and in many ways has tried to turn the Elder's evil designs to the good, in fact granted the apostles more spiritual strength because of their strong faith and sure trust, but not until their thoughts met with God's Thought[1] in their fervent prayer of thanksgiving.

The deceitful explanation of the disciples to Simon Peter concerning that which had happened gave rise to a movement – "the speaking in tongues" – which to this day finds proselytes among overexcited and highly strung people; a movement that has absolutely no foundation, since fanaticized people *can never think or speak with sufficient clarity and authority*. People who uncritically allow themselves to come under the spell of "the speaking in tongues" usually attract Darkness[2] to themselves and to their surroundings, whereby they frequently cause themselves and others great spiritual sufferings. On the other hand, the Light will flow more strongly and purely toward those people whose religious faith manifests itself without *selfishness, censoriousness or self-righteousness* as an unshakable trust in God, coupled with unselfish love and deep compassion for all their unhappy and suffering fellow human beings. These people will be able to provide their fellow men and women with truly helpful spiritual comfort and strength through well chosen words based on clear, logical and appropriate thoughts.

31.

The deep longing of the apostles for their beloved master and their constant hope for his early return, a hope stemming from their misconception of his speech[3] regarding the end of the world, together with John's Revelation – inspired by the *Elder* – are the reasons why many people even today expect The Second Coming, The Millennium, The End of the World, The Day of Judgment, and so forth.

So long as all of mankind has not reached the greatest possible earthly[4] perfection the end of the world will not come. And when the day comes, after millions of years, that the Earth disintegrates by the power of God's Will, all human beings will have left it; *no earthly being will be present on Earth when it meets its "death"*.

---

[1]) See Speech of Christ, pp. 117–18, regarding prayer.
[2]) Many of those who "spoke in tongues" were possessed by earthbound spirits, including the Eldest.
[3]) See Ardor's Account, pp. 58–59, and the Commentary, p. 221.
[4]) See Summary, pp. 306–07 and 322–23.

32.

Saul's vision of Jesus on the road to Damascus was a spiritual experience. Jesus did not appear before his earthly eyes in materialized form, but showed himself to him while Saul's body rested in sleep. The memory of what he had seen was so vivid for Saul that, as related in Ardor's Account, he received the impression that it was the radiance of light emanating from the body of Jesus that blinded him.

33.

Although the words and acts of Jesus left a profound impression on Saul, he was never able to reject entirely the ancient rabbinic teachings, so that the form in which Christianity appeared through his interpretation *became a complete distortion of Jesus' simple and beautiful teachings of love,* a distortion that resulted in part from Saul's great self-confidence, and in part from constant intervention of the Elder.

God, who out of deep compassion received the creatures of His fallen children into His Thought, and thereby bestowed eternal life upon mankind, *surely did not need to demand a blood sacrifice as atonement for the sin and iniquity of mankind.* The interpretation of Jesus' death on the cross as the "sacrificial lamb", in whose blood all sinners would be cleansed is therefore an entirely *blasphemous thought,* implanted in Saul's mind by the Elder.

The sacrificing of animals is such an ancient custom that it goes back to the Mlawayans in the Pacific Ocean, and even though Saul's original conception of Jesus as humanity's sacrificial lamb was intended to be symbolic, it is a symbol that can only be ascribed to the intervention of Darkness, *since God never has demanded, nor will He ever demand such acts in order to forgive the sins of mankind.*

The congregations founded by the apostles originally celebrated their Communions solely to commemorate the parting of Jesus with his friends. Only through Saul's interpretation did they take on a different meaning.

The words by which Saul tried to interpret the acts of Jesus were instilled in him by the Elder. These words were adopted by all the congregations which Saul had founded – and later by other congregations – and the words became so deeply imbedded in the minds of the people, that at the time of the Evangelists they were attributed to Jesus.

Communion was at first a symbolic act, but in its new form it grew more and more material until the bread and the wine gradually became the visible expression for "Jesus' true flesh and true blood" (John 6:53–56).

Christians who believe that they can obtain forgiveness of sin and partake of the bliss of heaven by "eating and drinking the flesh and blood of their god"[1] *place themselves on the same religious level as the so-called heathen,* even if they regard Communion only as a symbolic act.

People who take part in Communion out of habit, or because it is customary, *are all guilty of an immoral act.* And those servants of the Church who within themselves feel offended by this custom – whose dim origin is in ancient pagan rites – *carry a grave responsibility* if they continue to serve the communicants when the Lord's Supper is shared *because they lack the courage to reject dogmas conceived by human beings and established by human beings.*

Many Christians who take part in Communion according to the inherited traditions and with complete trust in *the truth of this Sacrament,* often feel comforted and strengthened. But the spiritual peace and strength that they receive is not a result of taking part in the "Sacrament", *it is due to their deeply felt remorse and to their prayer to God – or to Christ – for forgiveness of their sins;* for any sincere prayer coming from the depth of the heart will always meet with God's Thought, and the answer to the prayer will be felt as a profound, spriritual peace that passes understanding.

No human being can be delivered from the guilt of sin through Communion. Everyone must atone for his or her own sins according to God's Law of Retribution, either – if the sin is not repented – by being struck by the repercussions of the sinful thought or act or – if the sin is repented – by performing during later incarnations acts of love and compassion for the fellow human beings against whom he or she has sinned.

Transgressions against God or transgressions against the divine within the human being **can be atoned only through a deeply felt grief and remorse.** No human being can assume the guilt of sin of another, nor did the eldest of the Youngest by his death on the cross **assume the sins of mankind in any form, much less did he atone for them.**[2] But through a sincere prayer to God everyone can mitigate the lot that is about to befall a sinful fellow being, because *unselfish*

---

[1] Christ as the second member of that Holy Trinity that is the current Christian definition of God as the Father, the Son and the Holy Ghost.

[2] See Speech of Christ, p. 112.

prayer springing from the depth of a loving, compassionate heart will always draw the Light to those for whom the prayer is intended. This added stream of Light will then dispel the Darkness that envelops the sinner or the breaker of law and will enable the guardian spirit – the conscience – to exert itself and make it easier for the transgressor to heed its promptings. In this way human beings can extend much valuable help to one another.[1]

If Christians would observe the Lord's Supper in the *correct and proper manner* by making it *a commemoration* to be held on the evening of Maundy Thursday at church or in the home, they would afford the eldest of the Youngest much happiness; for then he would to a great extent have attained that which he had intended as Jesus of Nazareth: **to be remembered on that evening by all who love him.**

––––––––––

Further details of the more or less truthful accounts in the Gospels of the life and acts of Jesus and of the insertions and additions of later times cannot be given here. It would place too much, indeed, an impossible burden of work on the medium who serves as an intermediary. But with the foregoing as a basis, those who feel called upon to do so can themselves search for the true grains of gold that are to be found in all four Gospels.

Only this remains to be said: no one has the right to reproach the Evangelists for the erroneous, distorted or entirely false accounts that through them have been handed down to posterity, since it must be remembered that *nothing* was written down during the lifetime of Jesus – nothing was written until a generation after his death. During this time the words of Jesus and accounts of his life and the miracles he had performed passed by word of mouth. Something was added here, something omitted there, and it is thus fully understandable that it was impossible to produce a complete account that was accurate in every detail. Nor must it be forgotten that the Elder was to blame for most of the many distortions, contradictions and falsehoods. And although several of the Youngest who were disincarnated at the time gave the Evangelists much help through inspirational influence it was impossible, **so long as the Elder was still bound by the power of Darkness, to ensure that all was written down in strict accordance with the truth.**

None of the apostles was the author of any of the Gospels. The Gospel bearing the name of John was written by one of his disciples

––––––––––

[1] See Speech of Christ, p. 118, regarding prayer.

who was of Greek descent. It was compiled and completed after the apostle's death at the close of the first century. Minor fragments of this Gospel were, however, written down before his death and read at meetings of the congregations. Only a small part of the collected work was known and approved by the apostle John.

The Apocalypse has no claim whatsoever to be regarded *as a revelation from God.* It was inspired throughout by the Elder. The human author of the Apocalypse is not related in any way to the author of the Gospel of St. John.

The Acts of the Apostles and the many Epistles that are included in the New Testament should be regarded only as edifying reading of varying merit. Not all the accounts in The Acts of the Apostles are in accordance with the truth, nor did all the Epistles originate from the persons whose names they bear.

34–35.

The historic survey that Ardor has provided in order to link the past with the present has been made as brief and as simple as possible. Only the essential main points are included, since anyone who so desires may study the many available works on world and church history, and so gain insight into the gruesome religious wars and other conflicts of bygone times, as well as the rulers' tyranny and lust for power that drove them to commit the most hideous crimes in their quest for dominance.

Similarly may anyone who so desires study the many different sectarian deviations from the teachings of Christ and the resulting conflict, superstition and hypocrisy.

36.

When Ardor in his Account says: "A little more than eight decades before the eldest of the Youngest was born unto the Earth" – that is to say about eighty-one years before the birth of Christ – "God called for the first time upon the earthbound spirits", this number of years is given according to the traditional date for the birth of Jesus of Nazareth; but since that date has been set about five years too late, the actual birth of the eldest of the Youngest as the man Jesus took place about seventy-six years after God first called upon the earthbound spirits.

The centuries for God's callings did not coincide with the endings of the earthly centuries.

Christ and several others of the Youngest who had promised to assist him began in the year 1857 their toilsome journey across the Earth as disincarnated spirits in order to communicate directly with human beings via mediums, and in order with their help to try to influence the earthbound spirits, a task no human being can fathom or fully comprehend.

Because of the stream of Light that had been brought to the Earth through the work of the Youngest for humanity over millions of years, a faint dawn had gradually appeared on the astral counterpart of the Globe in place of the dense Darkness that had rested there at the creation of mankind. But in many places, especially where the earthbound spirits gathered in greater numbers, there were large, dense accumulations of Darkness that had the effect of compact cloud formations, and since astral Darkness is a reality for all disincarnated beings the Youngest on their journeys had constantly to penetrate these accumulations of Darkness with the help of the Light that streamed from their spirit-bodies.

In semi-Darkness, and frequently in complete Darkness that could only be dispelled by the Light that they themselves radiated, the Youngest had thus to journey from place to place in search of earthly helpers. They had also to endure the spectacle of the thousands upon thousands of wretched and evil-smelling earthbound spirits, who fled panic-stricken in all directions whenever the radiant figures of the Light appeared.

In these dismal surroundings Christ and his companions were obliged to remain without the possibility of returning to their dwellings in the sixth sphere to find peace and rest removed from the noxious vapours and horrible spectacles of Darkness. They had to abide on the astral plane of the Earth for several years until, after countless disappointments and many spiritual sufferings, they reached the goal that God had set for their journeying and mission there.

In the course of time some of the earthbound spirits began to understand that the spirits of the Light had come to help them escape their dreadful and captive existence on the Earth. These spirits therefore congregated in large numbers at the places where Christ tried to establish communication with the so-called mediums. This severely impeded them in their already difficult task, since the accumulations of Darkness that these human spirits brought with them enveloped everyone, the spirits of the Light as well as the earthly participants in the séance. During the first several years the messages from the spirits were therefore very faulty and misleading, and more often than not quite erroneous. In the vast majority of cases the mediums could not be blamed for this, but it naturally gave rise to much and justifiable doubt as to the authenticity of the alleged spiritualistic communications.

However, these distortions occurred mainly in those circles where the séances were not protected by the spirits of the Light, either because one of the Eldest was bound to the medium's human body as its spiritual self, or because the participants in the séance were themselves too earthbound in their thoughts and actions, or because the Elder and the disincarnated Eldest acted as the spiritual leaders of the séance in order in this way to counter the work of Christ. The Eldest would often assume the names that Christ and his helpers used, since they supposed – quite correctly – that most of the participants would be unable to determine whether they had a spirit of the Light or a spirit of Darkness before them.

The Elder tried constantly to induce mediums to experiment with trance,[1] materialization phenomena, and the like, in order thereby to gain greater control over them. He also urged the earthbound spirits wilfully to possess the medium and the séance participants, as a result of which many false messages appeared, since these spirits that were misled by Darkness did not scruple to appear under the well-known and high-sounding names of deceased persons. Séance participants who were exposed to such false and easily disproved messages were inclined to denounce everything as sheer falsehood and fraud.

However, many people who sought the spiritualistic circles very often did receive truthful messages from deceased relatives and friends, who without permission took advantage of such tempting opportunities to be remembered through the words, writings or materializations of mediums.

Through the persistent efforts of the Elder to counter the spirits of the Light, many spiritualistic circles were formed that frequently involved fraudulent mediums. Many of these circles formed by gullible people also acquired an unfortunate stamp of vulgarity, which caused great harm to the work that the spirits of the Light were trying to accomplish.

However, there were people who tried with true sincerity and unselfish interest to bring order to the spiritualistic chaos. Among these people Christ and his helpers found several who extended them

---

[1] Regarding trance and materializations, see pp. 241–45.

valuable assistance in their work to release the earthbound spirits and to present some of the truths of the Light, truths that were in many respects contrary to orthodox teaching. But the messages from the Youngest appeared sporadically at many different places, and always intermingled with the lies of the Elder.

When Christ and his helpers had found people who might be employed as intermediaries *for their special work,* they tried by various means to deepen their interest in transcendental communication, gradually introducing the séance members also to religious questions. But only a very small number of the spiritualistic circles[1] that they visited throughout the Earth were able to sustain an interest in purely spiritual questions and answers, and as soon as the desire for physical manifestations became predominant in a circle, Christ would regretfully have to abandon whatever ground had been won and search for other and more understanding intermediaries. To obtain a favourable result in this way demanded endless patience and deep love, a patience and a love that only Christ was fully able to evince. His unfailing patience and his unswerving trust in God's guidance sustained his companions when after the span of two decades they were *all* inclined to abandon the Shorter Road.

In those circles where the spirits of the Light had established communication Christ spoke under names that expressed or were in some way associated with his work among mankind. In this way he succeeded in gaining an audience, so that many of his ethical and religious principles were received, understood and believed. Only in very few cases did he venture to identify himself under the earthly name that he bore during his last incarnation, but the people to whom he thus revealed himself most often responded with doubt as to his identity. In a few instances where in the hope of meeting understanding he identified himself as Jesus or Christ he was promptly dismissed as if he were *Satan* himself – a strangely illogical notion, for if they were truly convinced of the realities of communication with spirits, Christian people should have realized that Christ, as readily as any other disincarnated being, must have been able to establish communication through an intermediary with those who believed in him and loved him – indeed, that in all probability *he* would succeed better than anyone else in establishing communication with good results. And since many circles open their séances with a prayer to God for help against the intervention of Darkness, the séance members at least should have remembered Jesus' words from the Gospel:

---

[1]) Christ approached only circles having few members, *never* those with a larger membership nor large public circles.

"...That if two of you shall agree on earth as touching any thing that they shall ask, it shall be done for them of my Father which is in heaven. For where two or three are gathered together in my name, there am I in the midst of them." (Matthew 18:19–20). In view of these words the members should then have ascertained – through questions and conversation with the manifesting spirit – whether they were in fact confronted with a spirit of the Light. And when they had been convinced of this, they would feel reassured that the name given was true, since a spirit of the Light *never resorts to falsehood*. However, many séance members will claim that despite their prayer for help against the influence of Darkness during séances, they have often been deceived by evil and wicked spirits. There is only one answer: *the prayers[1] that are not formed in complete trust and from deep in the heart, but are formed thoughtlessly or as a necessary and habitual precaution, are of no use whatsover.*

In order if possible to lighten the difficult task of Christ and his helpers, God arranged for several of the Youngest and some of the more advanced human spirits – men as well as women – to be incarnated in various places all over the world, so that as mediums they could establish the necessary link between the spirits of the Light and human beings.

In a small spiritualistic circle, some of whose members had been incarnated with a view to this purpose, Christ found at last the complete understanding and trust that God had set as a prerequisite for the success of his work.

In order to render Christ further effective help in carrying out this arduous task, God called upon the earthbound spirits some years before the allotted time had come. At a given time[2] in the latter half of October, 1911, God caused His voice to be heard by all who were bound by sin and vice to the astral plane of the Earth, and all of them except the Elder and his dual[3] heeded His call. (Ardor's dual returned at a later date).

Darkness had thus at last to yield due to Christ's perseverance, since nothing could discourage him and nothing could deter him. But that which still brought Christ forward and enabled him to overcome the opposing Darkness as well as human prejudice was his never-failing trust that God would not have shown him the "Shorter Road" had He not been perfectly certain *that the Shorter Road would lead to the goal.* The final victory over Darkness must there-

---

[1]) See Speech of Christ, p. 117.
[2]) The transcendental world does not wish to give the exact date. – Publisher's note.
[3]) At that time, disincarnated, she was in the ravaged Kingdom, the Hell-Sphere.

fore first and foremost be ascribed to Christ's unshakeable trust in God, to his profound love for the fallen brother, and to his deep compassion for the sinful human children of the Earth. It was this love and patience of Christ that gradually broke the power of Darkness, that evoked the grief and remorse of the Elder and that resulted in his return to God and to the Father's Home.

The eldest of the Youngest is, therefore, in the very real and the very deepest sense of the word, Christ – the Saviour and the Redeemer – not in consequence of any blood offering of atonement, but because of his unselfish and never-failing love.

Since Christ, by winning back his eldest brother, reached the goal that his Father had set for his arduous task among the fallen spirits bound by Darkness, the possibility *that Christ now or in the future will communicate directly with mediums or spiritualistic circles is out of the question, as such forms of communication would be superfluous.* Christ has once more returned to his dwelling in the outermost sphere, where as in the past he will seek to guide humanity and to establish order on Earth.

Mediums can act as intermediaries under the influence of *the Light* as well as of *Darkness.*

Apart from all the incarnated Youngest and Eldest, the more advanced human spirits are gifted with mediumistic talents while incarnated; but these gifts do not always reach the earthly consciousness of the individual. However, human spirits are only slightly gifted as mediums, but in order to serve the Light and if so desired by *the transcendental world,* their gifts or talents can be strengthened by the guardian spirit, who in various ways tries to support the medium, for example by strengthening the will to work for the cause of the Light, or by reducing the thickness of the insulation layer between the physical body and the psychic body, thus providing a stronger and more direct influence from the transcendental world. If mediums fail to heed the promptings of their guardian spirit and follow personal desires in order to satisfy their vanity, lust for power or other similar wicked motives, they will soon come under the influence of Darkness; which can readily be detected in the manifestations brought about with the help of such mediums.

It is easy for disincarnated spirits to determine which human beings are mediums. The radiance of the egg-shaped aura of the spiritual body is more luminous with these than with others; the aura of the Youngest is especially bright. However, if it is one of the Eldest who is bound to the medium's human body, the spirit as seen from the transcendental world appears as a jet-black shadow. These people are normally strongly physical mediums, *since practically all physical mediumism originates from Darkness.* The spirits of the Light obviously never use such mediums as intermediaries between themselves and human beings.

Physical phenomena that are produced with the help of Darkness include levitations of the medium or of the séance participants; irregular flickering light phenomena, such as larger or smaller phosphorescent spots, misty formations and the like; all genuine materializations and dematerializations during séances, violent explosive blows or noises and all irregular tappings and so on.

All regular tappings, with equal intervals between each knock, can be performed only by the spirits of the Light and therefore belong under the laws of the Light. These tappings can in the presence of very strong Light radiations ring with a clear and sonorous metallic sound, even though there are no metallic objects in the room where they occur. The spirits of the Light have often called upon their earthly helpers in this manner.

Materializations during séances are performed only by the earthbound spirits, including the Eldest. *None of the Youngest has ever appeared in a materialized state at any séance;* their appearances occur spontaneously and usually without the intervention of a medium, since they render themselves visible by the power of their will, that is to say, they let the Light-atoms of which their spirit-bodies consist oscillate with a reduced frequency – or they appear to clairvoyant people.

It has happened at materializations that completely honourable mediums in their earthly ignorance, and in the belief that they were acting correctly, have let themselves be used as intermediaries by unscrupulous spirits. These mediums have usually believed that they were doing a good deed in lending their assistance to such phenomena, partly so as to provide proof of life after death, and partly with the good intention of acting as intermediary between the living and the "dead". But since God has never permitted the earthbound spirits to make themselves known in this way, the spirits who have thus exploited and abused such mediums must carry the full responsibility for their forbidden actions. On the other hand, if the medium has been warned by the guardian spirit and has thus acted in defiance of conscience, *the medium* must bear the full responsibility for that which has taken place.

Many strongly physical mediums, the Eldest, can by the will of their spirit – and with no help whatsover from disincarnated spirits – produce levitation phenomena, such as the lifting of objects from a solid base or causing smaller objects to float about in the air. This usually happens without the medium's human brain being aware of it, since the spirit cannot influence its earthly body during trance with the same strength as is normally the case.

Only a very small proportion of the materializations and other physical phenomena known from séances are or have been genuine. Most often it has been sleight-of-hand and thus pure deception[1] on the part of the human medium, a fact for which all who meddle with the manifestations of Darkness must be prepared.

Certain kinds of trance phenomena will be described in the following. Under *deep trance* – a deep, insensible sleep – the medium's spirit was thrust aside from the human body while some earthbound spirit availed itself of the body's organs of speech. Many genuine results have been produced in this manner, and several truthful messages have been given by deceased persons to relatives and friends. These messages were nearly always confined to purely earthly matters, especially the recall of past events and experiences so as to make known the identity of the deceased. A number of earthbound spirits who were unknown to the séance participants have given exact proof of life after death by stating their name, occupation, place of birth, native land, year of birth and death and so on, these particulars having been shown by subsequent investigation to be completely accurate in many cases. The earthbound spirits could normally say nothing about life in the spheres, since the memory of this does not as a rule awaken until the spirit has returned to its dwelling in the transcendental world. However, a few have passed a number of obscure and confused messages describing this life as well as they could remember it; but the majority always tried to evade direct questions on life after death, as they were ashamed to say anything too definite about the sufferings of their dismal existence on the astral plane of the Earth. Only very few have given accounts fully describing the earthbound existence in Darkness, without peace and without rest.

The many different messages from earthbound spirits, who unaccompanied by the spirits of the Light had forcibly gained access to mediumistic communication, always occurred *without God's permission,* and therefore belong to the numerous manifestations of the intervention of Darkness.

Under deep trance the medium's own spirit frequently acts as communicator, without the medium being aware of this, a circumstance that can easily be verified by an acute observer, since such messages are usually coloured by the medium's own experiences and opinions. This is also a form of the influence of Darkness, for which the medium cannot always be blamed, since in most cases it is due to accumulations of Darkness that are introduced by one or more of the participants in the large séances. Séances should therefore *never* be made available to larger circles or to the public, since such "performances" only attract Darkness and adversely affect

---

[1] This also applies to photographs of spirits, of which only a few are genuine.

not only the medium but *all* the séance participants as well.

It happens not infrequently during *trance materializations* that the medium's own spirit by the power of its will appears in visible form and "poses" as various spirits, changing its appearance by strong will, showing itself in forms from earlier incarnations or assuming an appearance corresponding to images of beloved ones in the thoughts of the participants.

Under especially conducive circumstances – accumulations of Darkness – the medium's spirit can by the power of its will form a number of thought-images that resemble human beings – phantoms – and render these visible to the onlookers, who then easily mistake these images for spirits of the dead.

However, all this can take place only if one of the Eldest is bound to the medium's body, since no human spirit possesses such a strong will that it can bring about such manifestations.

The so-called *dark chambers* used with materialization séances are really quite unnecessary, which the many spontaneously occurring materializations clearly indicate.

Dark chambers have only caused harm to spiritualism, since so many fraudulent mediums have been able to operate under their cover of darkness. In order to ensure that genuine materializations were taking place during séances, the mediums *themselves* ought to have been the first to find, or propose, a procedure that precluded all fraudulence.

For example, the following procedure might have been followed: the medium should have lain stretched out on a mattress on the floor with the arms and hands somewhat extended from the body, the participants sitting in a circle around the medium at a distance of approximately one and one half metres, forming a chain by the holding of hands; the light should have been dimmed somewhat, but leaving *everything* in the room clearly visible.

If this procedure had been followed during a *genuine* trance, the medium would have remained on the mattress in deep sleep, while the materialized spirits or the materialized phantoms of thought became visible within the circle of participants or above the medium's body. But since the "spiritual control" of most[1] materialization mediums has been the medium's own spirit or one of the disincarnated Eldest, it is understandable that everything possible has been done by *them* to keep the mediums in ignorance of the facts of the situation, and this has unfortunately succeeded only too well.

Since all materializations during séances occur under the influence of Darkness, and are therefore not permitted by God, everyone is strongly advised against such experimentation. (See also pp. 247–51).

During *somnambulistic trance,* which is induced by hypnosis or by self-hypnosis, the medium's spirit is released by the will of the hypnotist or by the medium's own will. In this released condition, the medium's spirit can move about freely, but it

---

[1] The controlling spirit has in a few cases been the spirit of a human being.

still remains connected with the physical body by the cord. If the medium's spirit is one of the Eldest or one of the Youngest, then it is able to move far afield from the body. Upon waking from an authentic state of trance the medium can give descriptions of the places, landscapes, houses, rooms, persons, and the like, that the spirit visited during the trance. If it can be determined by investigation that the medium's reports are correct and that the medium in a normal state does not know the persons concerned and has never been to the places described, such a somnambulistic trance can give good evidence that a human being does not consist of a body alone, but has in addition an independent spirit which can think and act on its own, independent of the physical body.

During *ecstatic trance*, which stems from religious ecstasy or excitation, the spirit can similarly undertake excursions by itself. Memories of these journeys in the spheres or on the astral plane of the Earth can often be retained and recalled when spirit and body are later re-united. The medium and hypnotist bear full responsibility for these two types of trance. When the medium feels that such actions are taken contrary to good conscience, these should be stopped at once, since repeated separations of the spirit from the body can often cause great physical harm.

Semi-trance or false trance manifests itself as a dreamy, sleepless state or as a form of religious fervour,[1] or over-enthusiasm; in both cases it is *always the medium's own spirit* that acts as speaker or intermediary. All that appears in this way as spiritual accounts is therefore characterized to a greater or lesser extent by the medium's *own earthly beliefs,* even though such messages occasionally appear to lie a few degrees above the individual's human intelligence and insight. In those circles where spiritualism is made into a sectarian religion by religious gatherings, the mediums often speak in such false trances. The spirits who are said to manifest themselves through these mediums exist therefore only in the imagination of the persons in question, made in no way more real by the well-known names under which these products of fantasy appear. This form of religious fervour has in fact very little or nothing to do with mediumism, since all spiritually enthusiatic persons will be able to express themselves with greater strength when they feel themselves moved by the subjects on which they are speaking, when because of this enthusiasm or excitement they clarify their train of thought, choose their words with greater care, and thereby to some extent elevate their personalities above the day-to-day level, which makes their speeches or orations seem inspired, even though there has been no direct spiritual influence.

Without being mediums, preachers and orators have often been inspired by their guardian spirits, since the guardian spirit by its presence provides the speaker with greater spiritual clarity and authority. However, such inspired orators, who are not spiritualists, will never claim that this or that well-known deceased person has

---

[1] Religious fervour must not be confused with ecstasy, which can lead into somnambulistic trance, nor with hysterical excitation, which can lead to "speaking in tongues".

spoken through them, even though they did have a distinct feeling of being under a spiritual influence.

Spiritualistic circles are therefore strongly admonished never to employ *"mediums"* – neither men nor women – as religious speakers, *since the spirits of the Light never have appeared through mediums who are in the aforementioned states of semi-trance or false trance.* If spiritualistic religious speakers were to appear at the meetings under their own names, they would receive help from their guardian spirit, as do all others who serve the Light. *But so long as they act under false pretences and wrong assumptions, the spirits of the Light can give them no assistance.*

However, mediums who speak in semi-trance are not always aware of perpetrating a fraud.[1] They usually act in good faith, since the arbitrary conduct of the spirit is rarely perceived in any definite way by the medium. But if the medium has been warned through the conscience and thus becomes aware of the fraud, Darkness will be attracted more and more – and the medium will become totally unfit to serve the cause of the Light.

Thus: *all materialization, dematerialization and the like at séances conducted in darkness or dim artificial light (though occasionally by daylight), all levitation of persons, animals or objects and all speech in trance or semi-trance have always taken place and still take place without the permission of God.*

The following forms of communication can be employed both by spirits of Darkness and by spirits of the Light: 1) Thought-inspiration[2] through mediums who have a capacity for intuitive perception. 2) Direct speech to receptive (i.e., clairaudient) mediums. 3) Writing that is to a greater or lesser extent automatic, including mediumistic drawing, painting and inspired musical achievement. *From the form and content of such communications anyone should be able to determine whether these originated from a spirit of Darkness or from a spirit of the Light.*

Intuitive thought-inspiration, when employed by the spirits of the Light, requires mediums who are absolutely truthful and understanding people, who are very much aware that except for being a usable instrument their own selves have *nothing* to do with the messages. And since a thought-inspired medium is *never* in trance or even semi-trance, but is fully alert and awake, it will always be

---

[1]) These frauds are often due to auto-suggestion on the part of the mediums.

[2]) All human beings are receptive to thought-influence, either from Darkness or from the Light, but to a varying degree. However, in a very few people the gift of intuition is so highly developed that the spirits of the Light can employ them as intermediaries to receive extensive and continuous thought-messages.

very easy for the medium to determine which thought-images and ideas originate from the self and which must be ascribed to outside intelligences.

If a medium has unlimited trust in God's protection and guidance, the form and content of the messages received will be characterized by a lucid and stringent logic infinitely beyond that of the medium's earthly personality.

A form of communication that can be employed only by *the spirits of the Light* is the following:

In cases where the intelligences who manifest themselves wish to be recognized through the words, expressions, modes of speech, and so on, that characterized their former personality on Earth, they can resort to a procedure which in every detail accurately reproduces their particular usage of words and expressions.

While the medium's physical body is at rest in *natural* sleep, for example at night, the guardian spirit - with the permission of God - releases the medium's spiritual self, who in the released state then learns and memorizes the subject matter - be it prose or poetry - to be transmitted to the earthly world. The following day, at a predetermined time known to the medium, the spirit in question, present on Earth, transfers the acquired learning from the medium's psychic to the physical brain. Through strong, concentrated radiations of Light, the thickness of the casing - or the insulation layer - between the psychic and physical brain is reduced. Once the thickness of the casing is reduced to 1/16 of a millimetre the transfer itself, which cannot be explained to human beings, takes place. Gradually as the transfer progresses the memorized subject matter emerges in the medium's physical brain, following which it can be written down in the sequence in which it appears. If a medium in the released state has not memorized the poetry or prose correctly, that is to say, if the psychic brain is unable to recall every single word, a "void" will appear in the transferred text. The missing word can then be given orally if the medium is sufficiently clairaudient; otherwise the medium must during the next release learn the forgotten subject matter, which is then transferred - when the medium is awake - and inserted at the right place in the previously written text.

This procedure is exceedingly difficult and demands great patience as well as great care and attention on the part of the spirit manifesting itself, for which reason to this date it has been attempted with only one medium in a case where the transcendental world - with God's permission - wished *to prove irrefutably* the truth[1] of the

---

[1]) This refers to a collection of poems presented by several deceased Danish poets.

statement that human personality endures after the death of the physical body.

Several other forms of mediumistic ability, for example psychometry, hypnotism,[1] hypnotic suggestion and so on, as well as many other forms of communication with spirits have been known and practised since the dawn of history. Some of them are still known throughout the world, even among the primitive peoples, among whom the Eldest have often been incarnated.

Further comment on these matters would be too circumstantial, for which reason it will merely be pointed out that it can be most harmful to allow oneself to be used in hypnotic experiments, and especially harmful for those who are easily influenced and dominated by a stronger will, since through extensive training with such a person the hypnotist can gain complete control over the subject, who thus becomes a compliant tool in the hands of the hypnotist, both during hypnosis and at all other times.

Hypnotic suggestion can sometimes be practised successfully in cases of nervous disorder, but the practitioner must be a person of absolute integrity if all possible abuse is to be precluded.

One more form of communication with spirits should also be mentioned, a form that has been much practised by the earthbound spirits, and which the spirits of the Light, the Youngest, have also employed when no better means were at hand.

When the séance participants had seated themselves around a small table,[2] their hands were laid lightly on the table top, while one of the participants posed the questions they wished to have answered. The manifesting spirit would then, by the power of its will and through the help of the séance participants' psychic and physical radiations of Light and Darkness, lift one side of the table until one of the table legs was raised a little from the floor (i.e., not complete levitation). The séance leader then slowly recited the alphabet, so that by letting the table leg fall to the floor when a particular letter was reached the spirits were able to carry out quite long conversations. However, one or more mediums had to be present. This procedure was inordinately slow and hardly satisfactory for the spirits of the Light, but was indispensable for the earthbound spirits, since this was their best and easiest means of communication when trance possession could not be employed. When the spirits of the Light had established communication with human beings, many wretched earthbound and sin-bound beings, with God's permission and accompanied by one or more of the spirits of the Light, have received great spiritual help and

---

[1] See also Commentary p. 282, regarding hypnotism.
[2] A planchette – a board of wood or cardboard on which the alphabet is inscribed, equipped with a rotating pointer – or similar means have been employed.

comfort at these table séances through sympathetic and understanding human beings.

Where help to the earthbound spirits, provided in this way or by other methods, has been associated with larger religious gatherings as a kind of soul-saving work, the help has in most cases only led to a negative result, since the majority of these sinful beings were ashamed to mention anything in public about that which plagued and tormented them. When they manifested themselves at such gatherings they refrained for this reason from telling of the true reason for their restless life in sin and in Darkness.

Religious societies are often founded with the purpose of bringing help to the sin-bound spirits, but as indicated, they have not had the intended effect. And since the mediums on these occasions have sometimes been in a trance,[1] the spirits who have spoken through them did so without God's permission, and hence unaccompanied by the spirits of the Light. In cases where those who manifested themselves were moved by a sincere and deep-felt remorse, the Youngest have later tried to bring them the help they yearned for, partly by exerting their own influence on them if that were possible, and partly by bringing them to small séance circles where they could more easily talk of that which burdened their hearts and thus come into closer contact with the Light.

Since earthbound spirits no longer inhabit the astral plane of the Earth, and since *all* the spirits of the dead are led back to the spheres within a few hours of the death of the earthly body, all help through table séances or similar forms of assistance will in the future be quite superfluous and unnecessary, for which reason all people, both mediums and non-mediums, are most earnestly advised *never themselves to call upon deceased relatives, friends or strangers.*

In the years[2] that have passed since 1911, when the earthbound spirits at God's request all returned to their dwellings in the spheres, it has many times proved to be difficult for the majority of the young and undeveloped human spirits to escape the strong, longing thoughts of the bereaved, which often, much against the respective spirits' will and desire, drew them back to the Earth once more. In the early years only a few of the disincarnated spirits were attracted back to the Earth, but after the outbreak of war in 1914 it became more and more difficult for the guardian spirits to prevent this unlawful journeying back to relatives and friends left behind on Earth.

---

[1] Very often the mediums would not be in a trance, but only pretend to be. In such cases the mediums themselves "performed" as spirits, and would then carry responsibility for their fraud.

[2] The above communication was received in the months of April and June 1918 and was added to the earlier messages pertaining to the relationship between mediums and the deceased. It was included at the request of the spirit responsible for the Commentary and was received and written down under his guidance. – Publisher's note.

Each time the immature spirits of human beings let themselves be lured to the Earth, (most often with the assistance of the medium's strong invocations of thought), it became more difficult for them to escape the calling thoughts and demanding claims of the bereaved. Many of the spirits were drawn to the various séances, where, blinded and bound by Darkness, they delivered messages that were not always in accordance with the truth,[1] especially when those on Earth demanded information on occult matters.

Because *eighty-five percent* of the spirits of human beings are young and undeveloped, it is obvious that their returning to the plane of the Earth can in no way benefit either themselves or the living, since they will only exert a disturbing influence on the earthly state of affairs, and *hamper their own development* as well. The inhabitants of the first four spheres closest to the Earth will never be able to give satisfactory or accurate answers to questions of a transcendental nature asked of them by human beings.

Imagine, for instance, parents on Earth asking their young children in the lower classes of school to give comprehensive and precise answers to questions of how pupils are instructed in the higher classes, or demanding that these children give accurate information on social, political or commercial matters, or other such circumstances in their country. Reasonable parents could not regard any messages or information obtained in this way as anything other than *childish prattle*. Similarly, it should be obvious that disincarnated spirits from the lower or lowest spheres can at best give information on what they know from their own sphere, and many cannot even give that. Hence, they will give only mediocre and vacillating answers, convey false messages or give information on objects and experiences seen from their own narrow point of view.

The next *ten percent* of spirits of human beings, from the fifth sphere, are stronger personalities, in that their will is more developed. It is therefore easier for them to resist invocation by human beings, although only by exerting the full power of their will. But in the end, despite their exertions to the contrary, many have let themselves be lured to Earth by the grief of relatives or the calling thoughts of mediums.

Only the remaining *five percent,* the inhabitants of the lowest circles in the sixth sphere,[2] have with few exceptions succeeded in remaining in their dwellings with no appreciable effort.

---

[1] However, many have described their earthly existence in great detail, and thereby given further proof of a continued existence after death.

[2] The uppermost circle or plane of the sixth sphere is inhabited exclusively by the Youngest, who have their dwellings there while they work for the progress of humanity.

As time went by and the spirits noticed that on their repeated, un-lawful visits to Earth they met with greater and greater difficulty each time they wished to return to their sphere, these spirits under-stood that in the end they would have to remain entirely earthbound and thereby create a new lower class of spirits. Since the memory of earlier earthbound existences between incarnations on Earth stood before them *all* as a dreadful scene of horror, they turned to God and in their distress and their fear they prayed to Him to help them, *so that none could come to Earth without His permission.*

God answered their prayer and in order to provide effective help to the weak and immature human spirits He created, by the power of His Will, a barrier across the Passage[2] of Light to the Earth. *Spirits from the first four spheres are not able to penetrate this barrier.* But so that human spirits should not always remain as immature and passive beings, subject to influence from the Earth, God ordained that when they had reached a certain degree of spiritual maturity and strength they should try on their own to free *themselves* from the cal-lings and the demands of human beings. This spiritual maturity *should* be reached when the spirits entered the fifth sphere. For this reason God has arranged that the impenetrability of the Light-Barrier gradually diminishes for the inhabitants of this sphere as they ascend within the sphere's planes or circles. As the impenetra-bility of the Light-Barrier diminishes, the human spirits, whose spir-itual strength increases proportionally, must themselves give greater and greater attention to the steeling of their will for the purpose of remaining in their dwellings, rather than responding to the demands of human beings to let themselves be drawn to the Earth. All neces-sary help will, of course, always be given to everyone who desires it. The guardian spirits will thus constantly seek to strengthen and to guide those who still show weakness toward earthly attraction. But no restraint whatsoever will be imposed to hold back those who despite all help break one of the laws given by God *by visiting the Earth without permission and without escort.*

Far into the future, many spirits from the fifth sphere and some from the sixth will probably let themselves be lured to the Earth by the demanding thoughts of human beings in spite of all good inten-tions and efforts to remain where they belong; and since each viola-tion is inevitably followed by a repercussion, a punishment, God has ordained *that all those who against their better knowledge and without permission return to the Earth, will each time this happens have a period corresponding to one earthly year deducted from the*

---

[1]) This Barrier does not prevent the Light from reaching the Earth.

time otherwise allotted them for rest and development in the spheres. This stipulation goes into effect automatically without questioning and without judgment, and it gives the transgressors, those who themselves do not seek to steel their will, their next incarnation sooner than normal; an incarnation for which they consequently lack *the necessary spiritual preparation.*

Thus, in order to create the best possible conditions for the disincarnated spirits, all human beings, and in particular *mediums,* are hereby seriously admonished *never* to attempt to call upon the "dead" through any form of séance, be it by conversation, materialization, psychometry, or by any other means.

In order better to understand the disturbances and the disorder that enter the astral world by such invocations on the part of human beings, the following example provides a comparison with conditions on Earth:

Would any principal of a school permit or even tolerate that the students placed under the school's supervision and care time and again should be called from their classroom during class hours by parents, relatives or friends, so that these might inquire into the welfare of the students, their scholastic progress in the various subjects or obtain information on the operation of the school, and so forth? If requests to cease such interruptions were not heeded, the only recourse of the school principal would probably be to appeal to those authorities responsible for the maintenance of the general order of society and request them to help end such untimely interruption of the work.

Therefore, if mediums having learnt the facts as here set forth do not respect this appeal from the transcendental world, *the authorities[1] of the various countries should prohibit public spiritualistic séances.*[1]

If mediums are prevented from appearing in public, and if the concept of "private spiritualistic circles" is limited to the medium's immediate family, that is, parents, brothers and sisters, husband, wife and children, *and no one else,* the mediums will probably soon lose the urge to perform, since *the large majority of mediums are motivated* by a desire for public limelight. And since material gain also plays an important part for many people, it cannot be emphasized too strongly *that all spiritualistic séances, public as well as private, to which there is an admission fee always have been and always will be under the influence of Darkness.*

---

[1] The prohibition of public séances does not violate personal free will any more than does the prohibition of assault, burglary, theft and so on. Public séances are a disorder that should not be permitted.

Mediumistic gifts were from the beginning given by God to facilitate contact between the disincarnated spirits of the Light – the Youngest – and human beings through a medium, an intermediary. But these gifts were not given for human beings to abuse by establishing contact with the dead at their own discretion or by procuring information on occult matters through experimentation. These gifts are not to be used until permission to establish such communication or to obtain such information has been given according to God's insight and Will to those who have *already* been chosen, and who in their earthly lives fully submit to the guidance of the spirits of the Light.

Only one in about 10,000 mediums[1] can be employed consistently as an intermediary between spirits of the Light and human beings. Of the remaining 9,999 only about ten to twelve can be employed spontaneously, i. e., without any preparation on the part of human beings, and of these ten to twelve perhaps three or four can be employed more than a few times. The reason for this is that most mediums lack the necessary humility, the necessary understanding of their own unimportance, and hence will at once make more demands or be steeped *in self-admiration and lust for power* and continue to experiment, which will very soon bring them under the influence of Darkness.

The mediumistic talent of the remaining number is so slight that there will always be a danger that these mediums will fall under the confounding influence of auto-suggestion, although on occasion, one or two genuine[2] communications might be established. Among these is a number of the Eldest, who can *never* be employed by the spirits of the Light.

By means of the messages that have been received through the numerous mediums who in the course of time have been in communication with earthbound spirits or with the disincarnated Eldest, many people have been led to believe that their departed dear ones would always remain nearby, that they were able to help by offering advice, giving warnings, and so forth, and that this was a natural relationship *permitted by God*. But since communications through mediums *on Earth* had their beginnings with earthbound spirits and the disincarnated Eldest *without God's permission,* it should be obvious to all in view of the information given that any such rela-

---

[1] Very often a much higher number of mediums must be rejected before the spirits of the Light can find one who may be repeatedly employed by them.

[2] In the past, mediums of slight mediumistic talent have often been employed by earthbound spirits and the Eldest. Many genuine connections have been established, but they were under the influence of Darkness, an influence under which most mediums practise and which explains the numerous false and confused mediumistic messages of the past.

tionship is abnormal and contrary to the laws given by God for the progress of humanity. Human beings must therefore abandon this misconception and in the future remember: *that the departed ones live in the various spheres that they have reached through their struggle out of Darkness and toward the Light; remember that the disincarnated human spirits no longer walk among them, because according to God's laws they must not stay upon the Earth; remember that sojourn in the spheres is a time of rest and of learning, and that the spirits will only be held back and bound by the selfish yearning and demanding thoughts of the bereaved.*

Conversely it should also be remembered that every thought of love and gratitude, free of all selfish grief and bitter yearning, will reach the beloved in the spheres and bring them great joy – a joy that passes human understanding; for the *greatest* that a person can achieve during life on Earth is this: *to awaken a pure, sincere and unselfish love that can remain intact and be faithfully remembered beyond death.*

Should God need human beings as helpers or intermediaries in the future there are numerous ways in which the spirits of the Light can call upon human beings and communicate with them whenever this may be desired. Now as in the past there are also many ways in which mankind can be warned of threatening dangers.

For example, if a human life is threatened by attack from Darkness and if it is not deemed appropriate that the person concerned should be exposed to a sudden or premature death, then this person can receive a warning through his or her guardian spirit. For this purpose the guardian spirit, in the future as in the past, can employ a human spirit who in life on Earth was a relative or friend of the person to be warned. By the power of the guardian spirit's will[1] the deceased is made visible in the earthly world, and with this sudden appearance the warnings are lent stronger force and made more credible. Many have in dreams[2] or while awake thus seen a dear departed friend or relative, who through the help of the guardian spirit has warned the person concerned in words or in images, so that death through shipwreck, railway accident, earthquake or similar disaster has been avoided.

Under the Law of Retribution, people who are not warned but die in catastrophes of this kind have exposed themselves through actions in previous incarnations to suffer death in such ways, or to endure the sufferings resulting from such accidents and misfortunes.

---

[1]) Mediums are not always required for these purposes. Where it is absolutely necessary for the guardian spirit to act without an intermediary, this is done by the power of the guardian spirit's will.

[2]) See Summary, p. 291.

People who spontaneously or more regularly receive messages or information from the transcendental world without having *requested* them will always, directly or indirectly, receive at the same time such proof that they can never doubt the identity of the originator, nor that the communication received is given with God's permission. When communication with human beings is established on the initiative *of the transcendental world,* this is normally because these particular human beings before their life on Earth began were selected to assist in spreading knowledge and understanding of life after death through writings, lectures and the like. People who have been called and chosen in this way should not let themselves be intimidated by their fellow human beings' poor judgment, their materialistic views, their prejudice or their scanty insight in these matters, but should boldly come forth with their knowledge, whether they have received this knowledge through their guardian spirit by ordinary inspiration, through their own mediumism or through that of others. But it must be clear to all *that information concerning the transcendental or the occult is given only to* **very few,** *and only to those who through their greater spiritual development – the Youngest or advanced human spirits – are able to act as spokesmen for the spiritual world.*[1]

Thus: *people, including mediums, should never themselves call upon the dead; but should human beings be called*[2] *upon from the transcendental world, then the call must be answered, and the person addressed should seek to comply with the caller's wishes.* All conceivable support and all spiritual help will be extended to those who without fear of human judgment work for the advancement of the truth and the Light.

But all who act as intermediaries between this world and the transcendental, without a calling from God and against their better judgment, will for each occasion on which a disincarnated spirit is drawn to Earth have deducted, in the same way as the spirits, a period of time corresponding to an earthly year from the time of rest and learning to which they would otherwise be entitled after completion of their life on Earth. If mediums do not heed the warnings that are hereby given them, many will expose themselves to the danger of immediate reincarnation after earthly death, **without any spiritual preparation.**

Finally, *prescience* and *clairvoyance* will be discussed.

Mediums who are in full possession of the rare ability to foresee

---

[1]) See Speech of Christ, p. 119.
[2]) See Supplement I, p. 18, Question 4.

the future are in the minority. By the foretelling of things to come these mediums take upon themselves an exceptionally heavy responsibility, since the abstract events that through the predetermination of the Elder[1] *have been,* and through human thoughts *constantly are,* recorded by the oscillations of the ether do not always become realities on the plane of the Earth. With the predictions of these seers, knowledge of possible future events becomes accessible to large numbers of people, and through the thoughts of those who are incessantly preoccupied with such forecasts, the still abstract recorded images are frequently brought into the existence that is real for human beings. This often hinders the Youngest in their determined effort by means of their strong thought-influence to prevent some of the adversities that the Elder has determined for mankind, or that people create for themselves by their sinful thoughts and lusts; adversities that the Youngest – the guardian spirits – could often alleviate and perhaps partly or even entirely prevent.

These ether-recordings[1] relate to individuals as well as to entire nations. Such and such a thought, such and such an action determines such and such a future event, for the individual as well as for the many. *Through their own thoughts and actions human beings thus create in the truest and deepest sense their own lives and the lives of their descendants.* But with the voluntary help of the Youngest, God tries to guide the will of human beings for the good, and many criminal and evil deeds have thereby been prevented from entering the plane of the Earth as real events. Where only the individual is concerned, it is easier for the spirits of the Light with their influence to annul a few or many of the threatening abstract events. Where, on the other hand, entire nations are concerned, it is often very difficult to guide the rulers and leaders onto the right path and draw them away from thoughts and actions which can convert threatening abstract ether-recordings to earthly, concrete events. Very often the Youngest fail, especially when they are confronted with people of a strong individual will, since in such cases it is nearly impossible to guide, for example, heads of state, diplomats and leaders of people away from the erring paths of hate, lust for power and envy and onto the difficult paths of toleration. The disputes among nations that so often lead to bloody, brutal and senseless wars, could many times have been prevented if the leaders had in each given instance *always* followed the guiding voice of their conscience, instead of succumbing to the desire to take things into their own hands.

Predictions of things to come can often counteract the work of the

---

[1]) See also Summary, pp. 307–09.

Youngest for a brighter and happier existence on Earth, bring about *the very thing* that the Youngest with such great effort try to prevent.

Only in those cases where the one who can foresee the future feels compelled – through the conscience – to share such knowledge with others should the "vision" or the readings in the ether-waves be revealed.

Second sight, or clairvoyance, means that a human being can see with the spiritual sight, either sporadically or more regularly. If necessary for some specific purpose this ability of clairvoyance can be developed by the power of the human will or with the help of the guardian spirit.

The Youngest have occasionally appeared to clairvoyants, but this should not be confused with the true apparition that is seen with the eyes of the physical body.

In earlier times most clairvoyants were able to see the earthbound spirits, and through clairvoyants many people have received descriptions from which they recognized the deceased. It should be noted, however, that in most of these cases it was not the *spirit* of the deceased that the medium described, but the *thought-phantom* of the subject involuntarily created by the inquirer. Only in cases where the medium was able to reveal facts that were totally unknown to both the medium and the inquirer, and which further investigation proved to be in accordance with the truth, can one be sure that it was the spirit itself and not a thought-phantom. But as previously stated, (pp. 251–52), *human beings should in the future never seek information about the dead.*

The casing, or insulation layer, between the spirit and the body that is cast off at death has often been mistaken by clairvoyants for the spirit of a deceased person. A spirit, even the most sinful, will always look like a living being, whereas the cast-off casing most closely resembles a mask. In places where there are great accumulations of Darkness the casings are often preserved for long periods of time, since they can be dissolved and absorbed only by the Light. In the course of time many clairvoyants have seen these casings, which can best be described by the term "ghosts".

The casings of the Eldest are dissolved only by Darkness and therefore remain for a long time in places where there are strong Light-radiations, since the Light cannot absorb the Darkness of which the casings are made until the radiations of Darkness have dissolved them.

CONCLUDING SUMMARY

Through all eternity God was impersonal, until the moment Thought and Will met and became united in a harmony of perfect beauty. Then He arose as a personal Being, as the Master of the Light and Victor over Darkness, limited in His personal Being, unlimited in His supreme Will, containing time and space – limited as well as unlimited – in His all-embracing Thought. A Divinity and a Power, whom no human being can even begin to comprehend. Even the most glorious, the most exalted image of God is but a faint reflection of His true glory, omnipotence and wisdom.

All human beings carry in their thought a reflection of God. The younger and less developed the human spirit, the fainter and more obscure will be the reflection, and the more human becomes the divine ideal, since all ideals that spring from the human imagination are tainted with purely human emotions and human qualities. Therefore, the more obscure the reflection, the more the individual cloaks the divine in mysticism, in order perhaps to cover up or explain away the incomprehensible, that which cannot be seen with earthly eyes or conceived of by the weak, the undeveloped thought of human beings. But if the spirit is older and more developed, then God and the divine will be reflected more purely, more nobly and more gloriously in human thought, and the better will the human beings be able to conceive of an exalted, divine ideal, with which they seek to become one in the fervent devotion of prayer.

Not only the sublimity and omnipotence of God are reflected in the thought of every human being, but also His Fatherliness, His fervent, profound and all-embracing love. The thoughts, actions and lives of truthful, right-minded and pure human beings will therefore clearly reflect God's compassionate love, and in their hearts they will carry the complete trust of a child in a distant, invisible Father, in whose keeping they feel happy and secure.

But the young, the undeveloped human spirits, who are still strongly influenced by Darkness, are only dimly able to conceive of God as the gentle, loving and just Father. Only too often does He appear to them as the stern, masterful ruler, a terrifying, avenging and demanding deity, who grants nothing without suitable tribute in the form of blood sacrifice or sweet-scented offerings – a divinity with whom mankind must constantly barter to attain the desired blessings. But also the many who now live in slavish fear of their God and Father will sometime in the future, through the many progressive incarnations, be able to feel the child's unswerving faith and trust in Him.

Many people carry in their thoughts and in their hearts a glorious and clear reflection of the Divinity, but *man-made* dogmas, handed down from generation to generation, have veiled and obscured the original image that they carried with them from their existence in the transcendental world. These people should search their innermost selves, should reject all false assertions and wrong conclusions, until the veil is lifted from the divine reflection, that it may again stand clearly in all its radiant beauty.

But with the passing of time and as century is added to century and Darkness is slowly eliminated, more and more human beings will begin to understand God's boundless love, His justice, His kindness and compassion, and they will realize that they have belittled God by endowing Him, the Highest One, with mere human qualities, which must be removed before His image can once more stand exalted, pure and noble.

Every human being should strive to understand this idealization of the Divinity.

When Christ in his Speech to humanity (see p. 109) says: "My words shall sound unto all the peoples of the Earth. All shall hear them, and they shall reach unto the farthest regions of the Earth", he does not mean that those who are *now* able to understand and to rejoice in his Gospel of Love should forthwith go out into the world and proclaim his words to others holding different ideas and beliefs. Rather, he said this because he knew that sooner or later *all* people, some in their present and others in their future incarnations, will be able to achieve acceptance of his message with heartfelt joy and with deep understanding.

But even though that time still lies far in the future, when all existing religions will have merged into one common religion, human beings themselves can do much to shorten this time by not striving *against their inner convictions,* by not assuming a posture of indifference and hostility to this message that is presented to them from the transcendental world. They should strive to make it known and to propagate it from individual to individual, from people to people, in a *calm* and *dignified* manner, without *compelling* propaganda or *fanatic* missionary zeal; for this message can be of great help to *the human spirit so that in its earthly existence it can become the mirror that captures and radiates a purer, stronger and more beautiful image of the Divinity than has been the case in the past.* But it must be clear to all that the human reflection of God and the divine, no matter how glorious it may become in the earthly existence of human beings, can never fully reach its exalted ideal.

God's children who sprang from His Fatherly bosom – the Eldest, the Youngest and the human spirits – have *all* received the gift of eternal life; but since God never compels anyone to receive His gifts, He has also endowed every created spirit with a free will, with the right of self-determination; *but He has thereby limited His own Will and His own Knowledge.* On reaching a certain level of maturity all God's children can by the right of self-determination themselves decide whether they wish to receive the gift of eternal life or whether they choose to sink back into God's Fatherly bosom.

This truth has been applied in an erroneous manner in Buddhist doctrine, in which according to some interpretations the human spirit, upon attaining the highest perfection, sinks back into "Nirvana" – into the Divinity. Buddha himself originally taught that when the human spirit through numerous rebirths had attained perfect freedom from all earthly influence and all earthly desire, it then returned to the source – to the Divinity – from which it sprang. This absorption, or reversion, was not considered by Buddha as the annihilation of the individuality but as an indissoluble bond with the divine, whereby the reverted self could follow the earthly drama in serenity and contemplation. This absorption into the Divinity could sometimes be recognized in fleeting moments by certain highly advanced spirits in their human existence, and was then an indication that the spirit was living through its final incarnation.

All creation, the primary (the transcendental) as well as the secondary (the star universes) and all that has been called forth from Darkness through the fall of the Eldest, can at any time God chooses be dissolved once more by the power of His omnipotent Will into the elements from which it was created or evolved.

Since all being and all life exist only by virtue of *primal Thought* and *primal Will* – the source of all creation, the first cause and first beginning of all that is – God, who emanated Himself and through His emanation became capable of creation, can at any time He chooses dissolve His own Being as well as all creation; in other words: *revert Himself together with all that He created to that which*

He was, without beginning and without end – Thought and Will.
Cosmos will continue to exist only so long as God maintains the created through the all-embracing laws of His Thought (gravitation, cohesion, adhesion, centrifugal and centripetal force, and so forth).

*In theory God can thus let Himself and all creation sink back into
"Logos"; in practice He will never do so, since through His unending love for all His many children He has bound Himself for all
eternity by giving them the promise of eternal life.*

At the moment God emanated Himself, He drew Darkness under
the Light in a mighty circulation through His flaming Being, that
Darkness should thus be absorbed and purified by the Light.

When God resolved to create the star universes, Darkness was far
from absorbed and eliminated, it existed with latent poles as a weak
undercurrent in the swirling waves of the Light.

Since even the highest[1] oscillations of the Darkness that is
enclosed by the Light are much slower than the lowest frequencies of
the Light, Darkness will always precipitate, so to speak, in the sea of
the Light, for which reason God had to form the innermost core of
the four mother suns from the less rapid oscillations of the Light –
imperceptible to the human eye – which once more enclosed the
Darkness, with its still lower frequency of oscillation. From the
innermost cores of the globes to their outermost limits the oscillations increase in speed. As its frequency increases the Light also
increases in concentration of strength and in ethereal radiance, for
which reason the outer layer becomes like a radiant corona – not perceptible to the human eye – though without attaining the degree of
concentration and ethereal radiance emitted by those oscillations of
the Light that, through the power of God's Will, created His own
Kingdom (the Central Globe).

Since all of the globes in the star universes have directly or indirectly originated from the four first-created mother suns, they are all
identical in their structure. But since the ether (the Light, and the
Darkness precipitated in it) flows through and pervades all space,
and thereby all the globes in the universes, the darker cores of the
globes will gradually diminish as the waves of the Light in their circulation draw more and more Darkness away to be purified through
God's flaming Being.

When God had chosen the Earth as the dwelling place for the
beings He had thought to create, He formed from the higher –
ethereal – oscillations of the Light a world of perfect beauty that sur-

---

[1]) The highest frequency of the polarized Darkness separated at the fall of the Eldest was,
by contrast, about half way between the lowest and the highest frequencies of the Light.

rounded the Earth as a sphere, as a spherical shell. It was God's intention that those of His first-created children who were chosen to be the leaders of the inhabitants of the Earth should stay here while carrying out their task. The ethereal radiations from this transcendental world should according to God's plan and together with the ethereal-astral radiations of the corona of Light of the Earth's sun have regulated climatic conditions on the Earth itself.

But when the Eldest began to experiment with their attempts at creation, large quantities of Darkness were separated from the ether, and these ravaged the world of Light that God had created around the Earth.[1] This separation activated the Poles of Darkness, and as a portion of the separated Darkness slowly approached the Earth, the hitherto latent poles in the Globe's core of Darkness were gradually activated under the influence of the approaching, polarized Darkness. As the Darkness drew closer to the core, it intermingled more and more with the Globe's ethereal corona of Light, causing a significant reduction in the corona's frequency of oscillation. When Darkness reached the core of the Earth, the entire Globe[1] was darkened, and it appeared to be without any luminous corona (this corona was visible only from the transcendental world). But because the Light, through God's victory over Darkness, can never be extinguished or conquered, Darkness could not eliminate or destroy the Globe's ethereal radiation of Light, but could only contaminate and obscure it.

Although the frequency of oscillation of the corona of Light was reduced and moderated by the influx of Darkness, the radiation of Light was still strong enough to contain or fixate the Darkness that fused with the Globe's core of Darkness. Due to this fixation, the life-principle of the polarized Darkness fused with the seeds of life – given by God – that were in the Globe's corona of Light, and cells of various kinds emerged. Some of these cells were of dual sex, others were of single sex. The reproduction, or generation, of new dual cells took place, and still takes place, by the simple processes of division, ligation, and the like; while on the other hand the generation of new single cells took place, and still takes place, by a preceding union of two cells of opposite sex.

Some microbes can reproduce in two ways. For example, when certain disease-producing bacteria enter the body as parasites, they reproduce by a simple division that gradually reduces their vitality, and the illness is cured as the bacteria expire, or

---

[1]) Most of the globes in the galactic system to which the Earth belongs are contaminated by Darkness to a greater or lesser extent; many are completely saturated.

as their vitality is reduced to the point where they no longer interfere with the body's normal functions. But if the patient receives a new infection of the same kind before all bacteria have expired, a union of the present and former bacteria occurs, with the resulting divisions. If the new bacteria are sufficiently vital, the former ones are revitalized, whereby the illness flares up again, until the vitality of the bacteria is weakened once more through numerous divisions. The disease can of course be alleviated or cured in other ways, for example by the body's own antitoxin, by administering antidotes, and so forth. The foregoing refers only to the normal life-cycle of the bacteria.

Bacteria of related strains can also merge, or be absorbed by one another, with subsequent division as a result. In this way new strains appear that produce new diseases.

Each single seed of life that God by the power of His Thought and Will had implanted in the Earth's ethereal corona of Light carried within itself the prototype of the animal or the plant, i.e., the form into which these seeds – by the power of God's Will and at a time determined by Him – should grow forth in the world of Light that He wished to create on Earth. Since these seeds were brought forth to earthly life through a union with the life-principle of Darkness, they became subject to the distorting, malforming and degenerative influence of Darkness. But since the corona of Light had fixated the Darkness that transformed the Globe, the Light retained a regulating, elevating, differentiating and harmonizing influence on the single and dual-sexed cells and their reproduction, which had been produced by the fusion of the seeds of life with the life principle of Darkness.

The dual-sexed cells represented the lowest reproductive life form of Darkness, which could not lead to higher or more complex forms, and which for this reason were unable to produce even the weakest reflection of the prototypes that rested in the seeds of life given by God. The union of the single-sexed cells (male and female), controlled and guided by the regulating and harmonizing influence of the corona of Light,[1] is therefore a blind, mechanical simulation by Darkness of the *consciously-willed* union of primal Thought and primal Will that resulted in the emergence of God as a personal Being.

Under the influence of the corona of Light through millions of years, with the continuous cell division and cell formation resulting

---

[1]) According to the laws that God established by His Thought and Will for the eternal radiation of the Light's energy, the lawless and aimless chaos on Earth is re-directed toward order and purpose, toward greater usefulness, greater beauty and greater perfection.

from the merging of male and female cells, the more and more complex forms of life evolved, the various intricate tissues organized into bones, muscles, nerves, and the like, and into the various modes of digestion, reproduction, etc., both in the animal and in the plant worlds. All these forms continually strive toward the prototypes implanted by God in the original seeds of life. This striving was, and it still is, unceasingly restrained and disturbed by the degenerative tendencies of Darkness, and during this time when the power of Darkness over the Earth was so exceptionally much greater than the power of the Light, the formation of cells led to the most hideous and bizarre forms, for example through the animals' mating at random, so that in many ways they were departing from rather than advancing toward the prototypes[1] that were embedded in the seeds.[1] As the Light gains greater power over the "separated Darkness", these mutations of Darkness will disappear, which means that the many hideous and harmful animal species will slowly die out over the coming thousands or millions of years. (The same holds true for the plant kingdom).

When human intelligence began experimenting with creating new forms within the existing animal and plant species, human beings in many ways forestalled the influence of the Light. If these hybrids are to achieve a natural, independent and continued propagation within the developed forms, they must for hundreds, thousands or perhaps millions of years be exposed to the same care and the same treatment to which they are now subjected. Otherwise, when they are once again left to themselves, they will sooner or later revert to those forms they had reached under the slow but progressive ordering, elimination, adaptation and harmonization process of the corona of Light.

However, the earthly forms will never reach the perfection of the prototypes in the primary seeds given by God, partly because these, for example in the animal kingdom, had been destined to lead a life without propagation and without death, and partly because Darkness cannot be completely eliminated until the Earth itself is destroyed and has been dissolved.

When the Eldest created the human beings, it was their intention that the species they created should be maintained through reproduction. They endowed for this reason the male and female life-seeds of the human sexual cells with a characteristic, with a form,

---

[1]) As a result of the overwhelming influence of Darkness at that time, many of the primary prototypes given by God were completely destroyed, for which reason the creatures that evolved from the damaged seeds did not bear the faintest resemblance to the original prototypes.

that corresponded to the human type represented by the given seeds. These primary seed prototypes (invisible under any form of human observation) were thus to be the principal foundation for the creatures of the Eldest and, through reproduction, were destined to be reborn and maintained in the future generations so long as the Earth was in the power of the Eldest. But when God adopted the human race and endowed the physical body with a divine element, the body was brought under the harmonizing influence of the Light. And as an ever-increasing number of the Youngest were incarnated among human beings, the fulness of beauty that they all carried in their thought also began through procreation to exert a strong influence on the Eldest's primary prototypes in the human life-seeds. This influence was mostly directed toward the beautification and ennoblement of the physical body. During the many millions of years that the human body has been subject to the progressive and beautifying influence of the Youngest and of the Light, the primary prototypes of the Eldest have gradually departed somewhat from the original degrading stamp of Darkness. This ennoblement is especially noticeable in those races where the Youngest are regularly incarnated.

The human male and female life-seeds will also at any given time accurately reflect the personal characteristics of each individual. Thus, all outer and inner family traits and talents inherited by each individual from his or her ancestors, and all experience personally acquired in life on Earth, lie dormant both in the physical and astral life-seeds of the individual and can be transmitted to the offspring through procreation.[1] Through the coincidence of various internal and external circumstances, these latent characteristics and talents can be caused to reappear in the new individuals. However, outward characteristics as well as inner qualities can also, through various coinciding causes, be repressed through several generations, only later to reappear in new combinations in a few or in several members of the family.

Through the incarnations of the Youngest the primary human prototype is drawn further and further away from its original appearance, both the astral and the physical. But if the Youngest were to discontinue their incarnations, the ennobling stamp that they have left on the human body would soon fade away and the physical body would begin to resemble its original prototype. All the psychic enrichment that human beings have gained from the Youngest through the astral counterpart would likewise slowly fade away, almost to the point of vanishing. And if God in addition were to take

---

[1] See also pp. 274–75.

back the divine element, human beings would within an appallingly short time – a few thousand years – revert to the characteristics with which they were endowed by the Eldest, characteristics that would be far below and far more animal-like than those of the most primitive peoples of today, and the last trace of spiritual life that humanity has received through the incarnations of the Youngest would at the same time completely disappear. *Human beings would again be entirely the creatures of the Eldest.*

Therefore: in the animal and plant kingdom a slow *approach* to the primary prototypes is taking place under the upgrading and ordering influence of the Light, an approach to those prototypes that *God* at the creation of the Earth gave for the animal and plant life that He intended to call forth. However, in the human world a slow *departure* from the primary prototype is taking place under the ordering and beautifying influence of the Light and the Youngest, a departure from the *primary prototypes* that were given by the Eldest at the creation of mankind.

During the development of new individuals and through a combination of concurrent circumstances under the influence of Darkness, both astral and physical reversions toward the original prototypes can occur. The incursions of Darkness can likewise be so powerful as to cause deviations from these prototypes, thereby producing malformed offspring. If the incursions of Darkness go so deep as to impair the basis of the prototype, both astral and physical deviations, malformations and deficiencies can be inherited by the offspring. But should the human body for some reason become deformed or deficient during life on Earth, for example through amputations, surgical removal of organs, deformities caused by burns and the like, then the prototype is not changed. Only when Darkness intervenes directly and transmutes the prototype does the changed characteristic become heritable.

Because of the fixation by the corona of Light of the astral and molecular Darkness, all earthly life, all organic and inorganic substances arose as dualities, so that the forms that were due only to the molecular oscillations of the fixated material Darkness – oscillations of larger particles – assumed an apparently solid consistency in the earthly world, but appeared misty and unreal when seen from the transcendental world; whereas the counterparts that were formed from the fixated astral Darkness – faster oscillations of smaller particles – in combination with the reduced and muted oscillations of the polluted corona of Light assumed solid,[1] visible forms[1] and figures[1] when seen from the transcendental world, but remained in-

---

[1] Though not as firm in its consistency as that which is produced by the oscillations of the Light, as for example in the higher spheres.

visible to the eyes of human beings when they subsequently entered the earthly world.

Thus: the Earth's ethereal corona of Light fixated the Darkness that had fused with the core of the Earth; the faster and the less rapid oscillations of Darkness were thereby linked together, so that the molecular products of Darkness were strengthened through the somewhat faster oscillations, smaller particles and greater cohesive and adhesive properties of the astral Darkness. But the possibility was thereby created for the Light gradually to acquire a more regulating and balancing influence on the molecular products of Darkness on Earth, since the capacity of the molecules for stabilizing one another in the rotating oscillation, as well as their capacity for mutual adhesion – as for example, in the structuring of cells – was significantly strengthened through the fixation and reinforcement of the stabilizing, cohesive and adhesive properties of the particles of astral Darkness by the corona of Light. Where a pathological state – infection by micro-organisms or other abnormal conditions – might threaten to dissolve the bond between the molecular products of Darkness and their astral counterparts, the possibility was also created for the Light, through its strong vital force and stabilizing, cohesive and adhesive power, to counteract or arrest the incipient dissolution. And in cases where the cause of this incipient dissolution could be removed or eliminated, the greater stabilizing, cohesive and adhesive capacity of the Light would be able once more to bind the loosened bond between the molecular products of Darkness and their astral counterparts, whereby the complete separation that would otherwise result in death and disintegration would be prevented, so that, for example, the life span of earthly forms of animals and plants could be prolonged through the re-establishment by the Light of the bond with their astral counterparts.

Through fixation by the corona of Light of the Darkness that flowed into and over the Earth, and of the life-principle that existed in it, the life-potential of the molecular products of Darkness was thus improved and prolonged.

If the Globe's ethereal corona of Light had not been strong enough to fixate the Darkness, the Light would never have been able to gain any influence at all over the Darkness that had been separated by the Eldest; the Earth would then, if it had not been disintegrated and dissolved, have been brought completely into the power of Darkness, since the ethereal corona of Light, *which cannot be eliminated* by Darkness, would have been re-absorbed by the ether; in this case God would have had only one way in which to re-establish order amid the destruction: by the power of His Will to dissolve and annihilate the Earth, the ravaged Kingdom and His eldest, fallen children; for on account of the re-absorption by the ether of the ethereal radiations of the Earth and the ravaged Kingdom, the territory thus conquered by Darkness would have been completely precluded from all further connection with the Light. But since God had endowed all His children with a free will, and thereby limited His own power over them, He could never annihilate the Eldest, no matter how deep they had fallen, without breaking His promise. For which reason this means of restituting the fallen and the destruction that had occurred could never be realized, for if God had annihilated the existence of the Eldest, He would have done this *against their wish and against their will.*

In His omniscience God had foreseen this, and for this reason He had laid a world of Light around the Earth – the Kingdom ravaged by Darkness – formed from the rapid, ethereal oscillations of the Light, and endowed the ethereal-astral corona of the Globe with a strength of Light far greater than that possessed by the other suns and the stars and planets. The Earth's corona of Light thereby became so concentrated that it was transformed from the ethereal-astral into the ethereal, and thus became capable of fixating the in-flowing Darkness. Should any of God's children succumb to Darkness, the possibility was thus created of restoring all things to their proper order in the course of time through a steadily increasing influence on the part of God and of the Light, even though this reconquest from Darkness might take many aeons to achieve, for there could, of course, be no question of exerting any force against the free will of the fallen children.

With this provision God thus succeeded in saving His eldest children from absolute perdition.

The remaining astral Darkness that surrounded the Globe, and which had neither fused with the core nor been fixated by the corona of Light, partly absorbed the radiance from the earthly sun's ethereal-astral corona of Light, so that the astral counterpart of the Earth together with all counterparts of earthly life existing there was left unilluminated, without any appreciable difference between day and night. But the radiance of the sun's less luminous core, which consists of precipitated Darkness enclosed by the Light's slow oscillations, was able to pass through astral Darkness almost without resistance and to illuminate the earthly world, though it was not able to illuminate the astral counterpart of the Globe. (The slowest oscillations that enclose the sun's core will in the course of time become visible to the human eye).

In order to render the primordial state of the Earth's astral counterpart more understandable to human thought, the following comparison between astral conditions and an earthly scene may serve to illustrate the situation: during a storm – for example a thunderstorm, which to human beings is a visible manifestation of the powers of Darkness – the dark thunder clouds will, depending on the severity of the storm, to a greater or to a lesser extent exclude the rays of the sun that under normal conditions are visible to the human eye. Even though the sunlight has apparently vanished, the sun and its rays are still present behind the thick cloud cover. The astral Darkness around the entire Earth similarly held back the sun's ethereal-astral radiations of Light, so that they reached neither the Earth nor its astral counterpart.

According to God's plan, it was the ethereal-astral radiations of the earthly sun that should have illuminated and irradiated the Earth.

Neither the *weakest* rays from the sun's core of Darkness, nor the most strongly shining rays from the sun's corona of Light, will ever become visible to the eyes either of human beings or of animals.

Since the Eldest had decided to create beings who could make themselves masters of the Earth, they had to try to produce a creature that, without being an animal, nevertheless had the structure of animals as prototype both in astral and in earthly respects; to separate the molecular oscillations of the fixated Darkness and to create from these alone was impossible from the outset, because of the poor capacity for adhesion and cohesion of these molecules. Besides, the life-principle of molecular Darkness did not possess a sufficiently long-lasting vitality for this to form the sole basis for a sufficiently regular and continued reproduction. Thus, it became necessary for the Eldest to utilize the life-principle of both the astral and the molecular Darkness which had been fixated by the corona of Light and which, by fusing with the life-principle that was given by God in the corona of Light, had produced cells in all their various forms.

Being obliged to work with this "double material" to a great extent delayed the Eldest and complicated their aim, and since in the pursuit of their goal they constantly "forgot" various minor details that were essential to the whole, it was necessary for them to experiment for a long time with the design and assembly of cells into bone and organic tissue before they achieved a result that was satisfactory to *them;* a result that in several important and fundamental respects nonetheless turned out to be most unfortunate for human beings.

One of these many imperfections will be described in the following, since it is of especially great importance to human beings, namely: the earthly body's insufficient capacity for regeneration and reconstruction of the internal organs, bones, and so forth.

As mentioned earlier, some of the life-seeds that existed in the corona of Light before the wanton destruction by Darkness began were destined by God to appear on Earth, under the influence of the Light, as various animal species having an enduring life in the form once given, and not being subject to any manner of death or partial destruction. Hence, no law was given by God for the regeneration of lost parts or impaired organs, since such a law would have been entirely superfluous in a world of the Light. But when Darkness awakened the latent seeds destined to become animal forms, these became in various ways subject to death and decay, and for the higher species of animal there was no prospect of regenerating by new growth any damaged or lost parts of the body. And when the Eldest created human beings, partly with the existing animal forms as prototypes for their internal structure, they forgot, confused as they were by Darkness, to take this deficiency into account. For this reason the Eldest established no laws for a *more extensive* reconstruction of the human body.

Thus: in cases where human beings through accident or through necessary amputation lose an entire limb or part of a limb, the loss cannot be made good by any form of regenerative growth. Nor can anyone, no matter how highly developed the spirit, by the power of will or by the radiations of the spirit-body, cause new parts or new limbs to grow in the damaged areas. *Neither will prayers to God nor calls upon His assistance be of the least benefit in such cases; since God never violates the law for the construction and existence of the human body, the imperfect law that was established and followed by the Eldest when they formed and created the first human beings, and for whose deficiency they alone bear the full responsibility.*

The possibility that God would take upon himself any responsibility for so incomplete a creation as the human body, which in every respect is a very *poor imitation of God's own creation,* is absolutely out of the question.

Even if it had been God's intention by the power of His Will to improve upon the creatures of the Eldest by establishing laws for the regeneration of excised organs and amputated limbs, this would not have been the only change necessary, since the human body as it now appears from the hand of its creators is singularly imperfect in several other respects of importance to human beings.

However, if God had sought to relieve these deficiencies and to establish laws for the perfection and reconstruction of the physical body, He would thereby also have accepted responsibility for His fallen children's work of creation. *But God would no more do this than an artist on Earth would accept responsibility for the botchery and bungling of a pupil or an imitator. God will therefore never change that which was once given by the Eldest. But He tries, through the intelligence with which He has enriched human beings, to mitigate some of the many deficiencies.* (For example, through medicine or surgery; and where the medical arts do not suffice, human beings have learned to resort to mechanical aids).

———————

Through the many incarnations, the human spirit builds up its individual personality. Just as a mature or aging person can remember and look back upon thoughts and feelings and recall incidents and actions from early childhood, and yet as an adult in every way be able to identify with the child maturing slowly over the days and years, so can the released spirit remember as far back in time[1] as thought can reach and still feel a complete identity with all the human beings to whom it has given spiritual life. The gradual development of the self unfolds before the spirit as kaleidoscopic images, from the first feeble and weak personal beings to whom it has been bound, to those who through a slow progression have become more highly developed and more conscious personalities.

Therefore: *just as a human being at any given time represents the sum of his or her life, so does the individual personality of a released spirit represent the sum of the thoughts, feelings, actions and experiences of all its previous lives on Earth.*

However, the incarnations of the Youngest[2] present a different picture. When the Youngest promised God to become the leaders and mentors of human beings they were already highly developed personalities. When they look back on the lives that they have led as human beings, they feel – to use an easily understandable illustration from earthly life – more like actors and actresses who recall the stage figures to whom they have given life over the years by their art and talent. Actors always prefer the stage roles that most closely express their true selves and were brought to life in the portrayal because of the actors' distinctive character. In the same way will also the Youngest in their recollection of previous lives feel most attracted to and will most closely identify with those human beings on whom they have left the purest and most noble imprint of their spirit's exalted

———————

[1] In the same way that a human being is unable to recall the very first years of life, a released human spirit is unable to recall the very first incarnations.

[2] The Youngest are of course able to remember even their very first incarnations.

individuality. And like the actors who on leaving the stage will cast off their masks and reveal their true selves, so will also the Youngest, when at death they leave the earthly scene and once more awaken to full consciousness, cast off the human mask and appear as the highly developed individualities that they were before entering the earthly stage to take part in the great drama of the world.

The Eldest, who through their wilful embodiment as human beings brought themselves under the Law of Retribution, must – incarnation after incarnation – all restore their personalities, which were debased and distorted by Darkness. But in His deep compassion God extends the greatest possible help to these unfortunate beings by blotting out, as far as this is possible, the memory of all that they had experienced before the Earth came into being, so that to all appearances they are like human spirits.

Just as every released human spirit can look back upon its struggle out of Darkness and forward toward the Light, so can God follow His own struggle out of Darkness through past eternity until the final victory was reached. But to God it is not retrospection but experience in the present; for as He carries *all* time – finite as well as infinite – in His all-embracing Thought, the concept of time does not exist for Him.

The concepts of time and space are given by God for the use of all created beings; thus *all* of them are to a greater or lesser degree dependent on these concepts. The higher the spirit rises, the more it will be freed from these limiting concepts, but it will never gain full mastery over time and space. Since they were emanated by God through the power of His Will, even God's Servants cannot attain complete release from the concepts of time and space. Where God wishes to be, there He is, the same *instant* that the Thought arises; but for God's Servants some time must pass from the conception of the thought until it is carried out. It takes, for example, *three seconds* for God's Servants to cover the distance between God's Kingdom and the Earth.

In all that has been created or called to life on Earth there is a faint reflection of God's own struggle forward. Each planted seed lies enclosed in the darkness of the Earth until it inevitably sprouts forth toward the light. The human child and the mammal's young lie enclosed in the darkness of the maternal womb until the moment comes when they inevitably strive forward toward the light. The young of birds are enclosed in the darkness of the egg until also they inevitably struggle forth from the shell, and so forth. But the struggles of the seed, the child, the mammal's young and the young of birds from darkness into light, from *becoming* into *being,* these are unconscious, for it is the victorious power of the Light that draws them forth. These *unconscious* struggles are thus no more than involuntary imitations of God's *conscious* struggle.

Also in the struggle of mankind away from primitive, beast-like beings – caricatures of their creators – to the state of development now attained by the average human being can be seen a faint reflection and a likeness of God's own struggle out of Darkness.

The greatest likeness can be found, however, in the struggle forward of each individual human spirit through the many earthly incarnations from the deepest spiritual Darkness until certainty of the spirit's own sovereign will for the Light releases it from the Earth and leads it slowly to the goal – God's Kingdom – a goal that still lies far into the future for even *the most advanced human spirit.*

The unceasing struggle of earthly life away from Darkness and toward the Light is first of all due to the *Earth's ethereal corona of Light,* which by its fixation of the Darkness that was separated out at the fall of the Eldest became able to influence the earthly-material products of Darkness, and which by the strength that God had concentrated in its radiations became able to bring the chaotic life and distorted life-forms of Darkness into a more orderly state. Life on Earth as human beings experience it therefore became a ceaseless struggle from the *possibility to the reality of life,* an existence that on account of the short life span allotted to the material products of Darkness is constantly subject to decline, withering, death and destruction; a struggle and a cycle that will continue as long as the conditions for life on Earth obtain.

Even though the sun's role as the Earth's physical source of heat and light must not be disregarded, but must always be taken into consideration in connection with life on Earth, the solar rays could never have called forth the profusion of forms of life that exist on the Earth, had the ethereal corona of Light – the Earth's soul, or psyche – not existed. Nor would the radiance of the sun have been able to exercise any significant *regulating* influence on existing conditions, apart from the greater or lesser influence that is dependent on and arises from the various positions of the Globe in relation to the sun, and from the distance of the various regions of the Earth from its equator.

But since God, by the power of His Will, has formed an ethereal corona of Light around the Earth, its radiations of energy support and strengthen the radiance of the sun that penetrates the atmospheric layers to benefit the Globe, so that the influence of this radiance upon earthly life *thereby acquires a greater and more valuable significance.*

Since the sun has to a great extent been affected by the many collisions with accumulations of Darkness that drifted, and which still drift, about in space, *those* radiations that reach the Earth through the atmospheric layers are not of a uniform strength, because the rays from the affected parts are considerably weaker than the others. These differences influence the meteorological and climatic conditions.

The Ice Ages of the Earth were caused by the reduced strength of the sun's radiance after collisions with drifting accumulations of Darkness; but since the radiance from the sun's corona of Light and the surrounding Light-ether have eliminated large portions of the accumulations of Darkness that were depolarized by the collision, more normal climatic conditions prevail once more on Earth at this time, many thousands of years later.

The corona of Light also acts as a *condensing medium* for the radiance of the sun that reaches the Earth. If the corona did not exist, the solar rays would be refracted during their passage through the Earth's atmospheric layers, and would seem to earthly eyes to be broken and scattered. Since the corona not only now encloses the whole Globe, but has in addition fixated the Darkness to whose astral and molecular oscillations the earthly bodies and the earthly forms owe their existence, all luminous bodies and sources of light each separately appear, like sunlight, with a unified monochrome radiation of light. As the corona is cleansed of Darkness, which takes place exceedingly slowly, it will become better and better able to overcome the capacity for refraction and colour-separation[1] of the atmosphere, of water, glass and other materials. This slowly increasing resistance of the corona to all[2] forms of refraction and scattering will at some time in the future be of advantage to instruments for astronomic observations, when lenses will admit of significant enlargement without the colour tones of refraction interfering with the astronomic observations.

The Earth's ethereal corona of Light is the *vital energy* of earthly life, a stabilizing, sustaining, regulating, unifying, stimulating and renewing energy that constantly radiates power and strength to the smallest things as well as to the largest; an energy that can never be destroyed by Darkness, and which *never* diminishes, regardless of how much energy it radiates.

Thus: *life on Earth is primarily dependent on the ethereal corona*

---

[1] The colours will gradually etherealize, i. e., they will become purer and clearer until they finally disappear completely.

[2] The special refraction that causes the colour-spectrum at sunrise and sunset will become much more difficult for the corona of Light to overcome than ordinary refraction. The time period required will probably exceed the millions of years that in all probability are still allotted to earthly life. However, during the Earth's lifetime, mankind will be able to observe the etherealization of the colour-spectrum produced by this special refraction.

of Light that God in His providence created around the Earth, so that if any of His children should succumb to Darkness, He would be able to redeem them and their possible creations from the power of Darkness.

The astral counterparts of human beings, like those of all animals, plants and objects, are interwoven with the forms that are visible to human beings. In these counterparts – created from the fixated astral Darkness and from the Light that fixated it – are stored and preserved first and foremost all the human *primal urges* that are common to all people; next, the *instincts* acquired in the course of time that are *not* common to all, since these stem from each individual's various experiences in life on Earth. These acquired family instincts are the unconsciously accumulated memories and knowledge, partly of learned mechanical motions, and partly of feelings and impressions acquired through experience.

The primal urges that are preserved in the father's and the mother's astral counterparts, together with the instincts inherited from their ancestors, are passed on to the astral counterparts of their offspring through the human reproductive process, in the same way that the family characteristics of the physical body, its peculiarities, its weaknesses, disposition to illness and the like, are inherited from generation to generation.

Whether the offspring inherits mostly from the father and his forefathers, or from the mother and her family, depends on various psychological and physical conditions of the parents at the time during which the offspring is endowed with life. (Intercourse and pregnancy).

The Eldest were not able to establish completely regular laws for "parental inheritance". The present laws, still deficient in many ways, are therefore partly due to the regulating influence of the Light. But as Darkness disappears, these laws will become more discernible and more regular, as human beings can observe for themselves.

Thus, through the astral counterparts, human beings inherit first of all the lower primitive urges that stem directly from Darkness, for example self-preservation, the urge to propagate, the maintenance of the strong at the expense of the weak, and so forth; next, all that is acquired over time, mechanically or by experience, by means of the individual's evil, lawless way of life and action, for example bad physical habits, pleasure in inflicting sufferings upon other creatures, criminal tendencies, addiction to drink, the urge for lascivious excesses, and so forth. But since both the physical body as well as the astral counterpart stem from the Darkness that was fixated by the Earth's ethereal corona, human beings receive, also by direct inheritance from the astral counterparts, primitive urges that are due to the regulating and harmonizing influence of the Light, for example maternal care for the offspring, the impulse to protect the weaker, the individual's tendency to follow the leadership of one who is stronger or older, feelings for home and family, and the like; and finally, that which has been accumulated by experience from generation to generation, through such individual lives and actions as can be viewed as ethically proper, for example an instinctive aversion to all kinds of base habits, bloodshed, immoral and criminal acts, and so forth, together with motions learned by rote that stem, for example, from the pursuit of various occupations, and which are not affected by the influence of Darkness. All these primitive drives and acquired instincts for good or evil are accumulated in the astral counterpart and rest there in latent condition until they emerge, usually in response to some external cause, and give visible proof of their presence.

The *spirit* that is bound to the human body gives the individual self[1] its personal characteristic within the family; but since a constant inter-action takes place between the spirit and the body – both the astral and the physical – the spirit is able to eliminate part of the lower primitive urges and reduce the degree of strength of the bad and evil instincts that are inherited from the family in favour of the regulating and harmonizing influence of the Light. Every person who so *desires* can, by the power of his or her will, not only purify, elevate and improve the spiritual self, but can also subdue and ennoble the lower urges inherited through the astral body and eliminate the evil instincts and impart to the astral counterparts of the offspring new Light-inspired instincts, for example with respect to ethics. The more advanced the spirit that is bound to the human body, the better it will be able to control the lower, purely human urges and instincts. But even though a family through several generations has had its Light-inspired urges and instincts increased and ennobled and its lower urges and instincts subdued by the incarnation of highly developed or advanced spirits into the family, then it can experience a sudden attenuation of these Light-inspired urges and instincts and see a predominance of Darkness-inspired urges and instincts if a young, undeveloped and undisciplined spirit is bound to one of the family members. In most cases, this spiritual regression in

---

[1]) The self is the spirit and all the good and evil that is inherited through the astral counterpart.

18* C

the offspring will be due to either one or both parents, since all men and women who do not do their *utmost* to subdue the lower urges and instincts of the body, and who *do not strive* for higher personal *ethics,* but merely follow their inheritance without trying to improve on it, cannot expect to have advanced or highly developed spirits incarnated in the progeny that they bring into this world. This spiritual depravity is most striking in families where one of the *Eldest* has been incarnated. However, when such incursions of Darkness have taken place undeservedly, a countermove against the arbitrary incarnations of the Eldest, if this were possible, has often been made, whereby one of the more highly developed spirits – the Youngest – would be incarnated in some or all of the subsequent offspring in order if possible to counterbalance the influence of Darkness on the succeeding generations, inasmuch as siblings in their formative years often exert a beneficial influence on the brother or sister[1] to whose body a spirit of Darkness has been bound.

Where two people have been united, and where they are incarnated with a spirit of one of the Eldest and a human spirit respectively, the children of such a couple will usually be incarnated with highly developed spirits in order to counterbalance the influence of Darkness on the following generations. But in those cases where the Elder became the first[2] to bind one of his spirits to the expected offspring, the family has degenerated through several generations, and a great work has then had to be carried out by the Youngest in order to restore the upward trend. But where the effort has proved to be too great and has not shown any appreciable results, the Youngest, so as not to disperse their combined strength, have terminated their own incarnations in the families strongly afflicted by Darkness, and out of necessity allowed them to meet with extinction. In this way, many once prominent families have degenerated.

In those cases where a relationship has been established between two persons, whose spirits are one of the Eldest and one of the Youngest respectively, the influence of Darkness and that of the Light on the astral counterparts of their offspring would often strike a close balance between the urges and instincts of Darkness and those of the Light. The upbringing of the offspring would in those cases become a deciding factor in determining whether Darkness or the Light should gain the predominant influence.

---

[1] In some cases twins have been incarnated with a spirit of Darkness and with a spirit of the Light respectively.

[2] The spirits of Darkness are bound to the embryo in the third month of pregnancy.

The *physical brain*[1] is the instrument through which the astral counterpart's primitive urges as well as the instincts of Darkness and those of the Light manifest themselves in the earthly world. The brain is also the instrument through which the spiritual characteristics of the individual are revealed. However, there are significant differences between the ways in which the urges, the instincts and the spirit manifest themselves.

The basic primal urges of self-preservation, procreation and so forth, have gradually in the course of time become part of *the consciousness of the human spirit,* common to all humanity, for which reason the primal urges – of both Darkness and the Light – are contained not only in the brain of the astral counterpart, but are also present as faint memories and feelings in *the brain of the human spirit* (the psychic brain). For example, if for some external reason a human being should for the first time need one of the primal urges, it is automatically awakened at the same moment in those astral brain cells that store the latent knowledge of primitive urges. At this awakening the relevant astral cells vibrate; these vibrations of the astral cells are transmitted to the corresponding cells of the physical brain – interwoven with the astral brain – which thus receives the subconscious knowledge of the astral counterpart. The physical brain then passes the vibrations it has received on to the relevant nerves, muscles and organs; but at the same time as the vibrations from the astral brain cells are transmitted to the physical brain, the vibrations are also transmitted, through the absorption layer (the casing) to the spirit's psychic brain – the large nerve-centre – where they awaken the corresponding memory or feeling of the primitive urge in the spirit that is bound to the human body. A normal human being will therefore feel or act *consciously* after having received this double prompting, partly through the astral counterpart's subconscious knowledge and partly through the spirit's awakening conscious memories that stem from experiences gathered in previous earthly lives. With these memories as a basis, it becomes the task of the self to restrain – to bring under control – the primitive urges of Darkness, so that through the guidance of the spiritual self, such things as self-assertiveness at the expense of someone weaker can be subdued, or the urge to procreate can be ennobled.

---

[1]) By the physical brain is understood both cerebrum, cerebellum and medulla oblongata. It is, of course, not the object here to explain the function of the various centres of the physical brain, but merely to outline the interconnections between the psychic brain of the spirit, the astral brain of the counterpart, and the brain of the physical body.

From the foregoing must be excepted the urge of self-preservation, which in an infant child is clearly subconscious; not until later, when the spiritual self awakens to consciousness in the earthly world, does the individual become conscious of the urge.

It need not always be an *external* cause that occasions the awakening of the primal urges of Darkness, so that they manifest themselves in some way. If for example a very young human spirit, or one of the Eldest, is bound to the human body, their evocation not infrequently takes place through the spirit's memory. This memory, which appears in spirits unexercised in self-discipline, then affects the astral brain, which passes the received vibrations of thought on to the corresponding cells of the physical brain, whereupon the individual becomes conscious of the urge.

The purely instinctive influence on the physical brain is due *solely* to the subconscious accumulation of experience and knowledge of the astral brain, without the participation of the spirit. Instincts of Darkness or of the Light thus manifest themselves in actions and movements that are not based on any thought at the moment of their execution. For example, if a human being is assaulted with blows and the like, the individual will in most cases react according to the instinct of self-defence[1] and strike out without thought as to where the retaliatory blows are landing, or whether they are hitting anything at all. The action is then *purely* instinctive, but should the victim of the assault first think over the situation – even for a matter of seconds – to consider how best to ward off the attack, by hitting back, kicking or the like, then the spirit is involved and through the thought the ensuing action – the retaliatory blow, kick and so forth – is consciously performed. But with such consciously executed action the responsibility of the self for the result of the action is much greater than in the case of a purely instinctive response.

The spirit's independent communication of thought to the astral and physical brains takes place through the cord (the life-giving cord) which binds the spirit to the human body. The cord originates in the large nerve-centre[2] of the spirit-body – which corresponds to the physical brain. From there the cord passes through the casing and terminates in the astral brain, which as previously stated is completely interwoven with the physical.

---

[1] The instinct of self-defence has been acquired by human beings in the course of millions of years of struggle for existence, and must therefore definitely be regarded as an instinct and not as a primal urge.

[2] See Commentary, pp. 187–88, regarding the structure of the spirit-body.

The cord, which in this manner must serve as the thought-channel between the spirit's large nerve-centre and the human body's brain, is not completely interwoven with the various sections and ramifications of the nerve-centre, but only partly so. Which parts of the nerve-centre are to be included in the area connected to the cord – or thought-channel – depend on the spiritual level that the human being to which the respective spirit is bound is assigned during life on Earth. This provision is of special importance for the Youngest – the pioneers of mankind. If the Youngest upon entry into life on Earth were allowed to take with them all that lay within their spiritual consciousness of knowledge, experience, artistic genius and so forth, they would be totally unable to live among human beings. They therefore take with them only so much of their intrinsic individuality as will be of use during the forthcoming incarnation, whether they are now to acquit themselves as artists, scientists, inventors, religious reformers, great statesmen or rulers, and so forth. When the decision regarding the task they are to undertake on Earth has been made, and the spirit has been bound to an incipient human body, the cord is interwoven with those parts of the large nerve-centre whose spiritual power is to characterize the future human being and make it fit to carry out the task accepted by the spirit to which it is bound. If it appears that the human being is following the proper path and is capable, despite the onslaughts of Darkness, of greater service, beyond that which was determined before the incarnation began, then, by the power of God's Will, the interweaving of the cord with the spirit's large nerve-centre can be widened to include further areas, so that the individual personality of the human being can grow within its particular field of endeavour. Yet further areas of the psychic brain can likewise be interwoven with the cord during life on Earth, if it becomes necessary to enhance the human being's personality in these further spiritual areas, which in some way concern the field of the adopted task.

With the help of *the insulation layer* – the side of the casing that faces the spirit – the other parts of the spirit's nerve-centre are prevented from exerting their influence through the physical brain, so that only those parts with which the brain is in direct connection through the cord can impress their stamp upon the human personality.

All that is withheld of the spirit's knowledge, recollections from previous incarnations, learning and so forth, therefore lies outside the human consciousness. In cases where the insulation layer has been damaged in some way or another by the influence of Darkness, a greater or a lesser portion of that which has been withheld can penetrate to the human being's consciousness and cause disturbances in the individual's personality. A person will normally not remember anything from previous existences, because such memories would very often hinder the individual in utilizing the present life on Earth in the best way. For example, if someone has been a criminal in the previous incarnation, this memory would cause undue pain and hamper the spiritual development of the individual concerned; or, if the person has been a prominent figure, with many material goods and a life of idleness, perhaps with no consideration for less fortunate fellow human beings, and if that person is in the present incarnation a poor labourer, for example, then such an individual would be easily tempted to compare unceasingly the present with the past. The result would be a constant dissatisfaction with the present and a hindrance to *all* spiritual progress.

Only in a very few isolated cases, where it has been considered useful by the transcendental world, are human beings able to receive information regarding one or more previous incarnations. But such information is given only by the spirits of the Light, when all abuse of the information is entirely precluded. People are therefore strongly urged never to seek information themselves about their previous lives.

Information about future lives on Earth cannot be given by the spirits of the Light, since God *never* plans more than one life at a time for any human being, and the life planned is always based on the preceding life.

Human spirits have in the transcendental world a clear view over their earlier existences. (See also Summary, pp. 270–71).

The physical brain of a human being *plays an important role as receiver and communicator* of the experience and knowledge *unconsciously* accumulated in the *astral* brain, and of the knowledge, learning, and experience *consciously* acquired by the spirit during life on Earth.

The following serves to explain how the physical brain receives from its counterpart the accumulated memories and subconscious knowledge that through succeeding generations become instincts, inspired either by the Light or by Darkness.

If a person's vocation in life is that of a craftsman, for example a shoemaker, tailor, mason, carpenter, or the like, or is engaged in such daily physical activities as choreographic or plastic movements, sports, the exercise of technical or manual skills and so forth, the various motions of these activities or exercises are carried out with conscious thought while they are being learned. Through the organs of vision, *the physical brain* of a normal person receives an image of the task to be performed. This image is transmitted through vibrations of the physical brain cells to the *astral brain cells* and is then intercepted by the absorption layer (the side of the casing that faces the astral counterpart) and is transmitted from there to the spirit-body's large nerve-centre, the psychic brain. With the help of thought the spirit retains the image it has received, and through the thought-channel – the cord – the spirit lets the thought follow closely the motions performed during the task, in order to learn each detail; but once the physical body, guided by thought and will, has learned to perform the task, so that the thought no longer needs to be the directing agent, the individual movements become quite automatic and are performed without any thought-connection. As the astral counterpart is completely interwoven with the physical body, the counterpart learns the motion along with the physical body. Sub-conscious memory of these mechanically acquired movements is stored in the astral brain cells and is inherited by the offspring, with whom it remains in a dormant state until it awakens in the individual as instinct through an external or an internal cause. Even if in the first generations none is actively engaged in performing the task, whose mechanically or automatically learned movements rest latent in the brain of the counterpart, the memory of these can still be preserved by individuals in the immediately following generations[1] and will, if they are needed, reappear in one or another of the members of the family. The individual will then quickly and easily adapt to the task at hand, manipulate tools, perform motions, or assume correct positions as though they had already been learned. In contrast, an individual whose ancestors have never been accomplished in such tasks, will perform the same motions in an awkward and clumsy manner until the task has been learned with the help of thought.

However, there are exceptions, since human beings can be "trained" to perform simple tasks without the help of thought, in a manner similar to the training given to animals (tortures and beatings are, of course, excluded from this comparison). This applies to people who are mentally retarded or deficient, i.e., people with undeveloped or abnormal brains, so that the spirit cannot enter into sufficiently close contact or communication with them, either through the absorption layer or through the thought-channel.

Thus: *communications from the spirit to the astral and the physical brains pass through the cord, whereas communications from the physical or from the astral brains to the spirit pass through the absorption layer of the casing.*

Loss of memory that does not stem from illness, concussion, or from advanced age is usually due to a deficient use of the astral brain cells and the areas of the spirit's large nerve-centre in which the apparently forgotten subject-matter has been stored.

The knowledge, experience and so forth that have been supplied to the spirit's large nerve-centre through the physical and the astral brain is stored there in well-defined areas. These areas are connected to the cord – the thought-channel – through fine fibres, or threads, so that the spirit by the power of its thought and will can re-

---

[1]) These memories can fade away completely in later generations.

produce that which it has acquired and stored in the astral and the physical brain. If this reproduction of knowledge and experience is not maintained through meditation, retrospection or the like, the fine fibres in the nerve-centre loosen and thus become incapable of reproducing that which has been stored. The corresponding cells of the astral brain then cease to function and lose their elasticity, that is to say, they can no longer achieve the required frequency, and for this reason that which has been acquired and stored recedes into the memory or sinks below the boundary of recollection.

It is often possible through hypnosis to ascertain that apparently forgotten matter has not been lost but is still retained in the spirit's memory – the large nerve-centre – and that it can be recalled by a hypnotist; for the spirit, influenced by the stronger will of the hypnotist, will receive an additional energy that enables it to overcome the normal physical limitation. Through this strengthened interplay of energy, the spirit by its own will and thought is again able to reproduce that which has been stored – but normally only for as long as the hypnosis is in effect. Repeated hypnosis might restore so much strength to the fibres of the cord and the astral cells that the forgotten matter may even transcend the boundary of recollection under normal circumstances. But hypnosis repeated many times is not advisable, since it can cause the subject great harm in many psychic areas. For example, it can often be quite destructive in moral respects, since unprincipled hypnotists can take advantage of their subjects. By unscrupulously using these persons at proper and improper times, they weaken their will and subsequently make them completely dependent on *the will of the hypnotist.*

Forgotten matter can also reappear in the memory under narcosis or high fever, but the memory usually fades away again when normal conditions are restored. However, the temporarily recalled matter can sometimes remain as a faint memory.

The personality, represented by the visible human body, thus consists of three factors: 1) the psychic, 2) the astral, and 3) the physical brain. It naturally follows that of these three elements, only the latter is manifest in the earthly world.

1) The *psychic brain*[1] is the seat, or source, of thought and will, and also of conscious action, which is guided by thought and will. Everything the psychic brain receives in the way of knowledge, experience, learning, and so forth, can by the help of thought be transformed into both psychic and physical values and results, since the thought, guided by the will – for the good or for the evil – analyzes, co-ordinates, recreates, refines or sorts everything that it receives, and then radiates the resulting material in numerous more or less varied brightly shining facets, all in accordance with the preceding process of thought. The more advanced the spirit, whose psychic

---

[1] See Summary, pp. 312–13, regarding split personality.

brain is the main factor of human personality, the more prolific the thought process, the more diversified the nuances and the more brightly shining the radiance of the facets. Every thought process, no matter how brief or how faint, is perceived concretely by the normal person, since that human being to a greater or lesser extent can "feel" the thoughts working. All these thoughts that have been carefully considered become the permanent possession of the individual. The values that were derived during life on Earth from experience, learning, and so forth, are retained by the spirit from incarnation to incarnation and are increased with each new incarnation.

Through the process of thought each individual thus builds or shapes his or her own spiritual personality.

2) The *astral brain,* the human *automatic retention,* mechanically accumulates all impressions received during the earthly life of a human being, until it is given an occasion to reproduce that which it has received, *exactly as recorded, with no additions whatsoever.*

To make this more easily understandable, the following examples will be given:

A person is looking, for instance, at the ruins of an ancient castle. If the visual contemplation is accompanied by thought, an image of what is seen will be formed – through the vision and the physical brain – both in the astral and in the psychic brain. But if a person looks at the ruins and the surroundings without thinking,[1] as so often happens, then only the astral brain captures a reflection of that which is seen. The psychic brain remains unaffected, when the thought does not react to the vibrations of the astral cells. At some later time and for some external reason, for example by seeing a similar scene, the image of the ruin, which is recorded in the astral brain, automatically begins to emerge in the physical brain, reproduced there exactly as the astral brain once received it. If the thought now retains this emerging image, it will also impress itself upon the psychic brain, and with the emerging image of the ruins from the subconscious as a point of departure, the person can, for example, by the power of thought, create a splendid castle with ramparts, moats, and so forth – a probable reconstruction of the original castle now lying in ruins. It is thus *the thought* that has worked upon and utilized the image of the ruin that was preserved and automatically reproduced by the astral brain, since the latter is capable only of *repeating* received impressions, and not of *creating* from them.

The astral brain is influenced not only through the sight, but also through the other senses – hearing, smell and so forth. Impressions of experiences, events,

---

[1] The image that the physical brain cells receive through the eyes can be so faint that they are unable to impress it on the astral cells. In such cases what was seen cannot, of course, be reproduced by the astral brain.

sounds, tones and so forth can thus reappear on a given occasion, that is to say, *be reproduced exactly as they were received.*

An example is given here of the numerous automatic movements that human beings perform with the help of the brain of the astral counterpart in the course of everyday life: in a room are two washstands separated by a cupboard. Normally, a mirror hangs from a nail over one of the washstands. One of the room's occupants enters, his psychic mind at that moment engrossed in a train of thought far removed from the immediate situation. However, his eye catches sight of the mirror, which at that moment is lying, for example, on a table, where it does not belong. His astral brain immediately produces a mental image of the mirror hanging on the wall, and without interrupting his train of thought he takes the mirror – quite automatically – goes toward one of the washstands, holds up the mirror and lets it slide down the wall, so that the string can be caught up by the nail. The operation does not succeed and is therefore repeated three, four or five times, still quite automatically, but with this repeatedly performed movement the vibrations of the astral brain cells awaken the individual from his thoughts. The train of thought started long before is thus suddenly interrupted, and by the power of his will he redirects the interrupted thought. The hand holding the mirror is lowered, he looks up at the wall and through the concentration of conscious thought discovers that there is no nail upon which to hang the mirror, since the nail is located over the other washstand. The astral brain – the subconscious human being – was incapable even of the following reasoning: *that the mirror would not hang upon the wall because there was nothing upon which to hang it.* Not until the vibrations of several unsuccessfully repeated movements awaken the individual's *consciousness* – the spirit – can the *subconscious* error of the astral brain be corrected.

Finally, an example of the way in which a human being, to whose physical body an undeveloped spirit is bound can through autosuggestion believe that he has "seen" every detail of an event, even though he perceived it only in fragments.

The individual is an eyewitness, for example, to an accident that is due to several "coincidences". The shock of being present at the maiming or violent death of one or more fellow human beings causes the person involuntarily to close his eyes – possibly for only a few seconds. The image that through the sight and through the physical brain is registered in the astral and the psychic brains then becomes very deficient, since these receive an image only of that which the individual has "seen". Later, in recalling that which took place and what he has experienced, the individual tries by his thought to gather together the recorded fragments. As an "eyewitness" he should of course know what had happened, and since he has no recollection[1] of closing his eyes[2] – perhaps at the decisive moment – his thought sets about recon-

---

[1] The shock can delete this memory.

[2] A suddenly arising fear can for a moment paralyze a human being's consciousness, so that the physical and astral brain cells are incapable of vibration. What is seen is therefore not recorded so long as the paralysis persists. Voids can also arise in this way and disturb the total impression, even though the eyes were not closed.

structing a plausible general impression: it happened in such and such a way.... But with these constant thought-repetitions new images are registered – through the thought-channel, the cord – in the astral brain. These images appear every time the eyewitness repeats what he experienced, and supported by the thought they become steadily clearer, so that the individual becomes convinced that he saw every detail of the accident. Although he knows very well that his thoughts have been preoccupied with the subject for a long time, he is deceived by the succession of images composed by his thought. It is usually of no avail that another witness describes the event to him as it really happened, because he will in the vast majority of cases maintain that his own recollection is the true version.

Such uncritical thinking serves no other purpose than to repress the first exact reproduction of these fragments by the astral and the psychic brains, and to produce a succession of images composed by the self that have *nothing* to do with reality.

If a more advanced or a high spirit is bound to the physical body, such autosuggestion cannot occur, since the spiritual self will rapidly review the situation and understand that it has received only fragmentary impressions of the event. Should the individual attempt to gather these fragments into a complete picture, he will be well aware that *his own thought* has supplied the missing elements.

Thus: *the astral brain – the subconscious human being – will never be able to formulate, combine or create new thoughts on the basis of its subconscious store of knowledge – impressions, learning, motions, anything seen, heard or read and so forth – since it is only able to reproduce that which it has received.*

3) The *physical brain* – the receiver and communicator – is apparently the only factor in the human personality that, being an organ, is easily subjected to scientific investigation by human beings. But since the other two factors cannot be subjected to such material investigation as can the physical one, mankind has hitherto been unable to recognize these two non-visible but highly important factors – important, because very many aspects of human personality are and can only be explained and understood through their existence.

If the Eldest, when they created the human beings, had separated the material Darkness (i.e., the molecular) from the astral Darkness – as was their intention – and had undertaken their act of creation accordingly, human beings would have been in the possession of only a physical brain. (This refers to human beings without the spiritual consciousness that is given by God). This brain would have been able to receive, *but not to retain anything whatsoever.* Each new impression would at once erase the previous one, and even if the physical brain were exposed daily to the same impressions, these would each time be equally new to the individual. No experience, no knowledge, *absolutely nothing* could have been inherited by the children of such individuals. Human beings would then have become less than animals, whose astral counterpart's brain retains urges, instincts, feelings, and so forth, that can be inherited by the off-spring and thus have a regulating and improving effect.

However, since the Eldest soon convinced themselves that they could not create from material Darkness alone, they created from this double material,[1] and like the animals, human beings received an automatic retention – the astral brain – that through the vibrations of the physical brain cells receives and retains those values that would otherwise vanish as soon as they appeared.

When God had bound a spiritual being to the physical human body, the brain of the body also became an instrument for the spirit, so that the physical human being could be influenced not only by earthly surroundings, but also by the transcendental.

As previously explained, human beings can through the astral counterpart pass on to their offspring instinctive skills that in future generations can bring benefit and joy to the individual. Through this inheritance, human *talent* is created, whether it concerns a craft that can be enriched and ennobled by this talent or any of the forms of art, for example poetry, painting, sculpture or music. From the manner in which individuals achieve the fruition of their ability, talent or gift, it will be clearly and unmistakably revealed to what extent the individuals concerned, with the help of their spiritual selves, are able to open their creations to the influence of the Light and close them to the influence of Darkness. The better a talented person is able to approach all that is natural, beautiful, exalted, harmonious and pure, the greater is the influence of the Light on that which is produced; whereas unnatural, distorted and ugly forms and lines,

---

[1]) Since astral Darkness formed an integrated entity with the corona of Light, the Eldest were not able to separate it. The material with which they worked therefore appeared as if it were double, although it was composed of three elements: the corona of Light, the astral and the molecular Darkness.

The ability of the astral brain to retain the values and the impressions that are received through the physical brain is thus determined by the Earth's corona of Light, which fixates the astral Darkness. Even if the astral and physical brain cells are destroyed, the innermost principle of the astral cells cannot be annihilated, since it is created from the indestructible radiations of the corona of Light. Not until the physical body has died will the radiations of the Light withdraw. (See Summary, p. 295). Spirits who are bound to imbecilic people will through the Light-principle of the astral cells receive impressions that are transmitted through the absorption layer; but these impressions only become intelligible to the spirit when it is released from the physical body.

dissonant tones and impure and grating sounds demonstrate the influence of Darkness toward decadence. The same holds true for works of poetry that *reveal* and *glorify* all that is *ugly* in life, that *defend immorality* and stimulate degrading thoughts and ideas.

The same rule applies to all such creatively productive people: *through their works, they show themselves as they are - spokesmen either for the Light or for Darkness.*

The making of a contribution to an already existing form of art, science or the like, or the creation of something entirely new and hitherto unknown, be it in the arts, in science or in any other area requires the *genius* that only the *Youngest* or the *Eldest* possess. But from the creations of human genius it is also apparent whether the work is produced in the service of the Light or in the service of Darkness.

Talent can thus be passed on from generation to generation, whereas *genius can never be inherited;* but genius *can be brought forth from talent,* that is, the high spirits often let themselves be incarnated in families where with the help of inborn (inherited) talent, they can more quickly and more easily unfold their genius in the desired direction.

Gradually, as the *physical brain* develops with the growth of the body from childhood to a more mature age, it becomes a more useful instrument for the spirit that is bound to the physical body. The personal characteristics of the individual grow more distinct; the self acquires an ever greater ability to receive impressions through the physical brain, to bring to fruition through the thought-channel the abilities brought from the transcendental world, and by the power of the will to advance ethically and thus, if possible, to utilize the talents inherited from the family. But however well-developed the human brain *may* become, it will never be able to achieve any value whatsoever as an *independent organ* of thought, since the independent thought process derives solely from *the spirit* that is bound to the human body.

A person's physical brain - as an instrument for the spirit - can best be compared with a musical instrument, for example *a violin.*[1] Such an instrument cannot produce a single tone independently.[1] Tones are not produced until the moment the bow is drawn over the strings, and the sound which then issues will closely reflect the musical talent of the player. The genius will with the greatest ease pro-

---

[1] A violin can produce faint tones if the strings are activated by sound-waves from a piano, for example. But without some form of activation it cannot produce tones independently.

duce a wealth of tones and sounds and combine them to a whole of harmonious beauty, whereas an unmusical person on that same instrument – be it the finest of Cremonas – can merely call forth a succession of cacophonous sounds. Between the genius and the unmusical person lies a range of more or less musically gifted and accomplished individuals, each playing the instrument according to *his or her individual talent and ability.* But if a string breaks, even the greatest genius can call forth only harsh and grating sounds from the broken string. The physical brain is in the same way the instrument of the spirit. The more highly developed the spirit, the better and more fully can the brain be employed in the transposition of the thoughts of the spirit, so that they can appear in the earthly world. But if parts of the brain are impaired because of illness or old age, then even the most advanced spirit cannot effectively utilize the damaged cell tissue.

If a child shows signs of being gifted with an exceptional talent, those in charge of its upbringing should be careful not to develop this talent too early in life, since this will then take place at the expense of the remaining brain tissue, for the brain can easily be weakened if it is subjected to a one-sided development during the child's formative years; and the individual is then in danger of passing on a weak and non-perfectible brain to its descendants.

In the cases of defective or completely abnormal brains, the interaction between the spirit and the brain becomes more or less incomplete, and the more incomplete the interaction, the closer the behaviour and actions of the individual come to those of an animal. If the spirits of the Light during the development of an embryo become aware that the brain will be abnormal or predisposed to various ailments that in later life could partly or completely destroy or harden the brain tissue, they usually ensure that a younger and less developed spirit is bound to that individual. The spirit in question will therefore not suffer on account of the absent or deteriorating ability to absorb impressions or knowledge, or to assert the self strongly enough in the earthly world. But if an individual during an earthly life becomes *personally* guilty of leaving a feeble body and brain predisposed to illness as an inheritance to the descendants due to improper living habits, drunkenness, various bodily excesses, and so forth, the spirit in question that failed to discipline either the self or the body that was the visible representative of the self in life will according to the Law of Retribution again and again be bound to that family's partly or wholly degenerated bodies, of whose incipient destruction it had been the cause. In cases where a more highly developed spirit is the cause of decadence in a family, the spirit will *suffer* because of its missing or impaired ability to assert itself in life on Earth. As they gradually came under the Law of Retribution, many of the Eldest who through their wilful incarnations brought destruction upon otherwise healthy families have had to atone for their sinful and lawless conduct and way of life in previous incarnations by being bound to partly or wholly degenerated human bodies.

All the various abnormalities of the physical body are brought under the Law of Retribution whenever possible, so that the spirits that are bound to bodies that are to some extent defective have always in some way been guilty, in an earlier incarnation, of actions that can bring about retribution in the form of an impaired, malformed or deficient body.

If men or women, through no fault of their *own,* have contracted a physical disease that directly or indirectly can be inherited by the offspring, such persons should never bring children into the world *until the ailment is completely cured and all possibility of its being transmitted to the children is precluded.* If a person is fully aware of the heritability of this disease and procreates in spite of this knowledge, that person must bear the full responsibility for the suffering that is thus brought upon the family. According to the Law of Retribution the spirit that was bound to such a person's body will again and again be incarnated into the family whose disposition toward illness is due to lack of responsibility on the part of the spirit in that life on Earth during which the disease was made heritable.

However, if people are unaware of the heritability of their disease, they will be exempt from incarnation in the afflicted family, to whose members in such cases will be bound spirits that in one way or another have brought upon themselves an incarnation of bodily suffering.

Thus: *the same rule applies to all human beings: through the thoughts and conscious actions of the present incarnation the next one is created, so that it either takes the form of a life lived in greater or lesser spiritual and bodily sufffering, or becomes a life of health and happiness.*

The human being's *astral counterpart* cannot be separated from the physical body until death occurs. The so-called "double" that occasionally appears is therefore not the counterpart, but is either the spirit that is bound to the human body or a phantom – a thought-image – which the spirit has formed of the human being in question. However, it is very difficult for people to decide whether they are confronted by a phantom or by a spirit. If the double appears shortly before the corresponding person arrives, and if that person has thought neither about the people who saw the double nor about the place where it appeared, then it is *the spirit* that has gone ahead of the body; but if the person whose double appeared does not arrive, then the double is normally a *phantom*. The corresponding person has imagined himself at some place or another, and his thought-image becomes visible to the people who happen to be present at that place; but if it can be ascertained that the person concerned was *asleep* when the double appeared then it is normally the spirit[1] that is seen and not the phantom.

Only the Eldest and the Youngest possess this ability.

During *sleep* the body is supplied with renewed vitality through the influence of the Light, which replaces the loss of energy that is suffered by the body through spiritual or physical work in the waking state. The younger the body, the better and more easily is this loss made good by replenishment with new vitality; but if the body is older or sickly, the replenishment that can be provided is not so complete, because the bodily organism at an advanced age or in a diseased state cannot absorb the currents of the Light in the same measure as can the younger or healthier body. And when the time arrives that on account of age or serious illness the body is no longer capable of reacting to the influence of the Light, and is thus unable to renew its vitality, it begins to approach its dissolution, a dissolution that is completed through death.

While the physical body is growing, and as long as the rate of metabolism is high, the body needs much sleep so that it can develop healthily and harmoniously through the absorption of the currents of the Light from the Light-ether and the Earth's corona of Light. When growth ceases and the metabolism slows down, neither the fully grown nor the aged bodies can absorb the currents of the Light in the same measure as before, and as a result the older a person becomes the less sleep will be needed. However, about six hours of sleep should be the minimum, since insufficient sleep can prematurely weaken an aging body, unless it possesses an overabundance of good health. After prolonged illness the body needs somewhat longer periods of sleep than normal, so that the weakened body may acquire the needed amount of the energy of the Light.

Very old people can sometimes feel so physically tired in the last years of their life that they are constantly "dozing off". This need for frequent periods of sleep is usually due to spiritual lethargy; the self no longer has enough energy to keep itself

---

[1]) By the power of their thought and will the Eldest have often assumed the appearance of a living person, and by appearing visibly on the plane of the Earth have "acted" the part of that person's double.

spiritually or bodily active. This senile dozing does not strengthen the body, but only weakens it still more and thus accelerates its dissolution.

Sleep is thus the state in which the human body best comes into contact with the Light-currents of the surrounding ether. For this reason sleep should always be a sufficiently long period of real rest for the body that has been weakened by loss of energy. For a normal person sleep must also be a period of rest for the spirit that is bound to the body. If the spirit – which during earthly life is constantly wearied by its presence within the Earth's atmosphere of Darkness – does not receive the necessary rest and infusion of Light at the same time as the earthly body, the person will upon awakening feel *spiritually tired* and incapable of performing his or her earthly tasks with adequate spiritual interest.

During sleep the guardian spirit often gives warning to people who have strayed into paths that can lead them away from the plan that was laid down for their life on Earth. These warnings can take the form of visionary, symbolic dreams or cautionary words that sometimes upon awakening remain clearly imprinted on the memory. But not everyone can recall these admonitions equally clearly, whether they are given as visions or in words; but a feeling usually persists that something or other is not as it should be. By reviewing the recent past, or by reconsidering plans for the future, the person warned during sleep by the guardian spirit can very often find the reason for which the warning was given. It then becomes that person's task to correct the errors committed, to redirect the course of his or her life, or to make good use of the message in some other way.

The messages given by the guardian spirit through dreams can also be of a comforting, encouraging, reproving or prophetic nature.

Enticed and assisted by the Eldest or by the earthbound spirits, many human beings have released themselves during nightly sleep from the body to which they were bound and undertaken unaccompanied excursions. The impressions received by the spirit on these nocturnal trips – from association with the earthbound spirits, for example – were propagated through the cord to the brain of the sleeping body, and in that way produced images of that which had been experienced, images that were clear and coherent to a greater or to a lesser extent – or were utterly confused – and which sometimes through the astral counterpart's brain could be remembered in the waking state as dreams.

The disincarnated Eldest and the earthbound spirits have also tried to defile the human mind and thought through hideous, obscene dream-images in order to gain greater power over human beings.

Many dreams stem from physical ailments, or from the body's assuming a wrong position during sleep. This causes too strong a flow of blood to brain tissue, with the result that instead of resting the brain reacts to the increased pressure. Under this abnormal condition the astral brain produces a number of obscure memories that almost invariably can be ascribed to something experienced, seen, read or heard. Loud voices and sensations of heat or cold can likewise stimulate the astral brain to transmit visual memories. The more coherent dreams result from the thoughts of the waking spirit as it tries to correct the confused images that are being transmitted from the astral brain; but since the connection between the psychic and the physical brain is always somewhat slackened during the sleep of the physical body, the spiritual self is seldom able to bring satisfactory order to the chaos of the dreams.

In rare cases the psychic brain of a sleeping person can recall memories from previous lives on Earth.

As long as the spirit and the body are united, the "life-giving cord" that unites them cannot be seen from the transcendental world; but as soon as the spirit is released from the body, for example during sleep, the cord is extended or spun out more and more – like a spider's thread – by absorbing the aura of Light or of Darkness that surrounds the spirit-body. When all of the aura has been used up, or spun out, the cord tightens and retracts quite mechanically, and draws the spirit involuntarily back until it is reunited with the body; this reunion is also effected quite mechanically. The greater this aura of Darkness or the Light, the farther the spirit can move from the body. But since the auras of human spirits are not very large, these spirits can move only short distances from the body (30–60 up to 100 metres). The Eldest and the Youngest, however, can move inordinately long distances from the body; the Youngest can even reach their dwellings in the outermost sphere around the Earth. Since the cord is highly elastic it cannot break, but the spirit must take great care not to use up the entire aura, as it will then be drawn back involuntarily.

As stated above, many spirits of human beings have in the course of time learned from the Eldest how they may themselves release their spirit from the physical body during sleep; but after the return to God of the Elder – Ardor – normal conditions have been restored also in this respect, so that human spirits while the body rests can no longer release[1] themselves without help,[1] since God has blotted out this unlawfully acquired knowledge from the memory of their spirit.

In cases where a more advanced human spirit prior to incarnation has promised to be of help to the high spirits in some mission during life on Earth, the guardian spirit, having obtained God's permission, can release the spirit in question from the sleeping body in order to remind it in various ways of its promise, or to help it in the fulfilment of its promise by means of instructive discourse. If for some reason it becomes necessary, the guardian spirit can bring its charge to the home in the spheres, strengthening with the help of its own radiations of Light the human spirit's aura, so that the cord can be extended far beyond its normal reach.

---

[1]) During anesthesia, faintings, and the like, the spirit is often released, albeit quite mechanically.

Whenever they desire, the Youngest may leave the body during nocturnal sleep; but they avail themselves of this permission only when they are requested to do so by their guardian spirit.

The Eldest who were incarnated by Ardor and still live on Earth embodied as human beings have all during nocturnal sleep release been informed by the Youngest of Ardor's return. At the same time, each one was personally admonished to submit to the laws that God has given for the spirit while it is bound to the earthly body. Most of them promised voluntarily to submit themselves to these laws and, by the power of His Will, God eliminated so much of their spiritual aura of Darkness that like the human spirits they can move only short distances from the body, and can likewise only be released in the absence of help when body and spirit separate spontaneously on the body's sudden unconsciousness through illness, accident or anesthesia.[1]

Since God does not *compel* anyone to submit to His laws, *those few of the Eldest* who refused to comply are still able to move as far from the earthly body during sleep as they have hitherto. But in order to counteract as much as possible any harmful influence these may have on human beings, each of the Eldest is accompanied by one of the Youngest during all their nocturnal excursions.

In séance circles, where the manifestations of Darkness still occur, these incarnated Eldest[2] often appear under false names and with false messages and so forth. This cannot be prevented so long as human beings maintain their experimentation with Darkness; for which reason attention is once more directed to that which has been stated earlier (pp. 248–51) regarding the odious practice of séances, their unlawfulness, and the dangers to which mediums and participants expose themselves by submitting to the influence of Darkness. As soon as these Eldest have terminated their present lives on Earth, this disorder will cease for ever, as they will not be reincarnated again until they have advanced so far toward the Light that they will voluntarily submit to the laws of God.

When the Eldest created the human beings, they adjusted their organs of vision to capture and reflect the sun's more weakly shining rays that stem from the core of Darkness.[3] The human eye is therefore normally unable to see the astral-material radiations of the Light or the ethereal-astral corona of the sun, but gradually as the Dark-

------

[1]) See Commentary, p. 191.

[2]) These Eldest are scattered throughout the Earth, in many different countries. During their waking hours they usually remember nothing of their nocturnal excursions; but a few can at times remember them as dim, blurred dreams. During sleep release these spirits are able to participate in séances of materialization, dematerialization, levitation, and so forth.

[3]) The weakest luminous rays from the sun's core of Darkness cannot be perceived by the human eye.

ness about the Earth is eliminated, some of the sun's more strongly luminous rays that stem from the astral-material oscillations of the Light will be able to penetrate to the Earth, thereby intensifying,[1] beautifying and brightening the sunlight. The human eye will then slowly adjust to this stronger sunlight.

As the Eldest at a single point broke off the interweaving of the human astral and physical eye, they obtained the intended effect of human beings not being able to "see" the astral forms of Darkness, but only those forms and figures that pertain to the earthly world. Not until God had endowed the human body with a spirit were those human beings to whom the Youngest had been bound able occasionally or continuously to "see" with the eyes of the spirit. Later this was also the case for those to whom the Eldest or more advanced human spirits were bound.

The connection between the astral and physical auditory organs of human beings was also broken off at one particular point by the Eldest, so that the astral sounds might not be perceived. Clairaudients therefore listen with the auditory organs of the spirit and not with those of the astral counterpart.

All animals, unlike human beings, have double vision. The physical eyes of the body capture and reflect the earthly forms, while the eyes of the astral counterpart capture and reflect the astral counterparts. But inasmuch as animals owe their existence mainly to the molecular oscillations of Darkness and therefore lead their lives in the earthly world, their astral vision is the weaker, so that all they see in terms of astral forms are those released from the earthly material world, namely the counterparts.[2] Animals can also see the spirit that is bound to the human body, but they see it only as a misty extension of the contours of the earthly figure. The animals' astral organs of vision cannot, however, perceive the strong rays of Light emitted from the radiant spirit-bodies of the Youngest, nor can they see the ethereal-astral corona of Light of the sun and the stars.

When the earthbound spirits lived on Earth the animals were able to see them, but they could not distinguish between the living and the "dead" human beings.

The astral and physical auditory organs of animals are also closely interconnected, and for this reason animals are able to hear a number of sounds that are inaudible to human beings.

Like human beings, the animals have primal urges that in part stem directly from

---

[1] This will also happen to all other celestial bodies, also those that only reflect the sunlight (i. e., non-luminous globes). Over the centuries, the "stars" will thus gain in luminosity. Excepted are, of course, those stars so extensively damaged by Darkness that their luminosity is in strong decline.

[2] It takes approximately 48 hours for the released counterparts of larger animals to be completely dissolved; the smaller the counterpart, the shorter is the time of dissolution.

Darkness, and in part from the regulating and harmonizing influence of the Light (of the corona of the Earth). These primal urges are inherited from individual to individual in the various species and families through the astral counterparts.

During the past millions of years, the counterparts of the many different species and families have acquired a certain amount of knowledge through experience, and this can likewise be passed on from individual to individual. This acquired knowledge lies latent until the animal has occasion to use it. The animal's physical brain will then, if necessary, be stimulated quite automatically by the astral brain, and the subconscious knowledge will manifest itself in the earthly world as instinctive actions and feelings. Since *no spirit* is bound to the animal body, an animal will always act strictly in accordance with basic urges and instincts, i. e., it will never have any *conscious* understanding of why it acts or feels in such a way. Without exception, every animal acts and feels *only* as it is prompted to act and feel by the subconscious knowledge of its astral counterpart. Not even the most extensive training by human beings can evoke *independent thinking* in an animal. All skills that the higher animal species have acquired through training will for them continue to be mechanical, subconscious knowledge. The new experience and the new knowledge acquired by the individual animal during its lifetime will be inherited by its offspring and will always emerge for the benefit of the animal should the occasion arise.

The greater the care and kindness animals are given, the closer many of them can attach themselves to human beings, and they can then in all their behaviour display an immediate devotion and faithfulness that can hardly be equalled in the human world. But even these feelings and expressions of devotion and faithfulness are instinctive and often acquired from generation to generation through their close association with human beings.

On account of the regulating and adaptive properties and harmonizing influence[1] of the Light, the animal world has gradually been brought into a more orderly state, so that the animals in many ways live highly regulated lives.[1] This applies to all forms of earthly animal life, the higher as well as the lower. Through the ethereal corona of the Earth – the Earth's psyche – unconscious life is everywhere guided forward toward greater order and harmony.

(On the basis of the information that has been given concerning the knowledge unconsciously acquired by the human astral counterparts under the influence of Darkness or the Light, human beings can themselves draw comparisons with the lives of animals and investigate what is due to the regulating, purifying, separating and harmonizing influence of the Light, and what is caused by the eroding and destructive power of Darkness).

When earthly figures, forms and objects are destroyed by death, decomposition, burning and the like, their astral counterparts, as

---

[1]) Refers for example to the lives of ants and bees, the ingenious nest building of many species of bird, the migrations of birds, the migrations of fish between oceans and fresh water, etc. Countless examples exist everywhere in the animal worlds of the air, the land and the sea.

previously stated, are released; at the same time the radiations of the corona of Light withdraw and reject the counterparts that are released from the physical bodies, etc., and which are then absorbed by the accumulations of Darkness that constantly surround the Globe. With this continuous rejection of astral counterparts the Globe's ethereal corona of Light is gradually purged of the Darkness that erupted upon the Earth at the downfall of the Eldest. As the corona of Light is purified its influence upon earthly life increases; but since earthly life originates from the Darkness that was originally fixated by the corona of Light, the Globe will not be cleansed completely until all life on Earth has ceased – and when that time will be is known only to God.

When the accumulations of Darkness that have absorbed the astral counterparts are depolarized in one way or another, for example by inter-collision, by collision with the Earth's radiations of Darkness or in a similar manner, they are absorbed and eliminated by the Light-ether – but not by the corona of Light.

If collisions of polarized astral or spiritual Darkness take place indoors they can often be perceived by human beings who are not mediums. The sounds that are produced by these collisions differ widely. Depending on the size of the accumulations they can vary from the faintest crackle to a loud and short or more prolonged explosive sound. However, the Light-phenomena that always accompany depolarizations can only in very few cases be observed by persons who are not mediums.

When the Light, with the embodiment of the Youngest as human beings, was once more brought to the Earth, partly through the Passage of Light that God by the power of His Will had made through the ravaged Kingdom, and partly from the ethereal radiations of Light from the incarnated Youngest, several of the still latent seeds of life were drawn forth into reality in the earthly world. The astral counterparts of these animal and plant forms have a greater strength of Light than the others. (Seen from the transcendental world they are faintly coloured, while the others appear grey or black). When these earthly forms and figures are destroyed, the Light in their counterparts is separated and absorbed, partly by the corona of Light and partly by the Light-ether; the Darkness in the counterparts is absorbed by accumulations of Darkness in the normal way.

The Darkness that was separated from the Light-ether by the thought and will of the Eldest – when they had left God's Kingdom –

was concentrated on and around the Earth; but the destruction that it caused spread far and wide and affected the greater part of the star universe – the galactic system – that includes the Earth.

Certain anomalies in the planetary system to which the Earth belongs are thus due to experimentation by the Eldest with Darkness, whereby they succeeded in bringing a number of irregularities into the laws that were given by God for the orbits of celestial bodies.

Since none of the ethereal-astral coronas of Light of the suns and the stars are formed from the fastest oscillations of the Light, as is God's Kingdom, nor strengthened by a further infusion of Light in the same way as the corona of the Earth, these coronas were not strong enough either to reject or to fixate the separated Darkness that in large accumulations was spread far and wide in the star universe of the Earth. This Darkness drifted about, and still drifts about, in space without guidance;[1] when it approaches the globes of the Earth's universe the poles in the precipitated cores of Darkness in these globes awaken from their latent state and exercise an effect of attraction upon the steadily approaching accumulation of Darkness; at the moment of collision great catastrophes and anomalies arise, but the accumulations of Darkness are thereby depolarized, and can then be absorbed and eliminated by the Light-ether.

The globes that have not been destroyed but have been forced out of their original orbit after collision with accumulations of Darkness have often during their irregular motion through space been attracted and held by larger suns, which have then forced the vagrant globes into new, regular orbits. The globes that are not captured in this way continue through space until, for example, they collide with other globes or accumulations of Darkness and are destroyed.

Larger fragments of globes – the cores of Darkness – that have been disrupted through collision, and which by entering the Earth's solar system in their paths through space could expose the Earth to destructive collision, are forced by God into elliptical orbits with the sun at one focus and an astral, immaterial Light-centre emanated by the power of God's Will at the other focus.

If the accumulations of Darkness are attracted by the mother globe itself, partial eruptions come about, but these are not able to destroy the globe or to deflect it from its orbit; the accumulations are too small for this in relation to the huge dimensions of the globe.

---

[1]) God does not prevent the collision of accumulations of Darkness with the globes, since the Darkness is thereby depolarized and then eliminated; God intervenes only when the Earth is threatened.

The irregular destruction of globes occurs *only* in the galactic system that includes the Earth, and in which Darkness exists separated from the Light-ether. If globes in the other three systems disintegrate into their components, this takes place in accordance with *God's Will.*

When God had promised His fallen children that He would take the human beings into His care, He created six astral worlds, or dwelling places, around the Earth. These worlds were laid as six spheres, or spherical layers, around the ravaged Kingdom. The inner sphere was the darkest, although considerably brighter than the world of the Eldest, which had been defiled and obscured by Darkness. The second was somewhat brighter than the first, and so forth, until the outermost or sixth sphere, which was created from the rapid ethereal oscillations of the Light. The climatic conditions of the spheres are regulated from this Light-world through the ethereal rays of the Earth's sun, which are prevented by Darkness from reaching the Earth. The innermost sphere, closest to Earth, is partly dependent for its climate on the position of the Earth with respect to the sun; but since the rays of Light from the outermost sphere also irradiate these worlds, the conditions in these worlds are far better than on the Globe itself. Every sphere has its own atmospheric layer, which, like the spheres themselves, is not visible to the human eye.

Many people will maintain that since the celestial bodies in space are clearly and distinctly visible from the Earth, it is impossible for inhabited spheres to surround the Earth, because these spheres would in that case obstruct the view of the shining globes. For these people the following comparison based on earthly conditions may possibly make it easier for them to understand the presence of the spheres.

If one stands by a woodland pond, for example, and if the water is clear, the plant and animal life present in the pond can be distinctly seen. But no one can see the myriad life forms that teem in the water itself. On the other hand, if a drop of the water is examined under a microscope, a profusion of tiny infusoria is discovered, the existence of which would not otherwise be suspected. A similar situation exists with respect to the spheres; the physical organs of sight cannot perceive them, but to the spiritual – the enlarged – vision they are easily discernible.

The outermost world, the dwelling place of the Youngest while they lead mankind, was also created as an outer protection against the accumulations of Darkness that existed, and that still exist, in the encompassing universe, since God concentrated the radiations from this world to such an extent that in addition to absorbing the depolarized Darkness they could also repel the Darkness that threatened the Earth from outer space. Any new influx of Darkness was thereby prevented, so that no greater catastrophe that might have partially or completely destroyed the Globe could ever occur.

The so-called meteorites, which are small fragments of the condensed cores of Darkness from fractured globes, pass easily through all the spheres without causing any destruction. From the transcendental world these fragments appear as dark, misty accumulations; while traversing the spheres, especially the one farthest removed from the Earth,[1] their size is often considerably reduced under the dissolving influence of the rays of the Light (not of the solar rays). When passing through the atmosphere of the Earth, where the meteorites in earthly terms become incandescent, they often disintegrate still further, so that only few reach the Earth as larger pieces.

Because of the speed at which the meteorites fall, the radiations of Light from the sixth sphere cannot repel them as they can the accumulations of Darkness, but can only partially dissolve these fragments as they fall toward the Earth. But these fragmented cores of Darkness will never present a real danger to the Earth.

In advance of the wave of Light that God sent out, and which surged through the ravaged Kingdom at the time when the spirits bound by sin and bound to the Earth returned[2] to the spheres, a violent astral storm was called forth by the Will of God, whereby the remaining polarized Darkness was depolarized, so as later to be absorbed by the wave of Light, whose brightness was considerably reduced as a result of this absorption. This reduced brightness can best be compared to a faintly luminous dawn. But gradually, as the absorbed Darkness is purified and removed through the circulation of the Light-ether, the brightness will slowly increase over millions of years until the full intensity of the Light has once more been attained. How long this process of purification will take is known only to God; however, it will be completed *before humanity departs from the Earth.*

The effects of the more violent astral storms can often be detected in the physical world as greater or lesser disturbances in the terrestrial magnetism. However, the storms that rage outside the atmospheric layers of the Earth can be felt and detected only when they are especially violent.

Gradually, as the depolarized Darkness from the ravaged Kingdom is eliminated, more and more rays from the astral-material part

---

[1]) The spheres are located beyond the atmosphere of the Earth but within the lunar orbit.
[2]) In the year 1911.

of the sun's corona of Light will reach the Earth. Thus the sunlight will slowly – from century to century – gain in clarity and strength. This slowly increasing brightness of the sunlight will be observable from the Earth.[1]

In the future, the wave of Light that eliminated the ravaged Kingdom, and which envelops the entire Globe outside the atmosphere of the Earth as an insulation layer, will prevent the unattached accumulations of Darkness that drift about on and around the Earth – both inside and outside the atmospheric layers – from penetrating, darkening and completely destroying the innermost dwelling places – the spheres. Such destruction has often occurred in the past, thus obliging God time and again to purify and restore them.

Apart from the fact that Darkness, guided by the intelligence of the Eldest, has in many ways hampered and prevented the advance of the Light in a spiritual sense, it has also without guidance blindly and aimlessly wrought disturbance on the Globe itself through the many dreadful natural disasters that from the earliest times have caused death and destruction, which the Youngest could not prevent.

These natural disasters are mainly due to the radiations of Darkness of the Globe itself, which attract the accumulations of Darkness that are present in layers of varying density within the atmosphere of the Earth. The severity of the eruption depends on the innate power and density of the two mutually attracting and approaching forms of Darkness. At the eruption, which takes place the moment the radiations of the Globe meet with the attracted accumulation of Darkness, the two forms of Darkness are depolarized and can then be eliminated by the Light-ether.

Even though the Elder has returned to God's Kingdom, all the various forms of natural disaster will persist. But there is a possibility that they will diminish, in direct proportion to the depolarization and elimination of the Darkness.

Part of the depolarized – neutralized – Darkness was eliminated through absorption by the radiations of Light that were spread widely from the spirit-bodies of the incarnated Youngest before the ravaged Kingdom was annihilated by the wave of Light. But after the disappearance of the ravaged Kingdom,[2] the wave of Light,

---

[1]) See Summary, p. 294.
[2]) In the year 1911.

which has replaced it as a huge insulation layer around the Earth, also takes part in the elimination of the neutralized Darkness. From the insulation layer of Light the disincarnated Youngest have extruded fine strands of Light through those strata of Darkness that rest directly on and around the Globe; these strands of Light are led – also by the Youngest – to areas of neutralized Darkness in order to absorb it and in this way to remove it from the Earth, following which this Darkness is drawn into the great purifying circulation through God's flaming Being by the Light-currents of the ether.

The depolarized Darkness that after a certain time has not been absorbed and eliminated will gradually be mixed once more with the polarized Darkness, and thus after a period of latency – neutralization – revert to its original forms.

Although large quantities of neutralized Darkness are constantly eliminated by the Light, the process is exceedingly slow, since the Light can absorb *only* the depolarized Darkness that is produced by natural disasters such as, for instance, earthquakes, volcanic eruptions, thunderstorms and the like, or by many other manifestations of the numerous and highly varied forms of the powers of Darkness.

(Regarding the depolarization of *spiritual* Darkness, see Commentary, pp. 173-74).

Between the lowest and the highest frequencies of oscillation (i.e., rates of vibration) of Darkness extends an extremely wide range of rapidity, concentration and radiation that manifests itself in numerous material and immaterial forms, for example: 1) energy, i.e., electricity, electromagnetism, steam power, and so forth; 2) radiation, i.e., sunlight (solar rays of the lower and lowest frequencies originate from the sun's core of Darkness), phosphorescent light, artificial light (produced by electricity, gas, oil, etc.), heat, radioactivity, and so forth; 3) matter and substance; and a great many other forms as yet unknown to human beings.

At the time when God assumed the guidance of the creatures of His fallen children, He also took charge of the work of restoring order to the chaotic conditions that the incursions of Darkness had caused on the Globe; and as the Earth was gradually supplied with more and more Light – partly through the Passage of Light, partly through the ethereal radiations of Light from the aura of the spirit-bodies of the Youngest – Darkness was brought more and more under the regulating influence[1] of the Light and was thus forced to

---

[1] The Light that is supplied to the Earth in the above manner thus takes part, together with the Earth's ethereal corona of Light, in the great ordering, adjusting, segregating and harmonizing work in the earthly world of Darkness.

serve the Light by helping to restore the destruction that had been wrought through the downfall of the Eldest. Thus: the more *regular* a law is – whether it is a law of energy, radiation, matter and substance, or whether it is a law that directly concerns reproduction and propagation – the greater is the influence of the Light; whereas the more the law in question is encumbered with irregularities and exemptions, the smaller is the influence of the Light. And where human free will must be taken into consideration, *Darkness* generally has *the greater* influence on the established order. An easily understandable example of a law that is not completely regular, and in which human free will intervenes, is the following:

If the processes of conception and birth conformed to laws established by God, or if they had been brought completely under the control of the Light, a strictly determinate and standardized period of time would elapse between the instant of conception and the completion of birth. No abnormalities would occur during pregnancy, no premature or abnormal births would then *ever take place,* and the infant would in all respects be completely healthy, well-formed and capable of surviving. But since God did not make these laws, and since the bad habits and unhealthy ways of life of human beings make conception and birth highly dependent on the influence of Darkness, the regulating influence of the Light has still far from reached its full effect on these processes.

In the course of time the Light has gained a far more regular and ordering influence on procreation in the animal world – especially in the case of animals living in the wild state – than in relation to human beings; for animals, having no independent free will, simply give way to their urges and instincts and thus submit without resistance, albeit slowly, to the increasing influence of the Light. Whereas on account of the spirit that is bound to the human body, human beings live a *conscious* life and have a free will for good or for evil. And so long as human beings do not understand how to use their free will[1] in the proper way, so long as they allow Darkness to dominate them instead of voluntarily submitting to the Light, so long can the Light only imperfectly regulate the laws that determine, for example, the propagation of the human race and the liberation of the human body from abnormality and deformity.

All that to human beings may appear as the intervention of supernatural powers, all that human beings of undeveloped intellect and perception are unable to explain, has in the course of time been regarded as miracle, superstition, fantasy and the like. All these apparently inexplicable phenomena occur in accordance with regular *psychic and astral laws* – when they are *authentic;* but since human

---

[1] See Speech of God's Servant, p. 136.

beings have only a limited knowledge – in many cases no knowledge at all – of the various manifestations of psychic and astral powers, they neither *will* nor *can* understand that a natural explanation underlies the apparently "supernatural".

These laws for transcendental phenomena are known, and were known, both to the spirits of the Light and to those of Darkness, for which reason these laws, although permanent and regular in themselves, have often been used in an unlawful manner. One result of the use of these laws by an earthbound spirit *without God's permission* was, for example, the discovery of the healing waters of the spring at Lourdes. This event, which is known to many contemporary human beings, will as a typical example be further elucidated, since it has been described by some as a miracle and by others as pure superstition.

The French peasant girl Bernadette,[1] who was the intermediary between the sensory and the transcendental worlds when the existence of the spring at Lourdes was revealed, has given a fully truthful account of what she saw and heard. However, contrary to Bernadette's belief, the female apparition that appeared before her was not the mother of Jesus. This spirit, who was acquainted with the astral and phychic laws, appeared visibly and audibly without God's permission before the young girl, who was a clairvoyant and clairaudient medium. In her last incarnation this spirit had been a prominent Frenchwoman, whose conduct had in many ways been highly damaging to France. The anger and hatred of the people, combined with her own consciousness of guilt, had bound her, after the death of her earthly body, to wander about year after year on the astral plane of the Earth, unable to ascend to her home in the spheres. On her restless wanderings she discovered an underground stream that was visible to her and whose water contained certain radioactive substances. Since she knew that the water if used at the site – the radiations being very transient – would alleviate a number of bodily sufferings, and even partially or completely cure certain diseases, she believed that she could atone for some of her guilt toward the people of France by revealing her discovery to them. She therefore addressed herself to Bernadette, who as stated above was a medium, and in order to gain greater credence imparted her message in such a way that she could be mistaken for the Virgin Mary. Her words were: "I am the Immaculate Conception." She knew that this description befitted her no more than it did the mother of Jesus, but excusing herself by the so-called Jesuit adage that the end justifies the means, she had no hesitation in leading people to perceive her as the "immaculate virgin who conceived without sin" – the mother of Jesus. As must all others who are guilty of

---

[1] Those who have no knowledge of the spring at Lourdes are referred to the book "Lourdes" by the French author Emile Zola and "Lourdes" by the Danish author Johannes Jørgensen. Reference can also be made to the book "Lourdes" by Dr. Boissarie and to "Les Apparitions de Lourdes" by J. B. Estrade. – Publisher's note.

falsehood, she has had to atone in full for this deception; but the nature of her atonement is a matter between her and God.

Much use is made of the healing waters from the spring at Lourdes. It should be pointed out, however, that these healings do not result from the radioactive radiations *alone,* but are in many cases due to autosuggestion on the part of the patients. The absolute faith in being healed that many of them possess, together with the fervent prayers and intercessions for help that are answered by God, draw the healing rays of the Light-ether toward the patients, and the desired healing is then partly or completely achieved. Even if such prayers and intercessions are directed to the Virgin Mary, God will answer them when they are offered with fervour and in sincere trust. But only a few of the body's ailments can be cured in this way; and not all accounts of healings experienced at the spring are in accordance with the truth.

In view of the foregoing, the healings that occur through the application of water from the spring at Lourdes[1] can be regarded neither as miracles nor as cures based entirely on superstition, any more than can the discovery of the spring. The apparently supernatural in this case does have *a natural, lawful background;* but the laws under which the existence of the spring was made known to mankind were employed in an unlawful manner, that is *without God's permission.*

People have very often placed on beings from the transcendental world demands whose fulfilment was, and still is, in violation of the laws given by God. Thus it has happened, for example, that members of a spiritualistic circle have often demanded of spirits who manifested themselves during the circle's séances that they should prove their existence, their personal identity and their spiritual strength, or demonstrate that they were emissaries from God, and so forth, by performing materializations, dematerializations, and many other "feats" of this kind. Doubtless without being aware of it, these spiritualists have thus often demanded that their spiritual communicators should act *against the Laws given by God.* And when the spirits have not wished to act against these laws, and thus failed to produce the desired evidence, these people have forthwith labelled the spirits of their mediums as frauds, without being willing to investigate or respect the reasons for their refusal. Conduct of this kind by human beings is as foolish as that of a thief who would say to an honest person: *"Go and steal, and I shall believe in your honesty!"*

Human beings must learn in the future to respect the psychic and the astral laws, even though they do not understand them; learn that *they* must not *demand,* but only *pray;* learn to receive with gratitude the proofs that are given from the transcendental world *according to the insight and wish of God;* learn that *the spirits of the Light* will

---

[1]) Or from other similar springs.

not behave as *lawbreakers* simply because certain people *will not* understand until they have seen or received that which *they themselves demand.* And of one thing can human beings be certain: *the greater their demands, the less will they be given from the transcendental world. Only they who seek in prayer, with faith and in a completely unselfish manner, only they can achieve close contact with the spirits of the Light and receive the necessary help to find that for which they seek.*

The laws of lesser, greater or complete regularity that directly concern *purely earthly* conditions, whether relating to energy, to radiation, to matter and substance, and so forth, or whether to the psychic and astral laws that govern the contact of the transcendental world with the physical, *all* these laws are only provisional – temporary – which is to say that they apply only by virtue of the existence of the Earth, and only for so long as the Globe exists.

Through that intelligence with which God has enriched human beings, and through instruction from the incarnated Youngest, some of the forces of Darkness – electricity, electromagnetism, steam power and so forth – have been put to use in the earthly world and must therefore, being partly under human control, in many ways contribute to the easing and improvement of life on Earth.

Many toxic substances – organic and inorganic – that originate from Darkness have similarly been put to use in the service of the Light, for example as medicines and disinfectants, or utilized in many other ways, for example as pigments, etching reagents and so forth.

Several explosive substances that in the service of Darkness are used to cause death and destruction – for example as weapons of war – are also used to serve the progress of the Light, for example in the levelling of the ground, blasting of obstructions, drilling and so forth.

Also through the diseases of the body is Darkness forced to assist in maintaining the overall balance. An acute illness can relieve the sufferer of accumulations of Darkness – strain, germs, bacteria and the like – that threaten to destroy the body. The cure, which among other things is due to the healing influence of the corona of Light and the Light-ether, restores health to the body – the accumulated Darkness is eliminated and the balance thereby restored.

Through *the Laws of Retribution and Reincarnation,* which are also temporary, and which God has given to promote the progress of mankind on Earth, the spiritual destruction and disturbance that Darkness constantly causes among human beings is equalized and counterbalanced in many ways.

Through the Law of Retribution each evil thought and every evil or criminal act reverts to the person who conceived the thought or committed the act; in this way the originator must endure the same spiritual or physical sufferings as those intended for or brought upon others.[1] Balance is then restored through the sufferings endured by the originator.

Catastrophes that are due to the influence of Darkness on the existing order, and which intervene in the lives of human beings by causing disturbance and destruction, are similarly utilized by God to restore balance under the Law of Retribution, thus forcing Darkness also in these cases to serve the cause of the Light. For instance, people who directly or indirectly become victims of earthquakes, mine or traffic accidents or of fire disasters, of the devastations of war, such as maiming, disease, starvation, loss of property and so forth will always, because of the spiritual and physical suffering endured, have the guilt of misdeeds, killings, murders and other crimes committed in previous lives counterbalanced and annulled, so that their future lives on Earth become brighter and happier. For it must be clear to all: **that no human being endures any greater spiritual or physical suffering[2] than that brought upon himself or herself in previous lives,** and since God never lacks the means to intercede when this is necessary, people who have no guilt from previous earthly lives that can be expiated in the above manner will never be exposed to this kind of suffering. (See pp. 252–53).

God's mercy and compassion transcend the Law of Retribution. All who fully repent of their evil and sinful actions can through their remorse obtain God's permission to atone for their sins by one or more acts of love or compassion toward those against whom they have sinned.

Even death must serve life and the Light, since the spirit that is released at death, possessing the results of the accumulated experiences of the recently ended life on Earth stands prepared to acquire new experience and new learning through new earthly lives.

And when the many incarnations of humanity have come to an end, according to the Law of Balance of the Light, God will through a mighty cataclysm cause the remainder of the Darkness that has not yet been depolarized to assist in the dissolution of the Globe, which through the downfall of the Eldest was brought under the dominion

---

[1]) See Speech of Christ, pp. 111–115.

[2]) Sufferings of any kind that human beings bring upon themselves, for example by thoughtless or unhygienic ways of life, indifference, carelessness, wantonness, needless overexertion, and so forth, *are not counterbalanced;* in such cases human beings must suffer the consequences.

of Darkness. Then will the perfect and final balance have been achieved: *humanity will have been released for ever from the Earth – for millions of years the stage for human sin and grief and suffering; the Globe will disintegrate; the Darkness depolarized through the cataclysm will be absorbed and transported by the cycle of Light to its ultimate purification through God's flaming Being – and the saga of the Earth will have come to an end.*

All that has been stated concerning the oscillations, depolarization, radiations and various other manifestations of Darkness as well as the descriptions of the regulating and balancing influence of the Light have only been given in broad outline, since specific knowledge of the various branches of the natural sciences is required in order for the transcendental world to furnish a more thorough and detailed explanation. But people with scientific training who wish to proceed from this given basis can always be assured of receiving valuable help from their spiritual leaders – the disincarnated Youngest. Much that can be brought to light and utilized by human intelligence is still unknown and unresolved, while similarly a number of the powers of Darkness still remain to be brought under human control and made useful in many ways.

Since the Earth is a *world of Darkness,* human intelligence will be engaged mainly in utilizing the products of Darkness. But human beings will gradually learn to discern and determine *where the influence of the Light intervenes in the existing order.*

From the moment in the remote prehistoric past when the Eldest decided to oppose the incarnated Youngest in order to obstruct their guidance of humanity, the Elder has like God[1] laid plans in outline for the incarnations of the Youngest and the human spirits. In accordance with these plans the Eldest or the Elder himself sought to lead human beings astray and away from the paths of life desired by God.

The Elder has in the same way predetermined the fate of entire peoples, entire nations, in order to lead as many as possible away from the paths of the Light.

Since all thoughts[2] – evil as well as good – are received and reflected by the ether, the Elder's predetermining thoughts of future events were recorded as images in the ether of Darkness that surrounds the Globe.

---

[1]) See Commentary, p. 184.
[2]) The thoughts of God and the disincarnated Youngest are not recorded in the ether that surrounds the Globe.

20* C

Three different types of ether-image occur: future-images, present-images and after-images.

1) *Future-images* are the aforementioned records of the Elder's predeterminations for the fate and conduct of individual human beings and of entire nations. These future-images, which were meant to bring misfortunes and sufferings upon humanity, like everything else originating from Darkness have also been forced to serve the cause of the Light in accordance with the Law of Balance. The disincarnated Youngest – the leaders and guardian spirits of mankind – have thus been able to discern from these future-images what plots and designs threatened their charges at the hands of the Eldest. They have been able to determine, from the faintness or clarity of these future-images, whether the recorded events lay far out in the future or whether they were imminent, and have accordingly been able to take precautions if possible to avert or mitigate the destructive future events that threatened the individual or humanity at large.

Where nations were concerned the Elder normally outlined his predeterminations for several centuries into the future, so that by the time he returned to God he had recorded in the ether of Darkness that surrounds the Earth many future-images of the manner in which the lives of all the peoples and the nations on Earth for many years ahead should develop according to *his will*. But when some years before his return he understood that the Light must ultimately defeat him, he devised further appalling occurrences for the future of nations in the form of devastating wars, assassinations, yet more wars, misfortune and misery, etc., reasoning that hatred, envy and lust for power among human beings would help him draw Darkness closer about the Earth, and thus, despite the counteraction of the Youngest, postpone the day of victory of the Light over him. The Youngest, who were all aware of both these and the earlier predeterminations, did all they could to prevent them from occurring on the plane of the Earth as real events. At the time[1] that Christ succeeded in winning back his eldest brother, several of these ominous events had already come to pass as realities upon the plane of the Earth, while others were about to do so. The Youngest tried in many ways to divert or moderate the existing and impending conflicts between the governments of the various nations, and thus, if this were possible, to prevent the outbreak of the appalling wars in which such conflicts would otherwise result. But the many and energetic attempts by the Youngest to guide the leaders and the rulers into peaceful settlements of their standing disputes remained without

---

[1]) In the year 1912.

result, and numerous of the Elder's ether-recordings were called forth into reality in the earthly world *by the will for evil of human beings themselves.* But although the Elder carries the chief responsibility for the recorded predeterminations, human beings must also bear grave and onerous guilt for the horrors, murders and misdeeds that were committed through human malice, hatred, greed and lust for power, and which could have been avoided had human beings striven for the good and the true in life instead of heeding the promptings of revenge and injustice. And if the Youngest are to prevent the remaining threatening ether-recordings from being called forth into reality upon the plane of the Earth at the time appointed by the Elder, human beings, and especially their *leaders* and *rulers,* must assist by paying greater heed to the admonitions of their conscience, since the efforts of the Youngest will otherwise be in vain; **for God compels no human being to turn away from Darkness, and He compels no one to do that which is right.**

The Elder's future-images have often been seen by clairvoyant human beings, but through abnormal refractions in the ether these images have from time to time been perceptible to people who were not mediums. Several people have thus simultaneously seen ether-images – forewarnings – for example of marching soldiers, scenes of battle, murders and the like. The images have appeared in the open air (not unlike earthly mirages such as Fata Morgana) or in enclosed spaces, for example in the rooms of palaces, manor houses and ordinary dwellings that later became the scene of the crime foreboded by the ether-images.

Through similarly abnormal refractions in the sound-waves of the ether, sounds belonging to the future have been audible in the earthly world as omens, for example the sounds of battle, the crash of as yet imaginary train collisions, screams, sighs, groans, the sound of firm, stealthy or dragging footsteps and a great deal more.

No detailed explanation of these phenomena will be given, since they will all gradually cease as Darkness is eliminated.

Not all criminal deeds have their origin in the Elder's ether-recordings. In many cases they are due to the mutual hatred, envy and so forth of human beings. In the same way, by no means all the misfortunes that have occurred, and will continue to occur, can be blamed on the Elder. Many are due to human recklessness, indolence, negligence, dereliction of duty and so forth. Human beings who in these or in other ways cause the maiming or death of themselves or of others must bear the full responsibility themselves, and cannot lay the blame upon the Elder.

2) *Present-images,* in other words recordings in the ether of human thoughts that likewise in many ways affect the life of the individual and the existence of all humanity.

Since all thoughts are received and transmitted by the ether-waves, people influence[1] each other for good or for evil. Impure and evil thoughts are attracted by wicked and feeble persons, so that they often commit acts under the influence or compulsion of thoughts conceived by others. The one who transmitted[2] the thoughts must in such cases share the responsibility with the one who committed the act. But only God can determine whether the act resulted from the individual's own thoughts, or from thoughts that were attracted to or forced upon that person.

The principal psychic law, on which the telepathic power of thought is based, will not be disclosed to mankind from the transcendental world, since the ethical standard maintained by human beings is not yet high enough to preclude all misuse of this knowledge.

Through experimentation, human beings may possibly come to recognize and determine for themselves some of the more elementary laws for telepathy of thought.

3) *After-images* are reflections of human actions performed according to a conscious thought-plan, or according to thoughts that arise instantaneously from within the self, or that are attracted to or imposed on the self from the outside.

The moment a thought becomes action the thought-image fades and vanishes, and as the action is carried out, it is recorded or reflected in every detail. However, the image of the action seldom corresponds exactly to the image of the thought, since people virtually never carry out their actions precisely according to the thoughts that precede them, even if the conscious thought-plan is prepared with the greatest care, since many events unforeseen by human beings often interfere at the moment of action, whereby much can be changed or prevented.

The after-images that reflect evil human actions, such as murder or similar misdeeds, are often fixed for long periods of time in the accumulations of Darkness at the place where the crime was committed. These images dissolve and vanish when the perpetrators of the action have fully repented of their sin. But when those who have committed the crime do not repent during their earthly existence, or during the period of time for contemplation and repentance that is

---

[1]) Mass suggestion through thought can give rise, for example, to patriotism, war fever, revolutionary movements, the founding of religious sects, and so forth.

[2]) Since the thought has its seat in the large nerve-centre of the spirit-body, it is the psychic brain that is influenced, it being both the transmitter and the receiver of thought.

allotted to each released spirit at the time of death of the physical body, the image remains until the sin has been atoned for in some way in a new incarnation. It has therefore often happened that an after-image of this kind has remained in the same place for centuries.

In contrast to the thoughts, which are borne away by the ether-waves, the images of evil and vile actions are reflected in the accumulations of Darkness and remain there until they fade and disappear. Images of good deeds are reflected in the radiations of Light from the spirit-body.

The radiations of Darkness from after-images often produce a distinct feeling of uneasiness in sensitive people when they are present in places were crimes have been committed. Clairvoyants have often seen and described after-images of scenes of battle, murder, robbery and other evil deeds.

After-images of good or insignificant actions are dissolved and gradually fade away as the action withdraws in the individual's memory; but when the human spirit is released at death from the earthly body, everything – good and evil – remains recorded in the consciousness of the spirit.

In the same way that after-images are preserved in the accumulations of Darkness, sounds that stem from crimes already committed, such as screams, blows, the impact of an axe, stampings, shuffling footsteps and so forth, are preserved for long periods in accumulations of Darkness as after-sounds. These sounds may on occasion become audible in the earthly world in places where crimes were committed. The sounds can be so "real" that they can be heard by people who are not mediums. These sounds will cease as the respective accumulations of Darkness are eliminated.

Since human thought is a reflection of God's Thought, human beings are able by the existence of their thought to give form and shape to the products of their imagination, so that these can appear visibly on the *astral plane*. In contrast to the spiritual beings that God has created, the forms of human fantasy are not everlasting but only ephemeral, their existence being subject to dissolution and destruction.

The higher the spiritual self that is bound to the human body, the clearer and more firmly constituted are its thought-images or phantoms; but in most cases people do not shape or finish their thoughts completely, for which reason that which appears or is brought forth in the spiritual-astral substance normally resembles only misty, elusive and colourless sketches. All authors, painters, sculptors, and others who wish to translate their thoughts with the help of earthly materials, so that in some way they can be perceived and understood by their fellow human beings, consciously or subconsciously form or create in their thought one or more images of that which they wish to make accessible to sense perception. The clarity, brightness of colour and durability of the images and phantoms are dependent on the artist's ability to work with the spiritual-astral material. They normally fade away when the individual relinquishes the initial thought in order to let new images and new phantoms emerge.

Since clairvoyants can normally see these thought-phantoms but are not always able to differentiate within their field of vision between a phantom and a human spirit, numerous legends and fantastic tales of the so-called "elemental spirits" have come into existence in the course of time.

Ever since the earliest ages after the time when God had endowed humanity with spiritual life, i.e., thought and will, human beings – especially the most primitive, the least developed people – have imagined nature to be populated with invisible beings whom they believed capable of intervening in earthly existence in various ways, and of making themselves visible to the human eye. The forests, seas, rivers, lakes, mountains and so forth all had their own spirits – good-natured or evil-minded, helpful, mischievous or vindictive beings. In the forms created by human thought they were visible to clairvoyants. Many even believed that the elemental spirits ruled over and regulated the thriving of nature, that animal and plant life was dependent on the vigilance of these creatures. Since all natural life is subject to established laws, it is easy to see that all such beliefs belong to the world of fantasy. Gradually as human spirits mature, as their insight deepens and they lose all belief in *independently thinking and acting* elemental spirits, and as these spirits therefore no longer occupy their thoughts, the phantoms will dissolve and disappear.

Since all formerly earthbound spirits have been removed from the Earth, *possessions* by these spirits can no longer take place. If a person now appears to be possessed, the reason for that person's malicious, evil or irrational behaviour must be sought elsewhere. Three categories are described in the following:

1) *One of the Eldest* is bound to that person's body. (Many of the Eldest are at present still incarnated among human beings).

2) *Split personality,* i.e., memories from previous lives on Earth emerge in the person's consciousness, causing the individual to regress to one or more of its earlier personalities. This can occur where the insulation layer between the spirit and the body has been damaged by the incursions of Darkness, often brought about by the individual's own evil thoughts and sinful way of life; or this may be due to the misuse of mediumistic talent.

While the spirits of the dead remained on the plane of the Earth, split personalities[1] often originated from their malignant possession of human beings.

---

[1] Split personalities were not and are not always authentic, since they are often the result of a human desire to attract attention or to appear interesting.

The "dead" would thrust aside the spirit bound to the relevant body and then assume its place. But since the parasitic spirit was not bound by the life-giving cord, its energy would sooner or later weaken, thus obliging it to return the borrowed body to its rightful owner, who would only partly have been able to make contact with the brain of its physical body during the possession. The spirit that had thus been temporarily thrust aside could usually remember that it had shared its physical body with one or more intruding personalities. But in some cases the person had no recollection of having been seized by a parasitic spirit.

3) *Radiations from accumulations of Darkness* that gather around the individual, attracted by the Darkness emitting from that individual's personality. The encounter between these two forms of Darkness will then result in evil and impure thoughts or in criminal acts.

There is often a fourth category, in which the spirit that is bound to the physical body is not normally responsible for what happens. For example, if the physical brain[1] has been damaged in some way by concussion, sickness or old age, the spirit cannot enter into communication with the brain and therefore loses some and occasionally all controlling power, and the person is no longer "himself", i. e., he loses his individual personality.

———————

At the time when the Youngest at God's request decided to let themselves be incarnated on Earth, the human beings were still few in number, but they lived scattered over large parts of the Globe.

Since the Eldest had endowed them with almost no means of sustaining and defending themselves, their struggle for survival carried off thousands upon thousands of them at a very young age.

Several of the human types then existing were of such a low order that there was but the smallest possibility of leading these human creatures forward to greater spiritual maturity and greater bodily refinement, for which reason the Youngest from the outset declined to be incarnated among them. A few types were then selected, and the Youngest embarked on the monumental task *of leading human beings out of Darkness and forward toward their Father's Kingdom.*

Thus there are races of human beings in whose midst the Youngest have *never* been incarnated. The spiritual level that has now been attained by a number of these primitive beings is reached with the help of the divine element[2] that is given to every human being at the

———————

[1]) See Summary, p. 288, regarding the afflicted, abnormal brain.
[2]) See Commentary, p. 189.

moment of conception, and which always at each new incarnation endows the human spirit with a further spiritual enhancement. Newly created and young spirits are mostly incarnated among these primitive or fairly primitive peoples. Gradually, as God's need of these peoples for the first incarnations of human spirits diminishes, they will slowly become extinct.

When the first incarnations among the more primitive peoples have been concluded, as the spirit matures and its will becomes stronger, it is incarnated among more highly developed and finally among the most advanced human races. This happens so that the spirit in every aspect of life can learn to overcome evil in all its various forms. The human spirit must in this way experience *all* that is offered by life on Earth and thereby achieve a many-sided development of thought and will, although allowance must be made for the natural limitation that follows from the fact that a male spirit is always bound to a male body, and a female spirit to a female body. (However, exceptions to this rule have occurred with the unlawful incarnations of the Eldest. See Commentary, pp. 201–02).

Through millions of years, inconceivably slowly, step by step and generation after generation the Youngest led human beings forward, gradually providing them with new and greater knowledge, and with more and more aids and implements for use in everyday life.

In the beginning and through many ages the Youngest in their human existence were only little higher than human beings in intelligence and in spiritual development. Through their sense of beauty the female Youngest that were bound to earthly women endowed their progeny with ever greater bodily refinement.

At a certain time in the prehistoric past the Eldest began in manifold ways to oppose and hinder the Youngest in their efforts by constantly drawing across the Earth more and more of the Darkness from the ravaged Kingdom, and by directing it to the places where the greatest human progress was evident.

As stated previously, the first truly civilized realm,[1] which developed after millions of years, was situated in the Pacific Ocean. But many thousands of years before this realm was destroyed and disintegrated into island groups, the process of civilization[2] had started in other places on Earth, for example on the Island in the Atlantic Ocean, in the eastern part of Central Africa and in a few places in Asia.

---

[1] Ardor has mentioned only the prehistoric civilizations because human beings possess no historical accounts or traditions from those times; only legends exist.

[2] The Ice Ages that laid waste some parts of the Earth are not mentioned by Ardor, since they did not directly interfere with the work of the Youngest.

After the demise of the Island, the work of the Youngest was transferred mainly to northern and to eastern Africa and to the interior and southern parts of Asia.

At that time the majority of human beings still led a predominantly nomadic life, with no formal leadership. (The elders of the tribes usually acted as leaders in any tribal affairs). Laboriously they migrated with their cattle over vast distances; and thus were widely spread across the Earth many of the families that through the repeated incarnations of the Youngest had been endowed with greater nobility and beauty, both spiritually and physically, than had their forefathers. These families intermingled again with the peoples already living in the places where the wanderers settled for longer or shorter periods of their nomadic lives. The spiritual level of these peoples was higher or lower according to whether or not the Youngest had been incarnated among them. Through blood relations between the nomads and the original settlers there arose new human types, new races; some families were improved by this interbreeding, others degenerated and met with extinction.

When also the African realm perished and its inhabitants fled to various other places, the Youngest transferred their efforts to northeastern Africa – the area later to become Egypt – while a new process of civilization was begun in the southern part of Europe, and the work already under way in Asia was continued.

Until about half a century before the destruction of the Atlantic Island, the Youngest, despite the opposition of the Eldest, had brought all the peoples of the Earth, with the exception of the most primitive, forward in a reasonably straight line. But from the moment when the Eldest presumptuously began to incarnate themselves, they were able to offer an even stronger resistance to the Youngest, since the Eldest as human beings more easily gained power over their weak and immature fellow beings, with the result that the slow and relatively even progress of civilization and of the Light was supplanted by an erratic sequence of advance and retreat. For since the Eldest, as related in Ardor's Account, sought incarnation as human beings primarily where they could best achieve high positions[1] that would presumably satisfy their lust for earthly power and their urge to dominate, and since the great spiritual strength that was due to their inadequate insulation layer was especially prominent against the background of the low spiritual level of the weakly devel-

---

[1] This does not mean that *all* rulers were of the Eldest; both human spirits and the Youngest have often been bound to human beings who held high office, both ecclesiastical and secular.

oped human beings, it was necessary for the Youngest to counteract this domination by allowing still more of their spiritual strength and individuality to manifest itself in their earthly existence. In this way arose the great leading figures of history – both those serving the cause of the good as well as those dedicated to evil, represented respectively by the Youngest and the Eldest, men as well as women. These figures, who contrast so sharply with one another in their infinite disparity, can be found in all historical records, from the time of the earliest civilizations of antiquity to the present.

When the superiority of the incarnated Eldest became too great, the Youngest had to withdraw, but only to meet again as human beings in other countries and there to make an even greater contribution to the prevailing culture. In this way the many and mighty civilized empires of ancient times were created, and later fell into complete stagnation as the Eldest gained dominion and the Youngest were driven out. Sooner or later the culture of the Light declined, the independence of the people diminished, and many of the mighty realms were subjugated by neighbouring peoples and met with partial or complete extinction.

About 800 years before the incarnation of the eldest of the Youngest as Jesus of Nazareth, the Youngest were near to exhaustion and began to lose heart as the incarnated Eldest gained steadily greater power over human beings. Only few of the Youngest dared venture among them; but those who came brought with them an abundance of spiritual teachings, of new and noble thoughts and a wealth of artistic expression in colour and form, so that with all their strength they might take up the struggle against the Eldest.

To this era that extended to the birth of Christ belong, for example, several of the Jewish prophets,[1] a number of Chaldean, Arabian and Indian scholars, the two great religious founders Zarathustra and Buddha,[2] the great men of China, Lao-tze, Kung-tze and Meng-tze, some of the Greek poets, a number of scholars and philosophers, some of the most outstanding leaders of the Roman Empire in the field of spiritual life, and many other leaders in statesmanship, in the arts, in the natural sciences and so forth in all the civilized countries of the time.

---

[1]) Some of the prophets were of the Eldest, whose prophecies were inspired by the Elder or by his predeterminations. See Summary, pp. 307–09.

[2]) None of the great religious founders prior to Jesus is directly mentioned in Ardor's Account, because they were only to prepare the way, i.e., to make mankind more receptive to what was to come, and because the Account was intended to emphasize the work of the eldest of the Youngest on behalf of humanity. The Youngest who was incarnated as Zarathustra was later reborn as Mani; Buddha was reborn as Mohammed.

At that time, the astronomical sciences were especially highly developed in Egypt, Chaldea and in China, and were cultivated to some extent in India.

Astrology, an offshoot of astronomy, is an ancient "science", but has in fact absolutely no right to be called such, for the stars have **never** had any influence whatsoever upon the fate of human beings. If from time to time a horoscope were accurate this was because the astrologer who made the calculations had intuitively seen or read the Elder's recordings of future-images in the ether, or because the Elder often arranged his predeterminations in such a way as to coincide with the "laws of the stars", which the astrologers believed determined the fate of human beings.

Despite the great beauty and great learning bestowed upon mankind by the Youngest during this time, they were still not able to overcome the Eldest, who were growing ever more powerful; and the Youngest who resided in the spheres turned to God for more help and for greater strength.

When God in his discourse[1] with the Youngest had strengthened and comforted them, they set to work with renewed courage on the almost abandoned task, and thus about eight decades after taking counsel with God, the eldest of the Youngest was incarnated as Jesus of Nazareth.

Once again the Youngest were on the verge of despair, when after the return of Jesus to the spheres from his life on Earth his heirs proved incapable of completing the great task that had been entrusted to them: *to promulgate the teaching of Jesus in pure and unadulterated form,* and when Saul – or Paul – through the many false interpretations dictated to him by the Elder removed this teaching still further from its original form.

He of the Youngest who was bound to the physical body of Saul, and who before his incarnation had promised to open the eyes of the Jewish scholars to the truths in the teaching of Jesus, was a person of great authority and strong will, characteristics that in the earthly world are readily transformed into obstinacy. He was later reborn as the reformer *Martin Luther* for the purpose of cleansing Christianity of all the errors that he had imposed on the teaching of Jesus while he was incarnated as Saul.

Since Christianity spread primarily toward the northwest, and since the Youngest in their many attempts at restoring it to its true form had to be incarnated where there were the best opportunities for opposing the false doctrines implanted by the Elder, the culture of the Light spread more and more across Europe after the death of

---

[1] See Ardor's Account, pp. 31–32.

Jesus of Nazareth, but always accompanied by the degenerative and destructive countermoves of the Eldest.

Many of the Youngest were still of course incarnated in countries outside Europe, but most of them were sent to that part of the world.

Since the Youngest for many centuries had primarily emphasized *the purification of the teaching of Jesus,* it became impossible for them to continue their purely cultural work in the same forceful manner as before, and for this reason the incarnated Eldest, and with them Darkness, gained more and more power over mankind and thereby hampered and disrupted the endeavours of the Youngest to give guidance.

Some of the Youngest were in addition led so far astray by the Elder, and by the dense Darkness that he continually gathered about them during their human existence, that they often fought hard to defend precisely that which they had been sent to Earth to *oppose* and to *root out*. And again came a time when most of the Youngest were in favour of abandoning the task and letting human beings follow their own course. But Christ reasoned with them anew and again he made them pray to God for still greater spiritual strength and greater power of resistance in their earthly lives, so that Darkness should not overcome them all.

When God had once more[1] spoken to the Youngest, had shown them the shortcomings in their procedure and had pointed out to them how they would better be able to lead human beings forward by bringing them still more and still greater knowledge in various areas, as this would open their eyes to the numerous mistaken beliefs and cause human beings themselves to seek the truth, a multitude of the Youngest were once again incarnated, thus initiating the so-called Renaissance.

But since humanity at this point had populated large parts of the Globe, the tasks of the Youngest became greater in number and their work was made still more difficult. In addition to being incarnated, they also had to serve as guardian spirits, had to direct the incarnations of human beings and to instruct the human spirits during their sojourn in the spheres between their incarnations. And the work threatened to engulf them.

But those many of the Eldest[2] who had long since repented of their fall and of their sin – the creation of the human beings – and who now, having been purified, stayed in their Father's Kingdom

---

[1] See Ardor's Account, pp. 85–86.
[2] The Eldest who had returned at God's request; see Ardor's Account, pp. 14–15.

and followed the work of their younger brothers and sisters with profound and sincere gratitude, then asked their Father's permission to make their own contribution to this so very extensive work. In answer to their prayer God entrusted them with the task of assisting as guardian spirits for human beings, and of participating as leaders in the instruction given to human spirits during their stay in the spheres. And since in addition the Youngest of their own accord shortened the time of rest allotted to each of them after each completed earthly life, the work could proceed on its regular course.

But the Youngest had to endure severe struggles,[1] and especially those who had undertaken *to cleanse the teachings of Jesus* often suffered the greatest defeats. But despite all opposition they slowly made progress, though with varying success on different fronts – now the Light and the Youngest had the upper hand, now Darkness, the Elder and the incarnated Eldest.

After several centuries of persistent effort, conditions on Earth had improved to such an extent that Christ, the eldest of the Youngest, might succeed in crowning the work through another incarnation. As a human being with human emotions, but this time without human fear[2] of the Evil One he would be able to show compassion for the Elder – the Prince of Hell – and to pray from deep in his heart for his salvation. And by appearing as a religious reformer he would also be able *to restore to its original form* the teaching that he as Jesus of Nazareth had presented to humanity.

But God knew that despite Christ's resolve to do his utmost there would also in this incarnation be a possibility that Darkness might overcome him and thus expose his gentle mind anew to much deep and bitter suffering. And when God saw that despite the many acts of fraud on the part of the mediums more and more people tried in earnest and with understanding to communicate[3] with the dead, He decided – even though the spiritualistic connections were highly inadequate and misleading – to let Christ make an attempt, with human beings as intermediaries, to reach the intended goal in this way and thus be spared the many sufferings of a difficult life on Earth. With this decision and by this means, the unlawful application of astral and psychic laws by the spirits of Darkness could also be brought under control, so that the communications established be-

---

[1] The Youngest are often incarnated under humble and difficult circumstances in order to demonstrate to human beings how much a strong will and energy can accomplish in life on Earth.

[2] It was God's intention to let the eldest of the Youngest be incarnated in one of the many liberal-minded families which at that time existed in several different countries.

[3] In the middle of the 19th century.

tween the transcendental world and the sensory world might serve the cause of the Light rather than the cause of Darkness. In this way the spiritualistic *errors, misunderstandings, abuses and frauds* could also be attacked, exposed and rooted out, so that the elimination by the Light of the misuse of the astral and psychic laws by the disincarnated Eldest and the human spirits might if possible become final and complete. And God pointed to that Shorter Road by which Christ and his helpers after indescribable difficulties, sacrifices and disappointments have since reached the desired result: *the return of the earthbound spirits to their dwellings in the spheres, the absorption of the ravaged Kingdom by the wave of Light, the complete redemption of the Elder, his voluntary confession and his plea to human beings for forgiveness for all his sins against them, and the imparting of the message and teachings of Christ in the form of a speech to humanity.*

Since Christ has thus fulfilled the first part of his promise to his Father: **to deliver his eldest brother from the power of Darkness, to impart to human beings certain truths concerning life hereafter, and to provide clear and complete instructions on how life on Earth should be lived, God has relieved him of any future incarnation, so that he may devote himself entirely to the fulfilment of the second part of his promise: to guide human beings to the Home of Him who is the Father of them all.**

The constant ebb and flow of fortunes in the spiritual struggle on Earth between the incarnated Youngest and Eldest created circumstances that were not propitious for humanity. For since the Youngest were prevented from leading mankind forward in a straight line – that is to say, as far as possible bringing all human beings forward in a slow but constant cultural progress, whereby humanity might mature both inwardly and outwardly – they had to revise their methods, and as stated earlier elevate their individual personalities very many levels above the human beings in order to achieve even a relatively modest aim: *to hold the incarnated Eldest in restraint and to gain victory over them in the course of time.* For the average human being culture has thus become an outward gloss, an often mandatory facade that shatters easily on the least occasion and allows the true nature of the human being – *the human animal* – to be revealed. Especially in later and most recent times this disparity appears all the more incongruous against the background of apparently advanced spiritual culture in so many countries – a culture, however, that is sustained only by a minority, and which it will take ordinary human beings *hundreds, perhaps thousands, of years to attain and to assimilate.*

Should all the Youngest at some future time suddenly cease their incarnations, a general stagnation would result. Nothing significantly new would emerge in any area at all, and human beings would thus have to draw as long as possible (see p. 264) upon that which had already been given them of invention, natural science and poetry, of graphic, plastic and musical arts, and of much more besides, until the Youngest once again let themselves be born among them; for mankind will not in the future receive any innovations of importance from the genius of the Eldest, since *those* among them who have been incarnated since Ardor's return in 1912 have entered their incarnations under the leadership of God, and their genius has for this reason been withheld by the power of His Will so that they cannot become pioneers and innovators during life on Earth, but in every way appear as average human beings.

———————

The Eldest have in the course of time become divided into *three groups.*

1) Those who first repented of their sins and of their fall and returned to God's Kingdom without ever having been incarnated. *These Eldest never will be incarnated;* as stated earlier they atone for their sins against humanity by helping their younger brothers and sisters guide the journeying of mankind toward the Light.

2) Those who after a number of unlawful incarnations remained in the ravaged Kingdom. However, some of these let themselves be incarnated by the Elder from time to time, so as to assist him in his evil designs against human beings, and especially against the incarnated Youngest. These Eldest, of whom many are still incarnated, will in times to come be incarnated under the leadership of God, so as during new lives on Earth to atone for their sins and their crimes against humanity.

3) Those who could not endure remaining in the ravaged Kingdom and who have wilfully continued their unlawfully commenced incarnations. These have now progressed so far that they have all – long since – submitted to the leadership of God. The divine element that is bestowed at conception upon each future human being has been of great benefit to them, since with each earthly birth their darkened spirit thus receives a spiritual enrichment, whereby their struggle forward toward the Light has been considerably advanced

and facilitated – but they still have *much* to expiate before they return to God's Kingdom.

When the many thousands of the Eldest incarnated by the Elder who still live on Earth are released at death from their physical bodies, they are brought to distant astral dwellings in one of the other three star universes, where they must remain until the memories of their fall and of their many sins awaken, whereupon they will be incarnated under the leadership of God, so as to make atonement and to rehabilitate their personalities. When the last of Ardor's still "living" helpers departs from earthly existence, in about 50 to 60 years' time, human beings will be freed from the last remaining bond that binds them to their creators. A weak spiritual current[1] flowed into their creatures from the Eldest during their attempts to create them, and from the first appearance of human beings it has pervaded their astral counterparts, thus endowing them with a weak spiritual life and thereby freeing them from the destructibility[2] of Darkness. But the moment the last earthly body of these Eldest dies, this weak spiritual current will be broken off, and God will be released from the promise that He gave His first repentant children: *to let a divine element merge with the spiritual life bestowed by the Eldest, thereby to allow humanity to partake of eternal life and to release the counterparts so that upon death of the human body they can be dissolved and absorbed into the Darkness from which they were formed.*

Thus: **when the current from the Eldest is broken off, God will create no more spirits; the human spirits will then constitute a completed whole, with no further influx of newly created beings.** But in order to ease the journey of His many children to their Father's Home it is God's intention not to break off the divine stream of Light that flows from Him to humanity, but to allow it perpetually to infuse them all, so that in the future human spirits will *continue to receive with each new incarnation* a further spiritual enrichment as a gift from God. By this precious gift the spirit is endowed with ever-increasing spiritual strength and power of will to help it on the difficult journey. But millions of years must pass before the young and last-created human spirits can be released from life on Earth.

The number of incarnations for the human spirit is highly variable; in other words, it is not the same for all, since this number depends on the individual's free will toward good or toward evil. Human spirits who during their incarnations have

---

[1]) See Ardor's Account, p. 13, and Commentary, p. 178.
[2]) See Ardor's Account, p. 14, regarding human shadows.

been directly or indirectly responsible for the death of many fellow beings, whether by manslaughter, murder or accident, or who as earthly rulers have exposed their subjects to death in wars of conquest or religion, in family feuds and so forth, have been obliged to experience many more incarnations to atone for these many killings than those who have not committed such crimes. The longest time during which a human spirit has been bound to the Earth and its spheres before it could be released from earthly lives is approximately three million earthly years, and the shortest time approximately one and three-quarter million years; these periods include the years spent in sojourn in the spheres as time of rest and learning. Many of the first, the eldest of the human spirits, have long ago been released from all incarnation. These continue their journey on globes in the distant star universe, or galactic system, that corresponds to the one to which the Earth belongs. Here they slowly mature under the instruction of God's Servants until they can enter God's Kingdom, where they will be received by God, their Father.

These human spirits will never return to the Earth in order to participate in the work of the Youngest; even though their will toward the Light has overcome Darkness, their spirit is as yet too undeveloped for this purpose. And when after millions of years they have reached the goal of their journey, their help on Earth will be superfluous, since by that time there will no longer be any human beings on the Globe. The last of them will then have left this first stage of their journey, to continue on the distant globes.

The reason that the human spirits, after being released from life on Earth, are brought to the star universe that corresponds to that of the Earth is that most of the globes in the star universe of the Earth are contaminated by Darkness. Should God call forth life on these globes, it would have to be similar to that on Earth – a life of Darkness in worlds of Darkness, which could only hinder and oppress the human spirits. When these are released from life on Earth, they will therefore fully and for ever have dissolved the bonds of Darkness and will belong only to the Light and to the worlds of the Light. *The Earth is thus the only globe within its universe that sustains living beings.*

Although Darkness will never be able to bind human beings as it bound the Eldest – for the higher the spirit that succumbs to Darkness, the deeper and more lasting its fall – the power of Darkness over them is nevertheless very great, *since human beings arose from Darkness.* But through the will for the good, and by a fervent and sincere prayer to God for help, it is within the power of all human beings to free themselves more and more from the heavy yoke of Darkness. The stronger the will becomes to respond to the calling power of the Light, the lesser becomes the dominion of Darkness, and since Darkness no longer has disincarnated "servants" to bring human beings under its magnetic power, all who sincerely *desire* the good and the true will be able to avoid its influence more easily in times to come.

21* C

But for the present, the few who in every way submit with trust to the leadership of God can be counted as *one in a million,* and many generations must pass before the spiritual weapons of **love, justice and tolerance can gain victory over the murderous earthly weapons by which nations and peoples now settle their many disputes.**

In numerous areas and in many different ways the incarnated Eldest have drawn humanity downward, harming and opposing the work of the Youngest, since from remote antiquity when they were first incarnated, the genius of the Eldest has been employed in the service of Darkness.

Through writings in the natural sciences, philosophy, literature, and fanatical religion they led people astray and carried them away from the paths of the Light.

The Eldest bear the main responsibility for many of the inventions that have brutalized human beings, and which have caused destruction, torture and death; for example the ancient weapons of destruction, the many instruments of torture, gunpowder, the first firearms, and practically everything else that has developed from these inventions up to the present time.

A few of the inventions of explosive and destructive substances that have been brought forth with intent to *benefit* humanity are due to some of the Youngest who in their existence as human beings were led astray by the Elder.

But not only the Eldest have hindered the Youngest in their work, **human beings themselves have time and again proved to have no understanding of and to be hostile and unreceptive to the gifts and the truths that the Youngest have tried to bring them.** Rarely, if ever, have God's emissaries been understood while they lived among human beings on Earth. Not until the passing of one or more generations have the Youngest normally been even partly understood, which can be attributed to the fact that what they brought was *too advanced* to be comprehended by the immature human spirits, who even in the most advanced civilizations and societies have always been in the majority. During their human embodiment the Youngest have thus often been somewhat isolated. Time and again they have been exposed to scorn, anger, hatred and persecution; many have had to suffer various painful forms of death inflicted by human beings as a reward for their self-sacrificing work, their great patience and for the unfailing love with which each of them sought in every way to overcome Darkness and the influence of the Elder; and only the love and the thanks that they received after each incarnation from God, their Father, have helped them to endure *all the suffering, grief, disappointment and scorn inflicted upon them by the very beings for whom they sacrificed so much.*

Whether human beings in times to come will be able better to understand and more willingly to heed that which God's emissaries bring them, and whether they themselves will contribute to a development whereby *the culture of the spirit and the culture of the heart will unite in following one straight path toward the Light, must for the present time –* perhaps for centuries – *remain an open question,* until the time when human beings are able to answer it as it *should* be answered.

But in order for human beings themselves to take up the struggle against Darkness in earnest – not only against the Darkness that each individual harbours deep within the self in its own thoughts and feelings, and against the Darkness that surrounds all of them everywhere in the earthly world, but also against the Darkness that threatens them through the ether-recordings[1] of the Elder – they must first of all learn to tolerate the views and opinions of one another, since tolerance is *the basic element of love.* If people within smaller groups learn to yield to one another instead of mocking and deriding one another, it would be far easier for them to extend tolerance and thus love to the many, so that all human beings at some time – sooner or later – will stand united in their common struggle out of Darkness.

This applies first of all to the mutual intolerance among the leaders and followers of the higher religions, since it must be clear to all that the spiritual values of greater or lesser merit that have been imparted to humanity in the area of religious life have been given only in fragments, often at long intervals and always to some extent distorted[2] by the Elder, who at all times and by every possible means

---

[1] See Summary, pp. 307–09.

[2] Even the ancient myth of Adam and Eve imparts some of the truth despite its purely human form. During an earthly existence one of the Youngest tried through this myth to furnish human beings with an explanation of their origin: Adam and Eve are thus symbols of the Elder and his female dual. The serpent symbolizes the alluring, attracting and binding power of Darkness. The apple on the branch of the Tree of Knowledge of Good and Evil symbolizes the life-principle of Darkness, surrounded by and held fast by the Light. The serpent represents Darkness which tempted the woman to sin; the woman tempted the man to eat of the Tree of Knowledge, i.e., to gain knowledge so as to master the life-principle of Darkness. Removing the apple from the tree symbolizes the separation of Darkness and the Light. By their Fall, Adam and Eve – the fallen Eldest – were banished from the Garden of Eden, i.e., God's Kingdom. Cain and Abel symbolize the various types of human beings, who owe their existence to God's fallen children. Cain's murder of his brother is a symbol of sin and death, which through the birth, or creation, of Cain and Abel – humanity – was brought into reality in the earthly world.

has tried to obscure the pure and absolute truths in order to prevent human beings from gaining any precise knowledge. But those who wish and who are able to draw parallels between all religions from the earliest days to the present can find some of the truths of the Light in all of them, often the same truths repeated in somewhat different forms, *but all more or less obscured by human dogmas and clothed in human thoughts and misconceptions.*[1] No religious community therefore has the right to believe or to advocate that the religion adopted by their congregation is the only redeeming faith and that only they who profess it can lay claim to salvation, that only they are chosen and that they alone shall inherit God's Kingdom and be granted the gift of eternal life in glory and joy, while at the same time denouncing and scorning those of different views and different beliefs; for such narrow-mindedness, such self-assertion at the expense of fellow human beings *is the gravest of all religious delusions. Eternal life belongs to every human being who wishes to receive it; God's Kingdom is open to all; every human being shares in God's love; to all He shows the same patience, the same compassion;* **not to a single human being does He ever close His heart, nor to anyone does He close the portals of the Fatherly Home.** For to God, the Creator and Father of the human spirit, it is of no importance to what earthly belief the individual human being adheres in word and in action, but it is of importance that *human beings in mind and in heart, in thought and in action should live according to the faith that they profess, and not merely observe its outer forms or cling to its man-made dogmas or to that which is dictated by habit or by ritual, none of which has any spiritual value whatsover for eternal life.* **Only that which calls upon, evokes and maintains the best, the noblest and the finest in human thought and feeling, only that has lasting and inextinguishable value to the individual.**

No more than God forces a particular religion upon any individual does He demand honour and worship in any specific manner. Every religious community has the right to conduct its gatherings and its divine services according to the forms and rules that are in greatest harmony with its adherents' perception of beauty and of the exalted. But no one has the right to promote the form of worship accepted in his own community to the detriment of all other forms, as if it were the best and most perfect manner for the congregation to honour its God and Father and to attain communication with the

---

[1] In the ancient heroic legends and religious myths of many peoples, parallels can also be found that are due to the influence of the Elder – for example, gods that are also human beings, trinities, virgin births, and so forth.

divine. *All worship should therefore be voluntary, there should be no coercion of any kind, neither in one direction nor the other;* **for whether people meet in temples, churches, meeting houses or in their homes, God will always hear their songs of praise, their thanksgiving and their prayers when the devotion of their thought and of their heart is but true and deeply felt.**

Not only in the area of religious faith should people learn to yield to each other and to be tolerant of one another's views and opinions; but also in the areas of *social* and *political* life *should* they try to seek common ground between one another, seek in fellowship to cast off the yoke of Darkness, so that their common journey toward the distant goal may be accomplished under more favourable conditions than hitherto.

How can human beings themselves then help toward the achievement of this task?

Firstly *by never acting against better judgment, by always heeding the inner prompting of their conscience and by teaching the coming generations to work for* **truth, justice and peace on Earth.**

In bringing up the coming generation *women* have a special task, which many in recent times have partly or completely neglected in order to pursue the struggle for the equal rights of women. Women have a self-evident right to take part in social and political life according to their ability, but *only* if they have no infant children who demand their care; for if the woman is a mother, the task that she has thereby undertaken – the upbringing and maternal care of the young – will suffer on account of her work and duties outside the home.

Every woman who is a mother should know that by bringing children into the world she must also answer for their spiritual development.[1] It is the mother who moulds the spirit of the young child; with patience and with never failing love it is her task to weed out the shoots of Darkness that grow in the mind of every child; it is her responsibility to develop and to form the child's perception of that which is good and true in life, and to instil abhorrence of all that is impure, of falsehood, violence and disregard for the rights of others, and loathing for *all the abominations of warfare.*

Every mother should know that the first question that God will ask, when after the death of her earthly body she must render the

---

[1] This refers only to the upbringing of the children while they are within the home and not to the spiritual and other kinds of education that are given through schools and institutions.

account of her life on Earth, is this: *"How did you bring up your child, what spiritual values did you implant in its soul, and what example did you set your child by your own conduct?"* Many a mother has had ashamedly to answer: "I neglected my child, I left it to others to enrich my child with spiritual values, and by my own conduct I have set a poor example!" It is of no avail that such a mother can add: "But I have given much of my time and used many of my talents in the service of my country and my community." God's answer will then be: "You have not *served* but *harmed* your country and your community, for you have neglected and failed to honour the human spirit that was entrusted to your care, *and through your negligence you have given your country a poor and useless citizen."*

Mothers who bring up their children to be *truthful, just and peace-loving citizens* benefit their nation much more than those who leave the upbringing and maternal care of their children to others in order to participate in social and political life.

The father also has a great responsibility in the upbringing of children. First of all *he* must provide for their purely material needs; but if the children are many and the health of the mother is weak, or should she die leaving infant children behind, then it is also the father's duty to take charge of the ethical aspects of their upbringing.

Both parents have a very great responsibility, not only directly in the rearing of the children but also indirectly, it being their common task to make life in the home as bright, as peaceful and as harmonious as possible. It is not only the parents' task but also their *duty* to keep all their quarrels[1] and disputes away from the children, since nothing is so destructive of the growing generation as a discordant home. When a marriage is entered, in whatever manner this may take place, both partners must therefore be well aware of their responsibilities toward the coming generation. Husband and wife should have as many social and other interests in common as possible and so much spiritual kinship that on these they can build a deep and abiding friendship, so that they should not be tempted after some years to go their separate ways. Marriage should *never* be entered under duress or with the mental reservation that it can be dissolved, since divorce should be regarded as *a means of last resort*. However, if it is completely impossible for man and wife to yield to one another and to live together in peace and forbearance, then legal divorce is justified *for the sake of the children,* since in such a situation the children are far better brought up outside the home or in the home of the party with the lesser guilt.

All parents should strive both directly and indirectly to give their children the best possible upbringing, and should not permit them to suffer under the conse-

---

[1]) See Speech of Christ, p. 127.

quences of marital strife and discord, so that the coming generation[1] may be endowed with a pure, cheerful and tolerant disposition, and so that in all circumstances of life they may remember their home with happiness, and from the memories of their childhood derive strength to resist the temptations in life and the ways of Darkness.

In one area that is equally important to the upbringing of children – namely the area of *legislation* – human beings can themselves assist in improving conditions on Earth through the enactment of laws that have been carefully considered, laws that do not *restrain the initiative of the free will or compel the individual to act against the best and the noblest in every human mind.* For *laws of coercion* of any kind that are issued by the leaders and the rulers of the different countries serve only to promote the power of Darkness and to obstruct the progress of the Light. There must of course be laws to regulate the domestic and foreign affairs of countries and the postures of nations toward each other, but if it happens that these laws compel people to act contrary to their inner conviction, against their conscience, or if the natural development of the free will is impeded, then these laws will have only a destructive effect, and *the rulers will have abused their power.*

Among such laws of coercion must be counted, for example, *compulsory military service.*

So long as military service is only "peaceful", the many open air exercises and the discipline can in many ways have a beneficial effect on body and spirit, provided that the officers and superiors act humanely and do not abuse their authority in a degrading and improper fashion. But as soon as the game of war turns to deadly earnest and the soldiers are confronted with stark reality, facing living masses that will become fodder for their cannons, sabres, bayonets and other weapons, when they know that they will become the cause of the maiming or death of many people, then most of them must do violence to their conscience in order to act in the manner demanded by the leadership of their country. The best and the noblest in the souls of such human beings is often destroyed, since in order to deaden the rising abhorrence for the deed they are about to commit they let themselves be gripped by the din and the fury of battle and act blindly in order to avoid thinking of the horror that is before them. These human beings should never be compelled to commit such deeds, since very often it is they who in the battle's confusing

---

[1]) See Speech of Christ, p. 127, regarding the relationship between parents and children who are born out of wedlock.

and degrading turmoil commit the worst and entirely unnecessary atrocities.

But as long as the law governing compulsory military service exists, it is to no avail that single individuals or several in concert refuse to comply with the duty that is demanded by a country's government, since this kind of insubordination *only brings harm to the disobedient and in no way upsets the existing order.* In such cases there is but *one thing* to do: to submit to the duties that are imposed by society, even though performance of such duties clashes with one's innermost feelings. By acting in this way the individual stands *with a clear conscience,* while the responsibility for these compulsory actions will fall upon those *who originate and enforce such laws.*

These coercive laws should therefore be repealed by the leaders, the legislators and the rulers; when *they* realize that such coercion cannot be in harmony with God's desires and purposes, the time will have come for the existing laws to be repealed and replaced by new laws.

In order to provide a transition from present conditions to the time when a general and *universal* peace among all nations is an accomplished fact, all military service should be a voluntary[1] matter, with no compulsion whatsoever of the individual, *since responsibility for the many untimely deaths, the many murders and atrocities and the destruction is placed by God upon the leaders, the legislators and the rulers,* even though the individual soldier – the aggressor as well as the defender – must give account of all the unnecessary cruelties of which he is personally guilty. On the other hand, if military service is placed on a voluntary basis until further notice, then *the chief responsibility will be evenly divided among all the participants in war, the leaders as well as the soldiers in the field.*

All warfare is against God's Will and is in conflict with the laws of the Light, and it benefits neither one nor the other warring nation to call upon God's assistance[2] as supreme war lord; any supplication to God to bless the armaments or to bless the armies, so that under His leadership they may gain victory over their opponents, is therefore **a blasphemous prayer.**

Any conception of God as war lord or war leader must be rooted out, since all bloodshed, all destruction, all subversion *is completely irreconcilable with the nature of God.* Again and again God has sought to lead human beings to a complete understanding of love for their neighbours and respect for all that belongs to them. Time and

---

[1]) See Speech of Christ, p. 125.
[2]) See Speech of Christ, pp. 114–15.

again ever since the dawn of history God's emissaries have proclaimed to human beings: " **You shall not kill, nor take by force, nor rob, nor plunder!**" But so far the appeal has been in vain, human beings have not yet been able to free themselves from the primal urge of *brutish self-assertion through violence to the detriment of their fellow human beings.* So long as the individual members of the nations of the world do not unite and strive toward mutual peace and forbearance, so long as human beings cannot with complete faith in God's Fatherliness and Justice place everything in His hand and with trust submit to His leadership, *so long as the will of the many is not one with His Will, so long can bloodshed, violence and war not cease, and so long can the hope for peace not be victorious on Earth.*

Human beings must overcome the influence of Darkness, overcome hatred, curses, envy and lust for power through belief in God's existence and by trusting His guidance, rather than through prayers for help to crush their enemies and opponents by acts of violence – *for God never hears and never answers such prayers.*

If it could be conceived that an entire people were united in complete trust in God and in the absolute certitude that no evil arising from ambitious, envious or rapacious neighbours could befall them, then even the most evil of designs would fall to the ground, since it would be lost on so unanimous and complete a faith. *But where can such a people be found?* Humanity is still in its infancy, and centuries or millennia may pass before full understanding of such an unshakeable relationship of trust between God and human beings can be attained.

Thus, all warfare is rooted in Darkness and is brought about by the mutual intolerance of the various nations, which in turn can be attributed to the lust for power of the leaders and the rulers. If the human will for evil thus calls forth fighting and destruction and a war begins, *the nation that initiates the hostilities* must bear the responsibility for the war of aggression as well as for the war of defence forced upon the other nation and its allies, regardless of the forms that the war may take. And so long as the attacked nation limits itself to the defence of its country, of its rights, the aggressor will continue to be in the wrong. But the moment the defender extends the hostilities to the territory of the aggressor in order to attack rather than to defend, both sides must share the responsibility for whatever takes place from the moment the border into enemy territory is crossed. (The same laws apply if the battles are fought at sea or in the air).

The victory or defeat of the warring parties can in no way be attributed to God. Never does He take part in the hostilities, neither on the side of the aggressor nor on the side of the defender. *Only prayers for help to restore peace will be heard by God,* but His many and persistent attempts to speak to the leaders as their "conscience" are in most cases rejected.

The victorious party defeats its adversary by virtue of numerical or strategic superiority or the like, or because of the people's common hatred of the enemy and the people's common will to win; **but victory is never gained with the help of God.**

Any person – civilian or military – who *praises, defends and glorifies war* in writing or in speech, instead of evoking aversion to this deed of Darkness and enlightening his fellow human beings on the *degradation* and *brutishness* of war, is himself placing a heavy burden of responsibility on his shoulders and must, having ended his earthly life, *render a detailed account to God of the motivations for his actions.*

Even though human beings wage war among themselves, and even though God does not hear their prayers for victory, He never loses sight of them, but seeks either directly or through the disincarnated Youngest to awaken remorse among the leaders, just as He tries in many ways to instil in them an awareness of the injustice and the abuse of power of which they are guilty, so as to bring about a pact of peace *before one of the parties succumbs to the superior force;* but in the vast majority of cases also these attempts are rejected by human beings.

Many of the disincarnated Youngest gather where the fiercest battles rage in order to minimize by their presence the effect of the erupting Darkness and to divert those accumulations of Darkness that are inevitably drawn to the scenes of battle by the passions that are unleashed, and also to bring the thousands of spirits that were bound to the slain human bodies back to their dwellings in the spheres.

The Youngest will also try, for as long as a state of war obtains, to evoke feelings of compassion and to bring about acts of mercy among those directly or indirectly involved in the war, so as to counteract the influence of Darkness.

The love of human beings for their country[1] is under normal circumstances an excellent and exalted sentiment, but it is ugly and degrading when, aroused by the passions of war, it turns into egoism

---

[1]) Persons who despise or hate other nations or other races will in the next succeeding incarnations invariably be born among them, so that they may learn to love those whom they previously hated.

and self-worship. For regarding this self-overestimation and complacency, human beings must never forget that those men and women who from the earliest times and in the various nations have risen high above the average human being, and who *in the service of the Light* have exerted a lasting cultural influence on the peoples of their countries in the religious, ethical, scientific, social and political areas, *have all been the incarnated Youngest,* who under the leadership of God have let themselves be born at those places where at that time there were the best prospects for introducing innovations and improvements. *And as even the most advanced human spirits have not yet developed the ability to enrich their fellow human beings either spiritually or materially, nor yet succeeded in raising themselves above the purely human level in spiritual respects, humanity has no grounds whatsoever for self-overestimation or self-admiration, but reason only to thank God for the abundance of the gifts that He has given them through His emissaries.*

So that no government by the few, nor by a single head of state, should in the future be tempted through error of judgment or hasty decision to involve their own and thereby one or more other nations in ruinous and totally destructive war, all states should agree upon a common governing body, consisting of delegates from all the countries and all the factions, to act not as a peace conference meeting from time to time but as *a permanent authority*[2] whose members are elected for a longer period of office, and to whose hands all the disputes and entanglements of nations will be entrusted for joint resolution; for all disputes of any kind whatsover *can* and *should* be settled by peaceful, diplomatic means. **For in no respect whatsoever can humanity defend before God its presumed right to settle its disagreements by arms and by force.**

If all the nations, all the peoples of the East and of the West, would voluntarily meet in a joint endeavour to achieve a lasting peace, they would be assured of receiving all possible help from the transcendental world under the supreme leadership of *God.* However, it will be of no avail to establish a general world authority until *the will* exists in full sincerity and accord to fulfil the hope of "the eternal peace". But once such co-operation has been agreed upon and initiated it should never be breached, since the nation that deceitfully fails to honour its pledge thereby takes an unbounded responsibility upon itself; *because every vow that is broken draws Darkness to those who deliberately commit deceitful acts, and the*

---

[1]) Written in 1916. – Publisher's note.

*gathered Darkness will draw the Elder's recorded future-images
forth into reality upon the plane of the Earth and thus for long
periods of time hinder the toilsome journeying of mankind.*

These proposals for a general world authority or international
court of law have in various ways been put forward by human beings
in the past, but have not hitherto awakened the proper response and
understanding.

But with the permission of our God and Father this proposal is
hereby advanced from the transcendental world – from the spiritual
leaders of mankind – in the hope that those who are well placed to
advocate and implement some treaty of this nature will heed these
words in times to come.

And when the time comes that all human beings in full understanding should agree to enact an *inviolable* pact of peace, **all manu-
facture of all kinds of armaments and weapons of war should cease,
and never more be resumed.**

*Through an unbreachable treaty of peace between all the peoples
and the nations they will lay a firm foundation for an effective and a
fruitful joint endeavour between the children of the Light and the
children of the Earth, an endeavour that will in many ways be a
great help to the Youngest in their work for humanity, and benefit
especially those of the Youngest who are incarnated as human
beings.*

———————

"Lead us till we enter Thy Kingdom!" These are the words of the
ancient prayer that Jesus of Nazareth taught his apostles.

Under the supreme leadership of God must human beings themselves journey to the goal; the Kingdom of God can never come to
human beings on Earth; if God let His World's divine sea of Light
descend upon the Globe, all the weak and undeveloped human
spirits would without resistance be drawn back into His Fatherly
bosom, and everything there was upon the Earth, the living as well
as the lifeless, would at the same instant be absorbed and merged
into the waves of the sea of Light. However bright and peaceful the
conditions and existence on Earth *may* thus become, life there will
only be the faintest reflection of life in the Kingdom of God; and
since no human being can enter the presence of God without being
absorbed into Him who endowed the human spirit with the gift of
life, *Christ must not only be the guide of all human beings, but must
also be their Father's representative toward them,* until their spirits
have attained sufficient strength to enter the Fatherly Home.

Slowly, human beings advance on their journey to the distant goal, a mighty pilgrimage from all the realms and countries of the Earth; but in the vanguard journeys the most patient, the most loving and the most self-sacrificing of all leaders – *Christ, the Saviour and Redeemer of all human beings.* From his torch held up high, the shining light falls bright and clear on all the roads and paths that lead toward the goal; but if any should go astray upon the long and arduous journey, then Christ will seek until he finds those who have lost their way; for he has promised his Father to lead them all into His open embrace.

But how much time has yet to pass before mankind will acknowledge and receive Christ for what he is – *their faithful brother and leader* – and with his help unite in the common task of creating brighter and happier circumstances on Earth and thus improve the human condition, this no one knows – not even God – for *the free will of human beings for good or for evil must answer this question.* However, sooner or later the time will come when all will stand united and of one accord, *when the will of all is one with the Will of God,* so that fully, in the least as in the greatest, in spirit and in truth, He is the *God and Father* of all human beings. And then the ancient legend of the angels' song of praise at the birth of Christ will come true, then the words: *"Glory to God in the Highest, and on earth peace, good will toward men"* will rise in chorus from humanity and from the Youngest, their spiritual leaders.

The Youngest who were the companions and helpers of Christ while he fought the last severe battle with Darkness to win back their beloved brother now pray together to Almighty God: **"Father, bestow Thy blessing upon our task, that our words shall not sound in vain in the wilderness of human ignorance! Father, teach human beings to forgive our eldest brother even as Thou hast forgiven him, that in truth they may journey forward, toward the Light and toward Thy Kingdom!"**

POSTSCRIPT

In conclusion, an account will be given here of the manner in which this work came into being.

When the Elder had returned in repentance and had obtained forgiveness from God for all that he had transgressed against Him, the Youngest knew that their Father would assign to His eldest son the task of informing humanity of those truths that in the course of time had been distorted or withheld: *the truth concerning the creation of the human beings; the truth of how God, at the plea of some of the Eldest, bestowed spiritual life upon the astral counterparts of the human beings, whereby the human spirits were given eternal life; and the truth concerning the voluntary assumption by the eldest of the Youngest of the task of leading humanity to the Home of Him who is the Father of them all.*

The Youngest knew that the task that should be given to their eldest brother would be most difficult, nearly impossible for him, if they did not give him all the help that they could render. Christ and those who had assisted in the release of the earthbound spirits and the deliverance of the Elder from the power of Darkness therefore agreed to ask their Father's permission to sustain and to help their brother in the rendering of his account to human beings. God granted the desired permission without delay, and He also promised to be the Supreme Leader in the fulfilment of this task and to help them overcome all greater difficulties that might arise while carrying out this work of love.

With the permission of God they then turned to the spiritualistic circle whose few members,[1] two years before the return of the Elder, had received Christ and his companions with trust and understanding, when he had turned to this circle and established communication with them in his search[2] for earthly helpers.

---

[1]) The circle consisted originally of six members, but was later reduced to four.
[2]) See Ardor's Account, p. 100, and the Commentary, p. 238.

During the year that had been allotted to the Elder as a time of complete rest, Christ and his companions led some of the members of the circle engaged in psychic research onto some of the many questions that should be illuminated by the clear light of the truth. Thus it was essential to prepare the members of the circle before confronting them with the Elder, and especially to ensure that the medium who was to serve as intermediary had the insight and the willingness to accept those messages that contradicted the hitherto known Biblical traditions and dogmas of the Church. It is utterly impossible to establish effective co-operation if the attitude of the medium toward the spiritual manifestations is one of reluctance and reservation, whereas a greater understanding and readiness demonstrated by human beings will make it easier – for the spirits through inspiration, and for the medium through intuition – *to transfer the spiritual truths accurately to the plane of the Earth.*

The participating members of the circle had to promise not to write down the answers given to their questions. However, they were at the same time informed that at a later date all questions would be returned from the transcendental world, arranged in a particular order and with far more complete and coherent answers, which could then be written down as they would be received during the coming series of séances.

Christ and his helpers succeeded in conveying to their earthly assistants a broad but clear summary of the creation of humanity, of the work of the Youngest and of the deliverance of the Elder.

When one year after the return of the Elder, God requested[1] him to reveal to human beings his transgressions against them, and to try through truthful messages and statements to obtain their forgiveness, Christ presented him with those questions that he and his brothers and sisters had answered during the séances with their earthly helpers[2] in the course of the preceding year. It then became the Elder's task to arrange them in proper sequence and on that basis to form a coherent and consistent account.

Accompanied by some of his brothers and sisters, the Elder made his invisible presence known to the earthly members of the circle who were in attendance. So as to be recognized and accepted as his true self, he gave his name as *Ardor,* an approximate synonym for *Lucifer,* since he wished to appear in his confession under a name that was not feared and defamed by human beings.

---

[1] See Ardor's Account, p. 104.
[2] Only two members of the circle were present at the séances where questions were asked, except on one occasion when three were present.

From the very first séance, on *3rd March, 1913*, which was one year to the day after Ardor's return, an atmosphere of mutual trust and understanding was established between Ardor, the Youngest who had promised to support him, and the earthly helpers.

Through the medium's intuition Ardor's inspiring thoughts were formed into words and sentences, which were then written down by one of the séance participants as quickly as these messages from the transcendental world were recited by the medium.

The séances[1] were held once a week. Each meeting lasted about forty-five minutes, but the meetings were sometimes of longer and other times of shorter duration. After having been suspended[2] during the months of June, July, August and September, the séances were resumed, but this time they were held with greater frequency, usually three times every two weeks, until New Year, 1914, when they were again restricted to once a week. They ceased on the 3rd February, 1914, when the last words of the Account were written down.

Despite the thorough preparations of the Youngest during Ardor's year of rest he still met with many and great difficulties in carrying out the proposed task, since he who for millions of years had exercised his influence over mankind with the help of the magnetically attracting power of Darkness experienced great difficulties in successfully employing the radiations of the Light so soon after his deliverance. But the Youngest also helped him to overcome this difficulty by causing his thoughts, which were to be rendered by the medium, to pass through the waves of Light that emitted from their spirit-bodies, in order to strengthen and to clarify them. In those passages of the Account where God speaks to the Youngest or to Christ, one of the Youngest stepped forward to assist and guide Ardor; however, this should not be understood to mean that God *literally* spoke exactly those words. That which is said represents the quintessence of the Thought and the Word of God translated into earthly language, so that the past events of the transcendental world can be made accessible to human thought and comprehension. In the same way, Christ himself was present when his earthly life as Jesus of Nazareth was treated, in order to prevent any inaccuracies from occurring. Especially this part of the Account caused Ardor great difficulties, since he was overcome by emotion and deeply distressed by the recollection of the obstacles that he had placed in

---

[1] Three members were present at these séances.
[2] The members were absent on travels during these months. By summer, two of the six members had withdrawn from the circle due to illness.

the way of his younger brother while he lived on Earth as Jesus of Nazareth. Ardor's thoughts were therefore at times somewhat unclear, but with the help of Christ he also succeeded in communicating this part of the Account in full accordance with the truth.

Although the Youngest did their utmost to help Ardor in every possible way, his profound grief, his remorse and his despair often made it exceedingly difficult for the medium to follow the narration of his Account. As a result, not everything came through with equal clarity and continuity. But when all the questions had been linked together and answered, it turned out that the greater part of the Account had been expressed far better than any had dared hope, even though there were a few weaker passages here and there in the text, for example words that did not fully express Ardor's thought, several unclear sentences and a few answers that had been too condensed in the medium's repetition to give a satisfactory representation of the subject matter. In addition, among the many references to periods of time one clearly inaccurate reference occurred. This concerned the period of time that should have been indicated as "thousands of years", but which was erroneously understood by the medium as an "aeon" – about three million years – thus producing a quite incomprehensible idea of the course of time.

Some minor inaccuracies occurred in a few places through similar misconceptions on the part of the medium, but these were immediately pointed out from the transcendental world and then corrected.

However, the weaknesses of the Account must on the whole be ascribed to Ardor himself, since in addition to his aforementioned difficulties in communicating with the medium through the Light-waves of the ether, he also had to overcome his deep sorrow when the memories evoked by the narrative overwhelmed him.

Soon after the Account had been started, the spiritual guide enquired whether in the event of Ardor being incapable of shaping his thoughts clearly enough for his messages to form a consistent and coherent whole, one of the séance members would undertake the writing of the Account on the basis of Ardor's messages.

When the Account had been concluded and the guide had made the medium and one of the séance members aware of its deficiencies, they felt themselves incapable of revising or improving upon the less perfect passages, and Ardor therefore sought and obtained God's permission to undertake the necessary changes himself after about six months' rest. This was effected by the medium slowly reading several times through the Account in the presence of Ardor and two of the Youngest, during which certain words were replaced by more appropriate ones, several sentences rewritten to make them clearer and more explicit, and a few passages of three to seven lines inserted where the Account had been too condensed in its original formulation.

Since Jesus' relationship to suffering and grieving humanity had not, in Ardor's view, been elucidated with sufficient clarity through the questions posed by the séance members *themselves,* he obtained permission to insert at a later séance Chapter 18 – one among many incidents of which human beings have received no knowledge through the Gospels.

Revised and amended in this way Ardor's voluntary confession now appears in all respects in exact accordance with the truth and with that which in reality took place.

Since Christ had accustomed the medium through earlier séances to convey his thoughts in his own preferred form, partly by the answering of various questions and partly through the narration of parables,[1] it would have been an unnecessary waste of time to acquaint the earthly helpers with the contents of his Speech at preparatory séances. However, in order to create a perfect collaboration between the thought-inspiration of Christ and the intuitive capability of the medium, she was given permission to release[2] her spiritual self from her physical body during its nightly sleep, so as to acquaint herself with the various passages of the Speech. It thereby became easier for the medium's spirit to influence her physical brain during the séances, so that Christ's thoughts could be conveyed more quickly and more clearly than would otherwise have been the case.

While reading through the Speech, in accordance with the wishes of certain members of the circle a very few individual words were replaced by others that better expressed the underlying thought.[3] A few sentences that on account of the medium's fatigue had not originally passed her physical brain were also added, at Christ's request.

The Speech was commenced at a séance held on 10th February, 1914, and continued with one séance every week until its completion on 14th April of the same year.

In the reproduction of the Speech of God's Servant the medium again perceived a very long period of time as an "aeon", which was corrected from the transcendental world to "many ages". The re-

---

[1] See Addendum.
[2] See Summary, p. 293.
[3] The Danish text provides three examples of such modifications, whose pertinence would, of course, be lost in translation. – Translators' note.

mainder was rendered clearly and correctly. The medium had also in this case been acquainted beforehand with the contents of the Speech during sleep release.[1]

This Speech was given at a single séance that was held on 27th October, 1914.

Ardor's Account, the Speeches of Christ and God's Servant, and the Commentary were given through thought-inspiration and reproduced by the medium's intuitive perception. In order to achieve good results with this form of spiritual collaboration the medium employed must *be able to cease all his or her own thoughts and thus render the psychic and the physical brains receptive to the thought-images of the external intelligences.* The medium must necessarily also be in command of a certain vocabulary, so that the spiritual self can without too much difficulty translate what is given with as few and as well-chosen words as possible; for even though clear and concise thought-images are presented from the transcendental world, these do not suffice if the medium employed lacks the words to express the thoughts of the communicating intelligence. Since earthly languages often contain synonyms that can express the thought with varying degrees of precision, it is often very difficult for the medium's spiritual self to select at a moment's notice just those words that are best suited to transpose the thought into an easily understandable form. When the transcendental world desires an expression other than the one chosen by the medium, the words required are recited by the spirit manifesting itself or by the spiritual leader. They are then received by the medium's psychic ear and transmitted by sound-waves to the physical ear.

All of the higher and the highest spirits[2] can, of course, communicate in any earthly language they wish with attentive, responsive and sympathetic mediums. But in this case, where the medium perceived *mainly* through intuition – by way of thought – and was only slightly clairaudient, this procedure would present severe difficulty, since in the first place the frequency of the sound-waves that pass from the spirit that is speaking to the listening medium would have had to be very much reduced in order to be received at all. Then, in addition, every word would have had to be repeated again and again, until all the sound-waves had passed both the psychic and the physical ear clearly and correctly, with the result that the process of communica-

---

[1] Not trance, but natural sleep.

[2] God's Servants can when necessary transform their thought-vibrations into sound-waves by the power of their will, in the same manner that God can do this.

tion would have extended over a period of time greatly exceeding that required for thought-inspiration, thus tiring the medium quite needlessly and delaying the work. For this reason, direct speech was employed only when the medium was unable to find the best possible word or to understand the correct numerical quantity.

On the whole, thought-inspiration is the form of communication that is best suited to earthly conditions, whether employed during séances where several people besides the medium are present, or used when the medium is alone. This form of communication requires little or none of the medium's own psychic power;[1] on the contrary, the medium usually receives great psychic power through the abundant radiations of Light from the communicating spirits, and when as in this case a major integrated work is involved, whose appearance in the earthly world was of the utmost importance to the Youngest, it is obvious that the first consideration was to make such arrangements as would ensure that the medium to be employed as intermediary would not suffer, either physically or spiritually, under the many demands that would be made from the transcendental world. The method of direct transfer mentioned in the section concerning mediums[2] was for this reason not employed in the production of this work, since in the first place the medium's spirit could not have obtained the necessary rest required by any spirit bound to a human body, due to the numerous releases that would have been required for the memorization of such a work, even if it had taken place in stages. In the second place, the frequently repeated attenuation of the insulation layer, which accompanies transmissions from the psychic to the physical brain, would probably have resulted in some degree of rupture of the insulation layer itself, which, although it could heal again by the power of God's Will, would temporarily have exposed the medium to a great many spiritual sufferings. On these grounds, direct transfer has been used on only a few occasions for answering questions[3] in the Commentary, where it was quite impossible for the spiritual guide, by the method of inspiration, to give a clear understanding of the subject matter to be reproduced.

Automatic writing was not employed, since it will always be diffi-

---

[1]) If mediums nevertheless often experience fatigue during this kind of séance, it stems from the exertion that is always required to keep their own thoughts from interfering with those of the communicating spirit; this fatigue is only passing, whereas the fatigue that stems from loss of psychic strength is felt as a prolonged depression.

[2]) See Commentary, p. 245.

[3]) The many questions that were asked by the members of the circle while receiving Ardor's Account, and which could not be included in the Account, were deferred for later answer by the medium's spiritual guide.

cult, even for experienced mediums, to prevent their own thoughts[1] from interfering with the subject matter as it is written down and from influencing the given messages in some way.

It is hoped that this explanation will indicate why thought-inspiration was chosen in preference to all other forms of mediumistic communication.

A few of the questions in the Commentary were answered at conversational séances; but most of the answers were given to the medium alone under the inspirational influence of thought, one by one, as the questions were posed. Through co-operation between the medium and the spiritual guide the many answers were finally arranged in a sequence corresponding to the main questions in Ardor's Account.

The reason why the questions[2] in the Commentary have come to be answered primarily through co-operation between the medium, the spiritual guide and his helpers, without the presence of séance participants, was in deference to the wish of the Youngest to show mankind how much can be achieved by means of the inspirational method without resorting to the usual means employed at spiritualistic séances, and thus establish the point *that spiritualism is not the goal but only one of the ways by which the goal may be reached under the guidance of God.* And since the medium promised to place herself completely at the disposal of her spiritual guide, they succeeded after persistent work in translating those thoughts that were alien to the medium into words and sentences. This part of the work created a great deal of difficulty for the spiritual guide and his helpers to overcome, since the medium was neither familiar with abstract thought, nor did she have any experience in constructing or linking in proper order the questions that were to be posed. The questions were consequently presented in a very disjointed and inconsistent sequence, which made answering difficult, since very often too many interjacent questions were missing for the answers to be sufficiently satisfactory at the first attempt. But through calm, systematic work the spiritual guide and his helpers (several of the disincarnated Youngest) succeeded in eliciting the missing questions, either from the medium or from the other members, so that also this part of the work was concluded in accordance with the wishes of the transcendental world.

---

[1]) If a medium employs the method of automatic writing during trance, the spirit has greater control of the medium. But the spirits of the Light never employ mediums when they are in trance, i.e., the spirits of the Light do not coerce their mediums.

[2]) *All* the members of the circle, also those who withdrew, have contributed to making the questions so plentiful. At a number of meetings, the answers were read aloud, which usually gave rise to new questions – and new answers.

The answers to the strictly religious questions have been given in sufficient detail by the transcendental world, whereas several of the other answers have been provided merely as indications or pointers in the direction in which human beings *themselves* should continue to search, so that through a more profound study in greater detail they may achieve verification of that which has been stated here.

It is most likely that questions that have not been elucidated will occur to the individual reader of the Commentary, since it cannot be expected that all people will agree on asking exactly the same questions. Only that which *the transcendental world* has deemed to be of general interest is included, for which reason those who do not feel satisfied should continue to seek within the field of their particular interest. All possible help will at all times be given to those who seek. But one thing must be clear to all: *that the capacity, comprehension and understanding of the human spirit in the earthly world is limited, and hence that there will at all times be questions* **that cannot be answered.**

It is also likely that many will regard the answers to the questions as undocumented assertions. However, human beings can investigate several of these assertions on their own and thereby learn whether they are justified. But other answers cannot be investigated by human beings, since the transcendental world is necessarily beyond direct investigation; in these areas people must be content with the inner and logical consistency of the answers.

To the dogmatic, the fanatical and to the narrow-minded human beings and those to whom young and undeveloped spirits have been bound, the thought will in all likelihood occur that this book is the work of *Antichrist* (Satan[1] or his emissary). For the benefit of such people, the following will suggest how they should arrange that which is presented in this book, under the leadership of God and through the influence of the Light, in order to compare this with the ancient Scriptures, inherited traditions and orthodox dogmatism of human origin, all of which came into existence while Ardor was still striving to withhold from humanity as much as possible of the truth and of the Light.

---

[1]) This can of course be said with some justification with regard to Ardor, but it should be remembered that Ardor was not the representative of evil when he rendered his Account, and furthermore that it was at God's request that he communicated with human beings.

Which is the Mightiest, the Highest God?

He who hitherto has appeared in the human consciousness as the creator of the imperfect human body, of that world of sin and death in which human beings live; who caused one part of his divinity to appear as a human being in order through his blood sacrifice to reconcile the other part of his divine being with the fallen and sinful beings created by his whole self?

He who in His foresight arranged all things so that He could bring His fallen children and their creatures under the regulating influence of the Light, so as to win back His children and make their creatures His own; who in all ways, by every possible means, and along many roads tries to lead the human beings away from Darkness and sin and toward truth and Light?

Which God is the more Just?

He who judges the human spirit after one brief life on Earth; who demands blind obedience and belief without understanding; who demands, through his emissaries, that true faith shall be propagated by the sword; who sanctifies war; who is the supreme war lord to one of the warfaring parties, to the other or to all of them, and who thus contradicts himself; who selects one people as his own in preference to all other peoples?

He who allows human beings a sufficient number of earthly lives to mature their spirit and overcome the power of Darkness; who compels no one to blind obedience and blind faith in human dogmas; who through His emissaries calls constantly to human beings: you shall not kill, nor take by force, nor rob, nor plunder; who turns away in grief from human beings, when they wage deadly wars; who does not select one people, but who says: all human beings are equal before Me, all stand equally close to My Fatherly Heart?

Which is the more Loving, the more Compassionate God?

He who bestows the gift of eternal life upon a small chosen flock; who lets sinful human beings go to their perdition in an everlasting hell, that they may be punished, and that the joy of the blessed in the Kingdom of Heaven may be the greater in comparison with the sufferings of the damned; who demands that human beings must torment and confine themselves in narrow cloisters and hide themselves from life and from the Light; who demands that human beings shall recite prayers at given hours and according to prescribed rules; who must constantly be bribed with blood sacrifice, sweet incense, gold, silver and precious stones before granting any prayer; who demands Baptism, Communion and other Sacraments in order to receive the true believers and to forgive the repentant; and he who chains the Prince of Evil for all eternity in the darkest abyss of Hell?

He who bestows the gift of eternal life upon all who will receive it; who opens His Fatherly Home to all and bids all welcome when they have overcome sin and Darkness, and when their spirit has been purified by the Light; who seeks to open the eyes of human beings to all that is good and beautiful, that the joys of earthly life may help them bear its burdens of Darkness; who at all times has an open ear and a loving heart for the deepfelt yearning and the fervent prayers of repentant human beings; who gives without demanding tribute – or even thanks; who says: that which you have sinned against Me, that I forgive when you repent and when you pray; who has been able to forgive him that has sinned the most and fallen the deepest, and has opposed Him through millions of years?

In this way all that is now given to humanity through this work should be arranged and compared with that which has previously been given, and should there still be human beings who dare maintain that this is the work of Antichrist, then there is but *a single answer* to such an assertion: **also the spiritually deaf and the spiritually blind can through new incarnations come unto the knowledge of truth!**

When Christ and his helpers sought some years ago to come into communication with the spiritualistic circle whose medium subseqently took part in the transmission of this message from the transcendental to the sensory world, it was first of all necessary to find a spiritual guide in whom the medium had complete and unbounded trust. One of the Youngest, who in his last incarnation had been the medium's father, assumed at the request of Christ the spiritual leadership of the séances of the circle.

Since the medium before her incarnation had promised to try to act as the required[1] intermediary between the spirits of the Light and human beings, she was called upon from the transcendental world when her guardian spirit believed that she had attained sufficient knowledge of spiritualistic communication. The connection was thus established at the request of the spirits of the Light, and not in response to any demand or wish originating in the earthly world. The medium's guardian spirit had been the spiritual leader of the séances until the time when Christ made contact with the circle and the medium's "deceased" father took over the leadership.

The medium's unshakeable trust in God and absolute faith in the truthfulness of her spiritual guide, as well as the firm resolve of the séance participants to *seek* and to *find* the truth, together created the necessary co-operation that was a condition for the successful communication of this message to humanity.

Just as Ardor, Christ and God's Servant each separately vouch for the truth of the messages that they have given, so do I, who am the medium's spiritual guide, with the name that I bore in my last life on Earth, vouch for the truth of all the answers in the Commentary that have been given by me with the permission of and under the leadership of our God and Father.

R. Malling-Hansen

Late Pastor and Principal
of
The Royal Copenhagen Institute for the Deaf and Dumb
May, 1916

---

[1] See Commentary, p. 237.

Other translations:

QUESTIONS AND ANSWERS
Supplement I and II to "Toward the Light"
Additional Commentaries
from the transcendental world.

THE DOCTRINE OF ATONEMENT
A message from the transcendental world to all who bear
the name of Christian.

SOME PSYCHIC EXPERIENCES
Describes how communication with the transcendental world
developed and thus gradually established the foundation
for bringing humanity "Toward the Light".

For further information regarding these works, you are invited
to contact:

TOWARD THE LIGHT PUBLISHING HOUSE, ApS.,
"Vandrer mod Lyset"s Forlag, ApS.,
22 Købmagergade,
1150 Copenhagen K, Denmark